Cwragg
78

The Tumbling Sky

The Tumbling Sky

Hugh Halliday

First Published in 1978 by

CANADA'S WINGS
BOX 393, STITTSVILLE
CANADA K0A 3G0

ISBN 0-920002-03-X

Cover Design by Graham Wragg
Layout and Production by Rick Johnson
Printed by The Intelligencer, Belleville, Ontario

Contents

FOREWORD

During the First World War it was my privilege to serve as a fighter pilot on the Western Front, and to fly with men from throughout the Commonwealth. In 1918 I was involved in the Royal Air Force training programme in Canada. At the School of Aerial Fighting in Beamsville it was possible to apply the lessons learned over France to the training of new fighter pilots.

The Second World War saw many of those same lessons being relearned and applied in many theatres. The British Commonwealth Air Training Plan, which drew young men from the United States as well as the Commonwealth, was one of Canada's most important contributions to the war effort. As Inspector General of the RCAF I was able to see at first hand how aerial warfare had developed, and I met many of the trainees who subsequently became seasoned veterans throughout the globe.

Although there was much that was different between the two wars, certain aspects of fighter combat remained the same. Tactical advantage was of prime importance; so too was teamwork. Air combat was not a sport (though some masked their fears by assuming a cheerful exterior). It was a serious business, in which technology and skills were systematically refined.

Above all, however, the personal characteristics required of successful aircrew remained constant. Aggressiveness, a will to engage and to win, a readiness to take chances, tempered with the ability to recognize when such chances were foolish or unnecessary—all of these marked out the successful pilots and their supporting comrades.

Fighter pilots in both wars were the combat elements of a team. Behind them stood the designers who had given them their aircraft, the mechanics who kept them flying, the instructors who taught them how to survive and triumph, the planners who assigned them meaningful tasks. Canadians can be proud that their countrymen contributed greatly in all these fields, and gave this nation a record of accomplishments of which we can all be proud.

A.E. Godfrey
Air Vice Marshal

Introduction

The public acclaim of Canadian fighter pilots in the First World War had no counterpart in the Second World War. Whereas Canadians could run off a litany of famous airmen from the former conflict—Bishop, Collishaw, Claxton, Barker, McCall, McLaren—the same could not be said of their counterparts of 1939-1945. To a degree this is understandable; by 1939 aerial warfare was an accepted fact rather than a novelty. Moreover, the flyers of the First World War appeared to be the last romantic figures in warfare, easily contrasted with the impersonal gunners and massed infantrymen.

If writers have not chronicled the stories of the second generation of Canadian aces to the same degree as was done with the first, the subject has not been wholly ignored. John Gordon (*Of Men and Planes*) and Tom Coughlin (*The Dangerous Sky*) have contributed to the literature on the subject. Nevertheless, it is evident that there has been far more published on American, British and German fighter pilots. Such works occasionally mention Canadians in passing, but they have necessarily dealt with other nationalities in more depth.

This book, then, is intended to fill a gap, to serve as both a tribute and a memorial to the Canadian fighter pilots of the Second World War. It should also act to remind Canadians of a class of people who have been frequently overlooked in our search for national heroes. Many of the personalities mentioned may blush at seeing their names in print, or protest, "But I was only doing my job! " That, perhaps, was the most striking thing about them—their professional approach to a dangerous job that needed doing.

The term "ace" originated in the French Air Force about the spring of 1915. It was used to describe an airman who had destroyed five or more enemy aircraft. The process of marking out such pilots was copied by the German and American Air Services, which kept detailed, officially sanctioned lists of personnel and their victories in both world wars.

The British flying services (Royal Flying Corps, Royal Naval Air Service, Royal Air Force) did not follow this trend. Official British policy was that such practices gave undue prominence to fighter pilots over other aircrew or service personnel who had taken equal risks in less spectacular circumstances. It was an argument with some merit. This writer recalls a cartoon depicting a weary French infantryman climbing out of a trench, one foot on a German corpse. Peering at an airplane overhead he says despairingly, "I, too, have brought down my fifth Boche, but it will not be mentioned in today's communiques."

In view of the fact that the British and Commonwealth Air Forces kept no running tally of individual victories, it has been left to scholars and enthusiasts to determine the scores of Commonwealth fighter pilots, laying down such ground rules as the individual writer might apply. In this book the author has attempted to use, as far as possible, the best documentary sources available to him. It was decided that no distinction would be made between aircraft destroyed in the air and on the ground, provided that the latter were dealt with by gunfire. The reasoning behind this was that the hazards met in shooting up an airfield, heavily defended by anti-aircraft guns, were frequently as great as tangling with an enemy airplane in single combat. Indeed, in the closing stages of the war, it was probably more dangerous to shoot up a fighter on the ground than to engage in a dogfight with the same machine piloted by a raw recruit.

Before going any further, it would be worthwhile to note that the counting of victories was extremely difficult. Fighter pilots' claims were almost always made in good faith, and Intelligence Officers attempted to base the confirmation of claims on a solid factual footing, but often the number of enemy aircraft reported destroyed far exceeded the number actually shot down. This was most likely to happen when the aerial campaigns were particularly hectic or prolonged, as during the Battle of Britain, or when aerial fighting took place over enemy occupied territory.

Thus it was that during the Battle of Britain RAF and Allied pilots claimed approximately twice as many enemy aircraft destroyed as were actually brought down. On August 15, 1940, a day of particularly confused fighting, the RAF claimed 183 enemy aircraft destroyed, while on September 15 the total claimed was 185. Post-war examination of German records revealed that only 76 enemy machines had been lost on the former day and 56 on the latter.

In 1941-42, when the Allies were going over to the offensive, these discrepancies became even more serious. Between December 20, 1940 and June 13, 1941, a total of 50 Fighter Command pilots were lost in attacks on France and the Low Countries. The RAF claimed 72 enemy aircraft destroyed, but the actual number was 58. This was a comparatively accurate assessment. From mid-June until the end of July 1941, however, when the offensive was stepped up, Fighter Command lost 123 pilots, claimed 322 enemy aircraft, and actually destroyed 81. From March until June 1942 such offensive work resulted in the loss of 314 bombers and fighters. Claims of 205 enemy aircraft destroyed were not borne out by post-war research, which showed the enemy losses to be only 90. On August 19, 1942, during the air battle over Dieppe, 91 enemy aircraft were claimed as destroyed and 44 probably destroyed. In fact, the *Luftwaffe* lost 48 machines.

These instances of over-claiming were common to all air forces and for the same reasons. In the heat of battle it was difficult to follow the action. Smoke pouring from an enemy aircraft might be the result of battle damage, or it might be a ruse. An aircraft which spun after being fired on might be going down out of control, or its pilot might be taking voluntary evasive action. Flames flickering around an opponent's engine could indicate that his aircraft was on fire, or that the engine was merely acting up. Moreover, it was unwise to chase a victim down to ground level. Such action broke up formations and exposed the pursuer to an attack from above. In addition to over-optimistic claims, there were undoubtedly instances of double claims, in which two pilots, unaware of each other's work, might fire at the same target. Each would submit a "destroyed" claim, even though only one aircraft had been hit. It was the task of Intelligence Officers to reduce such errors to a minimum.

From this it will be recognized that the number of enemy aircraft *credited* to a pilot might often exceed the number which he actually *destroyed*. The problem is complicated when one realizes that the degree of over-claiming varied according to the circumstances. By the latter half of 1944, RAF and RCAF claims were remarkably accurate, what with ground troops present to witness some combats, and special sorties being flown to check out claims submitted from previous flights. There is no way to determine which combat reports were erroneous, and it would be manifestly unfair and inaccurate to slash scores arbitrarily. Collectively the fighter pilots exaggerated; individually their combat reports must be taken at face value.

This question of "scores" is, in any case, a rather sterile matter, for there were many facets to the pilots and their combats which deserve greater recognition than is generally given to them. Intruder crews, for example, performed minor miracles of navigation, frequently at night, invariably at low level, over blacked-out enemy territory. Some men had achieved great things even before they reached operational squadrons. Johnny Caine had struggled for two years to raise his educational level to that which would allow him to enlist. John Kent's pre-war work as a test pilot was at least as hazardous as his fighter sorties. To this day, Don MacFadyen believes that he contributed more to the war effort in helping to revise training manuals than in destroying enemy aircraft.

This book, then, aims at telling more than the combat histories of selected pilots. In the process of compiling it, the author has consulted a variety of documents and secondary sources, not all of which are of equal value. A review of these will explain much of the methodology while indicating possible weaknesses and strengths.

The best source of information on air actions has been the annotated combat report. After each combat a pilot submitted a report setting forth the circumstances of the action and claiming an aircraft as "destroyed", "probably destroyed" or "damaged." These were checked by Intelligence Officers from the squadron level upwards, and compared with data supplied by other sources. The claims might be allowed, upgraded or downgraded, depending on the judgement of the IOs and the supplementary information. During the war RCAF Overseas Headquarters kept copies of all such reports processed by Canadian squadrons, including No. 417 in the Mediterranean, as well as reports submitted by Canadians in most RAF units operating in Britain and Northwest Europe; for some unexplained reason, no reports of Canadians in No. 100 Group were filed. The reports later went to the Canadian Armed Forces' Directorate of History, where the author examined them.

A second source of information was the Squadron Diaries (officially known as Form 540 or the Squadron Operational Record Book). Again, in the case of RCAF squadrons, the author had direct access to these. They recorded a great deal of information besides combat claims, including the results of ground strafing, living conditions, even social events. However, they did not always note alterations in claims by Intelligence Officers, and while 99 percent accurate they were still subject to a small element of doubt, especially when they conflicted with processed combat reports.

Next there were the citations to decorations. These were written up by the immediate superior officer of the person to be honoured, but they could not be entirely trustworthy. Occasionally they ignored the downgrading of claims which the IOs had inflicted upon combat reports. At other times they were vague. As a blatant example, one may take the case of Flight Lieutenant Donald Morrison. The combat reports he submitted added up, after assessment, to 5 1/3 destroyed (four complete kills, two shared with another pilot, one shared with two pilots), 4 1/2 probably destroyed (four by himself, one shared) and five damaged. It is a fine record in itself, yet the citation to his Distinguished Flying Cross begins, "This officer displayed great skill and tenacity in air operations and has destroyed fifteen hostile aircraft." Citations, then, were used cautiously and wherever possible were compared with other material.

The press releases of RCAF Overseas Headquarters were also examined. These were useful in gathering anecdotes and background material on the aircrew. As with citations, they were less reliable than ORBs and combat reports, but were helpful in the absence of such documents. The remarkable thing in comparing PR releases with the best documents was the accuracy of the releases, but in the few cases of discrepancies there was no question as to which document was more reliable.

Secondary works were also consulted, and the author particularly leaned upon the works of Chris Shores (*Aces High, Fighters Over the Desert, Fighters Over Tunisia*) for information on pilots serving in the Mediterranean and Asian theatres. Mr. Shores is a meticulous researcher who has studied all RAF and RCAF squadron ORBs. Careful comparison of his findings and mine will indicate that we differ on a few points—most notably "Buzz" Beurling's tally—but it would not be too much to say that much of this book could not have been written without the aid of his works. Other authors of note were F.K. Mason (*Battle Over Britain*), E.C.R. Baker (*The Fighter Aces of the RAF, 1939-1945*), and Joe Holliday (*Mosquito*). Numerous British and Australian official histories proved invaluable for background material on campaigns.

The pilots themselves were prime sources of information. Beurling and John Kent I did not meet, but their books (*Malta Spitfire* and *One of the Few*) were the best sources of information about their own careers. Interviews with D.C. Fairbanks, R.G. Gray, G.U. Hill, A.U. Houle, G.C. Keefer, I.F. Kennedy, D.C. Laubman, J.H. Turnbull and P.S. Turner remain dearly remembered occasions, and correspondence with R.C. Fumerton, D. MacFadyen and R.I.A. Smith was also of great use. Far from spinning tall tales, they were genuinely reluctant to appear as "lineshooters"; at the same time they opened to me their log books, combat accounts, and, in the case of Houle, unpublished recollections.

When planning the format of this book the author was faced with the problem of dealing with a subject that encompassed more than 140 "aces". Quite arbitrarily it was decided to include a chapter on each man who destroyed ten or more enemy aircraft. In addition, chapters on Lloyd Chadburn and Robert Hampton Gray appeared to be merited, the former because of his distinction in twice winning the DSO, the latter for his Victoria Cross. Beyond that, a chapter was added, "Honourable Mention", dealing with a selection of other pilots who, though they destroyed fewer than ten enemy aircraft, were unique or interesting in some other way. Finally, as an Appendix, a listing of all Canadian aces with their scores has been included. Some may disagree with the figures given. Error on the author's part cannot be ruled out, although in some instances we may simply differ on the interpretation of documents.

In one sense it is unfortunate that so much stress has been laid upon "aces" and "scores", for the process invites comparisons which are inapplicable and creates false categories. One cannot compare the work of a night fighter pilot with that of one flying *Spitfires*, and a pilot flying in 1940-41 was operating in a vastly different set of circumstances than one flying in 1944-45. Many flyers won awards without becoming aces, and even those who gained no victories at all faced the same risks as their more prominent colleagues. It is hoped that those facts will be remembered, and that in reading the accounts of a few we may also honour the many.

The Fighter Pilots' Trade and Training

The science of aerial combat evolved during the First World War, and Canadian flyers won fame in this new trade. The most successful Commonwealth fighter pilot was Lieutenant Colonel W.A. "Billy" Bishop VC, DSO, MC, DFC, who destroyed 72 enemy aircraft, and right behind him was Major Raymond Collishaw DSO, DSC, DFC with 60 victories. Their names, and those of many others, became familiar throughout the country. Even lesser aces enjoyed regional fame; if W.E. Shields (23 victories) and Murray Galbraith (six) were not well known nationally they were common names around Lipton, Saskatchewan and Carleton Place, Ontario. The fighter pilots had become folk heroes long before George Drew's *Canada's Fighting Airmen* was first published in 1930, and their popularity was only enhanced by the rise of another type of hero, the bush pilot, for in the 1920s the two groups overlapped.

Yet for any boy growing up in Canada in the 1920s there was scant opportunity for following in the footsteps of these heroes. The Canadian Air Force (made "Royal" in 1923) was scarcely a military organization at all. Its primary task was "aid to the civil power", which meant experimental work, aerial photography, transportation for government officials, fisheries patrols, and a score of other duties. At various times the RCAF acquired some *SE.5a*, *Snipe* and *Camel* fighters from the RAF. They totalled 25; as of January 1, 1925 the force had

7

seven single-seater fighters which were used for training. In 1926-27 the RCAF acquired ten Armstrong-Whitworth *Siskins*. The *Siskins* gained their own measure of fame through an aerobatic team which performed at Canadian and American air shows in 1930-31.

The pacific stance of the Air Force was well-suited to Canadian needs from 1920 to 1938, when the RCAF contributed much to the development of Canadian aviation while opening the north to civil operators and commercial exploitation. After 1935, however, it became increasingly apparent that war was probable, if not inevitable. Reluctantly the government embarked upon a programme of re-armament. British and American aircraft were ordered while plans were laid for the production of both training and combat planes in Canada.

Many Canadians found the pace of military expansion too slow for their tastes, and several hundred enlisted directly in the RAF. Upon the outbreak of war in September 1939 there were actually more Canadians serving as aircrew in the RAF than in the RCAF, and most were either in the advanced stages of their training or already deployed in bomber, reconnaissance, and fighter squadrons. Thus, the first Canadians to see action were men wearing the uniform of the RAF. The first victory credited to a Canadian was chalked up by Flying Officer Howard Peter "Cowboy" Blatchford of Edmonton, Alberta. On October 17, 1939, while flying a *Spitfire* of No. 41 Squadron RAF, he shared in the destruction of an *He 111* 30 miles east of Whitby.

These "CAN/RAF" personnel fought with great distinction during the next five years of war. When German forces invaded Norway, three Canadians flew *Gladiators* in that northern theatre. Others operated during the Battle of France and helped to cover the epic Dunkirk evacuation. One RAF squadron, No. 242, was composed almost entirely of Canadian pilots. By the end of July 1940, when as yet no RCAF unit had reached overseas operations, these pioneering Canucks had been credited with the destruction of at least 68 enemy aircraft. Many lost their lives in flying accidents or in the first hopeless campaigns; during the Battle of Britain alone, twenty were killed in action, but the CAN/RAF pilots in turn destroyed more than 100 additional German machines.

In the meantime important events had been taking place in Canada. Early in 1939 No. 1 Squadron (RCAF) had begun to re-equip with *Hurricanes* which were delivered by sea to Vancouver. In June 1940 the unit, reenforced by personnel from No. 115 (Auxiliary) Squadron, sailed for England. Commanded by Squadron Leader Ernest A. McNab, a former member of the *Siskin* aerobatic team, No. 1 began to work up to operational standard. When its training had been completed, the squadron first saw action in the Battle of Britain. On August 26 No. 1 (Can) was scrambled to intercept a force of between

30 and 40 bombers. In the action that followed Squadron Leader McNab and Flight Lieutenant Gordon McGregor each destroyed a *Do 17Z*, while a third was shot down and credited to the squadron as a whole. Two *Hurricanes* were so heavily damaged that they had to force-land, and Flying Officer R. Edwards was shot down and killed. For the first time in history an RCAF unit had fired its guns in anger.

No. 1 (Can) Squadron remained in front-line service until October 9, when it was withdrawn to rest. During its involvement in the Battle of Britain its pilots were credited with the destruction of 30 enemy aircraft as well as damaging 43 more. Three of its pilots were killed and ten were wounded or injured in accidents. On October 22 Squadron Leader McNab became the first member of the RCAF to be decorated for gallantry when he was awarded the Distinguished Flying Cross. Three days later the DFC was also bestowed on Flight Lieutenant McGregor and Flying Officer B.D. Russel.

The number of RCAF squadrons in Britain soon began to increase. To avoid confusion with RAF units the Canadian squadrons were allocated a block of numbers running from 400 to 449. Existing RCAF squadrons overseas were redesignated in accordance with this policy, so that No. 1 (Can) Squadron became No. 401 while two army co-operation squadrons, Nos. 110 and 112, were renumbered 400 and 402. Other squadrons formed overseas or transferred from Canada to Britain were similarly numbered in the 400 block.

Initially the RCAF squadrons were led either by RCAF officers who had served in the pre-war, quasi-military Air Force, or by experienced RAF officers. Eventually, though, large numbers of Canadians who were trained under the British Commonwealth Air Training Plan became available for combat. Once they had been tempered by the air war over Europe and North Africa they began to take their places as squadron leaders and wing commanders. On March 9, 1942 Squadron Leader Lloyd V. Chadburn became the first BCATP graduate to command an RCAF squadron when he took charge of No. 416 Squadron.

By the end of 1943 the RCAF had 30 squadrons overseas, over half of them associated with one or another form of fighter work. Four were night fighter squadrons (Nos. 406, 409, 410 and 418), one was a Coastal Command fighter squadron (No. 404), three were army co-operation fighter units (Nos. 400, 414 and 430) and eight were day fighter units flying *Spitfires* (Nos. 401, 402, 403, 411, 412, 416, 417 and 421). With the exception of No. 417, which was operating in the Mediterranean theatre, all these fighter units were based in Britain.

Besides these there remained a dozen fighter squadrons in Canada. They had been held back to guard this country against possible direct attack by carrier-borne or long range aircraft. Most of them saw no action, and the months and years were spent in ceaseless training. Two

Kittyhawk squadrons, however, Nos. 14 and 111, operated in the Aleutian campaign of 1942-43, where they carried out escort and bombing duties. In this period they were credited with one enemy aircraft, a Japanese *A6M2-N* "Rufe" floatplane fighter shot down by Squadron Leader Kenneth A. Boomer, the Commanding Officer of No. 111 Squadron, for which he was awarded both the Commonwealth DFC and the American Air Medal.

By the fall of 1943, however, it was apparent that there was no longer any serious threat to Canada. Therefore, the strength of Canadian fighter forces in Britain was increased by the transfer of six RCAF squadrons from Canada to the United Kingdom. These became Nos. 438, 439 and 440 Squadrons, flying *Typhoon* fighter-bombers, and Nos. 441, 442 and 443 Squadrons, operating *Spitfires*. With their arrival RCAF fighter strength reached its peak.

Although these squadrons absorbed the bulk of RCAF fighter pilots in Europe, considerable numbers of pilots and observers served in RAF units. It should also be pointed out that many RCAF aircrew were American citizens who had enlisted in the force before Pearl Harbour. When the USAAF began to establish its fighter bases in England most, though by no means all, of these Americans transferred to their native air force. Besides those Americans who continued on as RCAF personnel, a handful continued to fly with RCAF units even after their formal transfer to the USAAF. This resulted in a curious situation with respect to two American pilots, Lieutenants J.F. Luma and A.A. Harrington, for although they wore USAAF uniforms, their combat reports were filed with the RCAF. Each man destroyed seven enemy aircraft, yet to this day their names do not appear on any official list of American aces.

During the war years the fighter squadrons operated in many different roles. Following the Battle of Britain the single-seat *Spitfires* had relatively little defensive work to do. Although there were sporadic "hit-and-run" attacks mounted by the *Luftwaffe*, especially after 1942, there were no further sustained daylight raids on Britain. Such defensive work as was required fell to RAF squadrons and night fighter units. This left the RCAF *Spitfires* free for offensive work over Europe. Eventually Canadian flyers operated over the continent in wing strength.

As early as December 1940, Fighter Command's aircraft had begun to carry out attacks on targets in France, and as time went by the scale of these operations expanded. The pattern varied, but generally speaking there were five main categories of work—Rodeos, Ramrods, Circuses, Roadsteads and Rhubarbs. A *Rodeo* was a fighter sweep in anything from squadron to wing strength, the aim of which was to entice the *Luftwaffe* to do battle and to destroy as many enemy aircraft as possible. Rodeos could be combined with *Ramrods*, in which bombers accompanied the formations. In a pure Ramrod the object was to destroy a target, and the primary task of the fighters was to protect the bombers. When the bombers were merely bait, and the intent was that the fighters knock down their German counterparts, it was a *Circus*. More specialized was the *Roadstead*, in which fighters covered a small force of bombers or fighter-bombers which were attacking shipping. Finally, there were the *Rhubarbs*—low level forays into enemy territory by two or four fighters shooting up any target they sighted. Often small Rodeos broke up into a series of Rhubarbs, and there were variations among the other types as well. About the spring of 1944 a new expression developed—"armed reconnaissance". These derived from the Rhubarb, but were carried out by up to twelve aircraft at a time. The expression was misleading, for they were hardly interested in "reconnaissance", their goal being to shoot up targets of opportunity.

The aims of these operations were numerous. One was the hope that the German fighter forces could be lured to battle and destroyed, although it is now apparent that the resulting actions were more damaging to the RAF than to the *Luftwaffe*. Following the German invasion of Russia in June 1941 it was hoped that a portion of the *Luftwaffe* would be drawn away from the eastern front. This, too, was not accomplished, for the bombing raids were light and directed at targets of secondary importance. When the Germans did withdraw fighters from Russia in late 1941 and again in 1942-43, they were responding to events in the Mediterranean (which became a bottomless pit sucking in *Luftwaffe* forces) and to USAAF daylight raids on German industries.

More important, however, was that in the absence of enemy daylight attacks on Britain the *Spitfire* squadrons would probably have suffered from stagnation, developing an airborne version of the "Maginot mentality". Offensive operations by Fighter Command maintained morale, nurtured an offensive spirit, trained new pilots, and permitted the evaluation of new tactics and equipment. At no time did the Command become a rusty sword. Admittedly its casualties were high, but even then the air operations could not be considered defeats. In some instances a great deal of damage was done to transport and shipping targets, and on other occasions the ends of the *Luftwaffe* were thwarted. The case of Dieppe provides an excellent example. On that occasion RAF losses were double those of the Germans, but at the same time the *Luftwaffe* was unable to hamper either the landings or the withdrawal of the assaulting troops.

In 1941-42 the struggle assumed a ding-dong appearance. Until the spring of 1941 the *Hurricanes* and *Spitfire IIs* had been able to hold their own against the *Bf 109E*.* The introduction into service of the

---

*While universally known to the Allies as the *Me 109*, this aircraft was referred to in all

Bf 109F virtually ended the days of the *Hurricane* as a fighter plane in the European theatre and threatened to inflict terrible losses on the *Spitfires*. Fighter Command regained technical parity with the faster *Spitfire V*, but by late 1941 the radial-engined *Fw 190* again upset the balance. The antidotes, the *Spitfire IXs* and *Typhoons*, set matters right again, and from early 1943 onwards the two sides remained about equal insofar as quality of equipment was concerned.

Prior to an offensive operation the pilots were called together and briefed by their Commanding Officer, Intelligence Officer, and any other staff officers whose information might be required. The nature of the objective would be given and the general aim of the operation disclosed. Then the tasks of the fighter pilots would be assigned. If they were to provide "close escort" to the bombers, the pilots would be obliged to break up attacks on their charges without being able to pursue the enemy. Fighters in the high level escort and target support wings would have greater freedom of action. Once the job had been explained, the pilots were briefed on other forces participating, expected enemy resistance, areas where flak was particularly heavy, routes, weather and Air/Sea Rescue facilities. Shortly afterwards they strolled out or rode to their aircraft.

Each pilot reacted differently to the imminence of operations. A few obtained pistols from the Intelligence Officer. Some immediately sought out their chaplains for a last moment of prayer. One man might hand a letter to a friend, to be mailed only if he went missing. Most simply studied their maps or recognition charts a little harder before departing. The first sortie for a pilot might be, for him, a dramatic moment; for the more experienced, going off on their fiftieth or hundredth sortie, it was a routine duty, tense yet undramatic. The "old boys" knew that most trips were uneventful.

Take-off was always a thrilling event as the *Spitfires* screamed down the runway. As they gathered speed their tails would rise and then they soared away, noses high. Once airborne they closed up their formations and headed for the rendezvous points. For the next hour or two the fields were quiet. In the Operations Room the radios crackled as the pilots communicated with ground stations and each other. Outside those rooms, however, the mechanics, cooks, and clerical staff had little idea of what was happening and they anxiously waited for the fighters to get back.

All eyes watched as the *Spits* returned, their engines humming,

---

contemporary German sources as *Bf* (for *Bayrische Flugzeugwerke*). This was applied to all aircraft designed before this company was reconstituted as *Messerschmitt A.G.*, including the *Bf 109* single-engined fighter, the *Bf 110* twin-engined fighter and the *Bf 108* communications aircraft. The *Bf* designation for these aircraft is therefore used in this book except in direct quotations from Allied individuals and sources.

their speed low. Was there any battle damage evident? Had the patches over the gun ports been blown away? Were all the aircraft back? If there was one or two missing, where were they—at an emergency field, down in a pasture, or lost in action? The first mechanic to reach a *Spit* which had touched down must have held his breath as the pilot paused before climbing out. Was he just tired, or was the delay due to wounds? Then, as the propeller ticked to a stop, the canopy would slide back and the pilot, pulling off his goggles and undoing his harness, would slowly emerge. His first words were with his mechanics, then with the Intelligence Officer. Perhaps, if there had been any combat, there might be a brief huddle to compare, congratulate, or console. Then the pilots were off to get a coffee or lunch before the next briefing.

As a typical action one might take a raid which occured on September 11, 1943. Late in the afternoon 33 USAAF *Marauders* set out to bomb a German airfield at Beaumont-le-Roger. The escorting force consisted of 120 *Spitfires* including 48 provided by Nos. 402 and 416 Squadrons (close cover) and Nos. 403 and 421 Squadrons (top cover). At eight minutes before six o'clock the bombs went down on the dispersal area of the enemy field. As the bombers withdrew about a dozen *Bf 109's* appeared northwest of Rouen. Two attempted to draw the top cover down on them and open the way for an attack by more *'109's*, but No. 403 Squadron, which had begun to dive on the *'109* pair, saw the trap before it could be sprung, turned into the German fighters which were attempting to take the *Spitfires* from the rear, and drove them off.

In the meantime Flying Officer Henry Dowding had been able to close on one of the decoys and opened fire. He saw strikes around the enemy's fuselage and engine cowling, then watched as the *'109* spun down out of control with black and white smoke pouring from its engine. Although he did not see it crash, he did observe a fire on the ground near where it should have hit, while another pilot saw the *'109* spin down and crash in flames. This was the only successful combat recorded on the operation, although twelve more German fighters attempted to pull up under the bombers. They were driven off by the escorts. All the Allied aircraft returned safely, but two *Spitfires* made emergency landings in England due to engine trouble.

In the spring of 1944 the *Spits* began to carry 250- and 500-lb. bombs, taking part in "softening up" the German defences in the West. On D-Day, June 6, every RCAF fighter squadron in Britain was active, and on D-Day plus one the *Spitfires* shot down 14 enemy aircraft in the vicinity of the Allied beachhead. By June 10 the three squadrons of No. 144 Wing (RCAF) were actually operating from fields within that same beachhead, and by June 27 the three RCAF *Spitfire* wings plus

No. 143 Wing, flying *Typhoons*, were all based on French airfields. Thereafter they followed the Allied advance through France, the Low Countries, and eventually into northern Germany.

German air opposition to the day fighters was spotty. The enemy had based few aircraft near the Normandy front, and at first the *Spitfires* found few aerial targets. In the third week of June, however, the *Luftwaffe* in France was beefed up with hundreds of fighters flown, for the most part, by indifferently trained pilots and backed up by an incomplete communications system. After days of uneventful patrols the Canadians suddenly found scores of targets, and a slaughter ensued. In August the German air arm was thrown in to support a panzer offensive, and when that failed the *Luftwaffe* attempted to cover the retreat of German troops over the Seine. Each event gave RCAF pilots more opportunities to score. When the Allies secured a bridgehead at Nijmegen the *Luftwaffe* was again committed to the fray, and on this occasion it suffered staggering losses. The RCAF *Spitfire* wings alone were credited with 99 enemy aircraft destroyed, three probably destroyed, and 43 damaged in the period September 25-29.

German air opposition then withered away for two months while General Galland, Inspector-General of the *Luftwaffe* fighter arm, hoarded his aircraft, pilots and fuel stocks. In December 1944, however, daylight battles became more frequent, primarily because enemy fighters had been called out to support the German drive into the Ardennes, but also because large formations were concentrated in western Germany and Holland for attacks on Allied airfields. On New Year's Day 1945 approximately 800 enemy aircraft attacked, intent on knocking out the British and American tactical air forces on the ground. The operation proved to be a disaster for the *Luftwaffe* because, while hundreds of Allied aircraft had been wrecked or damaged, relatively few aircrew personnel were killed. The Germans lost almost as many planes as they destroyed, and with them went 214 irreplaceable pilots. In the attacks that day the RCAF squadrons lost 37 aircraft and four pilots, but they shot down 30 German machines in the morning and seven more that afternoon.

Thereafter the destruction of the *Luftwaffe* was swift and terrible. Though it continued to offer resistance, its communications broke down. Allied bombing and Russian advances had robbed the Germans of their fuel supplies. Enemy pilots were now of two types—the "old pros" who had fought throughout the war and knew how to survive, and the newer ones, undertrained and relatively easy meat. RCAF fighters switched back to ground strafing, rail cutting, and general reconnaissance. The last RCAF aerial victory in Europe was scored on May 4, 1945 when Flight Lieutenant D.F. Campbell and Flying Officer T.L. O'Brian of No. 411 Squadron shot down a lumbering

He 111 northwest of Flensburg.

The preceding paragraphs are concerned almost entirely with the single-engined day fighters; the night fighters fought an entirely different kind of war. RCAF night fighter pilots went into action in the summer of 1941 flying *Beaufighters* equipped with the earliest forms of airborne radar. Later more sophisticated electronic systems were adopted which eliminated "bugs" and increased the range and accuracy of the radar sets. The *Beaufighters* were replaced by faster, more maneuverable *Mosquitos*. Gradually the element of luck was eliminated; night fighting became an artful science or a scientific art.

There were relatively few raiders with which to deal. By mid-1941 the German night bomber force had been scattered to other fronts. For more than two years the *Luftwaffe's* nocturnal attacks were delivered by forces of fewer than 50 aircraft, most of which, though fast and elusive, were unsuited to carry heavy loads. In these circumstances "kills" were few. The best hunting grounds lay inside enemy occupied territory.

Not content to wait for the enemy to come to them, the night fighter forces went over to the offensive themselves, although those aircraft carrying the latest radar equipment were restricted to flying over or near Britain lest the secret devices they carried fall into enemy hands. In the dark the *Mosquitos* began to haunt the skies of western Europe.

Special tactics were evolved and operations over enemy territory were carried out through five types of sorties, to which the name "intruding" was generally though erroneously applied. Properly, *intruder* patrols were offensive flights into hostile air space for the purpose of destroying enemy bombers at or near their bases. *Flower* patrols, flown in support of Bomber Command raids, were directed against German night fighter bases. When radar-equipped *Mosquitos* went out searching for enemy night fighters in the bomber stream it was a *Serrate* operation. If a radar-laden "Mossie" went out to intercept an enemy machine over Europe which was being tracked by radar in the UK it was a *Mahmoud* flight. Most dramatic of all was the *Ranger*, an operation by day or night in which one or two aircraft would try to track down any target within range, be it trains, ships, vehicles, barracks, or aircraft. The successful Ranger or Intruder crews planned their sorties to achieve the maximum surprise in a target area crowded with enemy aircraft, and such flights resembled the dramatic voyages of privateers. No. 418 Squadron's crews were so proficient in this that in a space of 30 months they destroyed 178 aircraft, 73 of them on the ground.

Early in 1944, however, the German night offensive was revived in retaliation for Allied bombing of the *Reich*. The "Little Blitz" never approached the proportions of the 1940-41 raids, but attacks did involve as many as 447 bombers in a night; the average was about 170 per raid. Though the night fighter crews still flew offensive sorties, they also found rewarding employment over England itself. Between February 3 and April 30, 1944, Nos. 406 and 410 Squadrons shot down 17 enemy bombers, about 14 percent of those destroyed by Fighter Command. Simultaneously RAF and RCAF intruder pilots harried the bomber bases, further contributing to the failure of the German campaign.

No sooner had the threat of renewed bombing been slapped down than, one week after D-Day, a new menace appeared. This was the *V-1* or "buzzbomb", a pilotless aircraft carrying almost a ton of explosives in its nose. Launched around the clock from ramps in northern France, they were used blindly in a frankly terroristic attempt to destroy or demoralize London. The *V-1's* were a major problem for British defences until the fall of 1944, when the Allied armies captured the launching sites. In the meantime Nos. 409 and 418 Squadrons formed part of the night defences against the *V-1*. By the end of August they shot down 92. However, at no time did they completely abandon their offensive patrols, which continued right up to the end of the war.

In the latter part of 1944 night intruding reached a new peak of efficiency. Credit for this must go to Fighter Command's belated approval of the use of A.I. Mark 10 radar over enemy-occupied territory. Even this presented problems, for although this equipment, when "looking" up, could easily detect enemy aircraft, it gave a confused picture of things lower down. RAF experience appeared to indicate that radar intruders could not operate below 5,000 feet. At lower altitudes German aircraft seemed indistinguishable from the ground "hash" which appeared on the scopes.

No. 406 Squadron, when switched over to intruder work in December 1944, proved that this was not inevitable. Tactics worked out by Russ Bannock and Don MacFadyen and their radar operators, C.J. Kirkpatrick and V.G. Shail, indicated that an enemy airplane could still be spotted at low level by the movement of some "hash" across the radar screens indicating an airplane changing its position relative to the ground. This would be particularly apparent if the intruder and its target were converging on a head-on course. Enemy aircraft normally approached their bases from a visual or radio beacon, flying rectangular left-hand circuits in preparation for landing. The *Mosquitos* flew a right-hand circuit nearby, or around the German beacons, and when they picked up a "blip" they converted a head-on approach into a stern chase, with devastating results.

There can be no better illustration of these tactics than to cite from a combat report. On the night of March 3, 1945, Flight Lieutenant H.G. MacKenzie and his observer, Warrant Officer I. Muir, went out to patrol around Rheine and Twente airfields. A revolving light beacon indicated that they were in the correct area. MacKenzie later described a textbook interception:

> We began right hand orbits around the revolving beacon at an average height of 1500 feet and at 2040 hours we picked up a contact at 4 miles range, and above, which crossed starboard to port at two miles.
>
> We did a 150° port turn and picked up the contact again at 4 miles and slightly to port. We closed in fairly rapidly and climbing, and cut the range to 1000 feet, obtaining a visual well above and on a course of approximately 300° at angels 4 [4000 feet]. I gave him a 'Bogey' challenge twice to which there was no response and no Type F was showing. I closed in to about 300-500 feet below and identified it as a *Ju. 88* which was confirmed by the navigator with night glasses. I dropped back to 400 feet and gave a short burst at 2248 seeing strikes on the port engine and a small amount of debris came back towards me. The enemy aircraft peeled off to starboard and down and we followed it in a hard starboard turn, losing height to a thousand feet and commenced an A.I. [radar] search but could not find a contact. Then at 2250 hours we saw the aircraft burning violently on the edge of a road with numerous explosions of ammunition.

MacKenzie had fired only twenty rounds of 20-mm ammunition to bring down the Junkers. The reader will note that, besides tracking the target, the crew took great pains to determine that it was hostile rather than friendly. A "Bogey challenge" was a radio message on RAF frequencies, demanding that the aircraft identify itself; "Type F" was a radar device, IFF (Identification, Friend or Foe).

All this appears simple, but it required masterful co-ordination between the pilot and his observer, the latter with his head *inside* the radar scope until visual contact had been made. The latter also had to be expert at sorting out all the signals on his screen, a job made more difficult by the fact that the RAF and *Luftwaffe* were waging simultaneous and mutual electronic warfare. MacFadyen paid high tribute to his partner when he wrote, "'Stubby' Shail was an exceptionally talented radar interception operator, who identified 'blips' in the ground returns where others simply did not try."

To achieve this level of effectiveness, the radar intruders trained constantly. When not on operations, the *Mosquitos* paired off over British airfields to practice these tactics. Their routine was a four-night cycle: two nights on ops, one night resting, and one night on exercises, doing low-level radar interceptions.

Not all Canadian fighter pilots served in Britain or on the Continent. In the Mediterranean theatre Canadians in the RAF were in action from the day in June 1940 that Italy declared war. CAN/RAF pilots flew in Greece and throughout the ding-dong battles which ranged up and down the North African shore from 1940 to 1943. In 1941 RCAF personnel began to appear in RAF squadrons, and in 1942 No. 417 Squadron joined the Desert Air Force. This unit remained in the Mediterranean until the end of the war. In its travels from Egypt to northern Italy its pilots knocked down 29 enemy aircraft.

Virtually all types of operations already described were carried out in the Mediterranean. One particular form of work proved to be especially hazardous, however. In the North African, Italian, and Aegean regions the enemy relied greatly on light coastal shipping to keep their forces supplied. RAF *Beaufighters* were entrusted with the task of suppressing this traffic. Operating at low level, the "Beaus" assisted greatly in strangling Axis garrisons, but in the process they suffered heavy losses through flak and enemy fighters, particularly during the fall and winter of 1942-43.

Malta, an island barely 60 miles south of Sicily, became a campaign in itself, and its story constituted one of the most heroic epics of the war. It was vital to the Allies as a base for ships, submarines and torpedo bombers which crippled Axis efforts to maintain forces in North Africa. In turn the Italian Air Force and later the *Luftwaffe* attempted to shatter the island base with bombing. For more than two years Malta was a fortress under siege, constantly lacking basic supplies while its defenders struggled against appalling odds. Pilots stationed there could count on three things—pleasant swimming, savage action, and dysentery. Although no RCAF unit served on Malta during its agony, CAN/RAF and individual RCAF personnel were present in substantial numbers, and the undisputed "top gun" of the campaign was Sergeant (later Flight Lieutenant) George Beurling. In all, Canadians destroyed or shared in the destruction of at least 160 enemy aircraft over Malta. Nineteen Canadians died in the defence of the island.

While the numbers of Canadians in the Far East was relatively small compared to those in the Mediterranean and Northwest Europe, this country was represented by men flying *Mohawks*, *Hurricanes*, *Spitfires* and *Thunderbolts* over Ceylon and Burma. Theirs was without a doubt the least publicized theatre of the war, yet it held as many dangers as Europe, and a few of its own besides. If enemy air opposition was less severe than over France or Italy, the chances of survival in the jungle after bailing out were less than encouraging.

The training of a fighter pilot was long and exacting, and up to three years might pass between enlistment and final reporting to an operational squadron. Having been sworn in and accepted for aircrew duties a trainee was sent to an Initial Training School where he received drill and lectures. On graduation he was promoted from Aircraftsman Second Class (AC2 or "Acey Deucey") to Leading Aircraftsman (LAC) and posted to an Elementary Flying Training School. Here he received *ab initio* flying training on *Tiger Moths* or *Finches*. After 1943 he might also be trained on *Cornells*. At these schools the hardest thing was learning how to land without tearing off the undercarriage, and the proudest moment was when the instructor climbed out of the airplane, turned to the student, and said, "Okay. Now see what you can do by yourself." The first solo was probably more important than final graduation.

From EFTS the student went on to more advanced training at a Service Flying Training School. The standard equipment at these was the *Harvard*, *Anson*, *Crane* and *Oxford*. Pilots trained on *Harvards* were generally destined for single-engined fighters while those trained on the other types were expected to proceed to twin- and multi-engined aircraft. The ways of monoplanes and retractable undercarriages, coupled with the secrets of cross-country navigation, were stressed here. Successful trainees received their wings at the end of the SFTS course. Wings parades were proud occasions when the school's Commanding Officer or a visiting dignitary pinned the flying badges on the trainees. The student was now promoted to Sergeant or commissioned as a Pilot Officer. However, he was by no means ready for combat.

Some graduates were retained in Canada to serve as staff pilots or instructors, particularly in the first two years of the war when the British Commonwealth Air Training Plan was being organized. Others might be posted to Canadian Home Defence squadrons, which were frequently used for advanced operational training. Others might be sent to the Operational Training Units at Bagotville, Quebec or Greenwood, Nova Scotia for training on *Hurricanes* or *Mosquitos*. Still others were posted overseas where they attended RAF Advanced Flying Units and OTUs for instruction in gunnery, tactics, aircraft recognition and even evasion techniques should they be forced down in enemy territory. Only after this intensive training programme was the pilot posted to an operational fighter squadron.

The pilot who now entered upon his operational career might be from any part of Canada, and could be short, tall or medium in build. He had at least junior matriculation and was in good health, something essential for any man who had to endure high speed maneuvers and still fight at high altitudes. He was almost invariably athletically-minded and played at physically demanding sports. This maintained both his wind and his reflexes. He had been taught much—how to fly and navigate; the recognition of different types of aircraft, ships and vehicles in order to distinguish friend from foe; how to keep station in a formation; how to keep a lookout for targets; how to evade an enemy aircraft; how to aim, to gauge deflection and to estimate the proper angle of attack. In short, he had been taught how to kill, how to avoid being killed, and how to protect his friends from being killed. In the end it boiled down to an elemental cliche: kill or be killed. Successful pilots added the final intangible elements of skill, courage and an extra dab of determination. A little luck helped, but the best made their own luck; chance was something that worked both ways.

The tactics which he had been taught differed with time and circumstances. Early in the war the RAF abandoned its No. 1 attack—line astern formation approaching the enemy from the rear—as this allowed only one aircraft a clear field of fire while enemy gunners had only one target with which to deal. By mid-1941 the "finger four" formation had been evolved (or rather, copied from the *Luftwaffe*) in which the aircraft operated in a loose, spread-out pattern, their positions being approximately those of the tips of four extended fingers. In a battle even these were split up, but the ideal situation was one in which an element leader did most of the shooting while his wingman covered his tail, warning of any enemy aircraft which might come too close. Some of the best pilots of the war had only modest scores; their achievements were the safe passage of their element leaders through a dogfight.

Different enemy aircraft presented different problems. Pilots attacking bombers were told repeatedly that their primary task was to get the bombers rather than escorting fighters. The *Ju 87* Stuka dive-bombers had very poor defensive armament, but with their dive brakes they could dive very steeply, yet very slowly, and were therefore difficult to hit. Fighter pilots were advised to attack them before they entered their dive. The heavy forward armament of the *Bf 110* practically ruled out head-on attacks on that type, but *Do 217* and *He 111* bombers were especially vulnerable to this tactic.

To escape from enemy fighters the *Hurricane* or *Spitfire* pilot was told to circle sharply and keep on circling in the same direction until he was either on the enemy's tail or the opponent broke off the combat. Reversing a turn was dangerous as it exposed one to enemy fire. These tactics were applicable to combats with German fighters, which could out-dive a *Spitfire* but had a wider turning circle. However, Italian fighters were more nimble than even the maneuverable *Hurricanes* and *Spitfires*. Against these it was advisable to outdistance the enemy, then turn and fight. Cruising below cloud was not recommended as the enemy, directed by a controller, might attack through cloud. Briefings on combat procedures were frequent and subject to change as new machines and tactics were developed on both sides.

Early in the war there had been some tensions existing between

Allied pilots and soldiers, stemming largely from the Battle of France and the evacuation from Dunkirk, when the troops felt, understandably but mistakenly, that they had been let down by the air forces. New respect was won for the Royal Air Force in the Battle of Britain, when Fighter Command turned the German invasion plan into an impossible dream. Thereafter the flyers took pride in the fact that, until June 1944, they (bomber crews included) virtually constituted the operational Western Front. Meanwhile, in North Africa, the Desert Air Force developed such close and effective support tactics that its pilots and the soldiers of the Eighth Army came to regard themselves as an integral team. The mutual respect thus engendered carried over into the Italian and Northwest European campaigns of 1943-45.

Yet the airmen were different from other servicemen. Their battle element was the sky, in which they fought both the enemy and the natural phenomena of wind, rain, hail and fog. The nature of their lives could suffer dramatic changes—literally "dining with the King in the morning—over France by four." Their forays into the sky were often brief, usually uneventful, yet never far from potential danger. Their uniforms and flying badges set them apart from others, and the respect accorded them was deep and sincere. Particular attention was paid to the "colonials", marked by the nationality badges on their shoulders, for they had travelled far to find their war.

Any group of specialized tradesmen develops its own jargon, and the airmen were no exception. Part of their language evolved from code words, but most of it seemed to grow mysteriously from nowhere, and to compile it all would be the task of a lexicographer. Thus, a "gong" was a decoration, "gen" was information, "ropey" and "dicey" were adjectives for dangerous (the latter from the expression "dicing with death"), and "duff" was another adjective meaning incorrect or unpleasant ("duff gen", "duff weather"). If there was a "flap" on, the situation was confused or unpleasant. On a patrol one might report a "bogey" (unidentified aircraft) which could turn out to be a "bandit" (hostile aircraft). If a man had been jilted by his girl the men would nod their heads wisely and say, "Poor old so-and-so. He was shot down in flames by his popsy." A flyer who had been killed or was reported missing had "gone west", "bought it" or "gone for a Burton" (Burton was a brand of beer). Supply officers were "grocers", mechanics were "erks", scientists were "boffins", the Intelligence Officer was referred to as "the spy" or "the Gestapo", soldiers became "pongos" or "brown jobs", and sailors were "blue jobs". Put together, this slang could be baffling to the uninitiated. Thus, a short statement might merit a detailed translation. "The kite was full of flak and we thought he'd have to use his brollie, but he made a belly-flop and off he went in the blood wagon" meant "The airplane was badly damaged by anti-aircraft fire and we thought he would have to use his parachute. However, he made a crash landing and was taken away in an ambulance."

The Canadian airmen looked, talked, and acted like professional flyers, yet few were so by nature. Most of them stepped forward from civilian ranks to join the Air Force, and most of the survivors returned to civilian life immediately following the cessation of hostilities. They had done their duty as free citizens responding to the wartime call. Not all of them came back, and some of those who did return bore physical and psychological scars from their experiences. A few—a tiny few—were unable to cope with peacetime situations. Most simply faded away into the crowd from which they had emerged, like Cincinnatus returning to his plough. Yet even today, as they carry out the routine of living, they still recall with pride the days when they heard the babble of the element leaders crackling in their earphones, when the smell of cordite filled the cockpit, and the tumbling sky was theirs.

Audet
Five in One Combat

Shortly after mid-day on December 29, 1944, eleven *Spitfire IX's* of No. 411 Squadron were lined up on Heesch airfield in Holland. They were to carry out a fighter sweep over Rheine, in western Germany, where *Luftwaffe* activity had been observed. It was a crisp, clear day, and the Battle of the Bulge was raging to the south. No. 411's pilots had been engaged during the past few days in shooting up enemy transport and in searching for German fighters which might attempt to strafe Allied troops.

At ten minutes to one (1250 hours in service time) the *Spitfires* began their take-off runs. Fighter after fighter flashed down the strip, their prop-wash setting the snow whirling at the edge of the runway. Then, their tails went up and they darted away, noses high, *Merlin* engines screaming, climbing eastwards in three sections. Leading the formation was Flight Lieutenant Elgin G. Ireland, the senior flight commander, who had two enemy aircraft to his credit. Behind, leading Blue Section, was Flight Lieutenant Robert M. Cook, whose score was two destroyed and two damaged. Heading Yellow Section was Flight Lieutenant Richard J. "Dick" Audet who, in spite of many hours of operational flying, had never yet fired at an enemy aircraft.

The *Spitfires* were circling at 10,500 feet between Rheine and Osnabruck when a distant controller, who was scanning the area by radar, advised them to turn westwards, towards Rheine. Moments later an *Me 262* jet fighter was sighted and then, ahead and to the right, a gaggle of about a dozen German fighters flying in line-astern formation slightly below the *Spitfires*. Yellow Section leader Audet eased his control stick forward and four fighters swept in to attack.

Audet picked out the last enemy machine, a *Bf 109*, and opened fire at a range of 200 yards. Cannon strikes flickered along the right-hand side of the victim's fuselage and around the wingroots. The *'109* caught fire, pouring forth clouds of dense, black smoke. Audet did not wait to see its fate. He immediately broke off the attack, but his wingman saw the Messerschmitt go down in flames. Number One.

By now Audet had lost altitude, and he circled to shake any enemy off his tail. The maneuver brought him up behind an *Fw 190* which he attacked. A torrent of shells blasted the enemy's rear fuselage and cockpit, and the *'190* caught fire aft of the engine. As Audet passed over his victim he could see the German pilot slumped over in his burning cockpit. Number Two.

Now he slipped in behind another fighter, this one a *Bf 109*. The German climbed sharply. Audet fired without observing any results. Abruptly, the Messerschmitt whipped over into a dive. Its pilot bailed out, apparently with his parachute shredded. Number Three.

Audet then spotted an *Fw 190* with a *Spitfire* on its tail, and behind the *Spitfire* another *'190*. He warned the *Spitfire* pilot of his danger, then jumped the rear-most Focke-Wulf. The enemy fighter went into a dive, but the young Canadian was able to close to 250 yards directly behind his target before pressing the "tit". Flashes along the length of the *'190's* fuselage marked his hits. Burning like a torch, the German fighter plunged straight into the ground. Number Four.

By now Yellow Section had been broken up in the wild dogfight, and Audet tried to reform his brood. He was flying at 4,000 feet when he saw an *Fw 190* some 2,000 feet below. Down went the nose of the *Spitfire*, but the intended victim saw him coming. The German turned sharply to the right, then bored directly at the *Spitfire* in a head-on attack. Audet throttled back and waited for the *'190* to come within range. At 200 yards, with only slight deflection, he thumbed a short burst. The Focke-Wulf flicked over and over, either its pilot dead or its controls severed, until it crashed. Number Five.

Audet had accomplished an incredible feat. In his first combat he had become an ace!

He scarcely believed it himself, and claimed only four destroyed and one damaged when he landed. His wingman, however, had seen each one go down. No. 411 Squadron was a jubilant unit that day. A total of eight German fighters had been shot down without loss, and "Dick" Audet was recommended for an immediate decoration. On January 14, 1945 it was announced that he had been awarded the

Distinguished Flying Cross.

He had waited a long time for his triumph. He had passed his training, endured hundreds of hours piloting a target tug aircraft, and had flown dozens of uneventful sorties, all this preceding a spectacular and tragically brief period in which he rocketed into the ranks of the RCAF's leading fighter pilots. Yet Audet was more than a deadly fighter pilot. He was so likable that he could almost have been invented for a recruiting ad. When he died, two months later, his squadron mates wrote his epitaph in their Operations Record Book:

> Modest and unassuming, he was just one of the boys and a real credit to Canada and her RCAF. His daring and keenness led to his presumed death. He was a leader, respected and admired by all. Just one swell guy.

He was born on March 13, 1922 at Lethbridge, Alberta, the youngest of six children. Though a native of Western Canada, he was of French-Canadian stock, his father having come from Baie St. Paul and his mother from Coaticook, Quebec. He was raised on a ranch near Coutts, not far from the foothills of the Rockies. He was addicted to sports and played baseball, basketball, badminton and tennis. Young Dick was a handsome youth with dark features, and he stood more than six feet tall. During the winter of 1940-41 he attended a business college in Lethbridge, and the following summer he worked briefly as a stenographer while his application for RCAF aircrew was processed.

From the outset he impressed all who met him. The recruiting officer charged with interviewing him wrote that he was a "clean cut lad, keen to be a pilot," and added the remarks, "possesses intelligence and personality. Alert, observant, well spoken and mannered. Looks good pilot material." On August 28, 1941 he was sworn in at Calgary.

Audet was posted to the Manning Depot at Brandon, Manitoba for outfitting and his first experience in "square-bashing". Then, for one month he acted as a guard at No. 12 Service Flying Training School, Brandon, pending an opening for him in the aircrew training programme. At length, in February 1942, he was sent to No. 3 Initial Training School at Victoriaville, Quebec. From there he went to No. 22 Elementary Flying Training School at Ancienne Lorette, just outside Quebec City, where he began training on the delightful Fleet *Finch* biplane. Finally, he was posted to No. 2 Service Flying Training School at Uplands (Ottawa), there to master the *Harvard*.

Throughout his training he proved to be an exemplary student who was popular with his fellows. On October 24, 1942 he was present at a wings parade held on Parliament Hill at which Prime Minister William Lyon Mackenzie King pinned flying badges on the successful students. Six weeks later, Pilot Officer Audet was in Britain.

There followed a period of waiting, and then five months of advanced and operational training. At last, in July 1943, he was posted to No. 421 Squadron at Kenley, Surrey. This proved to be almost anti-climactic. He flew four operational sorties with that unit, and though many enemy fighters were engaged during one of these, he himself had no opportunity to fire. Then, in mid-August, he was posted to Bournemouth.

If war is, as one writer has suggested, a period of great boredom interrupted by moments of intense excitement, Audet's experience in boredom was to become extensive. For a time he flew with an artillery flight. From December 1943 until July 1944 he operated as a tug pilot, pulling a drogue back and forth while anti-aircraft gunners practised their aim. His most outstanding success in this period was in a campaign which ended on July 9, 1944 with his marriage to an English girl, Iris Gibbons.

It was now mid-1944, and although he had been overseas for 18 months he was scarcely any closer to the war than on the day of his arrival. Finally he was posted to Kirton-on-Lindsey, where a month was required to polish up his operational flying. In August he was posted to the continent, and on September 14 he joined No. 411 Squadron near Brussels. Audet had finally found his war.

Nevertheless, aerial combat continued to evade him. Following the battles of August and September, first over the Seine and then at Nijmegen, the *Luftwaffe* had gone into hibernation. Audet's first combat sorties were uneventful patrols over the lines. Late in October the squadron embarked upon dive-bombing. In this he showed some flair; once his section achieved 100 percent accuracy in blasting a rail junction, and on another occasion his bomb cut a spur line and damaged a German factory. When enemy panzer forces opened the Battle of the Bulge, No. 411 took part in sweeps, looking for German aircraft on the northern flank of the battle. Audet had completed 52 sorties and had mixed only briefly in three dogfights up to the moment on December 29 when he suddenly and dramatically vaulted into the lists of "aces".

From then onward, as though he were trying to make up for the months of idle waiting, he became a tiger in the cockpit. A more Jekyll-and-Hyde combination would be difficult to imagine. On the ground he remained the diffident, likable boy from Alberta, yet once he was strapped into his *Spitfire* he became a whirlwind bent on engulfing the enemy.

If anyone thought that his quintuple victory had been a fluke, these doubts were soon resolved. On New Year's Day he blasted two *Fw 190's* into flaming wrecks, thus raising his score to seven destroyed. He teamed up with Flight Lieutenant J.J. Boyle on January 4, 1945 to shoot down three more *Fw 190's*, one apiece and one shared. On the 14th he increased his total to 9 1/2 when he blew another *'190* to bits over Enschede.

Death, however, flew perilously near each day, and on the 22nd Audet came close to losing his life. While patrolling near Osnabruck the long range fuel tank which hung beneath his *Spitfire* was hit by flak and exploded. Despite the damage to his aircraft he limped home. Next day he achieved another rare distinction; he became the only RCAF pilot of the war to destroy two enemy jet fighters.

That day he was flying an armed reconnaissance sortie when he spotted a line-up of aircraft parked on the west side of Rheine airfield, the hornet's nest where most of the operational *Me 262's* were based. As he dived to strafe the stationary machines, a tractor began pulling an *Me 262* towards the edge of the field. Audet aimed ahead of the tractor and at 1000 yards cut loose. The target ran into his stream of bullets, and the *'262* burst into flames.

He then pressed on to Osnabruck. Finding nothing of interest, he turned for home. Northeast of Rheine he saw a lone *Me 262* approaching the field with its wheels down. Audet dived from 8,000 to 4,500 feet, building up terrific speed as he went. As the distance narrowed between them, the German saw his pursuer and raised his undercarriage. The enemy jet accelerated slowly, however, and Audet was able to close to 300 yards range before jabbing the trigger button on his stick. The *Me 262* caught fire, spiralled into the ground, and exploded. Not far away the smoke was still rising from his victim of half an hour before. The amazing Dick Audet had now destroyed 11 1/2 enemy aircraft, all of them fighters, and all but one of them in air-to-air combat.

Next day, the 24th, he damaged another *Me 262* near Munster, but this time the jet outdistanced him. It was the end of his scoring. Once more the *Luftwaffe* faded away, hoarding its fuel and machines for the Eastern Front, where the enemy were trying to stabilize the Silesian battlefield. No. 411 Squadron reverted to strafing enemy vehicles and dive-bombing road and rail points.

Flak remained, however, and on February 8, 1945 Audet had another brush with this menace. While shooting up an enemy airfield his aircraft was hit and the controls damaged. Back at Heesch he found that the *Spitfire* would not level off properly, and thus was too dangerous to land. He climbed away, then bailed out safely. Soon afterwards he was granted leave and went to England to visit his wife. He returned to No. 411 on March 2.

In the meantime his continuing good work had brought further recognition, and he was awarded the Bar to his DFC with the following citation:

> This officer is an outstanding fighter. Since his first engagement towards the end of December 1944 he has completed numerous sorties during which he has destroyed a further six

enemy aircraft, bringing his total victories to eleven. Flight Lieutenant Audet has also most effectively attacked locomotives and mechanical vehicles. His skill and daring have won the highest praise.

The award was officially announced in the *London Gazette* on March 9, 1945, but Audet never saw it. Six days previously, while attacking a rail siding, his aircraft was hit by flak and burst into flames. From 500 feet he crashed into a wood near Coesfeld. He was not yet 23 years old.

Bannock
Buzz Bomb Destroyer

No. 418 (City of Edmonton) Squadron was remarkable for many things, not the least being that a large proportion of its aircrew actually came from Edmonton. It was not service policy to post people from selected regions to particular units, for if a squadron were to suffer heavy casualties then the incidence of losses would be more severe in one region rather than another. Mixing geographic backgrounds in a given unit ensured that casualties would be spread across Canada. Nevertheless, an unusually large number of Edmontonians found their way into No. 418, and three of the squadron's twelve aces came from that city. One of them, Wing Commander Russ Bannock, rose to command of the squadron.

It should be noted, however, that prior to 1939 Edmonton was probably the most air-minded city in Canada. From there aircraft probed into the north, eventually flying mail to the shores of the Arctic Ocean. Gilbert Labine, discoverer of Canada's first great uranium deposits, started by air from Edmonton. The city could—and did—boast of its aerial personalities. Mayor Kenneth Blatchford (later an MP) was probably the "flyingest" Canadian politician of the '20s. James Bell, the airport manager, was a single-minded character. There was also a host of the most famous of Canadian bush pilots—Leigh Brintnell, Louis Leigh, Paul and Jack Caldwell, Andy Cruikshank, Con Farrell, Elmer Fullerton, Vic Horner, Grant McConachie, George Gorman, W.R.

"Wop" May and C.H. "Punch" Dickens. Their exploits thrilled the world and put Edmonton in the forefront of commercial aviation. Much of this undoubtedly rubbed off on the youngsters who were raised there during the great, classic bush-flying era. Not only could they read of the latest aviation advances in their local papers, but they could see the principals about the city, and watch as the Bellancas and Fairchilds rumbled off into the wilderness. Anyone wishing to understand the impact of these events need only read *Airborne from Edmonton* by Eugenie Myles, which describes in detail the exploits of the flying pioneers and their overall effect on Edmonton.

One person much affected was Russell Bannock, who was born on November 1, 1919, the son of Austrian parents who had migrated to Canada. In fact, the family name was Bahnuk, which was changed to a more socially acceptable spelling in 1938. The ancestral origins also resulted in the odd situation of Russ Bannock having two cousins in the *Luftwaffe*.

His father was a railroad foreman, and young Bannock received his early education at Cooking Lake, Alberta. He attended high school in Edmonton itself, where he played a great deal of hockey and baseball. On leaving school in 1936 he worked for a variety of firms. He started with the Hudson's Bay Company as a freight purser on a steamboat in the Northwest Territories. Then he took up prospecting with Consolidated Mining and Smelting Corporation. That gave him the idea of becoming a flying geologist. In 1938 he took some courses at the University of Alberta together with flying lessons at the Edmonton Aero Club. The following year he qualified for his commercial lisense and was hired by Yukon Southern Air Transport to act as a second pilot on the run between Edmonton and Fort St. John. Flying Barkley-Grow transports, Bannock acquired considerable twin-engined experience before he was 20 years old.

On September 9, 1939, one day before Canada declared war on Germany, he enlisted in the RCAF. A measure of his professional standing at that time was that "Wop" May himself provided him with a reference. Soon he was training at Trenton and then Camp Borden. On February 28, 1940 he was awarded his service wings, and almost at once he was back at Trenton as an advanced instructor. The RCAF needed pilots to man the expanding British Commonwealth Air Training Plan and Bannock, with all his experience, was called upon to "teach teachers", showing pilots how best to impart their skills to the students who followed. For more than three years he carried on this work, rising to Squadron Leader in the process.

In November 1943, however, he was posted to No. 36 Operational Training Unit at Greenwood, Nova Scotia, where he once more became a pupil, this time learning the ways of the fast, deadly, and extremely beautiful *Mosquito*. Three months later he sailed to England, and after further training he arrived at Holmsley South airfield to join No. 418 Squadron on June 10, 1944.

No. 418 was then under No. 11 Group of Fighter Command (at that time burdened with the cumbersome title, Air Defence of Great Britain), carrying out intruder work. On the night of June 14/15 Bannock and his RAF observer, Flying Officer R.R. Bruce, attacked Avord airfield. In the face of intense flak and searchlights they burned out a *Bf 110* on the runway. It was a good start for beginners.

By this time, however, the Germans had begun lobbing *V-1's* at Britain, and for the next ten weeks No. 418 Squadron and Russ Bannock were very much concerned with these pilotless aircraft. Travelling at high speed and low level, the *V-1's* were difficult to track and shoot down, either with a fighter or with an anti-aircraft gun. Although they could neither dodge nor shoot back, the buzzbombs were dangerous to attack, for once hit they were liable to blow up in the face of a fighter pilot.

No. 418 Squadron was assigned the job of intercepting the *V-1's* at night. Although their "Mossies" carried no radar, the *V-1's* could be spotted by the pulsating flames of their ram-jet engines. The unit's aircraft patrolled over the English Channel in order to catch the "Doddlebugs" when their speed was relatively low; the buzzbombs accelerated gradually from a launch speed of 320 miles per hour until, by the time they reached the coast of England, they were travelling at nearly 400 miles per hour. Moreover, a *V-1* shot down over the sea could do no damage, whereas one downed over land might still kill or maim persons on the ground. To add incentive, higher authorities ruled that a *V-1* shot down over water would be counted as one aircraft, while one destroyed over land would be considered only half an airplane. The spur helped, for although the work had its dangers, it lacked the thrills of traditional intruder work.

The first *V-1's* shot down by No. 418 were destroyed on the night of June 16/17 by Flight Lieutenants D.A. MacFadyen and Colin J. Evans. By the end of the month the "City of Edmonton" Squadron had shot down 20. Bannock flew his first "Anti-Diver" patrol, as these sorties were called, on the night of June 19/20, when he saw three *V-1's* and shot one down into the Channel.

On the night of July 3/4 Bannock and Bruce attacked five *V-1's*. The first two engagements were inconclusive, but the next three buzzbombs went down as he fired short bursts from a range of no more than 200 yards. With four robot bombs destroyed, Bannock and Bruce were tied with the team of Colin Evans and S. Humblestone. Three nights later the squadron's crews shot down twelve buzzbombs. Evans landed to report shooting down three, but by then Bannock had already checked in with four, three of which he had hit over the Channel. In one attack he had shot out the *V-1's* engine at a range of 400 yards, and the device had exploded in the sea. Having gone into the lead, Bannock stayed out in front. By the end of July he had shot down eight more, and in August he added three *V-1's* to his score making a total of 19, almost a quarter of all those destroyed by the whole squadron.

The campaign forced the aircrews to adopt strange tactics. An excellent method of intercepting the "Doodlebugs" was to cruise near the French coast at about 10,000 feet until a flash heralded the launching of a *V-1*. The *Mosquito* would then cruise westward until the target passed slowly underneath, at which point the fighter dived almost vertically on the buzzbomb. It was a good idea to close one eye before pushing the trigger, so that after the *V-1* exploded with a blinding flash at least one eye retained night vision.

Bannock's most unusual *V-1* "kill" was the last one, achieved on the night of August 12/13. While chasing a *V-1* he scored several strikes with cannon shells, but although it slowed down, the robot refused to crash. Just before reaching the British anti-aircraft gun belt, the buzzbomb dipped its right wing and headed back towards France. Bannock followed, fascinated. Near Boulogne he opened up with his machine guns. The *V-1* plunged into a German military zone and exploded.

The *Mosquitos* of No. 418 Squadron at this time each carried a painting of an Al Capp cartoon character and symbols indicating the victories scored. Bannock's machine, "Hairless Joe", now carried a long string of miniature swastikas and *V-1's*. Meanwhile, other forms of recognition appeared. In July he was given command of "B" Flight; later both he and Bruce were awarded the Distinguished Flying Cross.

During the course of the Battle of the Flying Bombs Bannock did not altogether forget intruder work. In July he destroyed one enemy aircraft over France. Once the *V-1* launching sites had been captured, however, he was able to devote his time entirely to carrying out Ranger and intruder flights. He seemed to have a nose for trouble; between August 30 and September 27 he wrote five aircraft off the inventory of the *Luftwaffe*.

Typical of these was a Day Ranger flight to Copenhagen on August 30. Accompanied by another *Mosquito* piloted by Flying Officer S.P. Seid he attacked Vaerlose airfield at treetop level. With one short burst he set a *Ju 88* on fire. Then he spotted a *Bf 110* parked in a blast bay with a mechanic working near its tail. Bannock later reported, "After one look at us he broke all speed records during a sprint in an easterly direction." A short burst aimed at the enemy's port wing root set the Messerschmitt on fire. With the element of surprise gone, the "Mossies" hightailed it for home.

Bannock's aircraft did not go unscathed during these encounters. On September 27 he flew some 600 miles to reach Parrow airfield on the German Baltic coast. The outward journey lasted two hours. Arriving shortly after sunrise he tore into the airfield and blasted two *Bf 108* trainers into smithereens. Another *Bf 108* tried to ram the *Mosquito*, but Bannock pulled away. His port engine, however, had been hit by flying wreckage, and the temperature was rising fast. Then the engine caught fire. He pushed the extinguisher button, doused the flames, then feathered his prop. At low-level, with only one engine, he headed for Britain. The return flight lasted more than three hours, and the feat won Bannock and Bruce the Bars to their DFCs.

Yet Bannock also witnessed war in a different aspect. Early in September he and two other crews were despatched to Toulouse to escort a captured *He 177* back to Britain. The field was littered with wrecked aircraft, and snipers were still active in the area, which had been only recently liberated. There was incessant fighting between the *Forces Francais de l'Interieur* (FFI or Maquis) and those who had collaborated with the Germans. One of the navigators was virtually picked up by a pretty French girl. Before anything could happen, though, members of the FFI arrested her, explaining that she had been a Gestapo agent and would probably be executed. The flyers returned to England loaded with grapes and champagne, but they also carried memories of the seamier side of the war.

In mid-October Bannock was promoted to Wing Commander and given command of No. 418. A month later, however, he was posted to take charge of No. 406. There he was teamed up with a new observer, Flight Lieutenant C.J. Kirkpatrick DFC of Kindersley, Saskatchewan. Kirkpatrick was a quiet accountant who had won his "gong" while radar operator for Flight Lieutenant D.J. "Blackie" Williams.

Unlike some pilots, who were skilled in combat but baffled by staff work, Bannock proved to be a magnificent squadron commander, neither permitting himself to be permanently chairborne nor yet ignoring the routine duties of his job. He and Kirkpatrick destroyed two enemy aircraft and damaged two more before the latter was posted away in April 1945. Bannock then flew with Flight Lieutenant W.A. Boak, and in the last month of the war they destroyed two enemy aircraft and damaged one.

Intruding had its strange aspects. On the night of January 5, 1945, after downing an *He 111*, Bannock heard a sharp command in his earphones: "Waggle your wings, bogey." He immediately rocked the *Mosquito* violently. It was soon apparent, however, that he was not the intended victim, for about four miles away another airplane caught fire and crashed. Evidently a German pilot, not tuned to RAF radio frequencies, had failed to waggle his wings.

His last victory, achieved on the night of 23/24 April 1945, marked the climax of an exciting evening. He had been patrolling over several enemy fields without result and was approaching Wittstock airfield. As he did so the airfield lights flashed on as if to receive an aircraft. Bannock's own combat report best describes the events which followed:

As we approached the aerodrome, going full bore, and hoping to get a contact before the aircraft got in to land, we noticed the airfield lighting being flashed on and off frantically, no doubt an urgent intruder warning to the enemy aircraft in the circuit. Almost immediately we noticed an aircraft crash and catch fire on the final approach to the flare path . . . We concluded this aircraft crashed trying to do a low approach to avoid detection by intruders, and . . . we are very much pleased to think we may have been responsible for the prang. We flew over the crash, and . . . we could identify it as a *Ju. 88.*

At 0310, while continuing our counter-circuits, we obtained a head-on contact at almost minimum range. Height of fighter at this time was 400 feet, and position about one mile south of Wittstock airfield. Head-on contact was converted to a stern chase, and a visual soon established at 2,000 feet. We followed the aircraft visually through two tight orbits of the airfield, and then the aircraft started to take violent evasive action. We managed to stay behind and in anticipation of a port peel-off, we turned inside of the aircraft and closed the range until we got dead below him. He was easily identified as a *Ju. 88* in the bright moonlight. I dropped back to 500 feet, but just as I was about to open fire, the enemy aircraft went into another of his tight port turns. We followed, opening fire with a short burst and some deflection, managing to get strikes on the fuselage and starboard engine, which began to stream smoke. The target then went into a screaming dive. We followed at full bore, and fired a second burst at 1,000 feet range. At the same time the enemy top gunner opened fire with extremely inaccurate red tracer. Our burst resulted in a few more strikes, and immediately afterwards a parachute came sailing by our windscreen. A third short burst clinched the issue; the enemy aircraft caught fire, and crashed in some woods.

Wing Commander Bannock ended the war with a score of eleven enemy aircraft and 19 flying bombs destroyed. Shortly after the close of hostilities he was decorated with the Distinguished Service Order, an honour generally granted for qualities of leadership as well as bravery. The citation to his DSO noted his score and added that he had been largely responsible for No. 406 Squadron's efficiency and successes.

Later he attended the RAF Staff College in England and was offered a permanent commission in the post-war RCAF. He pondered the offer, then declined it. In 1946 he left the force and joined De Havilland of Canada.

As Chief Test Pilot of the firm, Bannock took the world-beating *Beaver* off the ground in 1947. By 1950 he had become a Director of the company, and in 1964 he was appointed Vice President in charge of sales. In 1968 he left De Havilland to form his own company, Bannock Aerospace Limited, specializing in sales and consulting services with respect to STOL aircraft. However, in August 1975 he returned to De Havilland in his former post, responsible for marketing. In January 1976 Russ Bannock became President of De Havilland Aircraft of Canada. The boy from Edmonton had come a long, long way.

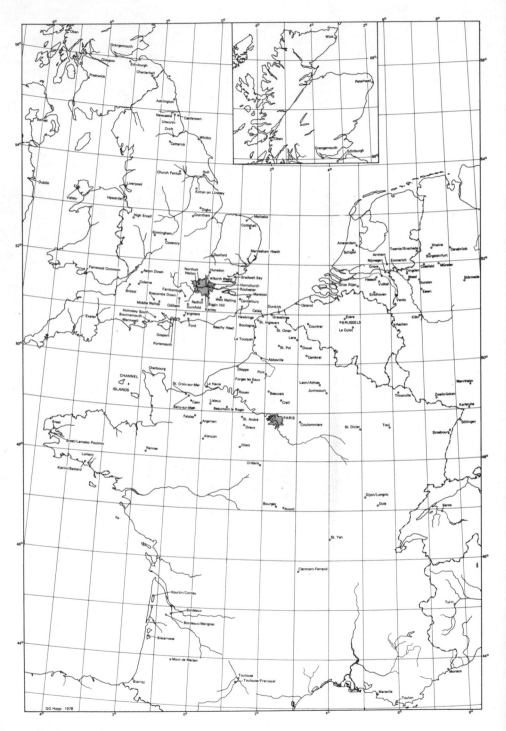

GG Hopp · 1978

Barton
Ex-Patriate Ace

Sometimes, for inexplicable reasons, particular communities produce an unusual number of successful flyers. In the First World War the village of Carleton Place, Ontario was home to three notable aces—Roy Brown, Stearne Edwards and Murray Galbraith—while in the Second World War, Kamloops, British Columbia was associated with four aces (Barton, Kipp, McElroy and Williams) plus one of the truly great Canadian bomber leaders, Wing Commander John Fulton.

Robert A. "Butch" Barton was born in that city on June 7, 1916, though he subsequently grew up in Penticton. In January 1936 he joined the RAF on a short service commission. As a pilot in No. 41 Squadron he became one of the first Canadians to fly *Spitfires*, and when the war broke out he was fully qualified on this aircraft. A fellow Canadian in the unit was Flying Officer H.P. Blatchford of Edmonton, the first Canuck to score an aerial victory during the war.

No. 41 flew numerous patrols during the opening months of the war, but few German raiders ventured over Britain, and the squadron experienced no combats. On May 16, 1940 Flying Officer Barton was posted to No. 249 Squadron, then forming at Church Fenton on *Hurricanes*. He was given command of "B" Flight, one of whose members was an eager Britisher, Flying Officer J.B. Nicholson, of whom more will be said presently. By this time the Allied armies in Europe had begun their tragic retreat, and by mid-June it was evident that their defeat on the continent was only days away. With the invasion of

Britain now a very real threat, the squadron personnel worked like Trojans to bring their unit up to operational standards. In June they flew more than 1,000 hours, and on July 3 No. 249 was ready for combat.

The fate of the Allied cause now, as never before or afterwards, hung on how well the RAF's Fighter Command stood up to the enemy. Thanks to heroic efforts in evacuating the British Expeditionary Force from Dunkirk, Britain had an army, but it was short of rifles, field guns, vehicles, and tanks, all heavy equipment having been left behind in France. The Royal Navy was incomparably stronger than its German counterpart, but operations in Norway and at Dunkirk had shown that naval superiority was a mirage unless it was coupled with air superiority.

In previous campaigns the Germans had developed a pattern of operations which made the future battle predictable to some degree. The first step was to knock out the opposing air force, if possible on the ground. Next came moves to outflank the main defence lines, either with airborne troops or panzer thrusts. Once that was accomplished, the enemy enveloped and destroyed their opposition. Round One in any invasion of Britain would clearly involve an attempt to destroy the Royal Air Force, itself mauled but unbroken after the Battle of France.

Fortunately the German High Command had not expected such rapid successes as had been gained in May 1940, and the speedy collapse of France took even the victors by surprise. Before any descent on Britain could be made, a blueprint for attack had to be formulated. Enemy planning went forward slowly, for Hitler hoped that Britain, fighting alone, might sue for peace. It was only when Prime Minister Churchill made it clear that the struggle would continue, that *Der Fuehrer* took an active interest in the invasion project. "Sealion", the proposed cross-Channel operation, continued to develop slowly, however, as the German Army and Navy disagreed on such basic matters as the width of any front for a landing and the number of troops to be employed. The first force to be ready for its part was the *Luftwaffe*, under its blustering chief, ex-fighter ace Hermann Goering. Goering was inclined to believe that "Sealion" was unnecessary; air attacks alone, he felt, would be sufficient to compel Britain to surrender.

This lack of agreement cost the enemy time, and in the interval Fighter Command was able to marshal its strength while building up some reserves of pilots and aircraft. Throughout July and the first week of August it was occupied mainly in warding off attacks on coastal shipping. Such operations nibbled away a portion of the reserves, but they also enabled Fighter Command to give some new pilots battle experience while the radar net was checked and co-ordination between ground controllers and fighters improved. There was also a stimulus to morale; for the loss of 150 fighters the RAF knocked down 286 German planes.

Nevertheless, on the eve of the Battle of Britain the odds appeared to be extremely unequal. The *Luftwaffe* was able to operate from fields which formed a semi-circle around the northeastern, eastern and southern approaches to Britain. *Luftflotten 2, 3* and 5 had at their disposal 1,370 long-range bombers, 406 dive bombers, 813 single-engined fighters and 319 long-range fighters and fighter-bombers. The Germans, moreover, held the initiative; it was they who would decide when and where the battles would be fought. To defend the whole of the United Kingdom Fighter Command had some 900 *Spitfires* and *Hurricanes*, but the most serious shortages were in pilots. The RAF, however, had two factors operating in its favour. The first was the chain of radar stations which would give warning of any enemy approach which would give warning of any enemy approach; the other was the fact that Fighter Command would be in action near its bases and over friendly territory. Another factor would also become important as the weeks passed; German intelligence reports were extremely inaccurate in assessing the organization of the defences and RAF losses.

The enemy's campaign to destroy the RAF itself began on August 13, when the *Luftwaffe* flew 1,485 sorties, mainly in co-ordinated raids on RAF fields. The next day, as the raids continued, No. 249 Squadron was moved from Church Fenton further south to Boscombe Down. This put the unit right in the middle of subsequent fighting, and the pilots wasted no time in taking advantage of the situation.

On August 15 the *Luftwaffe* launched attacks from all sides, including bombers escorted by *Bf 110's* from Scandanavia. The northern attackers were mauled by fighters from the Midlands. In the south the enemy gave Fighter Command a harder time, for there the bombers were closely escorted by *Bf 109E's*, the hottest fighters in the *Luftwaffe*. Several major raids were conducted, and at 5.19 P.M. No. 249 Squadron was scrambled to meet one estimated at 70 to 80 bombers with their fighter consorts.

Flight Lieutenant Barton was leading a section when he sighted a formation of between 30 and 50 enemy aircraft. He ordered the section to attack the rear of this force, but as the *Hurricanes* approached, the *Bf 110* escorts turned to meet them. Barton fired a two-second burst at one and saw smoke billowing from an engine. He then pounced on another, giving it two long bursts. Bullets poured into the *'110's* fuselage immediately behind the pilot and smoke streamed from its starboard engine. He followed it down and saw it crash.

The next day No. 249 was in action again. On this occasion Barton did not score, but it was a noteworthy battle, for in it Jamie Nicholson pressed home an attack on a *Bf 110* even though his own machine was in flames and a *Bf 109* was firing on him. He survived his wounds and was later awarded the Victoria Cross, the only pilot in Fighter Command to be so honoured, and one of only two Second World War fighter pilots to receive this award.

There was little activity on the 17th, and although the 18th was marked by bitter dogfights, the battle momentarily died down while both sides took stock of recent events. Assaults on Fighter Command fields were renewed on the 24th, however, and in the next four weeks the Battle of Britain raged varying only in the degree of ferocity.

On the 24th Barton was credited with a share in the probable destruction of a *Bf 109*; postwar investigation has led researchers to conclude that this machine, from *II./JG 2*, was actually destroyed. After that date most German raids were directed at targets in Kent, leaving No. 249 at the fringe of the battle. On September 1, however, the squadron moved to North Weald, which put it back in the thick of things.

On September 2 Barton became involved in an early morning battle with a score of *Do 17Z's* escorted by nearly 100 *Bf 109's*. The odds were 12 to 1 as the *Hurricanes* tore into the bombers. The Dornier formation split up, not because of the interceptors but because they had been assigned to raid several different airfields. Barton, accompanied by Pilot Officer J.R.B. Meaker, proceeded to chop a Dornier into little bits with burst after burst. His *Hurricane* was damaged by enemy fire, and the German crew ejected small bombs which fortunately failed to hit the fighter. At last the bomber crashed on Rochford airfield.

In spite of the victories that day, the Battle of Britain was not going well for the RAF. In the combat in which Barton had helped in shooting down the Dornier, No. 249 had lost one pilot who was wounded plus three *Hurricanes* destroyed and two damaged. The *Luftwaffe* was pressing hard, inflicting such damage on the sector stations that Fighter Command was barely holding its own. Between August 24 and September 6 the British fighters downed 380 German planes at a cost of 286 *Spitfires* and *Hurricanes*. Worse still, the supply of new pilots was falling behind casualties, and far too many replacement pilots had been rushed through training. Barton himself was shot down on the 5th, his *Hurricane* descending in flames, but he bailed out successfully. Next day the unit's CO, John Grandy, was wounded by *Bf 109's* and Barton became acting leader of No. 249.

Although its losses were larger than it could afford, Fighter Command was nevertheless accomplishing much. So long as it showed teeth and spirit, the German commanders, never really enthusiastic about "Sealion", were ready to delay and argue among themselves. Enemy aircrews, who had been assured several times that Fighter Command was on the verge of collapse, were becoming disspirited in the face of a force which was obviously still in fighting trim. Nevertheless, had the battle continued in the form it had been following, Fighter Command might well have been worn down and destroyed. That this did not happen was due mainly to the *Luftwaffe* itself.

On September 7, in retaliation for RAF raids on Berlin, the Germans switched their bombers onto London. Not only did this provide relief for the RAF's battered airfields, but it imposed near-intolerable burdens on the short-ranged *Bf 109* escorts. On the 7th, the first day that London was extensively bombed in daylight, the Germans lost 41 aircraft to the RAF's 28, and in the following days the *Luftwaffe* was, in its turn, to take larger losses than it could afford.

Barton was active throughout this period, taking part in many scrambles and assisting in the probable destruction of two Dornier bombers on September 15. Three days later he damaged an *He 111*. Then came September 27 which, for No. 249 Squadron, was the most successful day in the Battle of Britain.

Early that morning Barton was leading the squadron on a patrol south of London in company with No. 46 Squadron. Over Redhill they discovered twenty *Bf 110's* flying in a defensive circle. Barton led a diving attack from out of the sun, lined up a '110 in his sights, and delivered a four-second burst. His victim's port engine seemed to pour off steam (more probably glycol smoke) and pieces flew off. His own aircraft had been hit, however, and he had to break away for a landing at Gatwick. Another pilot reported that the *Bf 110* had crashed. In that dogfight No. 249 lost two pilots (one killed, one wounded), but they claimed eight destroyed and five probably destroyed. Before the day had ended the figures had risen to 21 destroyed and eight probables. One British flyer, Pilot Officer A.G. Lewis, was credited with six German machines that day. All this pushed No. 249 Squadron into second place in Fighter Command scoring, only No. 303 Squadron claiming more victories that month.

The Battle of Britain now petered out. Hitler virtually cancelled "Sealion" on September 19, turning his attention to a projected invasion of Russia. Although the battle had been conceded to the RAF, the victory was not immediately apparent to Fighter Command crews. *Luftwaffe* operations continued, although bombers were being switched over increasingly to night work. By day the enemy flew fighter and fighter-bomber sweeps over Britain. These were not particularly destructive, but they were difficult to intercept. Moreover, the Messerschmitts were being freed from the task of protecting bombers, and hence were more dangerous adversaries.

No. 249 Squadron flew many patrols in October, but few combats were recorded. On October 4, however, news arrived that four pilots had been granted awards, Barton receiving the Distinguished Flying Cross. Although he was entitled to wear the DFC ribbon from that day forward, it was not until January that he received the decoration from the hands of King George VI during an investiture at Duxford.

On the afternoon of October 29 Barton fought what was perhaps the most remarkable action in his career. The squadron was taking off from North Weald when a pack of *Bf 109's* dive-bombed the field. He caught up with the German "Tail-end Charlie" and let fly. The enemy plane began streaming glycol, but before Barton could finish off his victim the other *'109's* throttled back and it appeared that he would be swallowed up by the German formation. One by one, Barton engaged them, firing at six in all. One of them was hit and damaged, while another, taking a burst in the petrol tank, began trailing a plume of fire. The German pilot, *Oberstleutnant* Otto Hintze, bailed out safely and was taken prisoner. Hintze was a prize in himself; he was one of the *Luftwaffe's* top-notch fighter-bomber pilots and had been recommended for the Knight's Cross.

On November 7 Barton chalked up a probable kill in a wild melée with *'109's* over the Thames Estuary; No. 249 as a unit claimed five destroyed and four probables. Then, on November 11, he registered another confirmed victory. On this occasion he was leading seven fighters on a convoy patrol when they sighted an *He 59* seaplane and then what they identified as a *Ju 86* bomber. One pilot downed the Heinkel while Barton attacked the Junkers. The combat, just 200 feet above the sea was short and decisive. The bomber caught fire and dived into the Channel. However, one might question Barton's aircraft recognition. The presence of an obsolete *Ju 86* on this front appears unlikely. The victim was more probably an Italian *BR.20*, a type roughly resembling the *Ju 86*. The *Regia Aeronautica* was that day mounting an attack on Britain, more for political than military reasons, which supports the theory that Barton's victim was indeed a Fiat.

Early in December he was promoted to Squadron Leader and given command of No. 249. On the 29th he took part in the squadron's first offensive operation, a two-aircraft "Mosquito patrol" near Boulogne during which he shot up St. Inglevert airfield. On January 10, 1941 he returned to the same area when *Blenheims*, escorted by five fighter squadrons, opened the RAF's campaign of cross-Channel daylight raids. Nevertheless, his next victories were gained on a defensive convoy patrol rather than on offensive flying. On February 4 he and two other pilots were vectored onto two *Bf 110's*. The ensuing dogfight saw the *Hurricanes* weaving in and out of clouds, attacking head-on and then pursuing. Both Messerschmitts were shot down, one being destroyed by Barton alone, while the other kill was shared with a fellow pilot.

Shortly afterwards No. 249 began re-equipping with *Hurricane II's*. In mid-April notice was received that the squadron would be withdrawn from operations, effective May 1, for transfer to the Mediterranean. This was duly carried out, and on May 21 the unit arrived at Takali, Malta, bolstering that island's defences.

At this point the records of Barton's operational career become maddeningly scarce. During the siege of Malta his squadron maintained indifferent records, and some reports were lost or destroyed through bombing. It is known that on July 31 his engine failed soon after take off. He crash-landed in a field. In spite of second-degree burns he was soon back on duty. On October 31 he was awarded a Bar to his DFC after being credited with the destruction of four more enemy aircraft. His final score on that island was six enemy machines (one shared), including two Italian fighters in a single sortie and a *BR.20* bomber at night. His wartime tally was 13 1/2 destroyed, 4 1/2 probably destroyed, and at least nine damaged.

He left No. 249 Squadron on December 8, 1941, having been with the unit for more than 18 months. Throughout most of the remainder of the war he held staff positions, though in 1945 he flew some sorties in *Mustangs* while escorting American heavy bombers. He had been promoted to Wing Commander in February 1942, and in the summer of 1945 he was made an Officer of the British Empire (OBE).

Wing Commander Barton remained in the post-war RAF, retiring from that force on August 6, 1958. In 1965 he returned to Canada. He now lives in Hedley, B.C., with extended vacations in Arizona.

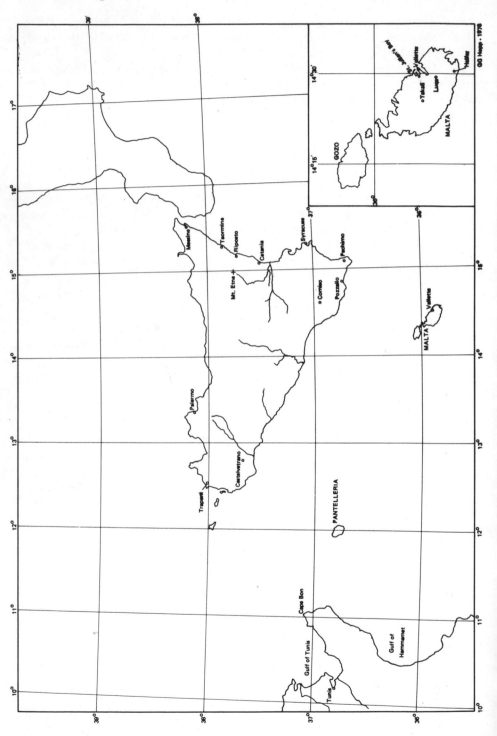

Beurling
"Screwball"

His favourite adjective was "screwball" and the word clung to him as a nickname. He was the most widely publicised Canadian fighter pilot of the war, and also the most controversial. He was a lone wolf, despising discipline and dedicated to flying and fighting. He virtually invited the wrath of senior officers, yet he won the respect of such aces as Group Captain Adolph Malan and Wing Commander J.E. Johnson. He twice refused a commission because he feared the responsibilities which would go with it. He was a poor leader and a mediocre instructor. One of the most successful pilots of the war, he was nevertheless "retired" six months before VE-Day. In the post-war period he made no effort to hide his contempt for the RCAF. In another age he might have been a pirate, a mercenary soldier, or a gangland hit-man. "Screwball" Beurling, known more widely to the public as "Buzz" Beurling, was a man of contradictions, and nothing could have been more ironic than the manner of his death. The great Canadian ace, survivor of terrible battles and mishaps, was killed in the crash of a *Norseman* light transport while en route to Israel, looking for another war.

He was born at Verdun, Quebec on December 6, 1921. As he grew up, his father hoped that he would become a commercial artist. Beurling, however, had fallen in love with airplanes as a child, and he often played hookey from school to haunt La Salle and Cartierville airports. When he was ten a man named Ted Hogan gave him a flight, and from then on Beurling loved aviation with a passion that bordered on mono-mania. He sold papers and did odd jobs to earn money for flights. When he was sixteen he began taking flying lessons.

Still he could not get enough, so he quit school, got a job, and sank as much money as he could into flying. He decided that he would like to fly for the Chinese Air Force. To get the necessary commercial license, he secured a job flying a Curtiss *Robin* transport between Gravenhurst, Ontario and Rouyn, Quebec. As soon as he had received his "ticket" he headed west, riding in empty boxcars. His trip to China ended in Washington state when he was arrested for illegal entry into the United States and was returned to his parents.

By now the Second World War had begun, so Beurling applied to join the RCAF. He was rejected for the lack of a complete high school education. An attempt to join the Finnish Air Force failed when his parents refused to give the required consent. Beurling came close to despair, until an acquaintance advised him to try in Britain, where the RAF was accepting pilot applicants with less education than RCAF re-cruiters. At an hour's notice he signed on as a deck hand on a munitions ship, worked his way overseas, left the ship in Glasgow, and was direct-ed by a policeman to an RAF recruiting centre.

The recruiting officer appeared interested in Beurling, but when the young Canadian was asked for his birth certificate he could not pro-duce it. A few hours later he was back on his ship, heading for Canada. Reaching Montreal, he secured the document, boarded the ship once more and arrived back in Glasgow, to be assisted by the same policeman and the same recruiting officer that he had met before. On September 20, 1940 he was finally sworn into the RAF.

Beurling was shaken to learn that, although he had more than 250 hours in his logbook, previous flying experience counted for nothing. He would still have to go through the routine of initial training school (complete with the hated spit-and-polish and parade square drill), followed by elementary and service flying training schools. Somehow he survived all these, but in the process he frequently rebelled against authority. Several times he was "on the carpet" for infractions of dis-cipline, unauthorized aerobatics and low flying. He made few friends and his first Christmas in England was spent alone beside the sea, watching the gulls. His fundamental, solitary nature had become fixed.

In September 1941 he earned his wings and put up the stripes of a Sergeant pilot. Following operational training he was posted to No. 403 Squadron. While there he was offered a commission which, after some reflection, he declined. In April 1942 he was posted to No. 41 Squad-ron. On May 1 he attacked and destroyed an *Fw 190* over Calais. Two days later he probably destroyed another *'190*.

Rather than being congratulated for these victories, Beurling was reprimanded again, for in achieving them he had committed the cardinal sin of European theatre air fighting; he had broken formation, leaving his leader's tail unprotected. Then, suddenly, he secured the ideal job for a man of his particular talents, methods and disposition. By trading postings with a newly-married pilot, he was able to have himself assigned to Malta. He was flown to Gibraltar where he embarked on the carrier HMS *Eagle* on the evening of June 7. Next day the ship sailed, loaded with *Spitfires* for that besieged island. Shortly after dawn on the 9th the fighters began taking off, and at 10.30 A.M. Sergeant Beurling landed at Takali to join No. 249 Squadron.

The blockade of Malta had been in progress for two years, and for the past six months the enemy had been tightening the noose. The intensity of Axis bombing varied, sometimes like a storm, sometimes a trickle; indeed, Beurling's arrival coincided with a relatively quiet period when fewer than half a dozen bombers ventured over each day. It was the logistical situation that was critical. Malta was short of everything—food, gasoline, ammunition, guns, spare parts. Supplies arrived in assorted ways—by aircraft, submarines, and fast minelayers. Nevertheless, these methods could provide the island with less than a quarter of its needs. Above all, Malta was kept operating by convoys run through the blockade at an appalling cost of ships and men.

Locked between Italian and German air fleets based in Sicily and Tripolitania, Malta, by this stage of the war, at least possessed an adequate number of *Spitfires*. It was apparent that the island would not fall through any action over its airfields. Rather the battle had shifted to the sea approaches to Malta; attempts to smash the RAF bases by bombing had faded away. The *Luftwaffe* had business elsewhere, notably in Russia.

If the enemy could make the blockade 100 percent effective, then Malta would wither on the vine. If, on the other hand, British merchant ships could again fight their way into Valetta's Grand Harbour and deliver supplies, particularly oil and gasoline, then the island could continue to serve as a forward base for the submarines and torpedo aircraft which rendered the Axis supply line to North Africa extremely hazardous. The enemy had to starve Malta to death, or their forces in Libya would themselves suffer such a fate. Those were the stakes when Beurling arrived to join the defenders.

He damaged a *Bf 109* within three days of his arrival, but thereafter the enemy neglected Malta, concentrating on a convoy which was being fought through to the island. The *Luftwaffe* was also busy supporting a renewed offensive by Rommel in Libya. The largest Axis operation was a raid on the night of June 21/22, when some 30-40 sorties were directed at Luqa airfield. It was the *Regia Aeronautica* rather than the *Luftwaffe* which showed the most interest in the island.

Events now demonstrated how confused the Germans were in their attitudes regarding Malta. It had been planned that Rommel's offensive would clear the British out of Libya, after which an aerial assault would be made with the aim of capturing the troublesome island. The seeming collapse of the Eighth Army, highlighted by the surrender of Tobruk on June 21, led Rommel to believe that he could follow through to the Nile itself. The attack on Malta was cancelled while the *Afrika Korps* pushed into Egypt, only to be halted at El Alamein. The German panzers were running low on supplies, just when a revitalized Malta was once more despatching aircraft to sink enemy ships.

Clearly, the Axis had to neutralize Malta if they were to exploit their recent victories. A force of 567 aircraft was assembled for another blitz. Malta then had about 200 aircraft, half of them bombers, the others *Spitfires*. After a few probing attacks on July 1 and July 5, the offensive opened on the 6th with a heavy raid which gave Beurling his first big chance.

He was one of eight *Spitfire* pilots who were scrambled to meet three *Z.1007* bombers and 30 fighters which were approaching Luqa airfield at 22,000 feet. The defenders tore through the fighter screen and made head-on passes at the bombers which promptly jettisoned their loads into the sea and fled. Beurling damaged one *Z.1007*, then saw a Macchi *MC.202* fighter on a *Spit's* tail. He went into a climbing turn, and as he did this he fired a single burst. The Italian fighter caught a load of lead in the engine and glycol tank and began to burn. Another Macchi tried to attack the same *Spitfire*, spotted Beurling's machine and dived away. The Canadian followed through a 15,000 foot dive. As it started to pull out, he fired from almost directly behind and the *MC.202* exploded. When Beurling landed, he learned that his fellows had destroyed another *MC.202* as well as damaging a second *Z.1007*. He also found his own *Spitfire* had been riddled by bullets, but he could not remember how or when.

Later that day he covered an Air/Sea rescue launch which was picking up the two Italian pilots he had downed. Then, just at sunset, he was off again with three other pilots to intercept two *Ju 88's* which were approaching under an escort of 20 *Bf 109's*. While two *Spitfires* headed for the bombers, the other two piled into the Messerschmitts. Two fighters got on Beurling's tail; he steep-turned behind them and one '109 tried to climb away. In a split second he had estimated the distance—800 yards—guessed the proper angle of deflection and made allowance for the drop of the cannon shells. A three-second burst did the trick; the '109, obviously hit in the coolant tank, began to stream white smoke, then burst into flames.

Beurling then attempted to catch two *Bf 109's*, but they outdistanced him and he turned back five miles from Sicily. En route home he narrowly escaped being jumped by two aircraft which he mistook for *Spitfires* but which turned out to be *'109's*. Back at Takali he reported his third "kill" of the day. He was proud but not jubilant; he had been on Malta long enough to know that shooting down enemy aircraft was his job.

He had, however, begun a meteoric rise which was to make him Canada's—and Malta's—top-scoring fighter pilot. On July 8 he shot down a *Bf 109* and once more came home with his fighter riddled. Two days later he added another *Bf 109* and an *MC.202* to his bag in separate scrambles, and on the 12th he destroyed three *MC.202's*, two of them in an action lasting only seven seconds.

Shortly afterwards he was awarded the Distinguished Flying Medal, the announcement being published in the *London Gazette* on July 28. He was always most proud of his DFM which, he felt, justified all the training, applications and ocean voyages. The remainder of his honours, when they came, he felt were to have been awarded naturally. The peculiar blend of modesty and arrogance is striking.

About this time Beurling was again offered a commission and again he refused, declaring that he was not officer material. Some distinguished aircrew were inclined to agree, but eventually officialdom triumphed. In August Beurling was told that, like it or not, he was being commissioned. For both the man and the service it was a tragic mistake. Tall, loose-limbed, with shaggy blond hair, he loved to play the fighter pilot to the hilt. He never did up the top button of his battle dress and he turned the collar up, regardless of his company. He never wanted to be an officer and, having been made one against his will, he refused either to act or dress like one. In the total democracy of a battle-hell like Malta this scarcely mattered, but in the future it would cause endless bitterness.

In the meantime he went on fighting and achieving fantastic results. To describe all his combats would be repetitious; they are discussed in great detail in the book *Malta Spitfire*, ostensibly written by Beurling himself, although Leslie Roberts clearly played a significant part. It is perhaps sufficient to say that before July had ended he had destroyed six more enemy fighters. In August, while suffering from vicious bouts of dysentery (the notorious "Malta dog"), he added one fighter and a share of a *Ju 88* to his "bag", thus winning a Bar to the DFM. Throughout September and October he shot down ten more enemy aircraft. His exploits won him a Distinguished Flying Cross and finally a Distinguished Service Order, the last-named being almost unheard of for a lowly Pilot Officer.

The scale of enemy attacks declined after July 14, and Malta's losses (39 fighters, thirteen pilots) were quickly made good by re-enforcements flown off carriers. The most serious difficulties were with maintenance, for of necessity the succeeding batches of *Spitfires* arrived without groundcrew. Army personnel acted as mechanics and armourers, but they could only partially make up for the lack of RAF specialists. Repeated pin-prick raids and sweeps inflicted little damage but did deprive personnel of needed rest. Food, fuel and ammunition remained critically short until August, when another convoy was run through the blockade, again with great losses. The only major *Luft-waffe* raids were in mid-August when a brief campaign was launched to keep Malta's aircraft from supporting the convoy.

Once Malta had been re-provisioned, RAF bombers and torpedo planes, assisted by reconnaissance aircraft based on the island, quickly created a logistical nightmare for Axis forces in North Africa. Knowing that a British offensive was imminent (the blow was to fall on October 23), the enemy resolved once more to neutralize Malta.

At the outset of the October "blitz" the Germans had 214 service-able aircraft (156 bombers) while the Italians had 163 (67 bombers). The RAF had 113 *Spitfires* and eleven *Beaufighters* but only 100 pilots. The campaign opened on the 11th with an estimated 80 bomber and 160 fighter sorties. By the 15th they had suffered so grievously that the ratio had changed to fourteen bombers and 100 fighters. By the 18th they had given up on bombers altogether, and after the 19th they halted the campaign. In those nine days the enemy flew 2,400 sorties and dropped 440 tons of bombs, yet no airfield on Malta was out of operation for more than 30 minutes. The RAF flew 1,115 sorties, with serviceability averaging 74 *Spitfires* and eight *Beaufighters* each day (although at one point barely 40 *Spitfires* were available). One *Spitfire* and one *Beaufighter* were destroyed on the ground while 30 *Spitfires* were shot down; in seventeen cases the pilots survived. The *Luftwaffe* lost nine fighters and 35 bombers; Italian losses were never satisfactorily tallied.

On October 14, just after noon, Beurling and three other *Spitfires* were scrambled to meet a raid. They encountered eight *Ju 88's* escorted by 50 *Bf 109's*. There was no option but to attack head-on, breaking up the enemy's formation. He personally tried to engage five *Bf 109's* but they dived away. Beurling then attacked a *Ju 88* and aimed at the "coffin corner", the starboard wing root where fuel tanks were located. The bomber caught fire and started to go down, but a fast-shooting gunner peppered Beurling's *Spitfire* as he dived after eight *Bf 109's*. Beurling was hit in the left arm and he now had two Messerschmitts on his tail.

The eight *'109's* he was after were chasing another *Spit*. In desper-ation he fired at a range of 450 yards. One Messerschmitt was hit and dived into the sea. Then, the two fighters behind started to take Beurling's machine apart. His *Spitfire's* tail and port wing were holed and the perspex hood above his head was shattered. Somehow he managed to climb out of the dogfight.

He then heard a call for help; two *Spitfires* were battling with 20 *'109's* immediately below him. He pushed the stick forward, dived under a *'109*, and shot off its port wing. Then he was clobbered again. The belly of his *Spitfire* was blasted apart and his right heel was shot away. A bullet passed under his armpit, nicking his elbow and ribs. Splinters stabbed into one leg. His controls were gone, the throttle was jammed open, and he was in a power spin. Now came the ultimate horror; flames began to spread back from the engine.

Exerting all his energy, he managed to slow the spin, then crawl out onto the wing and slip off, just before the *Spitfire* plunged into the sea. His parachute opened less than 500 feet above the water, and soon found himself floating about. Within twenty minutes a launch had rescued him and was conveying him to hospital.

Beurling spent two weeks in bed before being bundled into a *Liberator* which was heading for Gibraltar. On its arrival on October 31 the aircraft crashed, killing half the passengers aboard. Among the dead was Pilot Officer John Williams DFM, of Kamloops, who had destroyed nine enemy aircraft over Malta and who subsequently figured prominently in *Malta Spitfire* under the nickname "Willie the Kid".

Beurling spent more time in hospital. At the request of the Canadian government he was next posted to Canada for a publicity tour. He hated it. For him, to be non-operational was purgatory, but the tasteless idolatry showered upon him was hell itself. In Montreal he was enthroned in the Forum and presented with a bouquet of roses, one for each victory. Other heroes, put in similar circumstances, might have laughed and endured. Beurling responded with angry, undisguised contempt. Finally, after a tour of training establishments, he was sent back to Britain as an operational instructor.

That, however, did not appeal to him. He managed to effect a transfer to the RCAF and to wangle a combat posting. On September 5, 1943 he arrived at No. 403 Squadron, the unit with which his operational career had begun almost two years before. He wore only one full stripe, the mark of a Flying Officer, but within his wing he was a legendary figure, as famous as the formation leader, Wing Commander J.E. Johnson.

Beurling, nevertheless, was still a lone wolf. After Malta he found the routine of sweeps and escort sorties dull. What he *really* wanted to do was take a long-range *Mustang* and go hunting over Germany. On September 24, however, he became mixed up in a dogfight with some *Fw 190's* which were trying to intercept a force of *Marauder* medium bombers. A short, well-aimed burst tore one-half of one wing off a *'190*.

Soon after that he was promoted to Flight Lieutenant and posted to No. 412 Squadron. On December 30, while helping to cover *Fortresses* returning from Germany, he shot down an *Fw 190*, the last victim in his long tally. His tour ended in April 1944 with no further claims and he was repatriated to Canada.

Yet he remained undisciplined, devoted only to combat flying. A non-operational tour was intolerable. If he couldn't fly in action he wouldn't do anything. He wouldn't even look like an officer. To one superior he solemnly promised to toe the line, and promptly went off on a reckless binge of low-flying. He virtually dared the RCAF to court-martial him. Rather than risk bad publicity, the Air Force granted him an honourable discharge in October 1944. A service spokesman blandly explained that Beurling, having already done more than his share in the war, was being given an early start at rehabilitation. In fact, the RCAF was pulling a thorn from its flesh.

But what sort of man was he? How did he achieve his remarkable record of "kills"? His career was the outcome of extraordinary dedication and qualities. For one thing, he had uncommonly keen eyesight. On one occasion, when on the ground, a swarm of aircraft appeared on the horizon. While others were barely able to discern the aircraft in the haze, Beurling announced that they were *Fortresses*—56 of them. He was right. This ability served him well in combat.

Moreover, he worked at perfecting his gunnery to an extent which few other men displayed. He spent hours with pencil and paper, calculating speeds, distances, and angles of deflection required to bring down a plane. He taught himself trigonometry. Though he had never completed high school, he might well have been a professional mathematician. In a dogfight he applied his theories so expertly that almost all his victories were gained in the same manner—a short, expertly-aimed deflection burst. After his victory of September 24, 1943 he complained, "I aimed at his fuselage but knocked off his port wing. I must be losing my touch".

One of the strangest displays of his prowess occured in England in 1943. With another officer, he was out hunting when he fired at a rabbit which dropped dead. As they walked towards the animal, Beurling remarked, "I aimed two feet three inches in front of that rabbit to get all the shot in the head. That way, the meat won't be spoiled for eating". His companion was skeptical until he saw the rabbit. Two pellets had hit an ear, another was lodged in a forepaw, and all the rest were in the head.

Beurling often lectured his fellow pilots on deflection shooting, and as an instructor he was fairly effective. One ace, Squadron Leader A.R. Mackenzie DFC, later attributed all his victories to the tips Beurling had passed on. Yet he was exacting too. After one jubilant pilot reported a victory, Beurling asked, "Were you aiming at a wing, the fuselage, or the pilot?" The surprised victor exclaimed, "Good heavens, man, I was just trying to hit the damn thing."

Above all, he was devoted to flying. As one of his flight commanders remarked, "That Beurling was never happy unless he was in the cockpit of a *Spitfire*. That boy could really fly a *Spit*, and was never content to stay on the ground. He acted as if he was part of his aircraft." Beurling, in short, was as near to being a perfect combat pilot as is possible. Unhappily, he could not adjust to anything else. Playing the ruthless, reckless ace, he shed a great deal of his humanity.

Stories about Beurling were legion, and even in his lifetime it was hard to sort out fact from fiction. Part of the problem was his fame. Like many pilots, he apparently indulged in some "lineshooting", but whereas other men could relate their yarns to a closed circle of friends, in Beurling's case there was almost always a reporter around.

After the war he related one hair-raising tale which is typical of his swash-buckling adventures. According to Beurling, he had been instructing in England and had given a student some advice about how to catch an enemy aircraft if it spun away. After reviewing the procedure, he and his pupil went up to practice.

After some preliminary dogfighting, Beurling went into a spin. His student duly caught up with him, but with excessive zeal the tyro did more than use the gun camera; he also hit the gun switches. One bullet hit Beurling's glycol tank. He bailed out safely—and never reported the student, saying merely that the tank had sprung a leak. Since the *Spitfire* was completely destroyed in the crash, no one was able to discover the truth. Nor did he and the student ever discuss the incident.

It is a terrific story—so wild that it fairly reeks of "lineshooting". Nevertheless, in June 1943 when Beurling was on instructional duties with the RAF, his engine was reported to have caught fire following a practice dogfight and he was forced to bail out at 1,400 feet. So far the facts add substance to his story. The only odd item is that the student was Flight Lieutenant R.A. Buckham—a very experienced pilot who had already become an ace. Was Buckham the man who shot down Beurling? Did someone else accidently shoot him down? Or did Beurling embellish the story of his bail-out by attributing it, three years after the event, to some freakish circumstances? Both Buckham and Beurling are dead, so we shall probably never know the truth.

His wartime victory total is generally given as 31 1/3. This figure tallies with his own account given in *Malta Spitfire*, with the addition of the two victories gained in 1943. Other records, including Air Ministry accounts and citations to awards, are not in complete agreement, either with the book or with each other. Beurling stated that his "probable" *Fw 190* of May 3, 1942 was later upgraded to "destroyed", for which there is no evidence other than his own word. He may have heard a rumour to that effect, but the combat report held by the Canadian Armed Forces' Directorate of History indicates no upgrading. This author, after carefully weighing all the evidence at his disposal, is inclined to credit Beurling with 29 1/3—still a remarkable achievement.

The end of the Beurling story was as extraordinary as the war years. He acquired a commercial license and attempted to do barnstorming, carrying passengers and performing aerobatics. He got married, then divorced, his wife complaining that he put flying ahead of her. Finally, he decided to become a flyer-of-fortune and set out for Israel. Before he left, he was quoted as saying, "I will drop bombs or fire guns for anyone who will pay me, except the Russians." To a reporter friend he declared that he was now more mature and thus a better pilot, less inclined to take chances, but then he added, "I'll send you a telegram when I knock off my first one." There was a rumour that he was going to be paid $1,000 a month.

He arrived in Rome on May 5, 1948. There he was delayed, apparently waiting for an airplane which he was to ferry to Israel. The aircraft, a *Norseman*, flew in from Nice on the 18th, but it needed repairs. Once these were completed, on the 20th, Beurling and another pilot volunteered to test it.

They had scarcely taken off from Rome's Urbe airfield when the engine sputtered and failed. Beurling then committed Cardinal Sin No. 1—with no power he turned sharply to regain the field, stalled, and crashed. The intense flames burned both men beyond recognition.

When he heard the news his father, Fred Beurling, reached into his grief to sum up his son: "This is the way I expected his life to end—in a blaze of smoke from the thing he loved most—an airplane."

Caine
Intruder Par Excellence

In the darkness the German pilot of the *Me 410* did not even know he was being followed. A slim, twin-engined *Mosquito* slipped in behind him and jockeyed for a firing position. As the two approached Athies airfield the *Mosquito* pilot centred the Messerschmitt in his sights, then pressed the trigger button. Nothing happened! He checked his safety catch, then tried again, but through some technical fault the guns refused to fire. Seething with frustration, the "Mossie" pilot broke away while the *Me 410* landed. The date was most appropriate; it was February 13, 1944.

It was certainly the German crew's lucky night, however, for the intruding pilot, Johnny Caine, seldom missed. Indeed, he became the RCAF's most outstanding intruder pilot, destroying 21 enemy aircraft, including two machines shared, in two operational tours. While so doing, Caine won the Distinguished Flying Cross no fewer than three times, a distinction he shared with only five other members of the force. He was, indeed, the RCAF's intruder pilot *par excellence*.

He was born on August 2, 1920 at Edmonton. When he was four years old his father established a fur ranch and the younger Caine grew up with the business. As his father's health declined Johnny assumed greater responsibilities. He left school with an incomplete Grade IX education. As a boy he played hockey extensively. He was a handsome fellow, six feet tall, whose features were dominated by a mop of thick black hair and bushy black eyebrows.

On the outbreak of war he attempted to enlist as a pilot in the RCAF and was bluntly informed that his education was inadequate. Rising to the challenge, he embarked on a programme of Canadian Legion correspondence courses. Over the next thirteen months he struggled through until he had achieved Grade XI standing, then presented himself once more to the recruiters. Although he was qualified for little more than an Air Gunner, he was given a chance at pilot training.

At No. 11 Service Flying Training School, Yorkton, Saskatchewan, he particularly impressed the Chief Flying Instructor, Flight Lieutenant W.R. Irwin, himself a much-decorated ace of the First World War, who described Caine as "a smart, clean type of airman . . . very keen to be a pilot . . . self confident and cooperative." There were a few close calls, for he was weak in ground subjects such as mathematics and navigation, which had to be balanced against his excellent performance in the air. Buckling down to work, he passed the final examinations with good marks. On December 28, 1942 he received both his wings and his commission. In January 1943 he was posted to England where he arrived the following month.

There followed a delay of two months before he was pumped into the advanced training scheme, first at Grantham and then at No. 60 Operational Training Unit, High Ercall. There were two notable events at that place. One was his being teamed with Sergeant Earl Boal as observer; the other was his encounter with the CO, Wing Commander B.R.O. Hoare DSO, DFC, a one-eyed veteran who possessed what was probably the most prodigious moustache in the RAF; he claimed that the only proper moustache was one that could be seen on both sides of the head from behind.

Hoare's first words to the Canadian were, "I don't know how in hell you got here, but if you so much as scratch one of my 'Mossies', you are out!" Not long afterwards, Caine made a rough landing and bounced 20 feet into the air. The formidable CO was watching, and over the radio ordered him to go round again. Caine obeyed, landed, and then taxied to the dispersal area with very hot brakes.

Approaching his own blast bay (parking space), he found the brakes were not responding, and the *Mosquito* was in danger of banging into the wall. An alert ground crewman ducked under a still-rotating propeller and threw a chock under one wheel. The aircraft spun around through 180 degrees, and ended up facing outwards. Wing Commander Hoare arrived just as Caine was climbing out. "I suggest you take your ground crew to the pub tonight," said the CO. "That was what I had in mind, sir," replied Caine.

Teaming up with Boal was fortunate. Born in Ceylon, Saskatchewan, he had joined the RCAF as a radio operator in July 1940. In March 1942 he had remustered to aircrew and graduated from No. 3 Air Observer School, Regina, in September 1942. Since November 1942 Boal had been undergoing almost continuous training in Britain. He was a first-rate navigator who knew his equipment inside out.

Caine and Boal reported to No. 418 Squadron on October 5, 1943. Two weeks later they flew their first sortie. This was virtually a training flight to the Seine estuary. On November 9 they carried out a similar sortie to Rennes, after which they were employed in regular intruder work, notably Flower patrols, seeking out enemy night fighters when Bomber Command was conducting heavy raids.

The chief problem with these patrols was that, by 1943, the German night fighter arm had become so formidable that Bomber Command preferred dark, cloudy weather for operations. "Bomber night" conditions only increased the problems and hazards for the *Mosquitos*, which could not accomodate the heavy navigational aids carried by the larger *Lancasters* and *Halifaxes*. Moreover, the most recent radar equipment was not cleared for use over Europe, lest its secrets become known to the enemy. There was no question of putting the "Mossies" into the bomber stream, where collisons might occur and only chance encounters with *Luftwaffe* aircraft could be expected. Instead, the intruders would concentrate on German night fighter bases, hoping to catch their victims landing or taking off. The former was easier, for although the most numerous *Luftwaffe* night fighter, the *Bf 110*, was inferior in most respects to a *Mosquito*, the German plane could nevertheless outclimb its hunter. The frustrations inherent in this type of intruding were so great that the ambitious crews in No. 418 turned increasingly to Day Rangers—spectacular long range patrols that exploited the *Mosquito's* speed and firepower. As time passed the squadron hung ever-larger drop tanks under the wings of its aircraft, deepening its thrusts into enemy occupied territory.

Caine's first intruder sortie, carried out late in November, was washed out by solid cloud and rain. Even successful intruder flights were hampered by weather. Nevertheless, on the night of December 20/21, he destroyed his first enemy aircraft, an unidentified twin-engined machine, over northeastern France.

It was, however, on Day Rangers that Caine and Boal won distinction. No. 418 Squadron came to be specialists in this work. Curiously, the squadron was not a boisterous unit; its crews went about operations in a serious fashion. In the mess they were more inclined to frequent the bridge table than the bar. Such rituals as were peculiar to No. 418 were relatively tame. One was that when new Commanding Officers took charge, the retiring CO handed over his badge of office—a red flag. Another was that successful crews, after reporting to the

Intelligence Officer, then recounted their exploits to the squadron mascot, a horse named Hans, who was kept at a nearby farm.

Caine's career as a Day Ranger opened on the afternoon of January 27, 1944. Accompanied by a *Mosquito* crewed by Flight Lieutenant J.R. Johnson and Flying Officer N.J. Gibbons, he found numerous enemy aircraft near Bourges and Clermont/Ferrand airfields. Caine shot down a *Ju 88* and shared with Johnson in the destruction of two Junkers *W 34* light transports. Back at base, his cine-film stirred much interest for it clearly showed one *W 34* blowing up in a great sheet of flame.

In the early hours of February 26, 1944, during a Flower patrol, he destroyed a *Bf 110* as it was taxiing on a Munich airfield. This, and the aircraft shot down in December, were the only pure "intruder" victories scored by Caine; all his remaining "kills" were the outcome of Day Ranger sorties well inside occupied Europe.

Not all encounters with enemy aircraft were successful; his frustrating episode with an *Me 410* has already been mentioned, and on March 9, 1944 he was flying in company with the squadron's CO, Wing Commander R.J. Bennell DFC, when the latter was shot down and killed by anti-aircraft fire. Three days later, however, he blasted a *Ju 52* and a *Ju 86* which were parked at Clermont/Ferrand airfield. On this occasion he was accompanied by a *Mosquito* piloted by Flying Officer C.M. Jasper, who shot up another *Ju 86*, then had to shake an *Fw 190* off his tail. On March 23 the squadron diarist wrote, "Drinks are on Johnny Caine tonight, his DFC having just come through." Shortly thereafter Earl Boal, now commissioned, received the same award.

Like most high-scoring intruder pilots, Caine's score increased with large bites from the *Luftwaffe*. Thus, on April 14, in company with Squadron Leader Bob Kipp, he destroyed three and damaged one enemy aircraft. Two *Fw 190's* attacked the *Mosquitos* and Caine, forgetting to drop his long-range fuel tanks, narrowly escaped being shot down. His most successful day, however, was on May 2, when he destroyed no fewer than six enemy aircraft and damaged two more in what was probably the most spectacular single intruder sortie of the war.

Caine and Boal took off from Coltishall at 2.30 P.M. that day and set course at low level for the German Baltic coast. They were accompanied by a "Mossie" flown by Squadron Leader C.C. Scherf, an Australian Air Force ace who technically had been posted away from No. 418 some weeks before, but who liked to spend his leave doing Day Rangers with the squadron. There was a solid layer of cloud to hide the *Mosquitos*, and it began to rain as they approached their objective. It was perfect Ranger weather.

The two aircraft dropped out of the clouds over Ribnitz/Putnitz at 3.48 P.M. to find some 15 German seaplanes moored. Caine strafed four *Do 18's*, two of which blew up. Scherf had less luck; the aircraft he attacked were probably not fuelled up as they did not burn. The *Mosquitos* then headed for Barth airfield. Caine attacked first, exploding a parked *Ju 52*; he then fired at an *He 111* which Scherf eventually destroyed, then set a *Ju 88* on fire. The Australian set a *Do 217* on fire before vanishing into the clouds. As there were, however, still plenty of aircraft at Barth, the Canadian crew roared in for another attack.

The airfield was now in a shambles. Caine fired at a *Ju 86* and damaged it. With the "Mossie" almost cutting the grass, he made another pass, guns blazing at a *W 34*. The little transport exploded in a sheet of flame through which Caine flew. Finally he turned on the *Ju 86* previously damaged and pulverized it with gunfire. The Junkers blew up; Caine felt a thud as flying debris hit the *Mosquito*.

He now set course for the next objective, but five minutes later the port engine failed. Caine feathered the propeller and called for help, but Scherf could not find him in the overcast. Here was a fix indeed—500 miles from home, much of it over water, and only one engine ticking over! He climbed a bit to clear any hills, then headed north. Within five minutes, he and Boal had decided against internment and Swedish blondes. They altered course for Britain.

It was a long struggle home. At one point an enemy trawler blazed away at them but missed. Near Kiel they overflew a German convoy, but fortunately they were not fired upon. At last, at 8.05 P.M., they landed at Coltishall, where Scherf had arrived half an hour before. A comparison of notes showed that the two crews had destroyed a total of ten enemy aircraft—a rich harvest indeed!

On the night of May 8/9 Caine and Boal returned to the scene of their little blitz, this time in company with a *Mosquito* crewed by Flight Lieutenant J.M. Connell and Flying Officer D.J. Carr. Within minutes he had destroyed two more flying boats. Connell and Carr, however, were hit by flak and could not get home; happily, they both lived out the remainder of the war, though as POWs.

That was Caine's last sortie with No. 418. He was subsequently awarded a Bar to his DFC (as was Boal) and repatriated to Canada for leave and instructional duties at the *Mosquito* OTU at Debert, Nova Scotia. By then his score stood at 16 destroyed and five damaged.

He remained in Canada until March 1945, when he was posted overseas again, this time to No. 406 Squadron. The unit, led by Russ Bannock, was based at Manston, flying *Mosquito XXX's* with A.I. Mark X radar. Caine was assigned Flying Officer B.F. Tindall, RAF, to serve as radar operator/navigator. Shortly afterwards they were once more haunting German airfields, leaving a trail of enemy wreckage behind them.

Caine flew his first sortie with No. 406 on the night of April 20/21, 1945. Nothing happened. Four nights later, however, the Caine-Tindall team accompanied that of Don MacFadyen and V.G. Shail to Eferding airfield near Linz, Austria, some 700 miles from their base. It was a clear night with just a few patches of ground mist; a flare-dropping aircraft reported several enemy machines present on the field. The defences were on the alert. As Caine banked for a low-level attack, the pre-dawn twilight lit up as first one and then half a dozen anti-aircraft guns stabbed at the *Mosquito*.

An *Fw 190* caught one burst from his guns, but it apparently remained intact. Turning to port, he poured a torrent of shells into a *Ju 88* which went up in flames. Then he fired at another *'190* and damaged it. By now, however, the natives had become very hostile. There was a terrific bang and the *Mosquito* shook violently. A flak burst had smashed through the rear fuselage and tailfin, knocking two huge holes in the latter.

For the second time in his career, Caine found himself far from home, over hostile territory, with a badly damaged machine. Fortunately the control cables had not been cut and the engines were untouched. A three hour flight brought them to Manston, where they landed safely after experiencing some difficulties with the undercarriage.

Thereafter the weather closed in. Gales swept the continent, and on May 1, 1945 the squadron diarist wrote, "May begins under rather poor operational conditions with possible target areas shrinking daily and a recent period of bad weather preventing proposed sorties." The situation improved the following day, however, and on the night of May 2/3 No. 406 scored its last victories. At Marrebaek airfield in Denmark, Caine wiped out two *Ju 52* transports while Flying Officer J.H. Wyman destroyed four and damaged three enemy transports. These raised the unit's total to 64 enemy aircraft destroyed, seven "probables" and 47 damaged.

Then it was VE-day. Almost as an operational afterthought, No. 406's *Mosquitos* flew cover for Operation "Nestegg", the liberation of the Channel Islands, on May 9, 1945, almost five years after they had fallen to the Germans. May was an important month for Johnny Caine; on the 31st he married Jane Ford in England. Two months later he and Don MacFadyen travelled to London for an investiture ceremony at Buckingham Palace. No. 406 disbanded at the end of August, and Caine was soon on his way home to Edmonton where he would receive a welcome befitting the hero who had destroyed 21 enemy aircraft.

On October 19, 1945 the *London Gazette* announced that Flight

Lieutenant Caine had been awarded a second Bar to the DFC. Only six Canadians were so honoured during the war. Released from the RCAF in December 1945, he returned to fur ranching, breeding new varieties of foxes for the market. Caine Fur Farms were the largest operation of their kind in western Canada.

Johnny Caine now lives in retirement in Vancouver. His wartime decorations, mounted in a glass case, hang in his home, eloquent reminders of his adventures so long ago, so far away.

Chadburn
Fighter Leader Extraordinary

In November 1955, on the suggestion of Air Vice Marshal H.L. Campbell, then Air Officer Commanding the RCAF's No. 1 Air Division in Europe, a trophy was initiated for gunnery proficiency. This award was to be presented annually to the RCAF wing with the best record in air-to-air firing. This impressive trophy, which depicted two eagles circling each other, was won by Nos. 3 and 4 Wings before the changing role of the RCAF in NATO brought about the discontinuation of the award in 1961. Great concern was shown at the time that the trophy should be suitably named, and the names of such deceased pilots as Audet, Klersy and McLeod were considered. By general agreement, however, staff officers in Europe and Canada decided that it should be named the Chadburn Trophy, in honour of Wing Commander L.V. Chadburn, one of Canada's most brilliant fighter leaders of the war.

Although Chadburn's personal score was modest compared with those of many other pilots, he nevertheless combined, to a rare degree, flying skill and leadership ability. Group Captain A.E. McNab, Chadburn's immediate superior early in 1944, described him as "a superior fighter pilot . . . Has a personality that inspires those under him. He is loyal and completely trustworthy, an outstanding officer", while another senior officer wrote that he was "a first class operational Wing Leader who inspired complete confidence in all his pilots." It should be noted that the Distinguished Service Order was awarded as much for leadership as for personal courage, and Chadburn was one of only four RCAF officers to win this decoration more than once. His tragic death in action was considered to be a heavy loss to the service.

Chadburn was born in Montreal on August 21, 1919 and was educated at Oshawa and Aurora, Ontario. In 1938 he graduated from the Northern Vocational School in Toronto. He then attempted, unsuccessfully, to enlist in the RCN, the RCAF and the RAF. Turned down by all these, he worked for a time at General Motors and then as a bank clerk in Toronto. When the war broke out, however, he tried again. In April 1940 he was sworn into the RCAF. Initially he signed on as a gunnery trainee, but he was able to remuster to pilot. He learned to fly at No. 7 Elementary Flying Training School, Windsor, Ontario, and at No. 2 Service Flying Training School at Ottawa. He passed his wings test on October 2, 1940. Soon afterwards, Pilot Officer Chadburn was en route overseas.

He joined No. 112 (RCAF) Squadron—soon to be redesignated No. 402—in mid-December 1940. The unit was then converting from *Lysander* army co-operation machines to *Hurricanes* under Squadron Leader Gordon McGregor DFC, a veteran of the Battle of Britain and probably the oldest fighter pilot in the RCAF. McGregor watched as his cubs whipped themselves into shape. Chadburn was duly passed as fit for operations and on March 3, 1941 he flew his first patrol.

No. 402 was then engaged mainly in defensive operations and uneventful convoy patrols. "Chad's" most exciting experience with No. 402 occured during a camera gun training flight. He was at 3,500 feet when his engine failed. Nevertheless, he succeeded in gliding down and made a perfect wheels-up landing in a ploughed field four miles from Digby.

In July he was posted to No. 412 Squadron, then forming with *Spitfires*. That was a decided step up, but again operations were restricted almost entirely to defensive patrols. In September, however, he was switched to No. 19 Squadron. The highlight of his five-month tour with that unit occured on November 20 when he blasted a German "E" Boat into oblivion, 45 miles off the Dutch coast.

Late in February 1942 Chadburn, now a Flight Lieutenant with ample experience, was sent to Peterhead, Scotland, to take over a flight of No. 416 Squadron. Like most newly formed units, No. 416 was engaged in tedious defensive patrols. On March 9 he was promoted to Squadron Leader and given command of No. 416. He thus became the first graduate of the British Commonwealth Air Training Plan to lead a squadron, and at the time he was the youngest "Skew-Ell" in the RCAF.

Just as McGregor had shepherded the tyros of No. 402, so Chadburn now supervised as No. 416 converted to *Spitfire V's* while grinding through the routine of scrambles and convoy patrols. At last, in mid-July, the squadron moved south, leaving behind the excellent Scottish food and hospitality, but certain that action was in the wind. Instead, there was simply more defensive work which continued right up to August 18.

The next day, however, was Dieppe day. Four times No. 416 patrolled over the beaches and ships, and each time Chadburn was in the lead. The first two trips were uneventful, but the third provided excitement enough for everyone.

The squadron was approaching the Dieppe area at 6,000 feet when approximately fifteen *Fw 190's* appeared, approaching from above and behind. As the enemy fighters drew nearer, Chadburn swivelled his head, watching. Suddenly, the Focke-Wulfs began to dive on the *Spitfires*. Just as they appeared ready to fire, Chadburn called for the squadron to break. Twelve *Spitfires* turned steeply to port. The tables were turned; hunters and hunted had exchanged places. Within seconds three *Fw 190's* had been shot down.

No. 416 now re-formed over the ships. As they did so, four *Ju 88's* approached in a shallow "V" formation. Chadburn led the *Spitfires* into a left-hand turn that developed into a head-on attack on the bombers. He himself set one Junkers' engine on fire (it was assessed as "probably destroyed") and damaged another which vanished into clouds. All four bombers had been hit and the raid disrupted, while all the *Spitfires* were safe.

The engagement had been a brilliant success, despite his own modest score. The upshot was that on September 2 he was awarded the Distinguished Flying Cross, and on December 1 he received the decoration from the King at an investiture in Buckingham Palace. Shortly afterwards Chadburn handed over command of No. 416 to Foss Boulton and was repatriated to Canada.

He returned to action in April 1943. After serving for a fortnight with No. 403 Squadron, he took command of No. 402. Once more he showed outstanding leadership. On May 31, for example, the squadron was attacked by six *Fw 190's*. The bare statistics—one *Fw 190* damaged by Chadburn, one *Spitfire* lost—suggest a minor defeat. In fact, half the *Spitfire* pilots were able to fire on the enemy, an unusually high proportion considering the strike-and-run tactics of the day. His prowess won him promotion to Wing Commander and on June 13 he took charge of the Digby Wing, consisting of Nos. 402 and 416 Squadrons. As though to mark the occasion, he knocked holes in two *Fw 190's* that day, one of which was assessed as a "probable". Soon afterwards his score began to mount, and it increasingly included victims confirmed as destroyed.

His first task was to increase the efficiency of the wing. This he proceeded to do, calling for mass formation practices whenever possible, co-ordinating the squadrons so that they worked as a team, with every pilot having absolute confidence in his comrades. Soon the *Spitfires* were out in force, escorting *Beaufighters* on shipping strikes and *Marauders* on medium bombing raids. Because German fighters were deployed in Holland and Belgium to intercept American *Fortress* raids, some enemy reaction to these thrusts was normal, but seldom did a substantial enemy force intercept. Throughout the summer and autumn of 1943 the Digby Wing fought, not a battle, but a series of short, sharp skirmishes. Invariably, Chadburn was in personal command.

During this campaign, a surprising number of combats took place involving Chadburn and one or more inexperienced pilots, in whom he took a particular interest. On August 2, for example, accompanied by two young Pilot Officers, he shot down a *Bf 109* over the North Sea. The action was almost his undoing. One of the eager novices opened fire too soon, and when Chadburn landed he discovered a bullet hole in one of his propeller blades. Between June 27 and September 27 he submitted ten combat reports involving sixteen enemy aircraft which had been shot up in varying degrees. It was that sort of work which brought him, on September 2, the Distinguished Service Order, the citation for which paid tribute to his leadership, skill and fighting spirit.

Although, as noted before, most of these actions were skirmishes rather than battles, some brushes with the enemy did assume formidable proportions. The fight on August 2, for example, was a hard-fought action over an enemy convoy which RAF *Beaufighters* were attacking, and it netted four German fighters destroyed. Then, on September 5, came one of the biggest and most successful engagements ever recorded by the Digby Wing.

Nos. 402 and 416 Squadrons were escorting 36 *Marauders* which were bombing the marshalling yards at St. Pol. After dropping their loads, the bombers carried on about ten miles inland before turning for home. The *Marauders* were at 12,000 feet with No. 402 on the left and No. 416 on the right, at 16,000 feet and about two miles apart. At 4.36 P.M. some 15 to 20 enemy fighters were seen climbing behind and below the bombers. Chadburn, leading No. 416, turned towards the Germans and dived to attack.

Positioning himself behind one fighter, he blazed away, scoring strikes. The target, a *Bf 109*, was further damaged by Flying Officer A.H. Sager. By this time No. 402 had found some more Germans and the two massed dogfights blended into one. Another *Bf 109* went down and was seen to crash; this was credited to Chadburn and three other pilots.

In the confusion he had been separated from the other *Spitfires*.

As he headed back towards the bombers, he saw six *Spitfires* and, diving in behind them, a dozen yellow-nosed *Fw 190's*. Chadburn flashed a warning and the *Spits* broke to port while he roared head-on at the enemy leader. At 400 yards he opened fire and kept on shooting up to point-blank range, pouring lead into the enemy's big radial cowling. The *'190* flicked away under the *Spitfire* and crashed on the cliffs near Le Touquet.

It had been a "wizard show". One *Spitfire* had been shot down, but its pilot was plucked from the Channel by the Air/Sea Rescue Service. All the bombers were safe and the *Luftwaffe* was minus six aircraft.

Another large engagement took place on November 3, 1943. On that occasion Chadburn discovered over the rendezvous point that his charges consisted of two box formations of *Marauders*, rather than the single box expected. Moreover, they were heading for Schipol airfield, a target which would virtually guarantee a *Luftwaffe* reaction. He led No. 402 Squadron to cover the first box of 36 bombers while assigning No. 416 to guard the second box of 18. The arrangement was the best possible, but it meant that the fighter screen was dangerously thin. As another raid had preceded this one, the German defences would already be on their toes. Everything went well until after the bombing when the *Marauders* were leaving Holland. Small groups of German fighters began positioning themselves around the bombers. Chadburn broke into them and the fight was on.

Under the circumstances it was impossible for the squadrons to keep together, so the *Spitfires* broke up into two-plane elements with complete freedom to engage at their own discretion. For almost 15 minutes the battle raged over the sea. Chadburn saw a *Bf 109* shot down by the *Marauders*. Moments later he attacked a *'109* himself, gave a long deflection burst, and shot it down in flames.

He then covered a *Spitfire* which was pumping shells into another Messerschmitt. Turning north, he found a *Spitfire* chasing a *'109*, blissfully unaware of another *'109* on its tail. Chadburn made a hurried pass at the second Messerschmitt, firing two short deflection bursts before overshooting. As he steep-turned, he saw his victim going down on fire.

The *Spitfires* came dribbling back to Digby where the Intelligence Officer sorted out the pilots' accounts of the action. Twenty-three *Spitfires* had returned; Flying Officer W.H. Jacobs was missing. In all, nine German fighters were credited to the wing. Few enemy pilots had been given a chance to attack the bombers, only one of which was missing. Chadburn's score stood at five destroyed, plus shares in four others, six "probables" plus a shared claim, and six damaged on his own in addition to two damaged with other pilots. It was a record of teamwork.

In mid-December the Digby Wing was pulled from operations and Chadburn was posted away. That month he was awarded his second DSO. "It's a funny thing," he remarked. "When the boys put on a good show, the Wing Commander gets the DSO. They put on another and he gets the Bar."

Wing Commander Chadburn was posted back to Canada in March 1944. Like many other war heros, he was displayed prominently at Victory Loan Drives. More important to him was an address he delivered to some 60 Members of Parliament on the forthcoming problem of post-war rehabilitation. Even on home leave, he was still looking out for his men.

On his return to England Chadburn was assigned to No. 127 Wing which was composed of Nos. 403, 416 and 421 Squadrons. The wing's main task was escorting *Boston* and *Mitchell* bombers raiding tactical targets in France, but a few "rhubarbs" and dive-bombing operations were included. Despite the paucity of enemy opposition, the wing's pilots destroyed ten German aircraft in May, more than the other four RCAF fighter wings combined. The greatest excitement, however, was caused by the imminence of D-Day, the approach of which was marked by weather-proofing of vehicles, huddles over maps, studying of intelligence reports and finally, on June 5, the painting of black and white invasion stripes on the *Spitfires*.

Chadburn lived to see D-Day, but not much longer. On June 13, 1944, during a patrol over the beachhead, he collided with another *Spitfire* and was killed instantly, "The RCAF and No. 127 Wing lost a great pilot today," wrote the diarist of No. 416 Squadron, and No. 402's diarist added, "His loss will be keenly felt by all personnel who greatly admired him for his leadership ability and friendly personality."

In 1947 Chadburn was posthumously made a Chevalier of the Legion of Honour and awarded the French *Croix de Guerre* with palm. It was, however, his former squadron commanders, flight commanders and immediate superiors who agreed to honour a comrade in establishing the Chadburn Trophy.

Charles
Fighter Specialist

To the four *Bf 110* crews it must have looked like an easy target, a small cutter pilot boat in the English Channel, and so they peeled off to strafe the vessel with cannon fire. Help, however, was on the way and off Margate four *Spitfires* appeared. Minutes later two of the German fighters had vanished into the sea, one with four feet of wing completely shot away.

One of the *Spitfire* pilots was Flying Officer E.F.J. Charles, and the '*110* which he shot down was his first victim and his squadron's 100th. Over the next two years he would participate in shooting up, with varying degrees of success, 28 enemy aircraft—all of them fighters. That in itself was unusual, for most of the top-ranking Allied aces destroyed a mixture of bombers, fighters, transports and even enemy training machines. Fighters, though, were difficult to catch, dangerous to fight, always ready to turn the tables. Charles' score (15 1/2 destroyed, 6 1/2 probably destroyed, five damaged) was notable not only in itself but also because it was achieved solely at the expense of the German fighter arm.

Moreover, the fighters which he met in 1941 and 1943 were at least equal to the *Spitfire* and were flown by well-trained pilots. The decline in the *Luftwaffe's* fighter organization had not yet become apparent; the pilots encountered during his tours were several cuts above the half-trained recruits of 1944-45. Further, Charles fought during Fighter Command's offensive period, when combats took place over enemy territory with the Germans choosing the time and place for dogfights. It was probably the hardest aerial combat of the war and ultimately it shattered his health.

He was born in Coventry, England, on February 6, 1919, but came to Canada as a child. He was raised in Lashburn, one of the many "four-elevator" towns of Saskatchewan. Flying was in his blood; his father had been a pilot in the Royal Flying Corps and when the son joined the flying services he carried his father's wings as a talisman.

His first experience with military life was in June 1937 when he joined the 16th/22nd Saskatchewan Horse, a militia cavalry unit. In January 1938 he enlisted in the RCAF, took pilot training, then switched to the RAF in May 1939, with which force he completed his training. During the "Phony War" period and the Battle of France he flew *Tiger Moths* and *Lysanders* on communications duties.

By August 1940, with the Battle of Britain in progress, Fighter Command was looking to all possible sources for pilots. Trainees were being rushed through accelerated courses to get them into front line squadrons, in the pious hope that they would avoid being shot down long enough to acquire battle wisdom. On August 21 Pilot Officer Charles was posted to No. 7 Operational Training Unit at Hawarden. Instruction in fighter operations began the next day and ended on September 2, after which he was posted to No. 54 Squadron, flying *Spitfires* out of Catterick, Yorkshire.

That assignment was the best possible one for a green pilot like Charles. No. 54 had been active during the earlier stages of the Battle of Britain, but at this point it had been pulled out of the fight to recuperate while protecting the industrial Midlands. It gave Charles time to polish his flying and air firing before the test came in 1941.

In February 1941 No. 54 Squadron was transferred to Hornchurch, where it took over the *Spitfire II's* of No. 41 Squadron, the latter taking the place of No. 54 at Catterick. On the 26th Charles participated in the unit's first cross-Channel operation, an early afternoon sweep over Calais. Some *Bf 109's* were seen but they shied away, while flak claimed one *Spitfire*. From that date forward Charles was regularly employed in sweeps and Circuses over France, mixed with convoy patrols.

His first victim, one of the aggressive *Bf 110's* already mentioned, went down on April 17, 1941, after he had expended all his ammunition. In May the squadron re-equipped with *Spitfire Va* fighters, still with eight machine guns, and on June 17 he submitted his second claim, this one for a "probable" *Bf 109*. Once again he almost emptied his magazines. On June 21, while escorting *Blenheims*, he fired off all his ammunition in the act of destroying yet another *Bf 109*.

Not all of his combats involved so much shooting, but nevertheless, among the leading aces, "Jack" Charles was notable for his large expenditure of shells and bullets. It would seem, in fact, that he was an indifferent shot, and consequently he scored only one double victory. His victims fell one at a time, and his successes were due to two factors. One was his skill in stalking the enemy like a cat, which made his combats a duel of wits. The other was a willingness to press attacks home to very close range. This involved the added danger of sometimes having his targets blow up in his face.

On June 27 he pounced on a brace of *Bf 109's*, one of which he shot down after firing several bursts. It was his third confirmed victim, and it brought him the Distinguished Flying Cross for "exceptional zeal and immense enthusiasm during the many offensive sweeps carried out by his unit". The citation was published in the *London Gazette* on July 15, 1941. By that time he had raised his score to 5 1/2 destroyed. At the end of September it stood at 6 1/2 destroyed and a similar number of probables.

Typical of his combats was an action on July 9. Three *Stirlings* had been sent to bomb a power station near Lens and they were escorted by 16 squadrons of fighters. The enemy reaction was particularly strong, British radar tracking 75 German fighters. Most of the Messerschmitts refused to engage, preferring to fly in neat formation while waiting for an opening. Higher up, however, the British and German top covers clashed in the major action of the day. Charles later submitted a claim for one *Bf 109* destroyed with the following report:

> I was Blue One, flying at 28,000 feet towards the target and after I crossed the French coast, I saw four aircraft at two o'clock below me, one mile away, travelling east. I dived to attack these after I identified them as *Me. 109F's*, flying in line astern. I picked on the nearest enemy aircraft and when within about 200 yards, I opened fire, closing to 50 yards in a quarter deflection attack from astern. The enemy aircraft attempted to evade by turning quickly to the right, but as he turned, he flew through my line of fire. I could see my DeWilde ammunition enter the enemy aircraft and, with sparks and flames from the engine, a large piece of the wing fell off. Then it went spinning down with glycol pouring out and more pieces came away. I finally broke off combat at 18,000 feet and returned to Hornchurch at low altitude.

Throughout the action Charles had fired 2,000 rounds of ammunition. Similarly, on July 20 he expended every shell and bullet to destroy a *Bf 109* which spun into the sea. Yet the proof of the pudding was there; unexceptional shot or not, he was obviously bringing down enemy machines. His tour ended in September 1941 when he was posted away for instructional duties.

More than a year later he returned to action, joining No. 64 Squadron in January 1943. While with that unit he damaged one enemy fighter. On March 27 he went to No. 611 Squadron, then flying *Spitfire IX's* out of Biggin Hill, and four weeks later he was promoted to command the unit. The majority of operations were sweeps and escort trips to bombers, mainly American aircraft. The USAAF was sufficiently impressed by his work as to award him a Silver Star in July.

Charles soon hit his stride again. On April 18 he engaged an *Fw 190* in a head-on firing pass and shot it down with an unusually frugal amount of lead—24 cannon shells and 160 rounds of .303 ammunition. On May 14 he destroyed another *Fw 190*.

Biggin Hill, which had become famous during the Battle of Britain, had now claimed 998 aircraft, a situation widely publicized throughout Britain. A sweepstake was organized, worth 450 pounds, of which 300 pounds would go to the pilot who shot down the station's 1,000th German aircraft.

On May 15, in the mid-afternoon, the Biggin Hill Wing was off to escort *Bostons* to Caen. It was a fine day and the *Luftwaffe* reacted by scrambling some *Fw 190's*. Charles spotted two which were diving on the bombers and dived steeply underneath them. At 250 yards range he opened up and kept firing until he was only 50 yards away. He peppered the *'190's* starboard wing and fuselage, then overshot as the enemy pilot bailed out. Turning sharply, he attacked the second *'190*, fired a five-second burst, and shot it down in a vertical dive.

His first Focke-Wulf had certainly been Biggin Hill's 999th kill, but the second went down at almost the same moment as a *'190* that had been hit by René Mouchotte, commander of No. 341 (Free French) Squadron. The Canadian and the Frenchman gallantly credited each other with the honour. Finally, the Station Commander, Group Captain A.G. Malan, decided, like Solomon, that the prize should be divided. The money itself meant nothing; it was given to the ground crews. The occasion ended with a massive party, possibly the largest ever thrown on the station, and the celebrations spilled over into London itself.

Two days later another victory came to Charles, this one an *Fw 190* shot down while he was doing such a tight turn that he blacked out. On June 23 he chalked up another *'190*. By now his gunnery had improved, particularly in the first instance when he had used only 40 cannon shells. In the second he fired 134 rounds of 20-mm ammunition, the latter being about average for *Spitfire* pilots.

Early in July No. 611 Squadron converted to clipped-wing *Spitfire V's* for low-level work. They also left Biggin Hill for Matlaske. Then, on July 25, came Charles's only bail-out of the war. He was leading No. 611 over Holland when he attacked some *Bf 109's*, one of which he damaged. He next saw four *Fw 190's* and stalked them from behind. In his combat report he described the events that followed:

> I closed line astern on the No. 4; waited until I was 75 yards away from him and opened fire . . . There was a big flash in the belly and the enemy aircraft immediately blew up. I tried to avoid the bits by turning but felt some hit my aircraft. My windscreen and wings became covered in oil from the Hun. As I broke right to cross the coast, I noticed a white trail behind me. This I knew must have been glycol. I throttled back but had to open up again as I was attacked by a single *Fw. 190*. I evaded it by doing a wing over and dive. It did not follow me. At 10,000 feet 8 miles off the Dutch coast, my engine began to vibrate and then cut . . . I glided west. I notified my squadron of what had happened, gave a long transmission fix . . . and bailed out at 1,000 feet.

Charles was fortunate. He was soon picked up by the British Air/Sea rescue service and returned to his unit.

On August 9, 1943 he was promoted to Wing Commander and posted to Middle Wallop. On the 31st, during a dinghy search near Brest, he led four *Spitfires* into a scrap with eight *Fw 190's*. He fired at one and missed. However, the German pilot attempted to turn too steeply at low altitude, lost control and flicked into the sea. Four more *Spitfires* joined the fray to eliminate the odds. It was a sharp engagement all round; two Focke-Wulfs were shot down, but two *Spitfires* were also lost.

Wing Commander Charles was posted to Station Portwreath on September 16 to command the wing there. On the 24th he claimed his last victim, a *Bf 110* near Brest. The type was curiously appropriate; it will be remembered that his first victory, back in April 1941, had also been a *Bf 110*. Shortly afterwards he was assigned to staff duties with No. 10 Group.

In October 1943 he was awarded the Distinguished Service Order. The citation to this honour described him as "an inspiring leader whose great skill and tenacity have contributed materially to the successes obtained by the formations with which he has flown." It went on to describe his combat of September 24, and concluded by saying, "This officer, who has destroyed at least fifteen enemy aircraft, has displayed great courage and unflagging devotion to duty."

His subsequent duties included a lecture tour of Canada and a staff position with the Allied Expeditionary Air Forces which supported the liberation of the continent. In May 1944 he transferred to the RCAF. However, he never again flew on operations. Battle fatigue had destroyed his health.

Following the war he retired briefly to British Columbia. Subsequently he moved to England, taking up residence in Stratford-on-Avon.

F/L R. J. Audet, DFC and Bar.

This painting by Peter Mossman depicts Audet's Spitfire Mk. IXE on December 29th, 1944, the day on which he was credited with five confirmed victories.

The nose of Russ Bannock's Mosquito FBVI HR 147 of 418 Squadron which carried the code letters TH - Z. Note the "Hairless Joe" nose art and the symbols for aircraft and V-1 kills.

PAC PL-33532

S/L R. Bannock and his navigator F/O Bruce.

PAC PL-33041

Left: F/L R. A. Barton, DFC.

Below: Hurricanes enroute to Malta on board HMS Ark Royal.

Bottom: The Island of Malta, where a number of Canadian aces, most notably "Buzz" Beurling, made their names. This was the scene of some of the fiercest aerial fighting of the Second World War.

IMPERIAL WAR MUSEUM (IWM) CH 1947A

A. U. HOULE   IWM C 4301

Beurling's 403 Squadron Spitfire with 30½ victory markings.

"Screwball" Beurling, photographed in hospital with log book and trophies.

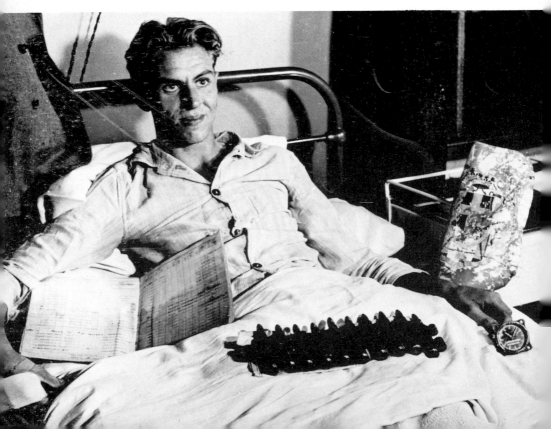

DeHavilland Mosquito FB VI which equipped 418 Squadron.

F/L Johnny Caine looking through the flak-damaged tail of his 406
Squadron Mosquito, 21 April 1945.

W/C L. V. Chadburn by a Spitfire bearing the cougar and maple leaf markings of 416 Squadron.

Chadburn's personal Spitfire V when he commanded the RCAF's Digby wing.

S/L E. F. J. Charles with his father's RFC wings which he carried as a talisman through the Second World War.

F/L H. D. Cleveland (right) and Sgt. F. Bays about to enter their 418 Squadron Mosquito, 21 January 1944.

PAC PL-10237

Left: F/L J. F. Edwards in North Africa.

Below: At war's end many allied airmen appropriated captured enemy aircraft. In the foreground a FW-190 bears Edward's initials while the Bf-108 in the background carries those of Stan Turner.

Cleveland
The Old Intruder

Russ Bannock, Johnny Caine, Howie Cleveland, Ross Gray, Bob Kipp, Don MacFadyen—these were the great names among the RCAF's intruder pilots. They had one thing in common, all began their combat careers with No. 418 Squadron. In addition, four were from western Canada and three rose to lead squadrons.

"Howie" Cleveland was the oldest of the lot—indeed, an old man as fighter pilots went. He was born in Vancouver on July 7, 1913, which meant he was over 30 by the time he went on ops. That was no obstacle to him; in five months he destroyed ten enemy aircraft on his own plus two more shared with another pilot.

He was raised in Vancouver, where his father was a civil engineer. The family had a cottage north along the coast, and in 1929 it was occasionally visited by an RCAF seaplane piloted by Flying Officer C.R. Dunlap. These trips were not entirely "official", for Dunlap was courting Howie's elder sister, but they also served to spark the youth's interest in flying.

In 1933 the younger Cleveland received a Bachelor of Commerce degree from UBC. He was also active in swimming, golf and rugby. In his graduating year he was captain of the All Star British Columbia Touring Rugby Team. Jobs were scarce at that time, so he shipped out for six months as a merchant seaman before landing a position as an advertising salesman. By 1940 he had risen to the position of sales manager with Neon Products Limited. He had other responsibilities as well; he had married in 1937.

For all his roots, Cleveland decided to enlist. He could have secured a commission in the Royal Canadian Navy; a senior officer almost begged him to look at that service. Nevertheless, he had his eye on the RCAF. Unfortunately, the reverse was not true. He was overage (25 years was then the limit for aircrew trainees) and married, which was also a disqualification at that stage of the war.

Just at that time, April 1940, James Duncan was appointed Deputy Minister for the soon-to-be created Ministry of Defence for Air. Duncan was looking for an Executive Assistant, and was advised that a dynamic young man named Howard Cleveland would fit the bill. Howie travelled to Ottawa on Duncan's invitation, and was interviewed. He was then advised that he was exactly the man whom the DM wanted.

Howie confessed to Duncan that he was not enthusiastic about the job; he had come to the capital hoping to persuade officialdom to waive the age and marital restrictions which blocked his enlistment. Could Duncan do something to arrange that? The latter agreed to try, and sent Howie to see Air Commodore Harold "Gus" Edwards, the RCAF's Chief of Personnel.

Cleveland possessed considerable charm and a forceful manner of expression, both of which he turned loose in equal measure on Edwards. He made it clear that he did not want to sit out the war as a desk-bound civilian. Edwards began by quoting the regulations; he ended up admitting that he was the officer that wrote the rules and that he could probably find ways of by-passing them.

The upshot of this interview was that Howie's application was reconsidered and he was accepted. In December 1940 he entered No. 2 Initial Training School, Regina, and thus began moving through the BCATP "pipeline." He proved to be an exemplary student. On June 22, 1941 he graduated at the head of his class from No. 33 Service Flying Training School, Carberry, Manitoba.

He was promptly commissioned, sent to Trenton for training as an instructor, then posted to No. 5 SFTS at Brantford. Keen yet cool, he was marked for accelerated promotion. One night in September 1942 he showed clearly how he would react in a crisis. He was Senior Duty Officer that evening when a heavy fog rolled in, blanketing the field. An *Anson*, piloted by a trainee, was caught away from the field. When the pupil called up for directions, Flying Officer Cleveland took charge. First he ordered the student to fly to Dunnville. That turned out to be fogged in, so he instructed the tyro to drop flares and find a field suitable for a forced landing. When no such field could be located, Cleveland radioed the student to fly clear of any towns, climb away, and then use his parachute. He even briefed the youngster on the proper bail-out procedure. Everything went smoothly; the pupil parachuted to safety and the *Anson* crashed in open country.

In June 1943 Cleveland was posted to No. 36 Operational Training Unit at Greenwood, Nova Scotia, for initiation into flying the *Mosquito*. A short period of leave followed, and then he was off to Britain, for more training, and assignment to No. 418 Squadron. He arrived at his new unit on January 1, 1944.

His first sortie, a training intruder flight to Rennes, was more exciting than most such tour openers. On that occasion he chased an enemy plane for six minutes at 2,000 feet but failed to catch it. He and his RAF observer, Sergeant Frank Day, flew eleven sorties during which nothing was seen but clouds and nighttime gloom. Then, on February 26, after careful planning, he took off on a Day Ranger—the ultimate opportunity.

A former member of No. 418 Squadron has described the Day Rangers as "gong-chasing games played by aggressive competitive pairs." There was that element to them, but they were also well-thought out exercises. Intelligence reports were studied to determine where concentrations of *Luftwaffe* aircraft were to be found, what defences might be encountered, and how important the various targets were to enemy operations. Routes were laid down to avoid flak nests, balloons, or single-engined fighter bases. Weather dictated timing; a clear day ruled out such a flight; low clouds or scattered fog made it more practical.

On this occasion Cleveland was accompanied by another "Mossie" piloted by Flight Lieutenant C.C. Scherf (RAAF), one of No. 418's crack intruders. The two fighters hugged the deck, roaring along under a solid cloud base, heading for enemy airfields in central France. Their first objective was St. Yan airfield, which they approached from the northwest. Scherf blasted two *Ju 52* transports; Cleveland fired at an aircraft he identified as an *He 177* bomber and set it ablaze. He was so low that in pulling up he cleared the enemy's tail by only ten feet.

The duo headed south as a ruse, then turned northeast for Dole airfield. They missed their objective and spent several minutes trying to locate it. Just as they found it a stupendous monster waddled into view—an *He 111Z* towing two *Go 242* gliders. The *He 111Z* was a gigantic airplane—two normal twin-engined *He 111*'s joined together like Siamese twins with a fifth engine added. The beast was one of the largest operational airplanes in the world, having a wing span of more than 115 feet. It was also slow and awkward—a huge pigeon.

The two *Mosquitos* climbed towards their prey with Scherf leading. So slow was the target, however, that the Australian stalled while trying not to overshoot. That left Cleveland with a clear field of fire. In his combat report he later described the death of the monster:

I opened [fire] at 300 yards closing to 50 yards. I saw the tow cable break and the rear glider almost stopped so that I nearly hit him. His nose went straight up and he dived straight down. Flight Lieutenant Scherf saw him hit the deck and crash into a house and hedge.

Flight Lieutenant Scherf then took the second glider, which flew into pieces, scattering him with wreckage. He then went in after the towing Bi-Heinkel and set the starboard outer and inner engines on fire. He broke away, and I began firing cannon and machine guns from 300 to 100 yards, setting the inner starboard engine on fire, with strikes on fuselage. Despite the amount of cannon (10 to 12 seconds) I had fired, and the fact that three engines were burning, and bits of wreckage flying everywhere, the Heinkel seemed to take a very long time before it started a slow spiral to the ground, with both *Mosquitos* after it.

Cleveland broke away to avoid a collision with his fellow hunter; Scherf saw the giant crash port wing down. The Canadian damaged another Gotha glider before they set course for home. Back at base they argued to the Intelligence "spies" that, as two *He 111's* constituted a single *He 111Z*, they should each be credited with one Heinkel destroyed. Fighter Command refused to buy that novel approach; the big glider tug was one airplane to be shared between two pilots. Cleveland later received a ribbing from his fellows when the combat films were developed. His "He 177" had twin fins and was, in fact, a much more modest *Ju 86*. Incidents like that sent squadron personnel back to the books to brush up on aircraft recognition. Howie's mistake was not enough to prevent him from being promoted to Squadron Leader on March 7.

His score ran higher on April 16, 1944 when, at Toul airfield, he wiped two *Fw 190's* and a *Bu 131* trainer off the *Luftwaffe's* inventory. North of Thionville, Cleveland, assisted by a *Mosquito* piloted by Flight Lieutenant J.B. Kerr, destroyed a *Ju 87*. It also sounds remarkably simple, until one remembers that these daylight sorties were conducted at such low level that the "Mossies" were practically cutting the grass. On this trip, for example, Cleveland's windscreen was spattered by mud which had been thrown up by his own cannon shells!

Eleven days later, during a night intruder sortie, he attacked a twin-engined enemy aircraft that was landing at St. Croix de Metz airfield. Before he could fire a shot, the German machine swerved off the runway and exploded—literally frightened to death.

Not all his low-level flying was in pursuit of enemy aircraft. In the spring of 1944 he frequently flew down to Dunsfold where his brother-in-law, "Larry" Dunlap, was now commanding a *Mitchell* medium bomber wing. Dunlap always knew when Howie was coming in, for the Flying Control Officer invariably reported a *Mosquito* breaking every rule in the book, beating up the field and buzzing the tower.

One of these episodes was almost his undoing. His brother Ernest was an Army officer on liaison duties with a *Typhoon* wing. One day Howie took him up and began showing him what a "Mossie" could do, including fly on one engine at 500 feet with the dead propeller feathered. He reached to restart the engine, but accidently killed the one functioning *Merlin*. Suddenly he was sinking without power and the ground coming up fast. Cleveland probably set a record at restarting his engines.

On June 2, 1944 the *London Gazette* published the announcement that Cleveland and Day had been awarded the Distinguished Flying Cross and Distinguished Flying Medal respectively. They would have appreciated the citations had they been able to read them, but by then the former was in a Swedish hospital and the latter was dead.

They had gone out on the afternoon of May 16, again with Scherf as a hunting partner, to harry the German Baltic coast. The Australian shot down an *He 111* and an *Fw 190*, after which they separated over Kubitzer Bay. Cleveland and Day headed south to Parrow airfield. There they found a parked *Do 217* which exploded and burned after their attack. Immediately ahead of them they saw an *He 111* approaching the field to land. Howie lowered his flaps to keep his speed down, attacked from astern, and blew off the Heinkel's port wing.

From reconnaissance photographs he knew that there was a canal nearby with several German seaplanes moored. He spotted these and banked to strafe them. Unfortunately, his course took him between two hangars, and his speed was fairly low as a result of the attack on the Heinkel. Two 37-mm guns mounted on the roofs of the hangars caught him in a cross-fire at point-blank range.

Cleveland winced as a piece of shrapnel stabbed into his right leg. The instruments were blown away and the starboard engine riddled, the roundel on that wing being blown right out. Holes appeared in the fuselage. The controls were sluggish, one *Merlin* was dead, Frank Day was wounded, and home was 600 miles away. Cleveland reported his two "kills" to Scherf before setting course for Sweden.

Normally an aircraft in trouble could enter neutral airspace by indicating that it was a cripple seeking refuge. There was a pattern for signalling this fact, including flares and lowering the undercarriage. Cleveland had two strikes against him. Day was too badly hurt to assist, and the "Mossie" was so heavily damaged that to lower the wheels for any extended time would endanger the aircraft. Nevertheless, he tried, but on this occasion Swedish flak batteries did not recognize his plight and opened fire. If he kept on going he would either crash with his wheels down or be blasted with them retracted.

Banking around, he headed back over the Baltic. In his mind there was a desperate plan. Obviously he would have to ditch; if he did so he might as well do it outside the three-mile limit. That way he might escape internment by pleading that he was a "distressed mariner." Fighting for control, he put the "Mossie" down on the waves.

He couldn't pull it off. With so many holes in it, the aircraft began to settle in the cold water. Then the tail section broke away and the *Mosquito's* nose dropped, with the machine sinking like a rock. Under water, Cleveland managed to drag himself and Day clear of the "Mossie". His lungs were near to bursting as he struggled to the surface and inflated the two dinghys.

He tried to get Day into one craft, and used up precious energy without success. With a final surge of effort he flopped into his own dinghy and lost consciousness. He was revived by someone pouring rum down his throat. Suddenly he was awake again, swearing at a Swedish fisherman who had rescued him. Only then did he discover that he had been adrift for three hours. Day had drowned; he may well have been beyond help before they reached the surface of the water.

Cleveland was taken to hospital. While recovering from shock he was visited by a British diplomat, to whom he explained his theory that he should be treated as a "distressed mariner". The gentleman doubted that the argument would gain sympathy, but he promised to use it on Howie's behalf. The Swedes were co-operative, however, and on June 17 he returned to Britain, riding in the bomb-bay of a *Mosquito* which was being used for courier duties. Soon afterwards he rejoined No. 418 Squadron. He shot down one more aircraft, an unidentified twin-engined type, on the night of July 27. He was then considered tour-expired and sent back to Canada.

By January 1945 he was back in the UK, where he was attached to the headquarters of the American Ninth Air Force, serving as a liaison officer. In April he went to RCAF Overseas Headquarters, and on May 24 he was assigned to No. 418 Squadron once more, this time with the rank of Wing Commander. He was the last overseas CO of the unit, assigned to close up the shop and send the boys home. Without the challenge of wartime duty to act as glue, he nevertheless kept No. 418 sharp and happy to the end. In September it was his turn to go back to Canada, and on November 6, 1945 he was demobilized.

Cleveland was one of many distinguished aircrew who immediately returned to their pre-war surroundings. He rejoined Neon Products Limited, and subsequently became President of the company. He also established Seaboard Advertising in Vancouver, and became prominent in the business community of that city. He has since retired from his firm and spends most of his time in Spain.

Edwards
Desert Ace

The first time that "Stocky" Edwards went into action he was an NCO pilot flying a *Kittyhawk* of No. 94 Squadron in North Africa. On that day, March 2, 1942, he opened up on a *Bf 109*, a type he had hitherto seen only in recognition books, and had the satisfaction of seeing it blow up after one burst of fire. Yet he was still very much of a new pilot, and a few days later he narrowly escaped being shot down by four Messerschmitts.

Edwards was born at Nokomis, Saskatchewan, on June 5, 1921. He played a great deal of hockey before joining the RCAF in October 1940. He took his early flight training at No. 16 Elementary Flying Training School, Edmonton, then went on to win his wings at No. 11 Service Flying Training School, Yorkton. In August 1941 he was posted overseas as a Sergeant pilot. Once he was in Britain his association with the RCAF became tenuous, for his next three years were to be spent almost exclusively in RAF units.

He took his operational training at No. 55 OTU, Usworth, and there, on October 1, 1941, he committed a blunder which probably delayed his being commissioned. He was descending through cloud, flying a *Hurricane*, when his engine failed at 3,000 feet. Edwards force-landed in a field, then reported to the police. Investigation showed that he had taken off on his reserve fuel tank and had failed to switch over to his main tanks.

He was duly sent to West Africa, from where he ferried a *Hurricane* to Cairo, arriving there on December 22. The following month he joined No. 94 Squadron, a *Kittyhawk* unit engaged both in ordinary fighter operations and in the hazardous task of ground attack, strafing and lobbing 500-lb. bombs at enemy vehicles.

The *Kittyhawks* lacked the level speed of the *Bf 109F*, but their speed in a dive was equal to that of the enemy fighter and they were capable of absorbing tremendous punishment. With six .50 calibre guns their armament was better suited to fighter-vs-fighter combat than that of their opponents, whose two machine guns were supplemented by a single 20-mm cannon. The *Kittyhawk* squadrons held their own against the *Luftwaffe*, and Edwards became the most successful *Kittyhawk* pilot in the RCAF.

On March 23, No. 94 Squadron, in company with No. 260 (another *Kittyhawk* outfit) was escorting twelve *Bostons* when a swarm of *Bf 109's* intercepted. A ding-dong dogfight raged over the desert. Two enemy fighters were shot down, one of them by Edwards, but two *Kittyhawks* were also lost. Four bombers went down as well—three to Messerschmitts and one to flak.

In April Edwards went to No. 260 Squadron, with which he proved to be an exceptionally proficient fighter pilot. He rapidly advanced from Flight Sergeant to Warrant Officer (First Class). During this period he was recommended for the Distinguished Flying Medal, but the paperwork was slow in reaching the proper levels. This didn't faze the slightly-built, tawny-haired Westerner, who went right on knocking down Axis aircraft with frugal, well-aimed bursts. Fellow pilots considered him to be a master of deflection shooting. One of his CO's remarked, "Edwards' secret lies in his uncanny shooting, which he displays not only in the air but also with rifle and shotgun, in addition to his good standard as a flyer."

His score mounted steadily—a *'109* "probable" on September 15, an *MC.202* confirmed on October 21, a *'109* destroyed on the 22nd, another "probable" *'109* on the 26th, and then a Messerschmitt destroyed on the 28th, along with one "probable". The fighting was intense as the Desert Air Force beat the *Luftwaffe* to a standstill over El Alamein.

Edwards was commissioned in November 1942, although the promotion was backdated to August 10. Within weeks he had become a Flight Lieutenant and was appointed a flight commander in No. 260 Squadron. His leadership left nothing to be desired. On December 30 he shot down another *Bf 109*. He was leading seven other *Kittyhawks* shortly after noon when they spotted half a dozen *Bf 109G's* bombing forward troops near Bir el Zidan, western Libya. A hail of anti-aircraft fire was being thrown up, but the eager *Kittyhawk* pilots ignored that hazard and sailed into the enemy fighters. Edwards later recounted the story:

> In a few moments the enemy aircraft and ours, and the cannon and machine gun fire of both, were whizzing in all directions in an atmosphere thick with shells and bullets from the ground. We got the *MEs* by surprise and hit them hard. I got a deflection shot at one, hit the engine, and saw the aircraft turn over on its back as the pilot bailed out, but he was too near the 'deck' and crashed before his 'brolly' could open.

No. 260 claimed five Messerschmitts destroyed in that action, which led to Edwards being recommended for the DFC. The new year started well when he shot down yet another *Bf 109* on January 2, 1943.

Honours soon began to pour in. Early in February he was informed that the long-delayed DFM had been approved. On February 16 the *London Gazette* announced that he had been awarded the DFC. The citation for the latter noted that he had destroyed eight enemy aircraft and that he had "invariably displayed outstanding gallantry and devotion to duty." The two blue-and-white ribbons beneath his pilot's wings constituted impressive proof of his record.

No. 260 Squadron was heavily involved in the pursuit of Axis forces across North Africa to Tunisia. About this time the unit acquired a captured *He 111* which they used as a transport. Edwards was able to log several hours in the Heinkel, when he wasn't smashing up enemy transport vehicles. However, he did not submit any further aerial claims until April 8, 1943, when he put three bursts into an *Fw 190* which nevertheless escaped.

Although it was too late for the enemy to hold Tunisia, they nevertheless increased their efforts, with the *Luftwaffe* flying about 150 sorties per day. On April 15 Edwards led his squadron down onto a dozen *Bf 109's* and *MC.202's*, taking them by surprise over the Gulf of Hammamet. Coming in at an angle, he fired a short burst at a *'109* which poured smoke and hit the shoreline. Swinging astern of another, he fired two quick, accurate bursts. His second victim caught fire and went into the sea. He then damaged a third *'109*. The successful ace later commented, "I shall never forget the way the second Jerry left a long trail of black smoke as he fell, just the way they used to do it in the movies when I was a kid."

It was, however, his last victory that year which was probably the the most unusual. In mid-April the hard-pressed Germans attempted to fly supplies from Sicily to Tunisia in support of their flagging armies. The result was a series of actions—more accurately described as mas-sacres—in which dozens of lumbering Axis transports were shot down. On April 22 about 20 *Me 323's*—giant six-engined aircraft, each carrying ten tons of fuel—attempted to break the Allied blockade under a heavy escort of fighters. Seven and a half squadrons of *Spitfires* and *Kittyhawks*, spearheaded by Nos. 4 and 5 Squadrons, South African Air Force, intercepted. One by one the transports were hit and exploded, until not one was left. No. 260 Squadron arrived near the end of the battle. Edwards saw a lone *Me 323* bent on escape, followed it, and shot it down into the sea.

A little more than a month later his tour ended. With more than 200 combat hours to his credit, he was posted to the Middle East Central Gunnery School, El Ballah (Egypt), where he served a non-operational tour setting up the course for pilots in the "Med". In December 1943 he returned to action, first with No. 417 Squadron and then with No. 92, both *Spitfire* units. It was with No. 92, then based at Marcianise, Italy, that Edwards pounded two more enemy fighters into oblivion, the last of his aerial victories.

The first of these was on February 16, 1944 when he and a South African pilot shot down the 299th and 300th aircraft credited to the squadron. From 500 yards, a range at which most pilots would not even consider wasting ammunition, he blew an *Fw 190* to bits. On the 19th he bagged another *Fw 190* in a battle which raged to within 20 feet of the ground.

On March 6, 1944 he was promoted to Squadron Leader and given the command of No. 274 Squadron. There was little chance for him to make a mark. On March 17, after crossing the lines to strafe enemy transport, he discovered a glycol leak in the *Spitfire*, probably caused by ground fire. The area was too mountainous to allow a bail-out, so he selected an open area and attempted to force-land. He had switched off his engine, but moments before touch-down his aircraft exploded. Twelve hours later he regained consciousness in an ambulance which was bumping him back to an Allied hospital. No. 274 Squadron left Italy in April 1944, and Squadron Leader Edwards went with them. They were assigned to Hornchurch, where he supervised the unit's conversion to *Tempests*. He led No. 274 throughout the Battle of the Flying Bombs but claimed no further victories. His second operational tour ended in August, at which time he returned to Canada.

Following five months of staff duties, he went back to Britain. On April 6, 1945 he put up the third broad stripe of a Wing Commander and was assigned to No. 127 Wing as Wing Commander (Flying). In one of his last wartime sorties, he led a mass flight over Kiel to help discourage any die-hard resistance. In September he returned to England for the trip home to Canada.

Throughout his operational career Edwards had flown more than 350 sorties. He was highly regarded by his comrades and superiors. Group Captain Stan Turner described him as "an excellent officer and leader . . . a proud asset to any unit." He was generally credited with 13 1/2 enemy aircraft destroyed, five probables, and eight damaged, plus seven aircraft and 200 vehicles destroyed on the ground. His log-book recorded flights in a great variety of aircraft including *Kittyhawks* (600 hours), *Spitfires* (450), *Tempests* (20), *Bf 109* (three hours and 30 minutes), *Fw 190* (two hours and 45 minutes), *Ju 87* (one hour) and *Bf 108* (four hours).

On New Year's Day 1946 it was announced that he had been awarded a Bar to his DFC. The citation, published in the *London Gazette*, was terse and pointed:

> This officer has successfully completed a very large number of operational flights and has destroyed thirteen enemy aircraft. He is a keen and courageous pilot whose example and leadership has been most inspiring.

Edwards remained in the post-war RCAF. Like many other veterans he had to accept a reduction in rank, reverting to Flight Lieutenant on October 1, 1946. He was promoted to Squadron Leader on January 1, 1948, and on June 1, 1952 he regained the rank of Wing Commander.

Much of his later service reflected his experience as a fighter leader. In 1948 he was part of an RCAF aerobatic team flying *Vampires*. He was the first CO of No. 430 Squadron when that unit reformed on *Sabres* in November 1951, and he subsequently took it to Europe, where he relinquished command in January 1953. He was also closely identified with units in NORAD and Air Defence Command. From August 1966 until September 1971 he commanded Canadian Forces Station Baldy Hughes. At that time he retired from the force. Wing Commander Edwards now lives in Comox, B.C.

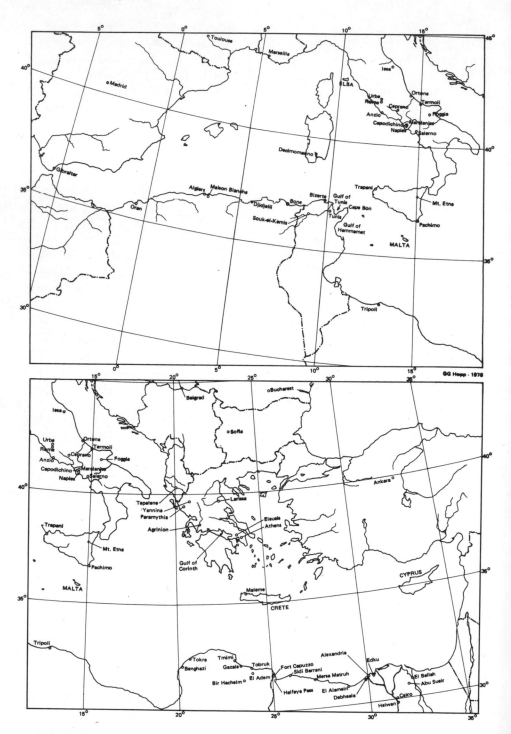

©G Hopp - 1978

Fairbanks
Tempest Tiger

December 17, 1944.

Time up and down: 1010 - 1135.

I was flying Blue One on a sweep to Rheine and we had turned on to 270 degrees at 2,000 feet . . . near Burgsteinfurt when I saw an aircraft about 1,000 feet below heading east. It passed under our formation and I immediately rolled on my back and gave chase. As I pulled out of the dive I recognized the enemy as an *Me. 109* and began to close in. The enemy aircraft pulled straight up and when I was about 500 yards behind it was in a stalled position standing on its tail. The pilot bailed out, the aircraft bunted and went straight into the deck and I saw the pilot land a short distance away in some trees.

I claim one *Me. 109* destroyed.

I rejoined the formation and we continued on 270 degrees at 3,500 feet and were about ten miles southeast of Emmerich when I sighted three *Me. 109's* at one o'clock to us flying in the opposite direction and at the same level as ourselves. I broke into them and they broke in our direction. I saw something fall away from the leading aircraft—it might have been the coupe or the pilot—I am not sure. I fired at this aircraft head-on from 600 yards. It put its nose down and passed beneath me. Then I broke round and picked out another Hun and got on its tail. I had a job staying behind it but managed to get in a few quick bursts with no results. The enemy aircraft was taking good evasive action and I overshot him once and ended up directly above him. I got behind him again and finally, firing from 150 yards, obtained strikes in his starboard radiator which immediately streamed glycol. His propeller started to windmill when we were down to 600 feet and a considerable amount of flak was coming up. The enemy aircraft circled in order to make a forced landing but I pulled up and attacked once more from 100 yards range and saw strikes on the port side of the fuselage in front of the cockpit. Then the enemy aircraft was at deck level and glided into some trees near Dingdon and exploded.

I claim one *Me. 109* destroyed.

I climbed again and with my section set course for Nijmegen. We passed near Emmerich and were just crossing the Rhine when two *Me. 109's* passed my starboard side slightly below at 4,000 feet and flying in the opposite direction. One was being chased by another *Tempest* and I broke into the second one. The enemy aircraft continued straight and level just at the base of cloud. I quickly closed the range from below to approximately 150 yards. I fired but only my port cannons worked. After a few bursts I saw strikes on the enemy aircraft's starboard wing. He did only a very slight turn to starboard and continued on. I rolled onto him again and fired until my ammo ran out. I overhauled the enemy aircraft and came right under his wing for a few seconds—the pilot was looking out the opposite side and did not seem to have a clue! He finally saw me and I pulled over the top of him, gave the finger sign and came home.

I claim one *Me. 109* damaged.

The author of this swash-buckling combat report was Flight Lieutenant (later Squadron Leader) D.C. Fairbanks of Ithaca, New York, one of hundreds of Americans who, long before Pearl Harbour, had realized that the Commonwealth's fight against the Axis was their fight as well and had joined the RCAF to play their part. Most had transferred to the USAAF when America entered the war. Fairbanks, however, had opted to remain with the RCAF, and later he was to convert his service association into Canadian citizenship.

The son of a Cornell University professor, David Fairbanks was born on August 22, 1922. In his youth he acquired an insatiable hunger for flying. He knew Thomas Morse, the distinguished American aircraft designer personally, and in grade school he read every book he could find which described the adventures of German and Allied aces of the First World War. He scrounged airplane rides and built model aircraft.

In his mind there developed an idealistic view of aviation and combat flying.

Little was required to impel him to join the nearest air force. From the outbreak of war in September 1939 he followed events with mounting interest and enthusiasm. While completing high school and after entering prep school his ambition to fly and fight after the manner of his heroes grew. At last, in January 1941, he could resist no longer. With two friends he ran away from home and headed for Canada. At the Peace Bridge between Buffalo and Fort Erie he was turned back for lack of funds—he had only 20 cents in his pocket—and he thumbed his way home, sleeping in barns en route.

His subsequent efforts were more conventional. He first convinced his widowed mother that he should be allowed to join the RCAF, then set out again, this time with sufficient money. In February 1941 he enlisted in Hamilton, and in so doing forsook the rich and comfortable existence which appeared to have been open to him.

Quiet yet alert, Fairbanks was an exemplary pupil. One of his instructors wrote that he was "amazing in quickness to learn." Moreover he was smart in drill, dress and appearance. It would be difficult to imagine a pilot more dashing in uniform, for he was blond and unusually handsome. He might have stepped from a recruiting poster or a movie screen.

The climax of his training came on November 21, 1941 when he received his wings at No. 9 Service Flying Training School, Summerside, Prince Edward Island. From there he was posted with nine other graduates to the Central Flying School at Trenton, where they learned the techniques of instructing. Like many other pilots of the early war years, he had been assigned to teach others to fly.

Fairbanks was sent to No. 13 SFTS at St. Hubert, just outside Montreal, to take up instructional duties. Restless, and ambitious for overseas action, he became a thorn in the flesh of his commanding officer. Once, following a brief absence without leave, he was threatened with a court martial. Fortunately his CO's superiors regarded the incident as trivial and Fairbanks escaped with a sharp dressing down. On another occasion, however, his high jinks led to his being made Orderly Officer for 30 days.

While at St. Hubert the young instructor indulged in numerous flying games with his fellow pilots. Night formation flying was not in the syllabus, so naturally they practised it. Another trick was to creep up on other *Harvards* at night while remaining blacked out, then flick on the navigation lights to signal a successful interception and "kill". This was hazardous in the dark and during one such flight Fairbanks came within ten feet of ramming another aircraft.

His year of mundane duties ended in February 1943 when he was posted overseas. He arrived in Britain in April, then went through the routine of advanced and operational training. At last, on January 12, 1944, he joined No. 501 Squadron flying *Spitfire VB's*. It was with No. 501 that he drew his first blood on June 8, shooting down a *Bf 109* and damaging another during an early morning sweep near Le Havre.

He left No. 501 in July and the following month joined No. 274 Squadron which was equipped with the latest RAF fighter, the Hawker *Tempest V*. This tremendous airplane represented the peak of British wartime piston designs. Powered by a Napier *Sabre* engine of more than 2,000 horsepower, it had a top speed of 435 miles per hour. The *Tempest* was armed with four 20-mm cannon and could carry an assortment of bombs and rockets weighing up to a ton. It was also the heaviest British single-engined fighter in service. This, coupled with its aerodynamically clean wing enabled it to pick up speed and catch German fighters in a dive, thus nullifying what had hitherto been the enemy's most effective way of breaking off a battle.

No. 274 was then at West Malling, where it had been stationed throughout the summer intercepting *V-1* "Doodlebugs". The onslaught of these sinister weapons was now tapering away as their launching sites were overrun, but Fairbanks managed to get a crack at some before the season closed. Two *V-1's* fell to his cannon, and in one instance the buzzbomb nearly took the *Tempest* with it. One moment Fairbanks was firing at his nimble target; the next instant he was flying in the midst of its flaming debris.

In September No. 274 moved to the continent to join the Allied Second Tactical Air Force. The *Tempests* found few enemy aircraft, so they were sent out to blast ground targets. It was in November that Fairbanks suffered his first battle damage. While attacking a locomotive his aircraft was hit by flak. For a moment he found himself upside down with the ground rushing up to meet him. Desperately he kicked the controls and righted the *Tempest*, but his troubles were far from over. One of the fuel tanks had been riddled and a fire was burning in one wing. Resisting the temptation to bail out, Fairbanks set course for base. The fire ate a gaping hole in the wing before finally dying out. He reached his field and landed safely. His exploit won for him his first Distinguished Flying Cross.

Then came his resounding triumph of December 17. Indeed, it was even more spectacular than he imagined, for in his combat report he had claimed only two destroyed and one damaged. Later it was reported that the third *'109*, whose inept pilot had been given the rude "finger sign", had subsequently been hit by an ack-ack crew and had bailed out. This victory was thus upgraded to "destroyed", with Fairbanks and the gunners sharing the honours.

Shortly afterwards he was sent to No. 3 Squadron, another

Tempest unit, with which he flew for a month. In January 1945, while serving with No. 3, he was credited with the destruction of three enemy fighters and also had a hand in shooting up a *Ju 52*. He also probably destroyed one *Ju 88* and damaged another, both while on the ground. For this work he was recommended for a Bar to the DFC.

No. 3 Squadron, however, was engaged primarily in low level strafing and interdiction, a job providing relatively little scope for air-to-air combat. New opportunities opened up on February 9, 1945 when Fairbanks was promoted to Squadron Leader and sent back to No. 274. In the next fortnight, while carrying out armed reconnaissance sorties, he was able to shoot down no fewer than seven German fighters.

One of his victims was an *Me 262* jet which he destroyed on February 11 over Rheine airfield. On this occasion he stalked the enemy machine for several minutes as they played hide-and-seek in the clouds. At last the German pilot settled down for an approach into Rheine, apparently satisfied that he had lost the troublesome *Tempest*. Just as the Messerschmitt's undercarriage slid down Fairbanks swooped out of the clouds and bored to within 300 yards of the jet. He thumbed the gun switch for less than a second. It was enough. The starboard *Jumo* engine flamed out and the *Me 262* plummeted down to explode in the centre of the airfield.

On two occasions—February 16 and 22—Squadron Leader Fairbanks bagged two enemy fighters in a single sortie. The German pilots were crafty flyers or, as Fairbanks expressed it in one report, "seemed to have quite a few clues", which was unusual considering the poor state into which the *Luftwaffe* had fallen. On the other hand, it should be remembered that in the closing stages of the war many experienced German pilots banded together, leaving their undertrained subordinates to fend for themselves. The result was that none of his victories came easily. In each encounter he was forced to wring the maximum performance from his aircraft with all the skill at his command. In one combat he saw tracer bullets whizzing in front of his machine, and in another action he had to put the *Tempest* into a vertical climb to bag a long-nosed *Fw 190D*. The brute power of his plane made things easier; no piston-engined German fighter could outrun a *Tempest* going flat out.

Early on the morning of February 28, 1945 Fairbanks took off leading five other *Tempests* for an armed reconnaissance in the Osnabrück area. Having shot up a locomotive they reformed at 5,500 feet between two cloud layers. Then they spotted a formation of 40 enemy fighters—a mixture of *Fw 190's* and *Bf 109's*—coming head-on towards them. Fairbanks' own words best describe the ensuing battle:

I called out a head-on attack and for the formation to drop long range tanks. Time was so short it was difficult to select a suitable target and lay off deflection. I don't remember any return fire from the enemy aircraft. I think they were just as surprised as we were and also didn't have enough time to line up a burst.

As soon as we passed the last man I called a left 180 degree break back toward the formation. As we turned around there were few aircraft to be seen. They must have scattered in all directions. I started to chase one but he went into a cloud and I lost him. Shortly after this I pushed my aircraft down into cloud and came out underneath and saw a *'190*. But this time my Number Two had lost me.

I closed the range on this aircraft and before I was ready to fire I noticed some tracers coming my way. I was near the ground and thought it was flak tracer. A few more tracers went by me and I was ready to fire at the enemy aircraft. I fired and hit the *'190* who burst into flames. The next instant I was hit hard.

It was not ground tracer I had seen but shells from the aircraft behind that hit me. I can remember seeing wing ribs and torn skin on the left and right upper wing surfaces and I was having difficulty keeping the aircraft level. The engine was missing and puffs of glycol were shooting by. No doubt my rad had been punctured. I held the stick hard over right to keep level and applied right rudder. With the controls in this position I knew I wasn't going home.

I decided it was time to bail out. Holding the controls with my right hand I tried to jettison the canopy with my left, but it wouldn't budge. I tried several times but didn't have enough strength in my left hand alone. I let go of the controls and pulled the jettison handle with both hands and away she went.

I can only remember that the canopy was gone and that I leaned my head to the left into the slipstream. The next thing I remember I was on the ground.

Fairbanks had bailed out still wearing his headset and oxygen mask, and in escaping he broke his nose. Otherwise he was unhurt. He was immediately surrounded by elderly German home guard troops who herded him at rifle point to a barn. There his hands were tied and he was led out again where a crowd of angry civilians began to jostle him. One man swung a pistol in his direction. "My God," he thought, "I'm to be shot like an animal." Desperately, at the top of his lungs, he began shouting practically the only German word he knew, "Kommandant, kommandant!"

"Are you hurt?" a friendly, accented voice asked. Turning his head, Fairbanks discovered a flak officer almost beside him. He was taken away and untied, then given a cigarette. The officer had been educated in England and spoke of the war in a sad, objective way. He finally turned his prisoner over to a local jail where Fairbanks spent two nights discovering all his cuts and bruises and aches in muscles he had never dreamed he had. He guessed that his parachute had not fully deployed before he landed; it was a miracle that he was alive.

It seemed as though a succession of miracles was required to keep him that way. Once in German custody he became the object of hate and contempt for civilians and ragged troops whose discipline had begun to vanish after the Battle of the Bulge. Twice more he came near to being shot out of hand and each time his captors failed to carry out their threats. After a week of this nerve-wracking treatment he was sent to the safety of a regular POW camp, but in April the Germans set the whole camp marching westward before the Russian advance. The enemy seemed unable to realize that their country was finished, that every prison camp was soon to be liberated, that captors and captives were soon to exchange places. And so it came to be that, late in April, advancing Allied troops freed Fairbanks and all his fellows.

In July 1945 he was awarded a second Bar to his DFC and was repatriated to Canada. Release from the RCAF followed in October. He then resumed his education and in 1950 obtained a degree in mechanical engineering from Cornell University. But where was he to stake out his career? His service contacts led him to more offices in Montreal than New York, so north he went to join the staff of Dominion Bridge. At the same time he enlisted in the RCAF Auxiliary where he took up flying *Harvards*, *Vampires*, and *T-33's*. In 1951 he switched to Sperry Gyroscopes, with which firm he worked four years. Two of those years were spent in England where he flew *Meteors* with the RAF's No. 504 Auxiliary Squadron.

In 1955 he landed a job as test pilot with De Havilland of Canada and moved to Toronto. The RCAF Auxiliary connection lasted until 1959 when he was forced to drop it through pressure of work. His assignments included demonstration flying from Canada to Kashmir as he took *Beavers*, *Otters*, and *Caribou* across four continents. Within the company he rose to become the Manager of Flight Operations, responsible for all test flying and all aspects of DHC's flight operations around the world. As an expert on STOL aircraft his advice was sought by regulatory agencies in Canada and the United States. Early in 1976 it was announced that, for his services to Canadian aviation, he had been awarded the Trans-Canada Trophy, better known as the McKee Trophy.

Tragically, it was a posthumous award. On February 20, 1975, David C. Fairbanks died in Toronto. The tiger of *Tempests* and sales-man of scores of aircraft succumbed to natural causes.

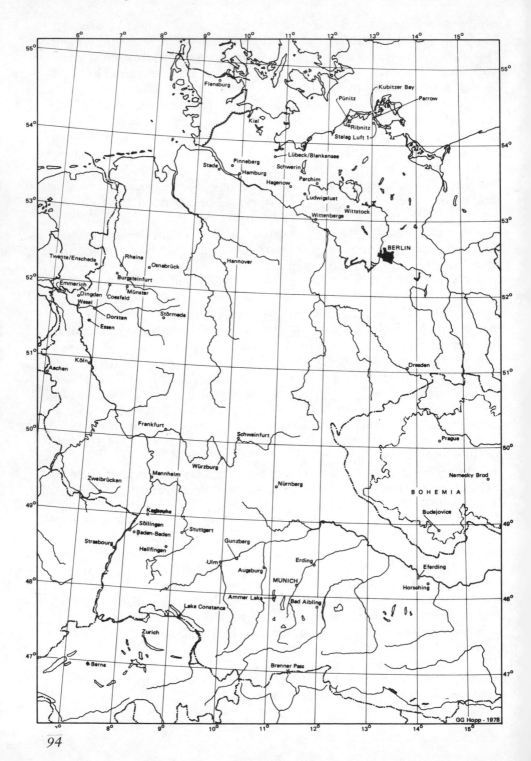

Fumerton
Night Fighter

Jerry was active. In the plotting rooms, WAAF girls chalked up the latest reports and moved counters over the map of northern England. Elsewhere, radar operators peered at their fluorescent scopes as the little dots which were German and Allied aircraft crept about. Controllers at their radio posts flashed reports to patrolling night fighters. A complex organization of men and cathode ray tubes was attempting to bring some of those dots together.

It was September 1, 1941. The Blitz, that terrible bombing campaign which had united the British people in their hardship and determination, had ended months before, but the few German bombers remaining in western Europe still probed the island's defences. Tonight there were about 40 of them, some off the coast, apparently minelaying, and about a dozen approaching Newcastle, obviously intent upon mischief.

Ten thousand feet over Acklington airfield, a *Beaufighter* orbited, waiting for instructions. The pilot, Flying Officer R.C. "Moose" Fumerton, was well aware of the problems involved in this sort of action. Much depended upon his radar operator, Sergeant Pat Bing, and on the ground organization which had to provide the initial guidance to bring him to his target. The radar set in the "Beau" was also a cause for worry. The RAF "boffins" (scientists) had been working with airborne radar for months, but the devices were still cantankerous. Sometimes they worked; as often as not they refused to pick up anything. Tonight was a typical one for headaches, only one of the set's two scopes was functioning.

Fumerton's headset crackled as instructions came through. Get well to the southeast of Brae—now head north—now west—now northwest—west again. He was flying northwest when Bing shouted in triumph. There was a target on the scope! Now they were on their own, stalking the "bogey" in the darkness. Then he saw it—a dark shape crossing ahead of him, flying at about 11,500 feet in a southwesterly direction.

The shape disappeared momentarily into clouds. Fumerton banked to port, following it through the murk and into the open again. Now it was silhouetted against the moon. There could be no mistake; the single rudder and forward "greenhouse" branded it as a *Ju 88*. The range shrank to 100 yards, then 50. Fumerton eased the stick back. From behind and below he cut loose and the *Beaufighter* shuddered as four 20-mm cannons and six machine guns belched out a storm of shells and bullets. Flashes marked the strikes on the Junker's fuselage and its starboard engine began to burn. There would be no losing the enemy now; the fire made it impossible for the German to hide in the night sky.

But the Junkers was not finished. It fell away to port, then straightened out. Fumerton was close behind. An enemy gunner opened up, but his own engine was in the way and the bullets were wide of the mark. From dead astern and slightly above Fumerton let fly again. Suddenly the sky was lit with a dazzling flash. The bomber had exploded!

Fumerton landed back at Acklington two hours and ten minutes after he had taken off. His victim had been the first shot down by himself, the first destroyed by an RCAF night fighter pilot, and the first victory for No. 406 (Lynx) Squadron. The next day the wreckage of the Junkers was located and a portion of metal with the *Luftwaffe's* black cross insignia painted on it was cut away. Then a small swastika was painted on the cross. As the war progressed and more enemy aircraft fell to No. 406's crews, the number of swastikas multiplied. Today, visitors to the Canadian War Museum in Ottawa can view the cross with its many symbols of victories scored in the darkness over Britain and Europe.

It is tempting to apply superlatives to fighter pilots, but in Fumerton's case they come even more easily than with most. Not only was he the "first" but he was "tops". Before the war had ended he had shot down 14 enemy aircraft. The figure was surpassed by many day fighter and intruder pilots, but by no Canadian pilot operating in the pure night fighter role.

Fumerton was a rugged man with a rugged background. He was born at Fort Coulonge, a small Quebec town in the Ottawa Valley, on March 21, 1913. He was educated there and at nearby Shawville, where he passed his junior matriculation in 1930. At school he played hockey, football and softball, and he also enjoyed hunting, an avocation which never left him. He grew to become a formidable young man, six feet tall, slim and muscular.

In 1931 he went to work as a timber cruiser. Two years later he was hired by International Nickle as a weigher and checker. Then in 1934 he went into prospecting. During the Depression he worked for three different exploration companies in Ontario and the Northwest Territories. Fumerton took correspondence courses in geology, mapping and surveying during this period, at the same time acquiring an extensive knowledge of aerial photography as it related to mapping. In 1939 he took up flying at the Sudbury Flying Club, went solo after five hours of instruction, and quickly acquired his Private Pilot's License.

When the war broke out, Fumerton returned home to Fort Coulonge to visit his family, then carried on to Ottawa where he enlisted. As the British Commonwealth Air Training Plan was not yet in operation, he was sent to Fort William to brush up on his flying with the Lakehead Flying Club. In March 1940 he went to Camp Borden, where his training continued on *Harvards*. At last he qualified for his flying badge, and on May 23 he and 28 other graduates received their wings from no less a figure than Air Marshal W.A. "Billy" Bishop, the most famous Canadian fighter pilot of all time. Fumerton and his comrades were among the first Canadian aircrew trained during the war and the next five years would leave their mark; of the men who had their wings pinned on that day, eight were to die in action and eleven would be decorated.

Unlike many other early entrants, Fumerton did not have long to wait before getting overseas. At the end of August 1940 he joined No. 112 (RCAF) Squadron in Britain. An army co-operation unit, No. 112 was flying awkward-looking *Lysanders*, machines already obsolete, and he had no opportunity to see action. Happily, he was sent almost immediately to a fighter Operational Training Unit. In October he went to No. 32 Squadron, a *Hurricane* unit at Biggin Hill. Theoretically he was merely on temporary duty, but his sojourn lasted almost two months, during which time he flew nine sorties.

In December "Moose" was posted to No. 1 (RCAF) Squadron (later redesignated No. 401) which was then operating *Hurricanes* in Scotland. There followed seven months of scrambles and patrols but no combats. Nevertheless, he had acquired a considerable amount of operational flying time before he was posted to No. 406 Squadron in

June 1941.

No. 406, which was then forming with *Blenheim* aircraft, was the first night fighter squadron in the history of the RCAF. Once its crews had acquired twin-engined experience on the *Blenheims*, they were given *Beaufighters*, the most heavily armed fighters flown by the RAF throughout the war. The pilots were paired with a new breed of men, the radar operators, and for his partner Fumerton drew Sergeant L.P.S. "Pat" Bing of Regina. They made an excellent team; the combat of September 1, recounted above, proved that. A week later they damaged an *He 111* in their final action over Britain.

Their greatest triumphs, however, were achieved elsewhere. In October 1941 Fumerton and Bing joined No. 89 Squadron, an RAF outfit which shortly afterwards was transferred, lock, stock and radar, to Egypt. At Abu Sueir, a field which 15 years later was to become familiar to Canadian flyers with the United Nations Emergency Force, No. 89 settled down to getting its ground and air equipment in order for the job of protecting the Suez Canal. Fumerton and Bing flew their first sortie on January 5, 1942. German raids were small and infrequent. Consequently, by the end of February, the Canadian crew had flown only five sorties, all without results.

Early in the morning of March 3, four *Beaufighters* were scrambled to meet an incoming raid and first contact with the enemy was made. In the moonlight Fumerton observed an *He 111* cruising over the canal. He bored in and opened fire, but the German crew was alert and an enemy gunner poured a deadly stream of bullets at the fighter. At close range the two aircraft hammered away at each other like a pair of boxers bent upon mutual destruction.

Fumerton's gunsight was blasted to bits. Some debris cut him about the right eye and cheek, a bullet hit him in the right leg just above the ankle, both of the *Beaufighter's* engines packed up, the undercarriage was damaged and the flaps rendered inoperative. The Heinkel, though, was taking a beating too. First one and then the other engine caught fire. The bomber finally crashed in the Mediterranean where its crew was plucked from a rubber boat two days later. The gunner with the keen shooting eye, it developed, was an interesting type in other ways. A "permanent force" member of the *Wehrmacht*, he had avoided the Nazi purges and remained in the forces in spite of his being a Jew!

Fumerton, for his part, had his own problems. He was within 200 feet of the ground when one engine picked up again, but his airspeed was only 115 miles per hour and he dared not turn lest the *Beaufighter* spin in. He managed to effect a landing on the Edku salt flats. It had been a magnificent show, and it won for Fumerton a Distinguished Flying Cross.

Three days in hospital followed, but "Moose" was flying the day of his release. Late in March he and Bing were sent to Edku, near Alexandria, where No. 89 maintained a detachment for the protection of that port. On the night of April 7/8 the team scored again. Over the city they jumped an *He 111*, set it alight, and watched it spiral into the sea while three crewmen bailed out. Minutes later they encountered another *He 111*. It too caught fire, but for a few minutes it flew on an even keel like a flaming log. Then it began to spin, one wing broke away, and the blazing wreckage smashed into the ground. Both victims had been from *II./KG 26*.

On June 22 the squadron established a detachment, known as "C" Flight, at Luqa on Malta. The unit had five *Beaufighters* and six crews. For operational purposes the flight was divided into sections, each of which operated for two successive nights and was then released for two nights. Malta itself drew enemy bombers like flies and Fumerton seized the opportunity. During the next two months he shot down no fewer than nine aircraft—a *Ju 87* and a *Ju 88* on the night of June 24, two *Ju 88's* on June 29, a *Ju 88* on July 1, another *Ju 88* the following night, a further *Ju 88* on July 22, an Italian *Z.1007* on August 14, and a *Ju 88* on August 28.

The last victory was scored in Sicily. In August the squadron had been given permission to operate intruders and two *Beaufighters,* stripped of their radar, had been allocated to these duties. Fumerton and Bing's final victim was destroyed on the ground at Castelvetrano airfield.

Not all sorties were brilliant successes. At times the "Beaus" had radar trouble which seemed to indicate jamming by a German transmitter. Fumerton suggested that they maintain absolute radio silence when airborne in the hope that the enemy would not know they were up and thus would not turn on their device. This had a curious sequel, which Fumerton himself recounted in 1977:

It was usually our custom when two of us were patrolling to do practice runs on one another. This particular night two of us were up—I was given a vector, we picked up the blip (no jamming). I was delighted. I closed in (it was a very dark night), pulled up and tucked myself inside the wing of the other "Beau" (*Hurricane* style) and prepared to wave at the other pilot. In one split second I realized it was a *Ju 88* and the horrified face I was looking at was German. Fortunately the reaction of the *Ju 88* pilot in doing a wing-over was so fast that the rear gunner, who couldn't have been more than 25 feet away and in perfect position, didn't get a chance to blast me.

During the course of another patrol, both of his engines failed and the Fumerton/Bing duo had to ditch in rough seas. They spent the night in a dinghy intended for one man and paddled to within five miles of Malta before being rescued the following morning. Bing, now a Pilot Officer, was awarded a DFC and Fumerton received a Bar to his decoration. Months later Bing got a Bar to his DFC as well, but that was long after the team had been broken up.

On September 23, four veteran crews of "C" Flight, including the two redoubtable Canadians, flew back to Abu Sueir. Over the next two months they were occupied with non-operational flying before December brought a posting home to Canada. In Ottawa Fumerton was mobbed by reporters and at Fort Coulonge he was given a hero's welcome. It was pleasant to spend Christmas with his family, but there was a touch of sadness to the occasion as well, for one face was missing. His father had died a year before, while Fumerton was still overseas.

In January 1943 he was assigned to No. 1 Operational Training Unit at Bagotville, Quebec, where he served for five months before being switched to staff duties with RAF Ferry Command. He was anxious to return to action, however, and in July he received instructions to proceed to England. There he brushed up on the latest night fighting techniques. On August 25 he was promoted to Wing Commander and given charge of No. 406 Squadron, the unit with which he had begun his string of successes two years before.

No. 406's fortunes were then at a low ebb. It was based at Anglesey, in northern Wales, and had seen virtually no action for five months. Its *Beaufighters* were now obsolete. Morale was poor. An indifferent administrator, Fumerton nevertheless knew how to deal with his men. From his opening address to them he inspired confidence. He began to lobby Fighter Command for a more advanced base and more modern aircraft. The first demand was met in November 1943 when the squadron moved to Exeter, Devon, but it was not until April 1944 that the first *Mosquito XII* aircraft were assigned to the Lynx Squadron. Its greatest campaign was to be carried out on the old "Beaus".

In December 1943 and January 1944 the *Luftwaffe* assembled its largest bomber force in western Europe since the Blitz, a total of 524 aircraft, ranging from four-engined *He 177's* and the new *Ju 188* through older *Ju 88's* and *Do 217's* down to a few *Fw 190* fighter-bombers. The objective was to strike massive retaliatory blows at Britain. Yet the bulk of the enemy crews were inexperienced; the few veteran pilots and navigators had been stolen from other fronts, particularly the Mediterranean. Nevertheless, on the night of January 21, the enemy struck at London, and from then until the end of May they launched 31 major raids against the British Isles.

Several of the attacks were effective, raising large fires in the capital. For the most part, however, the Germans failed to find their targets. Hundreds of tons of bombs were scattered over open country. The "Little Blitz" was painful enough—more than 1,560 civilians were killed and 2,900 injured—but the German bomber fleet was shattered. Some 329 enemy aircraft were destroyed by the defences or by accidents related to operations.

So long as the *Luftwaffe* concentrated on London, No. 406 remained on the periphery of the action. On the night of March 19/20, however, the Germans attacked Hull. The squadron scrambled three *Beaufighters* and shortly before midnight Squadron Leader D.J. "Blackie" Williams shot down an *He 177*, the first "Lynx" victory in exactly one year. Things were looking up and combats became more frequent. By the end of May No. 406 had shot down 12 raiders.

On the night of May 14/15 a force of about 35 bombers struck at Bristol and No. 406 scrambled six aircraft. Fumerton, flying a *Mosquito*, was vectored onto a *Ju 188* at 17,000 feet. It was a copybook interception, and though the Junkers took evasive action it could not escape the fleet "Mossie". From 100 yards range Fumerton opened fire and the port engine of the bomber exploded. The Junkers rolled over and plunged vertically into the sea—No. 14 for Fumerton. All round it was a rewarding night for No. 406, whose jubilant crews reported shooting down four raiders and probably destroying three more.

Although he was to gain no further victories, Fumerton would experience one further notable adventure. Three days after D-Day he flew a Day Ranger sortie to Lorient, but finding no enemy aircraft he decided to attack two light buoys in the harbour. As he was shooting these up, the blast of his cannons unexpectedly smashed the perspex nose covering. Bits of debris lodged in the coolant radiator, causing the port engine to overheat. He attempted to feather the propeller but that failed. The "Mossie" was barely 50 feet off the water and 200 miles from home; ditching appeared inevitable. Then the feathering mechanism ground back into operation, enabling him to return to base. Four Coastal Command *Beaufighters* escorted him back the last few miles.

The squadron was shocked to learn in July 1944 that Fumerton was being posted away. Repatriated to Canada the following month, he joined No. 7 Operational Training Unit at Debert, Nova Scotia, taking command of that unit. He remained there until June 1945. During that time he performed so capably that he was awarded the Air Force Cross. In July 1945 he left the RCAF.

In the post war years he returned to geology, but in 1948 he was approached by Russ Bannock of De Havilland with an amazing offer. Some 300 mothballed *Mosquitos* were being sold to the Nationalist Chinese government which was then rapidly losing its war with the Communists. Would "Moose" like to train the Chinese in their use? He jumped at the chance, recruited some veteran pilots (John Turnbull was one) and headed for Hankow.

His students, who had been flying *Mitchells*, were very earnest, but most were in their '40s. They were thrown into action almost as soon as they had learned the basics. Meanwhile, guerillas prowled around the airfield itself. Serviceability was erratic, and almost one-third of the aircraft had to be cannibalized for spare parts. Early in 1949 the war situation had deteriorated to the point that there was nothing to do but pack and run for Hong Kong and home.

The denouement of his career has been amazingly tame. On his return to Canada Fumerton became a real estate broker in Toronto. He settled down to raise five children, and now revels in Canada's great summer pastime—cottaging!

Gordon
How to Succeed and Get Shot Up

Contrary to popular myth, fighter pilots were not generally tall and slim. The cockpit of a *Spitfire*, in spite of its elegant layout, was a small, cramped workshop in which a short man had the advantage. Squadron Leader Don Gordon, described by recruiting officers as "massive", undoubtedly found it uncomfortable. Nicknamed "Chunky", he stood over six feet tall and weighed just under 200 pounds. With his trim, jet-black moustache he was a formidable figure.

He was equally fierce in the air. In two tours he shot down eleven enemy aircraft. Strangely enough, he was not a particularly good pilot; the record of his flying career is one of crashes and near-misses that would astound a flight safety officer. Nevertheless, he survived the war, only to die in 1949 following surgery.

Don Gordon was born in Edmonton on February 25, 1920, but spent most of his boyhood in Vancouver, where he completed his high school education in 1939 and attended a business college for one year. In the summer of 1938 he worked as a deckhand on a fishing boat and the following summer he was employed as a millhand. He was sufficiently interested in aviation to build model airplanes, but his primary activities were athletic. In 1938 he won the B.C. amateur light heavyweight boxing championship.

In October 1940 he enlisted in the RCAF in Vancouver. He was, wrote the recruiting officer who interviewed him, "keen on doing his bit". The same man noted that Gordon had "very quick reactions". He was certainly going to need them.

His first posting after Manning Depot was temporary guard duty at Prince Albert, but in January 1941 he went to No. 2 Initial Training School at Regina. No. 2 ITS was then presided over by Wing Commander H.J. "Hank" Burden, a burly man with a bristling black moustache, an impressive row of ribbons, and seventeen German aircraft to his credit from the First World War. Burden was a spell-binding leader and an inspiring example for impressionable trainees.

From Regina Gordon went to No. 8 Elementary Flying Training School at Vancouver. He passed the course, but not before experiencing his first accident when he groundlooped a *Tiger Moth* on take-off. From there he went to No. 10 Service Flying Training School at Dauphin, Manitoba, flying *Harvards*. The students there indulged in numerous high jinks. One pilot trainee won local fame when, in the course of some unauthorized low flying, he struck an outhouse, which was demolished, and managed to get back to base. He was court-martialled for this escapade and fined $75.00. During one spell of hot weather someone smashed in the screens in the airmen's barracks, supposedly to let more air in, and the result was a plague of mosquitos. Another anonymous genius then devised a smudge pot which drove both insects and airmen outside.

On July 14, 1941 Gordon received his wings and graduated as a Sergeant pilot. Within two months he was overseas and in November 1941 he reported to No. 65 Squadron, flying *Spitfires*. It was not long before he was having problems. On November 19 he damaged his undercarriage in a heavy landing. On December 26, during a Rhubarb operation, he was hit by flak near Cherbourg, bailed out over the Channel, and was duly picked up by an air/sea rescue launch.

In January 1942 he was posted to the Far East, and actually got as far as Ceylon before Singapore fell to the Japanese. Back west he went, and in May 1942 he reported to No. 274 Squadron, a *Hurricane* unit in the Western Desert. At this point things really began to pop. On May 22 he claimed a probable *Ju 87*. On June 21 he shot down a *Bf 109F* and probably destroyed an *MC.202*. In July he damaged another *MC.202*, and on August 3 he shot down his second confirmed victim, a *Bf 109F*. By the end of the year his tally stood at two destroyed, three probably destroyed, and three damaged. Late in December he went to No. 601 Squadron, a *Spitfire V* outfit. Between February 27 and April 21, 1943 he added a *Bf 109* confirmed to his score, together with an *MC.202* probably destroyed and two enemy fighters damaged.

There were other incidents as well, however. On July 6, 1942, while on an operational sortie, he noticed glycol trickling into his *Hurricane's* cockpit. The engine temperature was rising quickly, so he broke formation, heading for home. The *Merlin* began to belch black smoke. He switched it off and glided to Debheala airfield. His windscreen was covered with oil, but he nevertheless made an excellent landing, a feat which led the officer commanding No. 244 Wing to describe his actions as "a good effort." Soon afterwards he was commissioned.

He was less fortunate in other instances. On March 26, 1943 he crash-landed after a tangle with a *Bf 109*, and on April 2 he collided with a *Spitfire* on the runway, damaging both machines. Then, on May 20, he was involved in a road accident, knocked unconscious for 20 minutes, and sent to hospital. After treatment and a brief stint as a test pilot at a maintenance unit, he was returned to No. 601 Squadron. In August 1943 he was sent to No. 417 Squadron, with which unit he served until October, when his tour ended. From there he was posted to instructional duties in the Middle East. In the summer of 1944 he was sent back to England and then home to Canada for a rest.

Flight Lieutenant Gordon returned overseas in October 1944. On November 22 he reported to No. 442 Squadron, then at Warmwell in England. Three days later the squadron moved to Holland. It did not take him long to hit his stride; on November 28 he landed a *Spitfire* heavily, buckling the undercarriage.

Early on the morning of New Year's Day, 1945, No. 442 sent off twelve *Spitfires* for a sweep over western Germany. Shortly after take-off, Gordon's engine began running roughly, so he turned back for Heesch. He was at 7,000 feet and just south of his base when he glimpsed some anti-aircraft fire and an aircraft which he believed to be a German jet. Down he went to investigate. Suddenly he spotted a gaggle of 50-plus enemy fighters flying at tree-top level. The *Luftwaffe* was attacking Allied tactical airfields in strength that morning, and Gordon had run into one of the enemy's formations while on his own.

Selecting an *Fw 190*, he closed to 200 yards and fired a short burst with 60 degrees of deflection. He saw no strikes, but the *'190* flicked over, crashed and exploded. Immediately he shifted his sights to another *'190* and opened fire. The Focke-Wulf threw out black smoke, flew straight and level for five seconds, then nosed into the deck and blew up.

Suddenly his *Spitfire* rocked as a German pilot began knocking holes in Gordon's machine. Shell splinters wounded him in the back and head, and only his armoured seat saved his life. He plopped the *Spit* down in a farmer's field, skidded, then lurched to a halt. He scrambled out and began to run. Abruptly he was intercepted by an enthusiastic Dutch woman who rushed up, slapped him on the back, and exclaimed, "Happy New Year!"

It had been a remarkable day. The squadron lost one pilot killed that morning, but claimed six enemy fighters destroyed, two "prob-ables" and four damaged. Gordon was hospitalized and soon afterwards was awarded the DFC.

He returned to No. 442 late in January. Early the following month he was given command of "A" Flight. Then, on February 8, he had another run of good hunting. This time it was like shooting fish in a barrel.

No. 442 was carrying out an early morning armed reconnaissance when they discovered five *Ju 87* dive-bombers near Wesel. It was incredible; the Stukas had been obsolete four years before, and yet here were some operating on the Western Front. It was suicidal for the Germans, and No. 442 proved the point by shooting down all five. Gordon sent down two in flames and shared a third with Flight Lieutenant G.J. Doyle.

He scored one more victory with No. 442, a *Bf 109* which he blew to bits over Rheine airfield on February 25. In March the squadron returned to England to re-equip with *Mustangs*. "Chunky" did not accompany them; instead he went to No. 411 Squadron to take up a Flight Commander's position there. On April 16 he was leading the squadron near Parchim airfield when he discovered a *Ju 88* with an *Fw 190* perched pick-a-back on top. This was a *"Mistel"* combination—the Junkers, unmanned and loaded with explosives, was radio-controlled by the Focke-Wulf pilot. Gordon attacked just as the two separated. While his wingman tackled the *'190*, he proceeded to blast the Junkers. The robot crashed and exploded with a mammoth roar. His tally now stood at ten aircraft, including one shared.

The next day, Gordon was promoted and shifted to No. 402 Squadron, replacing Don Laubman who had been shot down and cap-tured on the 14th. Sewing on a half-stripe to denote his new rank, he led No. 402 through its last three weeks of operations, shooting up enemy transport and knocking down any German aircraft which were caught in the maelstrom of Allied air power. His last victories were relatively easy meat—an *He 115* seaplane which he destroyed at its moorings on April 27 and an *Fi 156* communications aircraft shot down in flames on May 3. The next day he flew his final operational sortie, an armed reconnaissance over southern Denmark during which two enemy vehicles were destroyed and ten damaged.

In July 1945 Squadron Leader Gordon was awarded a Bar to his DFC. The citation to this honour read as follows:

> Both in the air and on the ground, this officer has displayed outstanding courage and skill in operations against the enemy. Since the award of the Distinguished Flying Cross, he has destroyed five more enemy aircraft, bringing his total victories to at least nine enemy aircraft destroyed and others damaged.

He has led his squadron in many relentless attacks against enemy road and rail transport in heavily defended areas and has inflicted considerable damage on the enemy's lines of communication. At all times, Squadron Leader Gordon has displayed brilliant leadership, a fine fighting spirit and a great determination.

Although VE-Day had come and gone, "Chunky" Gordon had yet a few more adventures. On June 9, 1945, after a flight in an *Auster* light aircraft, he wrote in his logbook, "Got lost and ran out of petrol. Force landed in field. Finger trouble!" In August 1945 he was repatriated to Canada.

Gordon elected to remain with the post-war RCAF as a Flight Lieutenant. He was active with No. 14 Photographic Squadron, with which he suffered one more accident. In October 1945 he was taking off in an *Anson* when one engine seized, compelling him to force-land. In October 1947 he married Margaret Whitman of Ottawa, and in December of that year he was posted to Air Force Headquarters. With the exception of four months spent in Washington, the balance of his career was at AFHQ, Ottawa.

Tragically, there was little time left to him. Late in 1948 he began to experience deafness and he was sent to the Montreal Neurological Institute. It soon became apparent that the problem was but a symptom of neurological disease requiring radical surgery. This was carried out in June 1949 but proved unsuccessful. On June 26 "Chunky" Gordon died, and the career of yet another remarkable pilot was at an end.

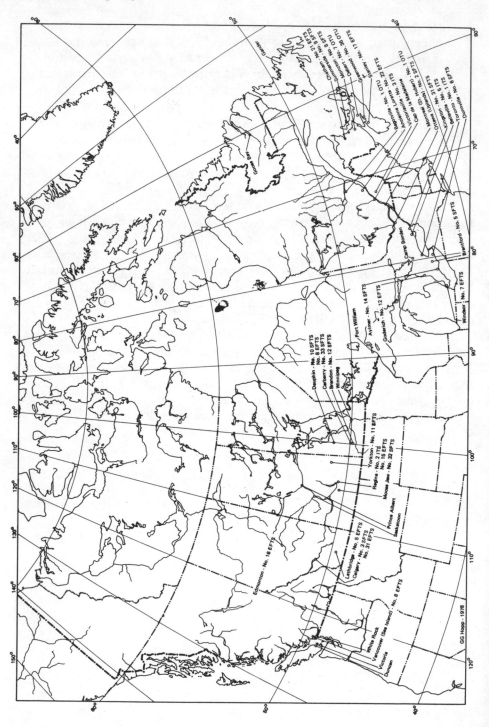

Gray
Five Times Lucky

Intruder pilots undoubtedly had the most opportunity for running up high scores in enemy aircraft destroyed. Their operations carried them to the heart of the *Luftwaffe*—its airfields—where they could attack the Germans while landing or taking off. Daylight Ranger operations provided the best opportunities by enabling pilots to see the enemy clearly and to assess results accurately. On the other hand, such sorties involved greater risks, for the *Mosquitos* had to fly at low level, well inside enemy territory and face heavy anti-aircraft fire. There was also the danger that they would be cut off by enemy fighters on the return trip. The Ranger pilot's chief protection lay in speed and surprise, and with these tactics he was frequently successful in chewing up the *Luftwaffe* in large bites.

One such pilot was Wing Commander Ross Gray, who destroyed ten and damaged 12 enemy aircraft in just three incredible sorties. His flights took him as far afield as Czechoslovakia, and on one occasion he limped home with his *Mosquito* riddled like a sieve. Yet ironically his closest shaves were experienced far from enemy action, in the skies over Britain itself. Today when he looks back on his flying experiences he can count five occasions when luck played an enormous part in his life.

He was born on December 15, 1916 in Edmonton. Following graduation from high school he obtained a Bachelor of Science Degree from the University of Toronto, then switched to law studies at Osgoode

Hall. He was nearing the end of his schooling when the war broke out.

Hitherto, he had shown no particular interest in aviation, and even today he finds it difficult to say why he chose the RCAF over the other services. Joining the Air Force in January 1941, he soon entered the ranks of aircrew trainees which were filling the flying schools in Canada. At No. 17 Elementary Flying Training School, Stanley, Nova Scotia, he was introduced to the Fleet *Finch*, and his first training flight was also his first time up in an airplane. From EFTS he went to No. 8 Service Flying Training School at Moncton, equipped with *Ansons*. He was most impressed by the Chief Flying Instructor, Squadron Leader Keith Hodson, a fine leader and a stickler for spit-and-polish efficiency. Hodson's theory, which Gray in time came to appreciate, was that a sloppy appearance was a symptom of a sloppy attitude, which could lead to flying accidents.

As the graduation date approached, Gray was called upon to fly a final wings test. He took off with the testing officer and went through the routine of steep turns, forced landing approaches, spins and stalls. Having completed these maneuvers he headed back to base and, as the old *Anson's* primitive retractable undercarriage had to be raised and lowered manually, cranked the wheels down for a landing. With the airspeed indicator reading 80 miles per hour he approached the runway, then realized that the *Anson* was not sinking fast enough, and that he was overshooting the field. Laboriously cranking up the undercarriage, he opened the throttles and circled for another attempt.

Once more he lowered the landing gear and held the airspeed indicator at 80, and once more the plane overshot the field. After three or four futile attempts at landing, Gray's arm was becoming stiff and sore from manually raising and lowering his wheels, and he began to wonder if the Army might have been a better choice. At that point the testing officer took over the controls and climbed away. Far from the school he stalled the *Anson* while checking the instruments, and discovered that the airspeed indicator was defective. It was reading ten miles an hour too low. With that knowledge Gray made another approach, landed normally, and passed his wings test. On October 10, 1941 he graduated from Moncton.

From SFTS Pilot Officer Gray was posted to Central Flying School, Trenton, and then to Calgary to serve as an instructor. For almost two years he was employed on these duties while nagging away at authorities for an overseas posting. The trouble was that just about every instructor in Canada was also lobbying for such a posting, and he was told repeatedly that he would have to wait his turn. In the meantime it was discovered that he had some legal training, and he was frequently called upon to assist defendants in courts martial.

By August 1943, when he was beginning to despair of ever getting overseas, the long-awaited orders came through and he was posted to Greenwood for operational training on *Mosquitos*, followed by the voyage to England. He arrived in Britain four days before Christmas 1943. More training followed, this time at No. 60 OTU, High Ercall, for instruction in gunnery, tactics, and combat procedures. Finally, on April 12, 1944, Flight Lieutenant Gray reported to No. 418 Squadron, accompanied by his observer, Flying Officer F.D. Smith.

Their first sorties consisted of night intruder flights to nearby French airfields, undertaken as final training before the really long-range operations were assigned. Following that came a half dozen intruder and Flower patrols over France and Germany during which nothing much happened, though on one flight his machine was holed by light anti-aircraft fire. Gray was discovering how difficult "cat's eye" intrusion could be, for the deep-penetration "Mossies" carried no radar. Trips like these might make the enemy nervous, but as long as a German aircraft flew with lights off, the odds were that no *Mosquito* would find him, barring moonlight or chance visual contacts.

Gray had his first victories in the summer of 1944, during the Battle of the Flying Bombs. He was able to fire on *V-1's* on half a dozen occasions, destroying two in the process, but his only combat with manned enemy aircraft that summer proved to be wildly frustrating.

In the course of a Night Ranger to Nuremberg he discovered several enemy aircraft in or near the circuit of a German airfield. Stalking one as a cat creeps up on a bird, Gray was just about to open fire when his quarry suddenly reversed its direction. Gray re-positioned himself and sneaked up again, but again the German machine, now identified as an *Fw 190*, carried out a steep turn. Surely the enemy had seen him! But no, apart from the turns, the *'190* took no evasive action, and meanwhile the airfield lights continued to burn.

Afterwards Gray concluded that the German pilot was doing nothing more than practising steep turns. With the wisdom of hindsight he decided that he should have ignored the fighter and gone after some of the aircraft in the circuit. Instead, he continued to follow his original target through one steep turn after another. Finally, his patience exhausted, he snapped off a quick burst, scoring a few strikes for a "damaged" claim. Alas, the *Fw 190* vanished into the darkness and the German airfield abruptly went black. He had muffed it!

July 1944 was a notable month for Gray. On the 18th he was promoted to Squadron Leader and given charge of "A" Flight. On the night of the 28th he had one of those near-misses which characterized his career.

It was a dark, dirty night with the cloud base at 800 feet. He was heading home after a Flower patrol, and his track led him over some English hills which rose as high as 1,000 feet. Perhaps it was fatigue or faulty navigation, but Squadron Leader Gray began to let down too early. He had scarcely emerged from the clouds when he saw radio pylons barely 20 feet on either side of the *Mosquito*. At the same instant he felt a slight shock. Pulling hard on the control column, he climbed back into the clouds, flew on for a few minutes, descended again near his field, and landed.

He did not even bother to check the airplane after touch-down but went straight inside to report his activities to the Intelligence Officer. Suddenly a ground crewman rushed in and urged him to look at the plane, so he trudged back to the *Mosquito*. Only then did he realize the significance of the shock. Outboard of either propellor dangled a hundred feet of cable which had cut into the wing almost to the spar. By all odds the cables should have fouled either a propellor or the ailerons. As it was, by hitting the cross-wires between the pylons dead in the centre, and just at the right height, he had escaped. Inches either way, up, down or sideways, and the "Mossie" would have been a fatal write-off. Once more, his luck had held.

Gray's luck was with him again on September 21, 1944. That day he took off for a Day Ranger sortie to Bad Aibling airfield, near Munich. He had a new navigator for the trip, Flight Lieutenant Noel Gibbons of Vancouver. Gibbons was one of the most experienced and competent men in the squadron. Six months earlier he had won a DFC for his work with Jimmy Johnson and Johnny Caine. Alongside them in another *Mosquito* were Flight Lieutenant Phil Brook and his navigator, Flying Officer Don McLaren. The cloud base was solid at 800 feet and there was a slight drizzle as the two *Mosquitos* approached the German field.

Everything worked. An enemy machine in the circuit filled Gray's gunsight, absorbed two quick bursts, and crashed in flames. In the murk below he spotted more enemy machines—he could not be certain what type they were—and followed through with two strafing runs, damaging a pair and sending one up in smoke. By now Bad Aibling was very much alive to the intruders and a torrent of flak belched forth. Momentarily Gray almost lost control as his machine was splattered by anti-aircraft fire. Shaken, he climbed into the clouds and set course for base.

The *Mosquito* looked like a Swiss cheese. The tail plane had been peppered and the port nacelle holed, damaging the undercarriage and bursting the tire. The starboard wing had taken a hit right through the fuel tank, leaving the gasoline exposed. The main spar was also damaged. Yet the "Mossie" kept on flying, and it did so all the way back to Hunsdon, England, where Gray landed safely in spite of one flat tire. Tempting fate was getting near to being an involuntary habit.

· On September 30 the team of Gray-Gibbons and Brook-McLaren conducted another Day Ranger into southern·Germany. Before reaching their objectives they twice had to shake off hostile fighters, once by weaving about in a steep mountain pass and once by turning to face their opponents. Having evaded these, they proceeded to beat up Erding, Eferding, and Horshing airfields. The result was three enemy aircraft destroyed (two of them Gray's) and seven damaged (four of them his). For Gray the most outstanding feature of the trip was Gibbons' exceptional navigation.

The big payoff, however, came on October 12. Once again, Gibbons was his navigator, but this time the accompanying *Mosquito* was piloted by Flying Officer R.D. Thomas with Flight Lieutenant R. McDonald in the right-hand seat. The two aircraft took off from St. Dizier, France, in the early morning hours. It was pitch dark, but they maintained formation as they flew on across the Rhine. As dawn broke they dropped to low level near Lake Constance. Thereafter a thick blanket of ground fog made navigation extremely difficult. Gibbons and McDonald, however, coped with this problem by navigating from the contours of the fog, truly an outstanding performance. They crossed the Danube without seeing it, but soon afterwards the mists began to thin out. At 6.40 A.M. they arrived at Budojovice airfield in Czecho-slovakia, dead on course, bang on time, to discover four Junkers *W 34* light transport planes parked about the base.

Gray attacked first, going into a shallow dive at 100 feet and pulling out "on the deck." With his first burst he damaged one and hit another which exploded. On his next run he riddled a third *W 34* which went up in flames. Thomas blasted the last *W 34* into wreckage. With that accomplished, the two *Mosquitos* high-tailed it for another German airfield.

Their next objective was hidden by fog, so they set course for Nemecky Brod. This turned out to be a grass field with many aircraft parked in blast bays. Southeast of the strip was a large, open dispersal area in which some 20 *Ju 87* dive-bombers were parked in staggered rows with about three wing lengths between each of them. Two machine guns on the ground opened up with inaccurate fire; apart from that there was no opposition, and the two crews were able to take their time. Making repeated runs over the dispersal area, they strafed up and down the rows of enemy machines until their ammunition was exhausted. It was almost impossible to miss, but also hard to gauge exactly what damage was being done. In his combat report Gray wrote:

> During the attacks I caused two aircraft to blow up, set another on fire, and hit a further one so severely that the fuselage broke and the aircraft generally disintegrated. At least five others were damaged with cannon and machine gun strikes. We believe that the number of damaged aircraft was more in the order of ten, but specific circumstances involving damage to but

five can be definitely recollected. We also believe that at least half the aircraft claimed as damaged are quite likely to have been destroyed, but due to uncertainty, claims for destruction are not being made . . . I claim four *Ju 87's* destroyed and five damaged at Nemecky Brod.

Having created such havoc, the *Mosquitos* climbed away. Gray and Thomas discussed the situation over the radio. It was broad daylight and they had no protective cloud cover. A return flight via southern Germany, including crossing the heavily fortified Rhine area, appeared inadvisable, so they headed for Italy. Fortunately they had the proper maps and encountered no opposition. At 9.35 A.M. they arrived at Iesa airfield where they refuelled and had lunch. That afternoon they flew directly back to England, passing through a violent thunderstorm enroute. At base they filed an amazing combat report. Once again, they had achieved much through expert navigation. Their total claim was eight enemy machines destroyed, one probably destroyed, and nine damaged.

For this sort of work there were rewards. Gray was recommended for the Distinguished Flying Cross after the trip of September 30, although it was not gazetted until January 9, 1945. The Czecho-slovakian raid brought another recommendation, and in June 1945 he got the Bar to the DFC. Thomas also received a DFC in June 1945. On February 12, 1946 the *London Gazette* announced that Flight Lieutenant Gibbons had been awarded a Bar to his DFC. This honour had been backdated to October 21, 1944, the day previous to his being killed in action while navigating for another pilot.

The trip to Czechoslovakia was Gray's last operational sortie. Late in October he was posted back to Canada to become the Chief Flying Instructor at No. 7 Operational Training Unit, Debert, Nova Scotia. Late in April 1945, however, he was sent back overseas. In May he joined No. 406 Squadron, which he soon took over from Russ Bannock with the rank of Wing Commander. He flew no operational sorties with the squadron; as its last wartime CO he had the trying task of maintaining high morale and discipline when everyone was impatient to get home.

Shortly after VE-Day Gray had another hair-raising experience. He was caught over Germany in a hailstorm which battered the leading edges of his wooden wings into splinters. Nevertheless, he made a safe landing. Then, on June 22 he went through another harrying flight. Once more his luck held.

The squadron was practising at Bradwell Bay for a flypast. One of the engines failed on Gray's "Mossie". That in itself was not dangerous. The *Mosquito* could easily maintain height on one engine, so long as the undercarriage was up. He began his landing approach and lowered his wheels, but the undercarriage would not come fully down. He decided to go around again, opened the throttle on the good engine, and ordered his navigator to raise the landing gear.

The aircraft was still sinking rapidly as it passed by the airfield. Emergency procedures called for a correct positioning of selector switches and the manual operation of a hydraulic pump. The navigator pumped furiously but the undercarriage was not retracting. By now Gray was over the Thames River. He recalled that only a few weeks before a *Mosquito* had been forced to ditch with the wheels down, and on that occasion the pilot had been killed instantly. Suddenly Gray realized that the selector switches were probably positioned incorrectly. He shouted to his comrade. A flick of the switches, more furious pumping, and the tide slowly turned. The wheels began to come up and the *Mosquito* lifted away. Soon they were safely back in the circuit, where they succeeded in getting the landing gear down and locked. It had been a near thing, though; at the crisis point Gray had been only four feet from oblivion.

He had no further opportunities to tempt fate. In August No. 406 was disbanded and he returned to Canada. At the end of October 1945 he was released from the RCAF and was able to take up his life where he had left off almost five years before. Today he is a Queen's Counsel and practises law in Ottawa. He scarcely ever thinks about his wartime experiences and rarely looks at his old logbook. Nevertheless, he realizes that he is extremely lucky to be alive. On or off operations, he faced and surmounted exceptional risks.

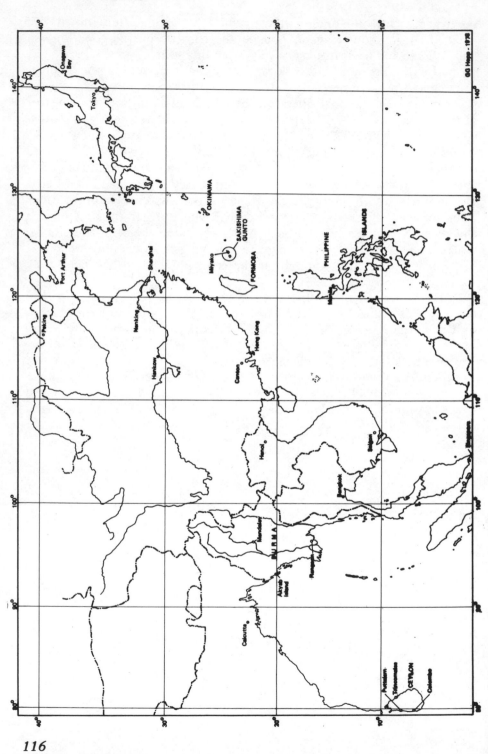

Gray
For Valour

During the Second World War three Canadian flyers were awarded the Commonwealth's highest honour, the Victoria Cross. It is a measure of the dangers they faced, the courage they displayed, and the standards to which recommendations for VCs were subjected that all three awards —to Lieutenant R.H. Gray, Flight Lieutenant David Hornell, and Pilot Officer Andrew Mynarski—were posthumous.

Robert Hampton "Hammy" Gray was born in Trail, British Columbia, on November 2, 1917. He was educated at Nelson, where he completed high school in June 1936. That fall he enrolled in the University of Alberta, but in 1937 he transferred to General Arts at the University of British Columbia. He was just beginning his final year when the war engulfed his generation. In preparation for the worst he joined the Canadian Officer's Training Corps that winter, acquiring reservist military experience. Having graduated with a BA, he hastened to the colours. On July 18, 1940 he enlisted in the Royal Canadian Navy Volunteer Reserve.

Gray, however, was not slated to become a common "tar". After a short stint at "square-bashing" and being initiated into the Navy's ways, he was posted to Britain. He was first sent to HMS *Victory*, a shore establishment at Portsmouth, and then to HMS *St. Vincent*, the Royal Navy's elementary flying training school at Gosport. On December 31, 1940 he was commissioned as a Temporary Sub-

Lieutenant, but his training was not yet complete. Sent back to Canada early in 1941, he was given six months operational training at No. 31 SFTS, Kingston, then passed to HMS *Daedalus*, the RN's Aircraft Training Establishment.

Gray, meanwhile, was advancing in rank. In December 1941 he became a Sub-Lieutenant (naval equivalent of a Flying Officer) and a year later he was promoted to Lieutenant. March 1942 brought a posting to No. 757 Squadron of the Fleet Air Arm in Britain. In May 1942, he was sent to East Africa. It appeared that action was not far off.

That was the terrible Spring when Japanese carrier fleets, fresh from victories in the Pacific and Indian Oceans, were viewed as a threat to British ports in eastern and southern Africa. Most of Gray's time was spent flying from shore bases in Kenya with Nos. 795, 803 and 877 Squadrons, although he did secure some carrier time aboard HMS *Illustrious*. Almost all his work was done on *Sea Hurricanes*, naval versions of the famous RAF fighter with strengthened undercarriages and arrester hooks.

Much to his chagrin, the Japanese did not appear off East Africa. Friends later reported that the lack of action made him bitter and impatient. His attitude was perhaps affected by personal tragedy, for in February 1942 his brother John was shot down and killed while serving with the RCAF.

Early in 1944 "Hammy" Gray returned on leave to Canada. In June, however, he was posted back to Britain. At that point, events took a turn for the better. He was given advanced training on Chance-Vought *Corsairs*, the most advanced carrier fighter then in service, and in August he was assigned to No. 1841 Squadron aboard HMS *Formidable*. With this he was brought to the threshold of his combat career. He was then 27 years old, of medium height and a bit chunky, yet still boyishly handsome. Fair-haired and blue-eyed, he looked far younger and less seasoned than was the case. A friend later recalled that,

> 'Hammy' was the quiet-looking type, the very picture of fresh, youthful innocence. Actually he was a ball of fire and a rare hand in a crap game. He was obviously the fighter type— aggressive almost to the point of recklessness. He had to be a fighter pilot and he had to be good to do the things he did and live as long as he did.

At the northern tip of Norway, in Altenfjord, deep inside the Arctic Circle, lay Germany's most powerful vessel, the battleship *Tirpitz*. A 45,000 ton monster, heavily armed and armoured, she was considered a constant threat to Allied convoys running to northern Russia. For more than two years the British and Russians had struck at her with heavy bombers, carrier planes, and submarines. Often hurt but never fatally, her bulk haunted Admiralty planners, who remembered how hard and costly it had been to sink her sister-ship, *Bismarck*, in 1941. Actually, the *Tirpitz* had been so crippled by British midget submarines in September 1943 that she could neither steam at full speed nor swivel all her main armament. Unaware of the extent of the battleship's wounds, the Allies continued to pound away at her.

Late in August a series of carrier strikes was laid on to keep *Tirpitz* in port and possibly knock out some of her vitals. No one expected that the light bombs toted by naval aircraft could sink the brute. Five carriers, *Formidable* among them, were assigned to the attack and the first strike, using 31 *Barracuda* bombers and 53 fighters, was launched on August 22. Dense clouds over the fjord spoiled the operation. That day only the *Hellcat* and *Firefly* fighters were able to get in a blow, the *Barracudas* and *Corsairs* having to turn back. On the 24th another strike went off—33 *Barracudas*, 24 *Corsairs*, ten *Hellcats* and ten *Fireflies*. The attack was a costly failure; five aircraft were lost to flak and only two hits on the *Tirpitz* were achieved, one of them by an armour-piercing bomb which penetrated deep into the bowels of the ship and failed to explode.

Several days passed with fog and gale-force winds preventing any further attacks, but on August 29 conditions were favourable and one more strike was delivered. The Germans, however, were able to smother the *Tirpitz* in a smoke screen which made all bombing a matter of guesswork. Having failed to achieve any significant results, the carriers returned to port. The battleship continued to glower in Norwegian fjords until sunk by RAF *Lancasters* in November 1944.

Throughout these operations "Hammy" Gray was leading a section of *Corsairs* which attacked German shore defences. On August 29 he also strafed three destroyers in Altenfjord. Flak severely damaged his aircraft, shooting away most of the rudder. Returning to *Formidable*, he circled the carrier for 45 minutes, burning up his fuel before making a successful landing. For his work that month he was mentioned in despatches.

Late in 1944 the Royal Navy had begun to assemble a large Pacific fleet for operations in conjunction with the American Navy. This brought *Formidable*, No. 1841 Squadron and Gray to the Far East theatre. The British Pacific Fleet commenced operations in the East China Sea in March 1945, attacking islands between Formosa and Okinawa. The ships were subjected to fierce *kamikaze* (suicide) attacks by Japanese aircraft. *Formidable* was initially held in reserve, but on April 12 she relieved *Illustrious* and thenceforward Gray was in the forefront of operations, shooting up airfields and dive-bombing targets of opportunity.

Early in May the fleet's activities bacame more important as the Okinawa campaign intensified. On the 3rd *Formidable* was hit by a *kamikaze* which destroyed eleven aircraft and killed eight of the crew. Fortunately the carrier's armoured deck protected her; within six hours she was back in action.

After the capture of Okinawa, *Formidable* was involved in attacking targets around the Japanese home islands. On July 18 Lieutenant Gray led a flight of *Corsairs* which braved bad weather to strafe airfields near Tokyo. Six days later he led a strike on a merchant ship, after which he shot up an airfield and two seaplane bases. On the 28th he scored a direct bomb hit on a destroyer in the Inland Sea. "Hammy" was becoming a specialist in attacking ships, and for these actions he was recommended for the Distinguished Service Cross. He never knew about this honour, for by the time it had been approved and published, he was dead.

Lieutenant "Hammy" Gray's last flight began on the morning of August 9, 1945. As his section of *Corsairs* thundered off *Formidable's* deck, they headed for the enemy naval base at Onagawa Bay, in northern Honshu. Approaching their objective, the pilots could see five ships anchored in the harbour. Puffs of black smoke began to appear as the vessels and shore installations opened fire. The fighters dived, then levelled out for a skip-bombing attack. As they did so the flak intensified. Far out in front of his comrades, Gray became the focal point of a cone of shells. His *Corsair* shuddered from at least two hits—one 500-lb. bomb was shot away. Moments later the aircraft was trailing flames.

What was he thinking? Was he a fatalist? Had he abandoned hope? Why did he not try to bail out? No one will ever know. What is certain is that, weaving and on fire, his airplane continued to bear down on a Japanese warship, reported at the time to be a destroyer but actually the escort sloop *Amakusa*. His remaining bomb slipped from its shackle and hit the target amidships. Then, like a comet, the *Corsair* and its heroic pilot vanished into the sea. Wracked by explosions, the *Amakusa* sank almost immediately.

On November 13, 1945 the *London Gazette* announced that Lieutenant Robert Hampton Gray had been awarded the Victoria Cross. The citation tersely described the dramatic action and concluded with the words, "Lieutenant Gray has consistently shown a brilliant fighting spirit and most inspiring leadership." His was the last VC action of the war. In addition to being the only member of the RCN to win this decoration, he was one of only two fighter pilots to qualify for the Victoria Cross. The cross itself carries a simple inscription, "For Valour", and this Gray showed throughout his operational career, to the end.

Hill
Nothing Fancy

George Hill had a knack for getting around and meeting people. He trained with some aces, taught others, and once in a POW camp he witnessed a friend's stunning aerial victory. An intensely social man, he went on to public service in the postwar years and even attempted to enter politics. When the 25th anniversary of the Dieppe Raid was observed, Hill was selected to represent the RCAF veterans at the ceremony in France. It was a fitting choice, for he received his baptism of fire during that historic action.

Hill was born at Antigonish, Nova Scotia on October 29, 1918, and was raised in the quiet little town of Pictou. He was a keen swimmer and yachtsman and boxed his way to several school championships. A popular youth, he was class valedictorian on graduating from high school. Later he obtained a BA from Mount Allison University. For funds he worked as a steeple jack, and on one occasion fell 40 feet from a roof. Fortunately he landed on a fairly steep slope, rolled to the bottom, and emerged unhurt. He had completed a year of pre-medical studies at Dalhousie University when the war broke out.

A close friend, Russ Johnston, had joined the RCAF in 1938. Hill decided to follow his example, signing on as a Provisional Pilot Officer in September 1939. His first posting was to the Halifax Flying Club for *ab initio* training on *Moths*. Then he was off to Camp Borden for advanced instruction. A fellow trainee was Russ Bannock. On February 28, 1940 they won their wings. Shortly afterwards posting instructions sent them to different points, but four years later their paths would cross in a most unlikely manner.

Throughout the remainder of 1940 and all of 1941, George Hill served as an instructor at Uplands, Saskatoon, and Summerside. His logbook noted the passage of many pupils, including Lloyd Chadburn and David C. Fairbanks. At Summerside he encountered Wing Commander Elmer Fullerton, a pre-war pilot who was mad about aerobatics and probably set a world's record for inverted flight in a *Finch*. Piling up hours and polishing his aerobatic flying, Hill acquired increasing confidence. At last, in January 1942, he was posted overseas. By then he was a Flight Lieutenant with more than 840 flying hours of experience.

Operational training followed, after which he was sent to No. 421 Squadron, then forming at Digby. He was made a flight commander, but as No. 421 was still non-operational he was attached briefly to No. 411 Squadron, acquiring some operational time on sweeps over France. A frequent visitor to Digby was Air Vice-Marshal Raymond Collishaw, the famous Canadian who had shot down 60 enemy airplanes during the First World War and who had remained in the RAF, becoming a legend in that force. Many times the young men of No. 421 sat around while the energetic "Collie" recounted his experiences. One piece of advice stuck with Hill: "Don't try any fancy stuff like deflection shooting unless it is absolutely necessary. Get in behind your target and get in close for sure shots."

George Hill followed that tip rigorously. On the few occasions when he did resort to deflection shooting he was almost invariably disappointed. His method, learned from Collishaw and his own trial-and-error, was to press in close from the rear and let fly with everything. It wasn't fancy, but it worked.

In June 1942 he went to No. 453 Squadron, an Australian unit which was reforming in Britain after having been destroyed in the Far East. Hill remained for two months, then moved on to No. 403 Squadron which was based at Catterick, Yorkshire. Almost immediately things began to pop. On August 17 the squadron moved to Manston in the southeast of England. Two days later the unit was flung into action at Dieppe.

No. 403 was out early that day, led by Squadron Leader L.S. Ford DFC, of Halifax. The *Spitfires* were circling the ships at 3,000 feet when a trio of *Fw 190's* appeared about 1,000 feet above. The enemy fighters dived to attack Hill's section, but once they had been spotted the Germans had little chance of getting a good shot. As they tore past the formation, Hill followed, accompanied by his wingman, Sergeant M.K. Fletcher. Two Focke-Wulfs got clear away; the third was less fortunate. Hill began pumping shells into this machine and the enemy pilot went into a loop. This gave Fletcher a chance to snap off a deflection burst. Both pilots made several more firing passes, on the last of which Hill came near to ramming the *'190*. Caught in a murderous cross-fire, the German fighter suddenly blossomed flame near the root of the port wing which then broke away. From 500 feet the *Fw 190* went straight into the sea.

There were more Germans about, however, and one dived on Fletcher. Hill turned into the attack, forcing the enemy fighter to break off the attack. Gas was running low, so the *Spitfires* headed back to England. It had been a grim action. One enemy aircraft had been destroyed (the Focke-Wulf shared by Hill and Fletcher) and another was claimed as probably destroyed, but three *Spitfires* with their pilots were missing.

Less than two hours later they were off again—twelve hungry *Spits* with Squadron Leader Ford at their head and Flight Lieutenants Hill and P.T. O'Leary leading Blue and Yellow Sections respectively. By now the Canadian troops were being withdrawn. All around Dieppe fierce fires were burning and dense smoke was rising to 3,000 feet. The *Spitfires* had been ordered to patrol at that height and ensure that the vessels below would not be molested.

No. 403 was prowling its aerial beat under a thin layer of clouds. Suddenly a dozen *Fw 190's* dropped out of the overcast above and ahead of the *Spitfires*. Evidently the enemy had not expected these sentries here; before they could position themselves for a strafing run the *Spits* were among them.

One turned in ahead of Hill who delivered a long burst allowing for deflection. The enemy plane began streaming a thin gray trail, but before Hill could administer the *coup de grace* it had pulled up into the clouds. Laying on power and lifting the *Spit's* nose, the young Canadian climbed after his victim. Emerging on top of the cloud layer, he saw no sign of the original *'190* but another was there. It ducked under the clouds. Hill followed in a stern chase.

He had to admit it; the German pilot was hot. Every time Hill fired the enemy flyer rocked his wings violently. Hill was hot too, though, and he could see flashes as he scored strikes all over his adversary. The enemy plane was heading inland, flying down a narrow valley, emitting puffs of gray smoke. Sighting once more, Hill jabbed the trigger button. Nothing happened; he was out of ammunition! Shoving the stick hard over and kicking the rudder pedal, he stood the *Spitfire* on its wingtip, wracked it around, and headed for home.

This time the results had been more satisfying. Hill was credited with one aircraft probably destroyed and one damaged. Other pilots in No. 403 claimed one destroyed and one damaged. Best of all, everybody was back.

At 4.20 P.M. the squadron was off again to guard the returning ships. This time Hill had no chance to fire his guns, but several of his friends did and the result was two *Fw 190's* sent into the drink. A fourth patrol just before sunset produced nothing at all.

It had been an exciting day, but immediately afterwards No. 403 was sent north again, far from any potential action. The weeks passed with nothing more worrisome than mock attacks on *Hudsons*. Several "gung-ho" pilots began to feel restless. Hill applied for a posting to the Middle East, but as he was a Flight Commander, Squadron Leader Ford was understandably reluctant to let him go. Hill's solution was ingenious; he waited until Ford had gone on leave, then submitted a request for a transfer which O'Leary, the acting CO, approved. In mid-December he was off to the Middle East.

On February 3, 1943 Flight Lieutenant Hill reported to No. 111 Squadron, then based at Souk-el-Kemis in northwestern Tunisia. It was a cosmopolitan unit in which Britons, Americans, Canadians, South Africans and Australians were serving. "Treble One" was fascinating, for it was peopled by legendary characters. Squadron Leader J.J. "Chris" LeRoux was one—a colourful South African who was reputed to be the most expert "lineshooter" in the Mediterranean. Another was Flying Officer John Draper, a gutsy Torontonian who once engaged an *Fw 190* in such a determined head-on attack that the enemy crashed after colliding with the *Spit's* tail section. Most squadrons adopted as their mascot a dog, donkey, or other common animal. Not "Treble One", which employed a huge tortoise as its talisman.

It took no time for Hill to be initiated into the squadron. The morning after he reported, his section was scrambled to intercept some high-flying *Bf 109's*. Ten of the enemy bounced his formation and in the melée that followed he damaged two of them. The fact that the Germans were rotten shots probably saved his neck. Then, on February 23, he shot down a *Bf 109G* in flames while escorting some *Hurricane* fighter-bombers. The following day he and Sergeant F. Mellor claimed an *Fw 190*. George Hill was back in his element.

There was never a shortage of dramatic moments in his Mediterranean tour. An example was the Great Stuka Battle. Early in March 1943 Field Marshal Rommel, fortified by a fresh consignment of fuel for his tanks, launched an offensive. The main thrust of the attack was in southern Tunisia, against the Eighth Army near Mareth, but secondary attacks were planned for northern Tunisia, where No. 111 Squadron operated. The German battle cry of *"Auf zum Angriff! Sprit ist da!"* ("Forward to the attack! Petrol has arrived!") proved to be a disastrous one, for Rommel's tanks were broken on British artillery defences while his air support was cut to ribbons by the Allied air forces.

Hill was carrying out a tactical reconnaissance sortie on March 4 when "Treble One" was vectored onto enemy aircraft over Beja. The nine *Spitfires* were at 14,000 feet when they spotted some 15-20 *Ju 87's* at 9,000 feet with ten *Bf 109's* flying at the same altitude as the *Spits*. While three *Spitfires* tackled the Messerschmitts Hill led the others down into the plodding dive-bombers. He nailed the enemy leader on his first pass, then shot down a second. He had just begun firing on a third when his aircraft shook violently. The engine temperature began to soar; his glycol coolant had been hit. Suddenly the *Merlin* engine seized and he was gliding in the middle of a dogfight with—of all things —a Stuka chasing him! Fortunately the enemy dive-bomber pilots had few opportunities to practise aerial gunnery and the German, making no allowance for deflection, sprayed the air behind Hill. Pushing the stick forward, he headed for the lines. He force-landed just inside the British defences where he was welcomed by grinning infantrymen who had witnessed the combat.

Then there was the Great Queue-Up of April 5, 1943. Hill had been carrying out a Rhubarb over the Bay of Tunis, had shot up two motor torpedo boats, and was heading for home on the deck when three *Bf 109's* appeared behind him, lining up for a squirt apiece. As he was alone at that moment he broke into their attack. He did this three times before another *Spitfire* joined him. The two pilots then kept turning to face the enemy, exchanging fire with them nine more times. One *'109* was hit and disappeared, damaged, but the other two hung on. The dogfight raged for 40 miles before the enemy fighters gave up the chase. Hill landed back at base with his fuel tanks dry.

The Glorious First of May was another hair-raising event. Hill had succeeded "Chris" LeRoux as CO only the previous day. On his first sortie that day, in company with four other pilots, he downed an *He 111* between Tunis and Pantelleria. That afternoon the squadron surprised fifteen *Bf 110's* accompanied by about ten *Bf 109's*. On his first firing pass Hill clobbered the lead German aircraft which must have been overloaded with gasoline as it blew up with a tremendous roar. Then, with assistance from first one *Spitfire* and then another, he bagged two more. At one point he found himself flying head-on towards a *'110*. The enemy plane carried two cannons and four machine guns in the nose, and Hill had a horror of all that firepower. He barrel-rolled over the German, flipped in behind, and let him have it at a range of 50 feet. The enemy pilot bailed out.

His last victory of the North African campaign came on May 6, 1943 when he shot down a *Bf 109*. The final surrender of the Axis forces in Tunisia on the 13th wrote *finis* to enemy air activity in that theatre. Nevertheless, the next few weeks were not uneventful. On May 21 the *London Gazette* announced that Hill had been awarded the Distinguished Flying Cross, and on June 1 the same publication reported his having won a Bar to the DFC. The citation to the latter award described him as a "courageous and skilful fighter".

In June his squadron moved to Malta to participate in the softening-up of Sicily. It was not until July 3, however, that Hill claimed another victim, a *Bf 109*. In the course of a dogfight between three *Spitfires* and twenty Messerschmitts he saw a parachute descending. Believing it to be a British pilot, Hill rushed to give protection while several *'109's* snapped at his heels. Skidding and twisting to avoid their fire, he finally succeeded in shooting one down into the sea. Shortly afterwards help arrived and the Messerschmitts fled. Ironically, it turned out that the pilot he had been trying to shield was a 19-year old German who had bailed out when his engine seized.

The Allied invasion of Sicily gave Hill his next chance at sustained combat, and also led to a startling coincidence. On July 12, 1943 he attacked what he took to be a speedy *Fw 190*. It was, in fact, an antiquated *MC.200* with which he nearly collided as he overhauled it. A jab of the trigger and the enemy machine went down in flames.

At that moment Allied flak opened up below. Hill's *Spitfire* was hit, and he force-landed at Pachimo, out of fuel and glycol. While waiting to be picked up and flown back to Malta, where No. 111 was based, he saw six aircraft approaching the field. The anti-aircraft crews did not fire. Suddenly the six machines cut loose, spraying the area in a fast, ragged strafing pass. Then the aircraft, *Bf 109's*, soared out of range. Hill located the major in charge of the gun crews and ragged him thoroughly. Allied flak, he suggested, was more dangerous to friendly aircraft than to the enemy.

Next day, just at dawn, Hill was patrolling near the invasion beaches. Against the faint light on the horizon he caught a *Ju 88*. It was perfect; the enemy was silhouetted against the dawn while the *Spitfire* was cloaked in darkness. Nothing fancy now; he swung in behind the bomber for a no-deflection shot.

His cannon shells and tracer bullets flashed out at the Junkers, and its port engine caught fire. Hill gently applied right rudder to have a whack at the other engine. The enemy rear gunner, however, was sharp and alert. Obviously aiming for the shadowy form of the *Spitfire* and for the gun flashes, the German let fly with a stream of well-aimed bullets. Hill's propeller was hit and the fighter began to vibrate violently. He broke away; the last he saw of the bomber it was descending with its whole port wing ablaze.

Obviously he could not get back to Malta with the engine threatening to tear itself out of its mountings, so Hill headed for Pachimo. As he set himself up for the final approach to the airfield, the anti-aircraft guns scattered around the perimeter belched flame and fury. Clearly he had been mistaken for an early morning intruder. Fortunately he was not hit and he rounded out to settle gracefully on the strip. Then he went in search of the officer commanding the ack-ack. He found him, the same major he had razzed the day before, haranguing his men for not having shot the *Spitfire* down!

Squadron Leader Hill's exploits were continuing to win him recognition. His final victories were scored on August 13, when he shot down a *Ju 88* and an *Fw 190*. Three days later he left No. 111 Squadron. On September 28, 1943 the *London Gazette* announced that he had been awarded a second Bar to the DFC. The citation noted that he had destroyed at least fourteen enemy aircraft, but did not differentiate between personal and shared kills. A review of his combats reveals that he had participated in destroying 16 enemy machines to that date, ten by himself and the remainder with one or more fellow pilots.

From "Treble One" he was sent back to Britain and thence to Canada where he received a hero's welcome both in his home town and in Ottawa. Photographs of the period show a grinning, boyish face surrounded by crowds. He seemed almost too young to shave. Yet the ribbon with two rosettes which he wore below the pilot's flying badge was proof of his prowess.

George Hill had seven weeks to savour his homeland. Then he was posted back to Britain to assume command of No. 441 Squadron, a former Canadian home-defence unit which had been despatched overseas. His first task was to work up the pilots to operational standards. By late March of 1944 No. 441 was ready for combat. He missed leading it on its first sweep over France on the 28th, but thereafter he flew with them faithfully. There was no sign of enemy air opposition, however, until April 25.

The squadron was out early that morning, covering the withdrawal of some 290 American heavy bombers which had been attacking Mannheim and enemy airfields in France. No. 441 was flying at 12,000 feet near Laon when six *Fw 190's* appeared ahead and at the same altitude. One section held back to serve as cover while the other *Spitfires* bored in. The "bounce" achieved perfect surprise; within minutes all six enemy fighters had been shot down. Hill, however, was in trouble.

He and his wingman, Pilot Officer R.H. Sparling, had sprayed a '190. The German fighter blew up, scattering debris. Sparling's radio was knocked out, and although he managed to get back within ten miles of England, nothing more was ever seen of him. Something lodged in Hill's engine which promptly packed up. He succeeded in gliding down to effect a crash-landing and immediately ran for some woods.

For more than a month he avoided capture. Linking up with the French Resistance, he obtained civilian clothes. Somewhere along the line, however, he seems to have been betrayed. He and a partner were waiting inconspicuously in a railway station when Gestapo agents entered and made straight for them.

Now began an ordeal of solitary confinement mixed with interrogations while in neighbouring cells he could hear the groans of tortured men and women. He never could decide just what the Gestapo wanted from him; as a mere squadron commander he had had no access to any important secrets. His months of solitude did have one striking effect; hitherto he had harboured no particular emotions about his opponents. Now he realized what the war was all about, and he learned to hate with reasoned passion.

At last he was turned over to the *Luftwaffe* and sent to *Stalag Luft I*, a prison camp on the shores of the Baltic. With plenty of time to think he became preoccupied with the problems of society and social justice. The outcome of this was a sense of political conviction which directed his post-war career.

Just north of *Stalag Luft I* was an enemy training field, and Hill could see German aircraft buzzing about the area. One day, September 27, 1944, he was idly watching this traffic when a new sound intruded —the high-pitched whining roar of *Merlin* engines. Into sight swept a lone *Mosquito*. Fascinated, Hill saw the "Mossie" sweep into the enemy circuit and shoot down two aircraft. Then it was gone. After the war he learned that the *Mosquito* pilot had been none other than his friend from Camp Borden, Russ Bannock.

In the Spring of 1945 George Hill was liberated by the advancing Allied armies, and on June 1 he arrived back in Canada. He left the service three months later, returning to pick up his life where it had left off six years before, in medical school. He married, then graduated from Dalhousie University in 1951.

Hill eventually established a practice at Orangeville, sixty miles northwest of Toronto, where he also raised a family of ten children. He was active in community and veterans' affairs. His energies seemed limitless. He was a member of the local school board for years and also served on the Dufferin Area Hospital Board. About the region he became known as a doctor who never refused to help or held back from making a house call, regardless of weather. He curled. He flew his own airplane for a time. On top of all this he found time to run as a candidate for the New Democratic Party, once in the Ontario election of 1967 and once in the federal election of 1968. The NDP organization around Orangeville was largely of his making.

On November 12, 1969 Hill visited his insurance agent to clear up some paperwork relating to his estate. Early that evening he was hurrying home to prepare for a curling match. Only yards from his laneway his car collided with another vehicle. He was killed almost instantly.

George Hill was a fighter all his life, as a boxer, pilot, and doctor. His body was flown to Pictou, Nova Scotia, where it was interred. As the services ended an RCAF *Argus* patrol bomber flew over and dipped its wings in salute to a very gallant gentleman.

Houle

The Battling Bantam

"Bert" Houle, now living just south of Ottawa in Manotick, Ontario, enjoys several distinctions. Not only was he a leading fighter of the war, but alone among the top RCAF aces he flew not a single sortie in Northwest Europe, his field of action being confined entirely to the Mediterranean theatre. Moreover, standing only five feet four inches tall, he was probably the shortest RCAF ace of the war. This, perhaps, was an advantage, for while other pilots were cramped in the tiny cockpit of a *Spitfire*, he felt right at home, and he proved it by shooting down no less than eleven enemy aircraft.

Houle was born on March 24, 1914 at Massey, Ontario, sixty miles west of Sudbury, where his father had chopped a farm out of the bush. In this hardy environment he was raised with his three brothers and one sister. Life was never idle or dull. Farm work occupied a great deal of his time, but he also indulged in sports and hunting, learning to handle a .22 at the age of ten. In winter the Houle boys set trap lines, and the money they earned from furs was used to buy skates, snowshoes, a rifle, or more traps. They often scrapped among themselves, but when faced by outsiders, such as a bully in town, they banded together to thrash their tormentors.

Money was scarce and the family realized that education was the key to advancement from the semi-isolated farm. Having completed his senior matriculation, young Bert enrolled in the University of Toronto.

While there he took up boxing and wrestling; in 1936 he won the Canadian Intercollegiate Wrestling Championship. The same year he graduated in Electrical Engineering. For the next four years he worked, first as a demonstrator at the U of T and then as an electrician in northern Ontario.

Early in 1939 he chanced to read George Drew's book, *Canada's Fighting Airmen*. In it he found vivid accounts of the exploits performed during the First World War by Bishop, Barker, Collishaw, and the other heroes who had made Canadian airmen the object of such great respect. His imagination was stimulated, and when the war began he applied to join the RCAF.

The paper work involved took a long time to be processed, and at one point he despaired of ever being accepted. At last the orders to report arrived. On Friday, September 13, 1940 he was sworn in at North Bay. The great adventure had begun.

There followed a long period of training and transfers. First there was the Manning Depot at Brandon, Manitoba for kitting and initial drill; then to Portage la Prairie to do guard duty at an uncompleted station; on to No. 2 Initial Training School at Regina; a graduation to No. 15 Elementary Flying Training School, also at Regina, where he graduated at the head of his class and won a gold watch which he wears to this day; finally, to No. 32 Service Flying Training School at Moose Jaw. For him, however, there would be no wings parade; on April 10, 1941 Houle, having passed his tests, gathered with eleven other graduates in a room and listened to a congratulatory talk by an instructor who simply handed them their flying badges. A month's leave followed, after which they were sent to Halifax and overseas.

Britain proved to be exciting. He liked the people, he liked the beer, but most of all he liked the bustle of a nation at war, the sight of sleek *Spitfires* parked on a tarmac, the throb of engines overhead at night. At No. 55 Operational Training Unit he learned to fly *Hurricanes*. On and off duty the instructors, almost all of them combat veterans, poured advice into his ear. "In a dogfight, get right in the thick of it," he was told. "The pilot who hangs around the edge of a scrap stands a good chance of being singled out and shot down."

Late in July Houle learned that he was being sent to the Middle East. After picking up tropical kit, he and his fellow pilots went aboard a carrier, HMS *Furious*. At Gibraltar they transferred to HMS *Ark Royal* which made a hurried sortie into the western Mediterranean. There a score of *Hurricanes* with long-range tanks were flown off the carrier for the 400 mile trip to Malta. They paused there a few days before continuing on, again using long-range tanks, to Mersa Matruh, in Egypt. Following orientation, Houle was assigned to No. 213 Squadron in Cyprus, to which unit he reported on September 17.

Nothing of any particular importance happened in Cyprus, which was a dormant front. Even after his flight was transferred to Edku, near Alexandria, he had scant opportunity to see action, although the constant operational training was later to prove vital to his survival.

In February 1942, however, he "put up a black" which almost cost him his operational career. Taking off on a cross-country flight in a *Magister*, he failed to check his tanks, ran out of fuel, and crashed near the Nile. It was a foolish mistake, but not an uncommon one. It came, though, at a time when several aircraft had been lost in accidents and the Air Officer Commanding in the Middle East personally hauled Pilot Officer Houle onto the carpet and informed him that he was being taken off flying permanently.

Houle was furious and bitter, for the judgement appeared to be both arbitrary and unfair. It was not until July, after much lobbying by himself and his Commanding Officer, that he was re-instated in flying. Ironically, it appears that when German forces advanced to within 60 miles of Alexandria, so many Allied documents were hurriedly burned that the records of Houle's aeronautical sin went up in smoke.

He had had one inconclusive brush with a *Ju 88* over Alexandria before being grounded, but for him the war really began on July 11, 1942 when he took part in a sweep over the El Alamein line. Thereafter, No. 213's *Hurricanes* were in the thick of the desert air war. Dogfights with *Bf 109's* were frequent and losses heavy. Happily, many pilots were able to bail out or force-land in the desert, then walk back to friendly troops.

The air war had many features peculiar to that theatre. Operations rooms, sleeping quarters and messes were all lodged in tents. Aircraft took off and landed in choking clouds of dust and sand which also drew the attention of enemy pilots patrolling nearby. The pilots of No. 213 had great respect for their Italian counterparts, who seemed to do aerobatics for the sheer joy of it and whose Macchi fighters were maneuverable almost beyond belief. Everything from gas and oil to soap and water had to be trucked to the airfields. Scorpions and spiders haunted the men. A favourite sport was watching chameleons stalking and catching flies. Dust storms frequently blotted out the sky, and even when the winds died down there was often a haze which complicated flying.

On August 31 Rommel launched an offensive against the El Alamein line. The air effort abruptly intensified on both sides. On the evening of September 1 a patrol of No. 213 encountered several *Ju 88's* and waded into them. Houle poured about 50 rounds of cannon shells into one bomber's starboard engine and fuselage. His guns then jammed and he broke away for home. Back at base he was warmly congratulated; another pilot had seen his victim crash and Houle had his first "kill".

Three days later he damaged a *Bf 109*. However, with the failure of the German ground push the *Luftwaffe* faded away to lick its wounds and hoard its precious fuel reserves, restricting itself to occasional fighter reconnaissance sweeps.

During the course of one sortie, Houle became engaged with an enemy sweep formation. He attacked a *Bf 109* head-on. Just as a collision appeared a certainty he broke left. The German pilot broke in the same direction. The two fighters missed each other by inches. On two other occasions, his *Hurricane* was shot up by *Bf 109's*; once the armour plate behind his head was dented by machine gun bullets.

On October 23, 1942 the Battle of El Alamein broke with a thunderous British artillery barrage. Minutes later the infantry began moving up; the offensive to clear the Axis out of Egypt had begun. The attack caught the enemy by surprise. *Luftwaffe* units in Egypt were short of gasoline and modern types of aircraft, but the enemy air force reacted as best it could. The RAF, however, ruled the skies. Nothing could stop this push.

The officer commanding the wing of which No. 213 formed a part conceived an idea. It was known that the enemy listened to RAF radio frequencies in the hope of learning when British fighters were patrolling the front. On October 26, about 90 minutes before dark, two *Hurricanes* took off and proceeded to make enough radio chatter to sound like a whole wing. After an hour they reported that they were low on gas and going home. At that moment two whole squadrons of *Hurricanes* were racing for the lines, intending to catch an enemy raid. Houle later described the outcome in his unpublished memoirs:

> It was getting dark by this time and, when about three miles from the line, we could see bomb bursts and ack-ack. We were having trouble maintaining formation on aircraft below. The controller called up and said the enemy bombers were going home by the coast at a low altitude. I was a little nettled at having missed them, so opened the throttle wide and dived through the ack-ack, our own and the enemy's, heading for the coast. Gordie Carrick, who was flying No. 4 in my section, called up to say that he was right behind me. This was a little moral support. When I hit the coast, I turned west just out to sea and about 800 feet above the water. For ten or fifteen minutes nothing showed up. Then I saw a Stuka at 11 o'clock above and reported it to Carrick who came back excitedly with 'Oi see it'. Roy Marples called up to ask where I was, and as I didn't know exactly and was just closing in, I replied, 'Down here.' Carrick and I were down in the comparative darkness near the sea. The whole skyline, a brilliant red from the setting sun, seemed to come alive with dots that were Stukas heading for

home, probably elated over the ease of their victory. I closed in on the first one to within fifty yards, stayed slightly below and gave it both cannons up the jacksie. Large pieces blew off; it belched smoke, turned on its back and went straight down. I didn't bother to follow it but veered slightly to starboard where there was another Stuka all unsuspecting, and poured cannon fire into it from close range. Its nose dipped slowly and it started down in a gentle dive. I followed, giving it an odd burst for good measure until it hit the sea. Pulling up behind another, I was able to give it a short squirt, knocking pieces off before it went over and down.

Just over the coast, I saw a few bursts of Breda [Italian flak] and a Stuka put on its navigation lights to show that it was friendly. I wasn't and pulled right in behind. I was so close that the bullets from my cannons, mounted in the wings, were going to each side of the Stuka's fuselage without hitting it. Then a high explosive incendiary bullet hit a wing tank and it became a blazing inferno. I pulled sharply to one side to avoid hitting it and I saw the pilot and gunner shrinking to one side to avoid the heat. The aircraft made a slow spiral and hit the deck, lighting up the whole countryside.

In the light of the flames from the burning Stuka, I was spotted by another Stuka which got on my tail. The first thing I knew four machine guns were tracing their patterns towards me. I immediately banked and applied sharp rudder to get below its level. It swung on inland, leaving me alone. I attacked another Stuka ahead of me and blew a few pieces off it. It started in a gentle dive for the sea. Fearing I might be short of ammunition and fuel, I turned for home. I was pretty jubilant as I taxied in and parked the aircraft.

He had reason to be jubilant; he had definitely shot down two dive bombers, probably destroyed one, and damaged two more. One of his victims was *Hauptmann* Kurt Walter, leader of *III./St.G. 3*, and holder of the Knight's Cross. The combat had been a fighter pilot's dream, the one Houle remembered most proudly, and it won him his first Distinguished Flying Cross.

By November 3 the lines had been broken and Rommel was on the run. Houle and his buddies now went over to ground strafing, harrying the retreating enemy columns without mercy. Then, in mid-November, Nos. 213 and 238 Squadrons took off, headed south of the main battle and landed at a temporary strip more than 100 miles behind the enemy lines. Hidden in the desert from the 13th to the 16th, the *Hurricanes* blasted everything within reach—trucks, cars, airfields—before a German armoured column was despatched to flush out this rat's nest. The fighters learned of the enemy's approach, however, and abandoned the field before the tanks arrived.

That short stretch of rear-area strafing was exhilerating—Houle burned out a *Z.1007* on the ground on the 15th—but the flak was hellish. On one occasion he heard the clang of shrapnel hitting his airplane while he raced at low level to get beyond the range of the flak piece. His aircraft was so badly riddled that, although he was able to fly 200 miles back to his landing ground, the *Hurricane* had to be written off. Another day he became lost in a sandstorm, put down in the desert, and lunched on his emergency rations. Four hours later the storm abated, enabling him to take off again.

On November 22 he was posted to command a flight in No. 145 Squadron, flying *Spitfire V's* from Gazala. Not long after his arrival he flew to Cairo, returning with a *Spitfire* into which he had crammed two cases of liquor, one case of concentrated lime juice and thousands of cigarettes. These were a treat for the *Spitfire* wing that Christmas. To give some variety to their diet, the pilots took to hunting desert antelope from jeeps. They might have to drive 60 miles to find a herd, then shoot the animals while the jeep was bumping along at 50 miles an hour, but the meat was a welcome change from bully beef and biscuits.

On January 5, 1943 the squadron moved forward and was immediately greeted by *Luftwaffe* fighters strafing the airfield. Houle got in his licks on the 8th when he knocked down a *Bf 109*. Just as he finished blowing off its radiator and holing its fuselage, his *Spitfire* was hit by "friendly" ack-ack and he turned for home. He had not seen the end of the *'109*, only a cloud of dust near where it should have crashed, so he claimed only a "probable". It turned out, however, that *Feldwebel* Friedel Behren, late of *JG 77*, had landed, burned his plane, and then been captured, so the "probable" was upgraded to "one destroyed."

By now Houle had been on continuous operations for six months and on January 28 he was posted away for a rest. He spent his first week away from operations by whooping it up in Cairo and Alexandria with a pile of accumulated back pay. The party over and the pay gone, he reported to No. 73 Operational Training Unit at Abu Sueir to serve as an instructor.

Unhappily, Houle found that the CO and Chief Instructor at the OTU were both non-operational men whose ideas on instructing clashed directly with his combat experience. He lasted two months before being posted away for a junior commander's course in Cairo. He kicked his heels there for a time, though he found the course extremely useful as it was tailored for potential squadron commanders. Then he went to an engine repair and testing depot where he was completely miserable.

By the Spring of 1943 he was lobbying for a posting to No. 417 (City of Windsor) Squadron, the only RCAF unit in the Middle East.

No. 417 had a bad reputation, not undeserved, for operational sloppiness, and was reputed to be the laughing stock of the Desert Air Force. The senior RCAF officer in the area, Wing Commander Patterson, resolved to correct this, for as No. 417 went, so went the reputation of the RCAF. He began rounding up experienced Canadian pilots to beef up the squadron and revitalize its leadership. Stan Turner was hand-picked to command the unit, and Houle was sent as "B" Flight Commander.

On June 11, 1943 Flight Lieutenant Houle reported to No. 417. Shortly afterwards he was flying sweeps over Sicily. When that island was invaded by Allied forces, No. 417 followed. Axis aircraft were seldom seen and never engaged, but life was not at all dull. Sniping and shell fire went on near the airfield. On August 3, Houle and Turner took a truck to scrounge tools from captured enemy sites. Just before noon the truck hit a land mine and was torn to pieces by the explosion. Houle was blown through the roof, seat and all. Miraculously, both officers survived, though they suffered from shock, lacerations and contusions. Both of Houle's eardrums were broken. It was not until September 14 that he was able to return to the squadron.

No. 417 moved to Italy that month. On October 4, during a patrol over Termoli, Houle destroyed an *Fw 190* and damaged two more—the first victories registered by the squadron in five months. Shortly afterwards he was posted to No. 145 Squadron, his old outfit, but on November 13 he returned to No. 417. A week later Turner became Wing Commander (Flying), No. 244 Wing. Houle moved up to Squadron Leader for the "City of Windsors".

His tenure as CO coincided with two major land battles, that of Ortona on the east coast of Italy and Anzio on the west. Bad weather hampered both ground and air operations but No. 417, based first at Canne and then Marcianise near Naples, was able to play an important part in both campaigns. Between November 30, 1943 and February 14, 1944, the squadron claimed fourteen aircraft destroyed, four "probables" and eight damaged. Houle's share was six destroyed and two damaged.

Houle's last run of victories began on December 3 when he attacked a gaggle of *Bf 109's*. One went down in flames and he shot the tail off another. Houle watched, fascinated, while his second victim tumbled through a series of crazed aerobatics before crashing. On January 22 he bounced four *Fw 190's* over Anzio, shot one down, then was attacked by another Focke-Wulf. On that occasion his *Spitfire* was hit in three places and the rear view mirror above his head was shattered. Five days later he again blew the tail off an enemy fighter, this time a *Bf 109G*, over Anzio and damaged a second. On February 7 he repeated a familiar pattern, jumping a *Bf 109* over Anzio, pumping it full of lead until it was pouring black and white smoke, then blowing its tail off.

The big pay-off came on February 14, 1944. Ten *Spitfires* took off that morning to patrol over the Anzio beachhead. One returned early with mechanical troubles so the patrol was conducted with Houle leading three other pilots at 7,000 feet while Flight Lieutenant Hedley J. Everard flew cover at 12,000 feet. Everard spotted six *Fw 190's* flying in line abreast formation and diving for the beaches with twelve more *'190's* not far behind. Houle plunged after the first lot while Everard tackled the others. At that moment, a dozen additional *Fw 190's* joined the fray. The German pilots had played their hand skillfully. Houle's section, the most heavily committed to an attack, suddenly found itself taken from the rear.

While turning to attack the first six Focke-Wulfs, Houle became separated from his wingman, whose job it was to guard his tail. He fired at one enemy fighter which began to smoke, then began shooting pieces off the tail of another. At that moment he felt a thud. Thinking it was a flak hit, he pressed on with the attack. Then all hell broke loose.

A burst of cannon fire blasted away the rear cockpit. The armour plate behind his head came loose, smashed him in the neck, and threw him into the instrument panel. He kicked the right rudder pedal and yanked the stick back to go into a steep climbing turn. This cleaned his tail, but he found that his radio was useless. His neck was stiff and the back of his shirt was sticky. Still, the engine was running and the controls were OK, so he headed home, landed safely, and was rushed to hospital. The doctors gave him anaesthetic. When he woke up he found his neck bandaged and a rag tied around his wrist. Wrapped in it was a heavy slug of armour plate which had been lodged against his carotid artery. A little more force behind the German shell and Houle would have bled to death in his cockpit.

From that combat he submitted a claim for two aircraft damaged. Ciné footage and the reports of army observers led to this being changed to one destroyed and one damaged.

Houle remained in hospital for nine days, after which he was sent back to No. 417. Nevertheless, he was not permitted to fly, and after a month of waiting he was happy to be posted away. Late in March he arrived in England where he learned that he had been awarded a Bar to his DFC. Eventually he received his decorations from King George VI himself at an investiture in Buckingham Palace.

In the Spring of 1944 "Bert" Houle returned to Canada where he took up duties as a fighter instructor at No. 1 OTU, Bagotville. In February 1945 he was released, but soon realized that he was mad about flying. Rejoining the RCAF in October 1946, he rose from Squadron Leader to Group Captain in nine years. In 1945 he had married Margaret Irvine of Edmonton, and in 1950 he obtained a

Master's Degree in Engineering. His postwar service career was closely associated with aviation research. His last position prior to his retirement in 1965 was that of Officer Commanding the RCAF's Central Experimental and Proving Establishment. Retirement enabled him to indulge in his favourite sport, curling. Idleness being impossible, he now works in the office of an Ottawa stockbroking firm.

The Canadian From New York

Keefer

Patrol El Adem area—squadron met 15 *Ju. 87's*, 12 Macchi *200's* and six *Me. 109's*—Destroyed one Macchi *200* and damaged a second. First crashed and exploded 15 miles Southwest El Adem—Squadron bag: 4 confirmed, 2 probable, 3 damaged, P/O Gains, P/O Sutton and F/L Hobbes missing.

With these few words in his logbook, Flying Officer George Keefer wrote the opening chapter in a long history of successful combats. The same day that he gained his first aerial victory, Japanese aircraft attacked Pearl Harbor, bringing his other homeland into the war.

Keefer was born in New York City on July 11, 1921, the son of a wealthy American insurance executive and his Canadian bride. The elder Keefer died when George was six, and the boy's life thereafter was divided between attending private schools in the States and spending the summers with his mother and her family in Prince Edward Island. The young man came to regard both countries as his own. During vacations he worked as a service station attendant in Charlottetown. Not surprisingly, he became deeply attached to "The Island" with its lovely green countryside and red sandy beaches.

In September 1939, just as Canada was declaring war on Germany, Keefer entered Yale University to take mechanical engineering. By the time he had written his exams the following Spring, Poland, Denmark and Norway had been invaded, the first clashes at sea had occured, and the British Commonwealth Air Training Plan had been launched. Keefer was drawn towards Canada and her involvement in the war. The catalytic event was his mother's death in the summer of 1940. With no immediate family left, he decided to enlist in the RCAF. On October 15 he was sworn in at the recruiting centre in Charlottetown.

His first "square-bashing" training was carried out in Toronto. Early in December he reported to No. 11 Elementary Flying Training School at Cap de la Madeleine, about mid-way between Montreal and Quebec. One of his fellow students was a tough, chunky lad from Melrose, Ontario, "Wally" Conrad, whom he had met at Initial Training School. The next three years were to see their careers running on parallel courses as they rose to command squadrons and destroy aircraft in the same theatres of war.

Keefer experienced the first flight of his life on December 11—40 minutes in a Fleet *Finch*. He proved to be an exemplary student, soloing after only four hours of instruction. The Chief Flying Instructor at Cap de la Madeleine was most impressed by the stocky American; in his assessment of Keefer he wrote:

> Exceedingly keen; no cockiness; absolutely no fear. Learns extremely readily. This pupil is definitely of the highest standard with a general great deportment. He has a lot of dash and pep.

From EFTS Keefer and Conrad went to No. 2 Service Flying Training School at Uplands, just south of Ottawa, for advanced training on *Harvards*. In April 1941 they graduated with their wings and commissions, Keefer at the head of the class of 63 students and Conrad in second place.

The two friends were posted overseas almost immediately. Throughout June and July they learned the habits of the *Hurricane* at No. 59 Operational Training Unit. In August they went aboard HMS *Furious*, sailed to Gibraltar, and transferred to the aircraft carrier HMS *Ark Royal*. On September 13 they took off from the deck of that ship and headed east, pausing briefly at Malta before hastening on to Libya and Egypt where they joined No. 274 Squadron. Two months later the British Eighth Army opened its November offensive, "Crusader." No. 274's *Hurricanes* were thrust into the battle, and with them went Pilot Officers Keefer and Conrad.

Keefer remained with No. 274 for eleven months, Conrad for ten. That period covered the second British advance into Cyrenaica, the German Spring and Summer counter-offensives, the Allied retreat into Egypt, and the First and Second Battles of El Alamein. They were months of heat, flies, sand, wind and thirst. They were months when, to pass the time between sorties, he devoured a book every two or three days. They were months when at night the mess tent, full of airmen's babble, would suddenly fall silent as they listened to the husky, haunting voice of Lale Andersen singing "Lili Marlene" for German and Allied troops alike. There were the infrequent leaves in Cairo and Alexandria when a lifetime was crowded into two or three days of touring, drinking in the finest service bars, and buying supplies of scarce food and liquor to take back to the squadron.

Crammed into those months were 179 sorties. A few entries from Keefer's logbook gives some indication of the variety of tasks he performed: "Scramble, forward area", "Patrol over armoured divisions", "Sweep—Mechili area", "Scramble—got a head-on burst at a *109F*—no apparent result", "*Boston* escort 10 miles east of Mechili", "Sweep—Gazala—Tmimi—Bir Hacheim", "Bombing Hun guns—Sidi Henish", "Scramble and patrol—El Alamein". Every flight was different and important. All of it was grim, grimy and dangerous.

In many ways it was a frustrating tour. The *Hurricane II* was inferior to the *Bf 109F* and could just hold its own against the *MC.202*. Keefer could never recall having a height advantage over the Messerschmitts. At night the desert airfields were frequently bombed by prowling *Ju 88's*. To gain the advantages of a slit trench, Keefer and Conrad, who were tentmates, dug a wide, shallow hole in the sand over which they pitched their joint habitation. "Wally", however, liked to sleep on an inflated rubber mattress. Keefer recalls that whenever enemy aircraft were heard approaching, Conrad would try to hunch down a little more by pulling the plug. For five minutes sleep would be impossible while the mattress deflated with a shrill, persistent hiss.

Then there were the combats which, as often as not, were inconclusive. Nevertheless, Keefer succeeded in shooting down four enemy aircraft, probably destroying one, and damaging six. Typical of these combats was one which occured on June 8, 1942. The squadron had just finished bombing some Italian vehicles east of Bir Hacheim when he spotted an *MC.202* fighter about 500 feet below. He dived on the enemy, closed to within 15 yards and cut loose. The Italian machine rolled over and went straight down, crashing on the desert floor about a mile away.

The sortie in which he took the most pride, however, was one flown on June 4, 1942. During a patrol over Bir Hacheim the squadron had been attacked by *Bf 109's* and scattered in all directions. Keefer was pounding for home when a smear of smoke arched out of the sands below. Someone had fired a Very pistol. Circling about, he saw a lone figure standing in the desert, waving a Mae West life preserver.

Selecting a bare stretch about 200 yards from the man, Keefer put the *Hurricane* down. The pedestrian turned out to be a South African pilot, Lieutenant John Lane, who had been shot down by '*109's*. Lane climbed into the cockpit and took over the seat. Keefer sat on Lane's lap. In this cramped position he managed to take off and bring them home. A month later he received a short, emotional letter from Lane's parents in Pretoria. He still has the letter, his most valued memento of the war.

Throughout the North African campaign Keefer was never wounded by enemy action. One morning, however, while scrambling into his trousers, he felt a searing stab of pain racing through his buttocks. A scorpion had crept into his clothes during the night. Hustled to the medical tent immediately, he submitted to treatment for his humiliating "war wound".

He flew his last sortie with No. 274 on August 12, 1942 before being posted to the Air Firing School at El Ballah for instructional duties. Presently he was joined by "Wally" Conrad. Things always seemed to happen simultaneously to these two men; on January 22, 1943 they were both awarded the Distinguished Flying Cross, on February 15 they sailed for England and on April 9 they reported to Station Digby for their second operational tours. Keefer took a flight commander's position in No. 416 Squadron while Conrad was given a similar job with No. 403. Air fighting now assumed a new form. Enemy aircraft were encountered less frequently than had been the case in North Africa, but now Keefer was flying his dream airplane, the graceful *Spitfire IX*.

Within a few days of their joining their respective outfits the two pilots were caught up in a violent shuffle. On May 13, while escorting *Fortresses* near Amiens, Squadron Leader Foss Boulton of No. 416 Squadron was nailed by flak and became a POW. In the juggling of appointments that followed, Keefer was shifted to No. 412 Squadron, first as a flight commander and then, in June 1943, as commanding officer, a position which he held until April 1944.

During his career with Nos. 416 and 412 Squadrons, Keefer logged more than 150 sorties, mostly escorting American medium bombers which were attacking targets on the fringes of *Festung Europa*. Throughout this period he encountered German aircraft on only six occasions, and in most cases he was unable to get close enough for a good firing pass. He did manage to knock holes in a couple of *Fw 190's*, damaging one on June 12 and probably destroying another on December 1, but the highlight of this tour was on July 27, 1943, the day he came near to being captured.

No. 412 Squadron had been carrying out a late afternoon Rodeo over northern France. Nothing out of the ordinary happened until the *Spitfires* had turned back from Abbeville. At that point Keefer's engine began to overheat dangerously. His aircraft had developed a glycol leak. While still 15 miles inland, the *Merlin* packed up and he found himself gliding in silence while the rest of the squadron gave cover.

Keefer stretched his glide westwards as far as possible, but at last he was down to 1,000 feet and just barely off the French coast. Undoing his straps, he climbed out on the wing and bailed out. The instant he hit the water he banged the release bar, struggled free of his parachute and climbed into his dinghy. His troubles were not yet over. It was 6.00 P.M., broad daylight, and he was so close to shore that he could clearly see the windows of houses opposite him. Fortunately no Germans appeared to have spotted the hapless flyer. He began paddling furiously, intent on getting back to England, even if it meant rowing there under his own power. This went on for four hours until he was about three or four miles from shore. Dusk was gathering and it seemed that he might have to spend the night in the Channel. Just as the last light was failing, the comforting throb of an engine reached his ears. A "Shagbat" (*Walrus*) amphibian grumbled overhead, swept round, and alighted beside him. Minutes later he was safe at Hawkinge airfield.

All in all it was a fairly unspectacular tour, but the steady and reliable execution of routine sweeps and patrols brought rewards. In April 1944 Keefer was awarded a Bar to his DFC, then promoted to Wing Commander and given operational charge of No. 126 Wing. He now led three crack *Spitfire* squadrons, Nos. 401, 411 and 412. One privilege which went with the position was that he could paint his initials on his aircraft, and GC-K soon had ample opportunity to knock down enemy machines. The invasion of Normandy triggered the hottest air fighting in more than a year.

The first and most spectacular brush with the *Luftwaffe* was in the early morning of June 7. Keefer was leading the wing in a patrol over the eastern beachheads when a dozen unescorted *Ju 88's* appeared, intent on bombing Allied ships. It was, in his words, "bags of fun". In a few blazing minutes eight of the Junkers were shot down, one of them by Keefer. That afternoon, during another patrol, the wing bounced six *Fw 190's*, one of which went down under Keefer's guns while another was claimed by Bill Klersy.

In mid-June the wing moved to Normandy to provide close support for the Allied armies. When the pilots were not flying, they were often poking around the battle area looking for souvenirs. On one such foray, Keefer and "Buck" McNair discovered a German anti-tank gun which had been abandoned in working order. Latching onto it with undisguised glee, they proceeded to tow it behind a jeep from one spot to another, banging off rounds in the general direction of the enemy's positions, much to the surprise and annoyance of the British troops who felt that the fly-boys had no business interfering in "their" battle.

There were plenty of other things to shoot at too. Ground strafing and armed reconnaissance patrols led to a huge harvest of enemy vehicles destroyed or damaged. On June 25 Keefer added a *Bf 110* to his score; two days later he shot down a *Bf 109*. Moreover, his overall leadership was magnificent. Between D-Day and July 9, when he flew his last sortie before going home, No. 126 Wing destroyed 56 enemy aircraft and shot up almost 400 vehicles. This tremendous showing led to his being awarded the Distinguished Service Order.

In mid-July he handed over his job to Wing Commander Dal Russel DFC, a veteran of the Battle of Britain, and headed back to England. A month later he sailed for North America aboard the *Queen Mary*, accompanied by several hundred tour-expired aircrew and his German shepherd, "Rommel". The dog had been smuggled aboard ship, drugged and stowed in a crate, and was not discovered until the vessel was well out to sea. When the captain learned of the dog's presence, which was contrary to regulations, he protested to the senior Air Force officer aboard (Keefer), declaring that "Rommel" would have to be put to sleep. Very well, Keefer replied, but if this was done no guarantee could be given about the behaviour and discipline of the airmen aboard. The matter was dropped; "Rommel" stayed.

Back in Canada, Keefer visited with relatives in Prince Edward Island, but the prospect of a non-operational tour did not appeal to him. In September 1944 he wangled his way onto a flight to Britain, explaining with a straight face that he had to get back to attend the RAF Staff College. Once in England he proceeded to pester everyone he could reach for a combat job. His chance came when an RAF wing, No. 125, lost its leader in action. On November 16 he began his third operational tour, this time on *Spitfire XIV's*.

The routine was much as before—ground strafing, armed reconnaissance sorties, escorting tactical bombers and covering Allied ground operations. Occasionally enemy aircraft including jet fighters were glimpsed, but few engagements took place until March 1945. Then, with the Germans being squeezed between the Anglo-American and Russian armies, the *Luftwaffe* was forced to react; it had no place left to hide.

Between March 2 and April 25, Wing Commander Keefer destroyed nine enemy aircraft, five of them in a single ground strafing pass. In one combat on March 19 he led No. 130 (Punjab) Squadron down in a "bounce" over Rheine airfield. In a rag-tag dogfight over this hornet's nest, *Spitfires* and Messerschmitts weaved in and out of stabbing streams of flak. Later he submitted the following combat report:

> I found two *Me. 109's* going round together in a tight turn. Eventually one straightened out and flew due east. I gave him a quick squirt from dead astern and saw strikes on the starboard wing. Closing in further, I fired again and this time there were strikes on top of the cockpit and I saw that the hood was dragging. The enemy aircraft slowed, pulled up, and he stalled

in from about 20 feet. I saw the enemy aircraft crash into a field.

His most spectacular sortie of this tour, however, was on April 18, 1945. Again he was leading No. 130 Squadron, this time on an armed reconnaissance. He was flying at about 6,000 feet when he spotted eleven *Bf 109's* neatly lined up on the runway of Parchim airfield. It was a big, juicy, tempting target and temptation got the better of him. With Flying Officer T.L. Trevarrow (RAF) for company, he dived to within 50 feet of the ground and headed for the Messerschmitts.

Almost immediately the flak started up, glowing tracers zipping past. Weaving was out of the question; that would spoil his aim. He gambled that, with his minimum height and maximum speed, it would be impossible for the enemy gunners to get a bead on him. Still, a lucky hit was very possible with all that lead flying around. No time to think about it, though. From 1,000 yards range he started firing, and once he saw the first strikes he kept his thumb jammed on the trigger.

It was utterly fantastic; the Messerschmitts must have been fully fueled and loaded with bombs, for normally a strafing pass by two *Spitfires* would not have produced such results. Four or five '109's began to burn. Packed together, the others caught fire too. There was a flash and a smoke mushroom; something had blown up. A series of explosions ripped through the lineup. Within minutes, all eleven aircraft had been gutted and a dense pall of smoke rose to 10,000 feet. Keefer and Trevarrow had no way of knowing whose fire had done the most damage so they simply agreed to divide the claim on the basis of six for the RAF flyer and five for Keefer.

Only four RCAF pilots received Bars to their DSOs, and Keefer was one of them. The honour was gazetted in July 1945 and the citation was virtually the story of his third tour. In part it read:

> Since his appointment as Wing Commander Operations, Wing Commander Keefer has led and trained his wing to a high pitch of keenness and efficiency. Under his leadership, the wing has destroyed 191 enemy aircraft and damaged many more. In addition, a great variety of enemy ground targets have been successfully attacked. During this period, Wing Commander Keefer had destroyed four enemy aircraft in the air, bringing his total victories to twelve aircraft destroyed. He has also destroyed at least 60 enemy transport vehicles . . . This officer has completed three tours of operational duty and has proved himself to be a leader of the highest order and a cool and fearless pilot.

With the end of hostilities in Europe, Keefer sailed home to Canada, but unlike most wartime pilots he did not immediately seek his release. Instead, he remained with the RCAF, serving at the Air Force

Staff College and the Canadian Joint Staff in Washington. By 1947, he had decided that the post-war Air Force was not for him. He left to take a job in commercial aviation. Starting with Canadian Aviation Electronics, he switched to Canadair in Montreal, first as supervisor of purchasing, then as Procurement Manager, and finally as Vice-President. Early in 1968 his enterprising spirit led him to embark on a new career. He resigned from Canadair and bought a plastics factory in Granby.

A Canadian citizen since 1945, former Wing Commander George Keefer, double DSO, double DFC, French Croix de Guerre, Netherlands DFC, flies no more except as a passenger on Air Canada. His marriage in 1949 included an unwritten agreement that he would do no further piloting. He is now preoccupied with his work, his four daughters, two grandchildren, and his reading. His bookshelves are crammed with works on flying—mainly with flying in North Africa—but like most wartime pilots, he scarcely glances at his operational logbook and albums. A dynamic individual, he has been far too busy to look back.

Kennedy
The Happy Warrior

When "Hap" Kennedy was growing up in the village of Cumberland, 15 miles east of Ottawa, he showed a burning interest in flying. He avidly read the books of W.A. "Billy" Bishop, while showing little interest in studying. One day a teacher asked him what he planned to do when he left school. "Fly airplanes," replied the boy. "Well", the frustrated teacher snapped, "you'll never get off the ground."

Such a comment did not deter Kennedy. He continued to plan, hoping to secure a Short Service Commission in the RAF. However, the outbreak of war changed everything. He and his brothers, Carleton and Bob, all decided to join the RCAF. On October 21, 1940, "Hap" was sworn into the force. He first soloed on *Tiger Moths* at No. 8 Elementary Flying Training School, Sea Island, B.C., and then went on to *Harvards* at No. 10 Service Flying Training School, Dauphin, Manitoba. On June 22, 1941 he won his wings. Shortly afterwards, Sergeant Kennedy was in England.

There followed the usual round of advanced training, in his case on *Hurricanes* at No. 55 OTU, and then he was off to No. 263 Squadron, operating twin-engined *Whirlwinds* on exercises and convoy patrols. During this period he was promoted to Flight Sergeant and then, on March 20, 1942, commissioned. Yet the *Whirlwind* would clearly be no match for a *Bf 109*, and he was happy when, in June 1942, he was sent to No. 421 Squadron, flying *Spitfires* out of Fairwood Common,

Wales. The result was more convoy patrols and sweeps over France. He did have one close call. One day, while flying at between 25,000 and 30,000 feet, his oxygen system failed. Anoxia knocked him out and he did not recover his senses until he woke up at 5,000 feet in a wildly gyrating *Spitfire*.

The war news and intelligence reports, however, emphasized that Malta was the hottest piece of real estate on the map. Flying Officer Kennedy applied for service there and the request was granted. On October 23, 1942 he left England, and on December 14 he scribbled "Malta at last" in his logbook. He was assigned to No. 249 Squadron. However, the siege of the island was over. Now the *Spitfires* were on the offensive, seeking out the enemy over his own territory.

His first sorties included escort flights for *Beaufighters* and dive-bombing Sicilian targets. For the first time he experienced being "jumped" by Messerschmitts. Then, early in the morning of February 7, 1943 he set out with Flight Lieutenant J.J. Lynch, a courageous but near-sighted American. Over Sicily they wrecked a train with bombs, then pounced on a *Ju 52*. Lynch made the first pass, setting fire to the German transport. Kennedy then attacked from astern and watched as the Junkers crashed in flames. The squadron reported the kill as one shared between the American and the Canadian. Kennedy himself concluded that the victory belonged to Lynch alone, his own bullets having been pumped into a flying corpse. Nevertheless, the incident gave him new confidence and, remembering his debt to Lynch, he too chose to give junior pilots who flew under him their share in future actions.

"Hap" now settled down to the serious yet exhilerating business of making life miserable for Axis aircraft flying between Sicily and Tunisia. He was neither a glory hunter nor a cold-blooded killer, but he took the war seriously, even if, in Malta, he was unofficially credited with having the biggest grin in the RCAF.

By mid-April he had added three tough, armoured *Ju 88's* to his score. On each occasion, in company with one or two other pilots, he set fire to the engines of the Junkers'. He had to admire the bravery of the German rear gunners who continued to fire at him even when their aircraft were going down. Each time, Kennedy found numerous bullet holes in his *Spitfire* when he got back to Malta.

On April 22 came one of his most thrilling combats. Just after sunrise he and Lynch, who was now the CO of No. 249, took off with long-range tanks slung under the bellies of their *Spitfires*. Flying "on the deck" to avoid detection by radar, they swept to the east coast of Sicily. Ten miles from Riposto, Kennedy spotted and reported a *Ju 52*, also "on the deck." Lynch failed to pick it out, so "Hap" peeled back, came in on the enemy's port quarter and shot it down with a single one-second burst. The two *Spitfires* then continued northwards, buzzing along just above the sea.

As they approached Taormina they turned northwest and began to climb overland. Although there were enemy fighters based in southern Sicily, the towering bulk of Mount Etna screened the *Spitfires* from German radar. Approaching the sea once more, they dropped down to wave height again. Then Kennedy saw them—three crawling dots. Once again he warned Lynch and again his leader failed to see them. Finally the American said, "Lead me to them," and Kennedy roared off in pursuit at full throttle.

The dots now resolved themselves into three lumpy shapes— unescorted *Ju 52's* whose crews obviously were not expecting RAF fighters so far north. Kennedy was overtaking them fast. Glancing behind, he saw Lynch was trailing in the rear. The first attack would be his alone.

As he approached the rearmost Junkers he glimpsed its upper machine gun pointing straight up in the "rest" position. Behind it sat a gunner, head down, cap over his eyes, obviously asleep. The Junkers filled his gunsight and he jabbed the trigger button. Moments later, two *Ju 52's* were going down in flames. Lynch, arriving late, polished off the third transport.

This done, the fighters turned south and began to climb, still using Mount Etna as a shield. At 22,000 feet they radioed base, reported their victories, and were told that "the whole German Air Force" was up looking for them. Unperturbed, the duo went into a shallow dive, heading for the enemy fighter base at Comiso. Swooping in at low level, they found the field deserted; the *Luftwaffe* was busy trying to escort transports to Tunisia. After buzzing across the field, adding insult to injury, the *Spitfires* scampered for home.

Back at Malta, the two pilots huddled momentarily. They discussed their first shared victory of February 7, and agreed to split these four evenly. Each claimed and was credited with two *Ju 52's* destroyed.

Kennedy added two enemy fighters to his score on June 10. In a sweep near Pozzallo he fired at a *Bf 109* which streamed white smoke, but he was not able to confirm its fate. Back at base another pilot reported that the German had bailed out. Later that day, while flying in the same area, he spotted a German seaplane picking up his earlier victim. He eyed it hungrily, but such aircraft were not fair game. An escorting *MC.202*, however, was legitimate prey, and thanks to "Hap" it also wound up "in the drink."

At the end of July, having been awarded the Distinguished Flying Cross, he was posted to Sicily, now in Allied hands, where he joined No. 111 Squadron. No more enemy aircraft came his way, however, until the invasion of Italy, which started another run of good fortune.

Between September 4 and October 15 he shot down five enemy fighters and probably destroyed a sixth.

The first two, scored on September 4 and 10, were both similar and contrasting cases. In each instance he chased an *Fw 190* which had been bombing Allied ships. In the former case he was flying a *Spitfire V*, which was slower than his opponent. Sheer tenacity and tactical skill enabled Kennedy to catch and destroy the better aircraft north of Messina. On the 10th, however, No. 111 was flying new *Spitfire IX's*. Following a dogfight over the Salerno beachhead, "Hap" pursued a *'190*, caught it easily, and clobbered it.

His wildest episode, however, occured on October 13. By then he was a Flight Commander with No. 93 Squadron. About noon he and another pilot were patrolling at 14,000 feet over the Volturno River. While stalking two enemy aircraft, a pair of *Bf 109's* dove in behind. The *Spitfires* turned, the Messerschmitts overshot, and the enemy headed for the deck. Kennedy chased one, caught up with it, and fired a burst from 50 yards. The German pilot bailed out at 600 feet, but that was too low; his parachute had not fully opened when he hit the ground.

The *Spitfires* climbed back to 8,000 feet. They were heading south when Kennedy spotted a dozen *Bf 109's* approaching from behind and above. There was only one thing to do—turn and face the enemy. In the next few minutes "Hap" lost track of his wingman and assumed he had been shot down. The battle now settled into a weird pattern. The *'109's* and the lone *Spit* formed a wide ring, all of them slowly circling and climbing. The German leader was behind Kennedy but not quite in a position to shoot; Kennedy was similarly placed behind the rearmost enemy fighter.

The situation was embarrassing. It was apparent that most of the German pilots were tyros. On the other hand, if Kennedy tried to escape, he would be bounced by a fast-diving Messerschmitt. Several times he radioed to other *Spitfires* in the vicinity, asking for help, and each time he received the same reply; "Hold 'em Hap, we're coming." By the time they reached 16,000 feet he had gained on the "Tail-end Charlie". At that point the German leader broke off the action and headed north, followed by his cubs. "I can't hold them," Kennedy reported. He waited until the last *'109* had dived away. Then he set out on a chase.

The *'109's* levelled off at 2,000 feet. After several minutes their black exhaust smoke vanished, indicating they had throttled back. Kennedy dropped down below them, hiding in their blind spot. He was confident that his position, plus the camouflage of the *Spitfire* at tree-top level, would render him invisible. He was right. At intervals the *'109* leader banked back and forth, yet the German failed to see the lone pursuer.

Then, as they approached their field, the unsuspecting enemy committed a fighter pilot's sin; in a war zone they closed up their formation into three tight, fancy boxes, suitable for a formal flypast but not for a battle. Kennedy squinted through his reflector sight.

As they swept over a grass airfield, possibly Ceprano, he cut loose. Only the starboard cannon and machine gun fired, causing his aircraft to swing. He applied port rudder, aimed off and fired again. His bullets cut through one fighter barely 50 yards away and its pilot bailed out. That done, Kennedy finally yielded to discretion by running for home. He landed at Capodichino to be greeted by his startled wingman. Each had assumed the other had been lost, and their reunion was a boisterous one.

As his tour wore on, however, he began to feel the strain. He was tired, yet he refused to admit it. Under such stress, pilots tended to "get the twitch." Some became over-cautious; consciously or unconsciously they would abandon sorties at the faintest sign of trouble. Others did the reverse and became reckless. Kennedy fell into the latter category. He was bored. Knowing what it was like to destroy aircraft, he wondered idly about the sensation of being shot down. One day he ignored a flak warning and flew over a defended zone. An anti-aircraft burst flipped his *Spitfire* over. He recovered control, but back at base he did not even mention the incident. A vigilant Medical Officer assessed the situation as combat fatigue and whipped Kennedy off operations. His first tour, double the length of a normal one, ended on December 3, 1943. He had flown more than 365 operational hours.

He should have taken more than six months rest, but while he was a gunnery instructor in southern England the invasion of Normandy occurred. The tug of all those ships crossing the Channel affected him, and he wangled a posting to No. 401 Squadron, which he joined at Tangmere on June 15, 1944. Three days later he was flying from French airfields.

Casualties were heavy. On the 28th some *Fw 190's* jumped No. 401 out of the sun and shot down two *Spitfires*, including "A" Flight's commander, but four Focke-Wulfs were clobbered, one of them by Kennedy, who subsequently took over "A" Flight. On July 2, in a dogfight with 30 *Bf 109's*, he shot down one German fighter. This one went down with its engine dead, but Kennedy could do no more as his guns had seized. He formated on the *'109* and waved at its pilot who looked back but made no effort either to maneuver or bail out. Possibly he had been injured by "Hap's" fire. In any case the Messerschmitt effected a reasonable crash-landing.

Lorne Cameron, the CO, had been brought down by flak on the 2nd, and the next day Kennedy was promoted to Squadron Leader in charge of No. 401. On July 22 he damaged another *Bf 109*, obviously hitting the pilot. He then forced it to turn around and head for Allied territory, but it finally crashed in the German lines.

Yet the old ghost—fatigue—was still there, made worse by the strain of patrols that ran to three a day. On July 26, ignoring the red circle on a map, he flew over the flak-infested town of Dreux. It was 4.20 P.M. He was leading the squadron at 9,000 feet when suddenly there was a puff of smoke to one side. Another puff appeared on the opposite side. The third one hit. In front of his feet the airplane splintered and the engine temperature zoomed. Someone yelled over the radio, "Get out boss, you're on fire!" Kennedy radioed back, advising his pilots what course to fly to get home. Then he bailed out.

He had put on someone else's parachute and the straps were loose. As the canopy opened with a crack, the harness momentarily cut into his flesh. Then he found himself floating under a white umbrella, drifting east. Glancing down, he saw an open German staff car tearing along the roads, trying to keep him in sight. The wind foiled them; each time they stopped, he sailed over their heads and was blown further east.

He landed near a farm house where a fat French woman was standing. As he scrambled out of his parachute, he shouted, "Ou sont les Allemandes?" She pointed west, then east, and cried out, "Courez-vite!" Then she scooped up the parachute and stuffed it under her dress. Kennedy ran to a barn, decided that that was too obvious, dashed through some woods and into a wheatfield, dropped to his hands and knees, and began to crawl.

His pursuers wasted several minutes checking the wood, then began beating through an adjacent field. At intervals they would stop to fire their guns into the air. It was unnerving, and he briefly considered standing up to surrender. As he lay low he heard the wheat rustling. Three children crept to him. They had risked their lives to bring him some cherries and bread.

The Germans continued to beat the area until dark. That night it rained. Kennedy kept reasonably dry by piling leaves on himself, but it was still uncomfortable. The rain, however, proved to be a blessing. Next day the enemy were back, this time with dogs, but the scent had been washed away. After three days the search died down.

"Hap" now sought shelter in the woods. There he met a Frenchman who demanded to know his name, rank, serial number, squadron, and other information. He gave only the first three items and told the man to go to Hell for the rest. Next day the Frenchman returned with a companion who spoke English. The same thing happened. The second man then explained that he had to have this information for his own protection, and at last the downed flyer answered their questions. His two visitors told him to remain in the woods, then slipped away.

Twenty-four hours later they were back. They had radioed England and determined that Kennedy was a genuine evader rather than a German "plant". They then took his picture for use on forged documents and arranged for him to stay in a barn. The owner of the barn did not know about his guest, though the man's wife did.

Hiding in the hay for more than two weeks was a nerve-wracking experience. There was little to do but think. He worried about his brother Carleton, who was now a bomb-aimer completing his training in Britain. Occasionally German troops entered the barn to drink the farmer's apple cider. Once he left the barn to stretch his legs. He was at one end of a garden when a German soldier walked in the other end. Reacting instantly, Kennedy dropped under a thick currant bush. He could hear the soldier approach, then stop less than a yard away. Again, he was tempted to betray himself and grab his enemy's ankle, but once more he held back. After several minutes the German left, unaware of the flyer's presence.

Finally the Maquis agents arrived with phony work permits and passports. Kennedy set out on foot, heading west, dressed as a farm hand. He moved by day, keeping to the roads but hiding if a German column appeared. He walked for a week, and as he approached the front he could hear the boom of artillery, then the rattle of machine guns, and finally the crack of rifles. The countryside would have been lovely, but the roads were littered with wrecked vehicles and the corpses of troops and horses.

On the evening of August 22, with the fighting raging nearby, he slipped into some woods. That night the darkness flashed with gunfire while figures darted back and forth in the gloom. As dawn broke, Kennedy peered out of his hiding place. A few yards away sat an American jeep. He was safe!

One might think that at that point he had had enough of the war, but he was ready for more. His successor as CO of No. 401 had already been shot down and he applied to Air Marshal Lloyd Breadner for his old job. First of all, though, he decided to visit Carleton. Perhaps they could celebrate the Bar to "Hap's" DFC, which had come through while he was down. Accordingly, he set off for Yorkshire. About midnight on August 31 he walked into the mess at Croft, the home of No. 434 Squadron, and asked if he might see Flying Officer Kennedy. The reply was brief and blunt: "You can't; we buried him today."

This shocking news did not deter him from seeking operations, but he was convinced by Breadner that he should at least return to Canada for a visit. In October he was repatriated and assigned to St. Hubert. He found himself virtually unemployed, and realized that, with the war winding down, he would probably not get another crack at combat. With nothing to do, he took direct action. He went absent without leave, travelled to Ottawa, and enrolled in night school to complete his high school education. Three months later a sympathetic Air Force granted him an honourable discharge.

"Hap" Kennedy entered the University of Toronto's School of Medicine in the Fall of 1945 and received his degree in 1950. Today he practises as a country doctor at Cumberland. The hands which so delicately handled a *Spitfire* now work to preserve life. The grin is still there, and in the lilting accents of the Ottawa Valley he recalls with pride his adventures in that far-away struggle. He is very much the Happy Warrior returned.

Kent
Leader of Poles

Canadian airmen have not been given to writing their memoirs—or have been singularly unfortunate in having them published! By contrast, British pilots have frequently had their recollections published, quite apart from autobiographies of retired "brass" explaining the intricacies of war at the top. The literary tradition within the RAF is remarkable both for its extent and the quality of work produced, the writer/flyers including such men as Richard Hillary (*The Last Enemy*), A.E. Clousten (*The Dangerous Skies*) and J.E. Johnson (*Wing Leader*). Fortunately a Canadian in the RAF was moved to write his memoirs, and so we have John Kent's *One of the Few*.

Kent was in every way a remarkable man—a brave fighter, a brilliant test pilot, a hard-driving commander who was nonetheless the object of hero worship on the part of his men. That was no mean achievement, for as a fighter pilot he was most closely associated with the Polish squadrons in the RAF—and what remarkable characters made up those units!

He was born in Winnipeg on June 23, 1914. One of his earliest memories was of a barnstorming aircraft in that city, and thereafter he was fascinated by aviation. He had his first flight, a birthday treat, at the age of 15. Shortly before he turned 17 he began taking flying lessons and soon had his private pilot's license. Two years later he obtained a commercial license and began looking about for an opening in aviation. At that time RCAF educational standards were so high that he was ineligible to join. He thought of hiring himself out to the Chinese Air Force, until he learned that their equipment was hopelessly obsolete. Finally, in 1935, he secured a Short Service Commission in the RAF.

Following aircrew training he was posted to No. 19 Squadron, flying Gloster *Gauntlet* biplane fighters. That was fun, but by 1937 the novelty was wearing off, and Kent thought of returning to Canada and becoming an airline pilot. He changed his mind when he was sent to the Royal Aircraft Establishment at Farnborough to become a test pilot.

It might be argued that Kent's most dangerous duties were carried out *before* the war. Part of his job involved flying different types of aircraft into balloon cables, initially to develop the balloon defences of Britain, later to test cable-cutting devices which RAF machines might use against similar German defences. The balloon cable program was difficult and dangerous, but Kent had volunteered for it, and he conducted it with such cool skill that in January 1939 he was awarded the Air Force Cross.

The experiments usually took place at 7,000 feet at speeds ranging from 150 to 330 miles per hour. The aircraft included the Fairey *Battle* and the Vickers *Wellesley* and *Wellington*. Over two years Kent deliberately collided with balloon cables more than 300 times, with the aircraft suffering varying degrees of damage. Late in 1939, while returning to base with 500 feet of cable dangling from one wing, he had a particularly close shave. As he approached the field for a landing, one end of the trailing cable became engaged in high tension wires. More than a decade later he recalled the incident:

> I felt a tremendous jerk and the aircraft spun through 45 degrees and the wing was pulled down at an alarming angle. I instinctively opened the throttle and gave full opposite control and the aircraft literally flew into the ground in a level position. The cable fortunately pulled clear of the high-tension wires. This sometimes, even now, causes me to break out into a cold sweat when I think of it. And I was very nearly arrested for putting a large part of South Devon into darkness.

In May 1940, now a Flight Lieutenant, he was posted to Heston where the RAF was experimenting with high speed, unarmed photographic reconnaissance aircraft. The "tests" were actual flights over Germany and France under battle conditions, and Kent had several near-escapes. During one of his sorties over the Rhine in a *Spitfire* he felt a bump, then another and harder one, followed by more of the same. For a time he thought that his controls were malfunctioning. Then he looked behind to see a string of gray smoke puffs—flak bursts which had been drawing ever nearer!

A detachment of the Photographic Development Unit operated from French bases in June, providing tactical reconnaissance for the armies. These flights were conducted at lower altitude than the earlier experiments, and so a brightly painted all-blue recce *Spit* was fitted with machine guns. Kent was flying that particular machine one day when some *Hurricanes* and *Bf 109's* started a brawl which spilled over in his direction. Almost by accident he found himself lining up his sights on a Messerschmitt. The enemy pilot saw him and reacted with a violent half-roll that whipped him away out of control. Kent later speculated that the German must have been doubly surprised; up until then no *Spitfire* fighters had operated in France, and the peculiar paint scheme of this specific aircraft would have suggested the presence of a deadly though eccentric ace.

Once the techniques of high speed reconnaissance had been worked out, Kent was posted away for a fast (13 day) course on fighter operations. There followed a week of confused orders when he was sent first to No. 257 Squadron, then back to Farnborough, and finally, on August 2, to No. 303 (Warsaw-Kosciusco) Squadron which was then forming at Northolt on *Hurricanes*. This, of course, was the famous Polish unit which was manned by pilots who had escaped their homeland following the German invasion. Most of them had fought in France before reaching England. For them the war had a special meaning and they were impatient to get into action.

Although the Poles had their own officers, an RAF commander, Squadron Leader R.G. Kellett, and two RAF flight commanders, Flight Lieutenants Kent and A.S. Forbes, were assigned to assist these flyers. The language barrier was formidable. Most of the Poles spoke some French, and communications between Kellett and Forbes on the one hand, the pilots on the other, were conducted in that language. Kent had very little French, and so he struggled to learn elementary Polish while his charges worked on their English.

The RAF officers had to teach the Poles how to fly *Hurricanes*. They also had to instruct them in the tactics which Fighter Command had evolved, particularly in co-ordinating aircraft movements with radar controllers. The task was complicated by the fact that the veteran Polish pilots felt they knew at least as much about air fighting as their mentors, which in some cases was true, their understanding of basic combat tactics being much more realistic.

The team which developed was remarkable, for there was patience and courage on both sides. The squadron included in its ranks such men as Witold Urbanowicz and Manfred Beckett Czernin, as well as an amazing Czech, Josef Frantisek. These three men alone would destroy 57 enemy aircraft throughout the war. Between Kent and the Poles there developed a great pool of mutual respect.

No. 303 went into action on August 30, when some *Hurricanes* on a training flight encountered a formation of *Do 17's*, one of which was shot down. Kent himself did not score for more than a week, although on September 6 he had to force-land after his engine caught fire.

On the afternoon of September 9 he was leading No. 303 in company with No. 1 (Canadian) Squadron which was also based at Northolt. Over the Channel near Beachy Head the *Hurricanes* met some 40 bombers under an escort of *Bf 109's* and *Bf 110's*. He dived on a straggling *Ju 88*. His bullets apparently killed the rear gunner as the Junkers fled for cloud cover. Three *Bf 109's* attempted to intervene, but Flying Officer Z.K. Henneburg covered Kent's tail as he chased his victim into the clouds. Emerging in the clear, the *Hurricane* pilots saw no sight of their original quarry. Instead, there was a solitary *Bf 110*. Kent swung in behind, silenced the German gunner, then set the enemy's starboard engine on fire. The Messerschmitt, belonging to *III./ZG 26*, turned gently back towards England but crashed into the sea ten miles south of Beachy Head. He was credited with one destroyed and one damaged—his first aerial victories.

About noon on the 15th Kent led twelve *Hurricanes* into the air. They were supposed to co-operate with No. 229 Squadron, but the latter unit was lagging behind when he met a bomber formation under an escort of 50 fighters. "Kentowski" sent nine *Hurricanes* down on the bombers while, with two companions, he tried to hold off the escorts. Although he accounted for no enemy machines in this action, his leadership enabled the Poles to claim ten aircraft without loss.

His next victory came on September 23, when he destroyed a *Bf 109* of *JG 3*. It was a long, drawn-out engagement in which his victim absorbed a tremendous pounding before the pilot bailed out over the Channel. In the same sortie he damaged an *Fw 58* which was obviously searching for downed German aircrew. On his return to base Kent found himself in the middle of a debate with the Poles as to whether he should have machine-gunned the *'109* pilot. On the 27th, again while leading No. 303 and No. 1 (Canadian), he shot down a *Ju 88* despite a determined gunner who damaged his propellor and put two bullet holes through the *Hurricane*—the only time during the war that his airplane was ever hit.

No. 303 was now the top-scoring unit in Fighter Command. During September its pilots had claimed 108 aircraft destroyed. Although this figure was certainly inflated by erroneous assessments made in the heat of battle, there can be little doubt that, drawing on their own experiences as much as that of their tutors, the Poles were among the deadliest of air fighters. Kent was impressed by the way they sailed into the middle of enemy formations, holding their fire until the last possible moment in order to conserve ammunition and ensure accuracy.

Kent's own most spectacular combat occured on October 1 when he became separated from his formation. As he attacked a *Bf 109*, he noticed tracer going past. Only then did he realize that he was alone in the midst of some 40 hostile fighters. Twisting and rolling, he snapped off several bursts. A *Bf 109* went down smoking furiously; it was a "probable". Another he raked with bullets and sent down in flames. This fourth "kill" was at the expense of *4./JG 26*.

In mid-October he was promoted to Squadron Leader and awarded the DFC. On the 26th of that month he took command of No. 92 Squadron, a *Spitfire* unit at Biggin Hill. While the opportunity to fly *Spits* was a welcome one, he nevertheless missed his Polish friends. It was not long before he was flying with them again.

In the meantime there was work to be done. The *Luftwaffe*, having abandoned daylight bombing, had now switched to nuisance raids by *'109's* carrying 250- and 500-lb. bombs. These attacks had little military value and served mainly to inflict scattered casualties on civilians. The fighter-bombers were difficult to intercept, and were nimble targets once engaged. In spite of this, Kent succeeded in shooting down three *'109's* and probably destroying a fourth in the first two days of November. Two of the confirmed kills, plus the probable, were registered in a single, tumbling dogfight over southeastern England in the mid-morning of November 2.

The pin-prick attacks continued for another month, but Kent gained no more victories. In January 1941 No. 92 Squadron moved to Manston. Shortly afterwards it was engaged in the first "Circus" operations over France. The highlight of the month, however, was the news that Kent, Kellett and Forbes, the three RAF officers originally attached to No. 303, had been awarded the *Virtuti Militari*, 5th Class, one of Poland's highest decorations—though to call it the Polish VC, as many writers have done, is stretching the point too far.

Squadron Leader Kent was taken off operations in March 1941 and sent to No. 53 Operational Training Unit as Chief Instructor. This appointment also entailed promotion to Wing Commander. The posting stood for only three months, after which he was returned to Northolt to command the fighter wing stationed there. The occasion was virtually a re-union with the Poles, for the Northolt squadrons were Nos. 303, 306 and 308. Leading these pilots, Kent was to destroy four enemy aircraft. Before the end of August he would run his final score to 13 destroyed.

His first sortie with the wing was an uneventful patrol on June 16. On the 21st the formation took part in a "Circus" composed of six *Blenheims* with 17 squadrons of fighters in support. Enemy opposition was extensive and determined, with yellow-nosed *Bf 109's* making repeated attacks on the bombers. The operation was one of the most successful carried out that year. Two *Spitfires* were lost, but the escorts claimed (and the Germans admitted) 26 aircraft destroyed. One of these was a *Bf 109* shot down west of St. Omer by "Kentowski". Six days later, while strafing a German airfield, he blasted another '*109* into a heap of scrap metal. In July he shot down two more *Bf 109's*, raising his score to 11, eight of which he had bagged while leading Polish formations.

The long association between Kent and these gallant exiles ended on August 2 when he was posted to Kenley, assuming command of the wing there. His final victories were on August 7th and 16th, on each occasion a sole *Bf 109* being the victim. The last combat was also a hair-raising affair. Near Gravelines, in company with No. 602 Squadron, he discovered three '*109's* attacking two *Spitfires*. Another *Spit* drove off one Messerschmitt, and Kent closed in on the remaining two. His own combat report described the events that followed:

> I was approaching the *Me. 109's* and the one which was firing half rolled away and I followed and got on its tail. The second *Me. 109*, however, managed to come down on my tail, but my No. 2, Pilot Officer Grant, succeeded in his turn in getting on its tail. He was unable to fire as I was in front of his *Me. 109* and as the second one did not fire, it is very probable that the same consideration affected him. But I fired several short bursts with cannon and machine guns in the dive, and eventually the *Me. 109* ahead turned slightly to the right and on its back at 3,000 feet. As I was not aware of the predicament the second *Me. 109* was in, not even really aware of its presence but merely suspicious, I turned very sharply to the left and blacked out, losing sight of my *Me. 109*. I was, therefore, unaware of the fact witnessed by my No. 2, that it crashed into the sand dunes in the vicinity of Gravelines.

Early in October 1941 Kent was posted to non-operational duties and awarded a Bar to the DFC. For the remainder of the war he served primarily as a staff officer and test pilot, with much time being spent in North Africa and the Mediterranean. In one instance while checking out a beaten-up old *Hurricane*, he was unexpectedly vectored onto a prowling *Ju 88* near Tokra in Libya. He set one engine smoking, but his cannons packed up, allowing the bomber to escape. On another occasion, flying a stripped-down *Spitfire*, he attempted unsuccessfully to intercept a high-altitude *Ju 86P* reconnaissance aircraft over Tripoli. He reached 41,500 feet, but the "bandit" was still climbing away. He snapped off a brief burst, but saw nothing for the *Spitfire* immediately stalled and spun. He dropped through four miles of sky before effecting a recovery.

Following the war he acted as Personal Staff Officer to Air Chief Marshal Sir Sholto Douglas, the Military Governor of British Occupied

Germany. In 1947 he returned to his old haunts at Farnborough as Chief Test Pilot. Other postings included a tour of exchange duties with the USAF and command of RAF Station Odiham, for which post he was promoted to Group Captain in 1952. In December 1956 he retired from the RAF. Like many former Air Force officers he worked for a time in the aviation electronics industry. With that passionate love of flying, he could not easily withdraw from airplanes.

Kipp
Four to One Hundred

Night. Out on the runway at Holmsley South, two _Mosquitos_ were taxiing at high speed, their tails up. Everyone in No. 418 Squadron was hoping for their success. That day, May 2, 1944, crews from the squadron had carried out a series of Day Rangers, had shot down eleven German machines, and had raised No. 418's total score sheet to 97 enemy aircraft destroyed. Now two of the squadron's best crews were off, one for an intruder probe into France, the other for a Night Ranger into southern Germany. Perhaps by dawn the squadron might have its 100th kill.

Throttles wide open, the two aircraft began to pick up speed. Smoothly they lifted away. The watchers on the ground could no longer see them, but they could imagine the wheels thudding into the nacelles as the _Mosquitos_ cleared the runway. The roar of the _Merlin_ engines died away. Now everyone waited.

Squadron Leader Bob Kipp was heading for Munich. On a long trip like that there could be little maneuvering to avoid enemy flak positions. He simply belted along a direct course while his navigator, Flight Lieutenant Peter Huletsky, map read and checked their position. Over the radio they picked up scattered fragments of German and British wireless traffic, but they themselves maintained absolute radio silence. It was almost one o'clock in the morning as they approached their objective.

Some 15 miles southwest of Ammer Lake they could see search-lights burning. That was curious; no Bomber Command raids had been scheduled for this region and as they were flying "on the deck" the enemy could hardly be looking for them. Then, at 5,000 feet, they spotted an *Fw 190*, apparently acting as a target to give searchlight crews some practice. With its navigation lights burning, the enemy airplane stuck out like a sore thumb. Applying full power, Kipp eased the stick back and began to climb.

Creeping in under the German's tail, he closed to within 150 yards. There was no indication that the "Mossie" had been sighted. Kipp jabbed the gun switches. For two seconds a hail of cannon and machine gun bullets laced the *'190*. No more was needed. The enemy fighter dived straight into the ground and exploded. No. 98 for No. 418 Squadron.

They turned eastward toward Munich, then northwest to Augsburg, but although several lighted enemy airfields were seen, there appeared to be no German aircraft about. The time allowed for patrolling the area was running out, so at last the *Mosquito* turned west, heading for home. It was 1.40 A.M. when they saw another aircraft approaching Gunzberg airfield with all its lights burning. In the moonlight Kipp could see it was another *Fw 190*. He made one pass, overshot, and circled around. The enemy pilot must have been green as grass, for he made no attempt to evade the *Mosquito*. A two-second burst did the trick; the *'190* exploded and crashed. No. 99.

By now Kipp's fuel was running low and he knew he would have to get home in a hurry. He set off once more, but at 2.05 A.M. he caught a glimpse of an aircraft off to the left and very low. Dropping down to 600 feet, he identified two *Fw 190's* flying in echelon star-board formation with navigation lights burning. Kipp was determined to get both. He maneuvered for several minutes before he was satisfied with his position. Settling in 150 yards behind them, he lowered his wheels to bring his speed down to 150 miles per hour. As the trailing *'190* filled his gunsight, he opened fire.

He let the German have it for two seconds, switched over to the leader and gave him an equal dose of lead. Two brilliant flashes lit the sky as the Focke-Wulfs exploded, one-two. The whole port wing of the first victim broke away and smashed into the leading edge of the *Mosquito's* port wing which stalled, sending the "Mossie" into a dive. As soon as he had some speed built up, Kipp fought it into level flight, barely 100 feet off the deck.

The trip home was incredibly difficult. At 180 miles per hour the port wing, its lift characteristics disrupted, would stall. Clearing the mountains of southern Germany proved to be a near thing. At last Kipp entered some cloud and stayed within its protective cloak until he reached the Belgian coast. He could not hope to get back to his base in one piece. Instead, he selected Manston for a landing, mainly because of its long runway. He needed all the concrete he could get, for the damaged "Mossie" had to touch down at 225 miles per hour. Safely down, he telephoned his squadron and reported his four kills.

The occasion clearly called for a party and No. 418 set about organizing a spectacular one. The date set was May 12, but before that day arrived several problems had to be overcome. It was almost impossible to lay in stocks of gin and whiskey in war-weary England. On the 10th Wing Commander A. Barker, the popular CO, failed to return from a sortie. The loss threatened to cast a pall over the festivities. The following evening, it was announced that Barker and his observer had been rescued from their dinghies off the French coast. This gave the squadron a double purpose to celebrate. The result was a party to end all parties, attended by such dignitaries as Air Marshal Sir Roderick Hill, Air Marshal Lloyd Breadner, and the former CO of No. 418 Squadron, Group Captain Paul Davoud. Seven kegs of beer provided the necessary lubrication. That night many a toast was drunk to Wing Commander Barker, Squadron Leader Kipp, and Flight Lieutenant Huletsky.

Robert Allan Kipp was born on October 12, 1919 in Kamloops, British Columbia, where he was educated and subsequently under-studied his brother, a pharmacist. Finding this not quite to his liking, he secured a position as manager and caretaker of the Kamloops Lawn Tennis Club, which he left in June 1940 to join the Air Force. Of medium but athletic build, he impressed the recruiting officer who wrote that Kipp had all the necessary qualities to make a good fighter pilot—an amazingly accurate assessment as it turned out.

He enlisted in Vancouver and shortly afterwards was sent to the Manning Depot in Toronto. Unlike many early wartime trainees, he did not have to waste time on guard duty at some lonely station while an opening came due in the flying program. Instead, he was fed directly into pilot training, first at No. 1 Initial Training School in Toronto, then at No. 7 Elementary Flying Training School at Windsor, and finally at No. 31 Service Flying Training School, Kingston. In March 1941 he graduated with his wings and a commission. Another pilot on the same course was a lanky, cheerful young man from Saskatchewan, "Buck" McNair.

Kipp was despatched to Trenton, Ontario, where he learned the techniques of instructing. In June 1941 he was posted to No. 11 Service Flying Training School at Yorkton, Saskatchewan, where he proceeded to lead countless students through the intricacies of flying *Harvards* and *Cranes*. At the same time, he came under the direct supervision of two former fighter pilots, Squadron Leader W.R. Irwin DFC and Bar, who had flown *SE. 5's* with No. 56 Squadron, and Group Captain G.R.

Howsam MC, an ace with 13 victories scored during the Kaiser's War.

While with No. 11 SFTS Kipp was a model officer. He crashed no planes and caused no disturbances to get overseas. Late in 1941 Group Captain Howsam wrote of him as:

. . . a very capable and intelligent flying instructor . . . He displays a keen interest in his work and carries out his duties with efficiency and good judgement. Pilot Officer Kipp is a well mannered young officer whose conduct has been very good. He takes a personal interest in his pupils and is very popular with his fellow officers.

His excellent record as an instructor brought him accelerated promotion to the rank of Flying Officer. His tour at Yorkton ended in January 1943, when he was given special leave before being posted to Britain. He arrived overseas in March 1943, the same month that he was promoted to Flight Lieutenant.

His first station was No. 12 (Pilots) Advanced Flying Unit at Grantham. From there he went to No. 60 Operational Training Unit, High Ercall, the factory for night fighter and intruder crews. There he was teamed up with his navigator, Flying Officer Peter Huletsky of Montreal. At last, training completed, they reported to No. 418 Squadron on November 2, 1943.

Hitherto, No. 418 had been concentrating on intruder work over French airfields by night. This had not paid off particularly well, for the Germans were intruder-conscious and usually doused all lights at the approach of Allied aircraft. Moreover, enemy bomber operations on the Western Front had been at a relatively low level over the past two and a half years, which meant that the roving *Mosquitos* could find very few important targets.

On November 28, 1943, however, a momentous event occured in the history of No. 418. That day an Australian pilot, Flying Officer C.C. Scherf, and another *Mosquito*, captained by Flying Officer J.R.F. Johnson, took off under cloud cover and flew to the southern coast of the Bay of Biscay. Their claims that day were modest—two *Ar 196* floatplane fighters damaged—but they saw no fewer than seven enemy machines. Moreover, they discovered that Day Rangers by two aircraft were easily managed; the navigator of the lead aircraft could handle all the navigation while the navigator in the second machine kept a lookout for enemy aircraft. The Ranger—both daylight and night varieties—was to become a specialty for No. 418 Squadron, thrusting it into the foreground of operations as breathless *Mosquito* sorties ran up fabulous multiple victories. The crews of the unit might try to understate events, but their combat reports read like the adventures of aerial corsairs.

The squadron operated its second Day Ranger on December 12 when four *Mosquitos* were sent out. One pair, bound for Toulouse, turned back when the necessary cloud cover thinned out, but the other machines, flown by Johnson and Kipp, encountered a solid cloud layer at 1,500 feet which masked them from the enemy. Near Bourges airfield, virtually in the centre of France, they pounced on an *He 111* bomber. The port engine of the victim caught fire. It cartwheeled into a field, breaking off first the port and then the starboard wing while several interested French farmers looked on. Proceeding to Avord, near Paris, they attacked another *He 111* and riddled it. They had to break off the action to avoid flying into German anti-aircraft gun range. Consequently they were unable to see the second Heinkel crash, but it was assessed as "probably destroyed" and credited jointly to the two fighter crews.

Over the next six months, the team of Kipp and Huletsky registered an impressive string of victories. Kipp himself showed such enthusiasm that in February he was given command of "A" Flight and promoted to Squadron Leader. Not all sorties were successful, of course. Routine intruder sorties against French airfields brought scant results—mainly fleeting contacts with enemy night fighters which evaded the *Mosquitos.* A lone high-altitude flight to Berlin in January 1944 brought no contacts at all.

On the night of February 18/19, however, as part of a renewed aerial offensive against Britain, the Germans launched a major raid on London, employing some 200 bombers. Kipp and Huletsky were scrambled to catch some of the enemy as they returned to their bases. At Juvincourt airfield they hit two *Me 410* twin-engined fighter-bombers which went down in flames. That feat was achieved in spite of a malfunctioning gunsight.

Another memorable sortie was on April 14, 1944 when Kipp and Huletsky carried out a Day Ranger over Denmark, accompanied by the redoubtable Johnny Caine. Over the Kattegat they discovered four *Ju 52's* which appeared to be conducting minesweeping operations using electronic equipment. While Caine disposed of two, Kipp lowered his wheels to reduce his airspeed and blasted the other pair. Flying only ten feet off the sea was tricky, and at one point he thought his wheels had actually touched the water.

Proceeding to an airfield near Copenhagen, the two crews set about strafing parked enemy aircraft. Kipp sent two *Do 217's* up in smoke and damaged a third. The *Mosquitos* then headed for home. Before reaching the North Sea, they were attacked by two *Fw 190's* which opened fire on Caine but missed. The enemy fighters broke off the action as soon as the coast was reached.

Air fighting was, of course, a highly impersonal business. In one's mind, one fought machines rather than men. Even when enemy crewmen were seen to bail out, imagination could be dulled. Those floating, broken bodies were not humans; they were appendages to the machines. On one occasion, however, Kipp came face to face with the enemy. It was a strange, dramatic, touching event.

On the night of March 24 a German bomber was shot down over Ford airfield. The German crew bailed out and one man was seen to alight on the 'drome. Kipp was not flying that night so he went out in search of the downed flyer. He found him, alive but lying like a shattered doll, suffering from terrible injuries. The German's parachute had failed to open properly. The man was rushed to the station's sick quarters. He mumbled in German a great deal, but did manage to say in English that he was sorry before he died an hour and a half later.

Kipp's four-in-one-night success on May 3, 1944 put the squadron's tally up to 101, and Flight Lieutenant Don McFadyen made it 102 by destroying an *He 111Z* the same night. The famous party of May 12 was followed immediately by news that Kipp had been awarded the DFC. Shortly afterwards, Huletsky was honoured with the same decoration. Yet there was no looking back, no time for self-congratulation. The work of intrusion and hell-raising went on. Two more victims were to fall to this skilled team.

The first was an *He 177* encountered over France during a Night Ranger patrol on May 15/16. The giant bomber absorbed three slashing attacks before it finally exploded, leaving only a cloud of debris through which the fighter plunged. The 13th and last victim was an *He 111* shot down on June 14 during a Day Ranger over the Baltic coast, a hunting ground much favoured by No. 418's crews. That was Kipp's 35th and final sortie. At the end of June he was posted away to serve as an Intruder Controller with Fighter Command Headquarters. In mid-July he was attached to the American Air Force as a liaison officer. It was about that time that he learned he had been awarded the Distinguished Service Order, while Huletsky had won a Bar to his DFC. The citation to Kipp's DSO noted his quadruple victory over the *Fw 190's* and went on to say, "His genius for leadership has always been apparent and his example has been most inspiring".

Squadron Leader Kipp spent the rest of the war on staff duties. Though slated to return to operations early in 1945, he was kept out of further combat flying by an attack of appendicitis in January of that year. He finally arrived back in Canada in September 1945 and was released a month later.

He had planned to open a tourist service in British Columbia, but in 1946 he changed his mind and rejoined the RCAF. He was an extremely capable officer who experienced no difficulties in the transition from a wartime to a peacetime force. In January 1949 he was given command of No. 410 Squadron, the first jet fighter unit in the RCAF, flying De Havilland *Vampires*. On July 25, 1949, while practising low-level aerobatics in preparation for an air show, he crashed and was killed. A week later he was buried near Kamloops. He was home at last.

Klersy
Ram Squadron Ace

Top-scoring fighter pilots seldom remained with the same squadron throughout their careers. The successful pilot would soon be marked for promotion, and would be posted to flight commander and squadron leader positions as vacancies occured in other units. This ensured that these duties would be carried out by flyers who had been promoted on the basis of skill rather than simple seniority. Thus, although many "aces" might be closely associated with a given squadron, few would serve exclusively with any one unit. A remarkable exception was W.T. Klersy, whose entire operational career was served with No. 401 (Ram) Squadron. Klersy must be regarded as the "top gun" of No. 401 which he flew with, eventually led, and finally died with over a span of less than two years.

He was born in Brantford, Ontario on July 30, 1922, but the family moved to Toronto shortly afterwards. Early in his youth he became fascinated with aviation. In his dreams he saw himself as a bush pilot. To achieve that end, he began taking flying lessons at the Toronto Island Airport, paying for them with money earned during summer vacations. He was not particularly fond of school, but he was above average in athletics, particularly in team sports.

The war ended all thoughts of bush flying but opened new opportunities. In June 1941, having completed high school, he enlisted in the RCAF. For another year he was a student training on *Tiger Moths*,

Yales, and *Harvards*. On June 19, 1942 he qualified for his wings at No. 6 Service Flying Training School, Dunnville, but his hopes for an immediate overseas posting were dashed. In July Pilot Officer Klersy was sent to No. 130 Squadron at Bagotville, Quebec. Although No. 130 was designated as a fighter squadron, it was actually more a training unit in which Klersy piled up flying time on *Harvards*, *Kittyhawks* and *Hurricanes*.

His training continued in other ways as well. Bagotville was also the home of No. 1 Operational Training Unit. Through the station trekked a long line of tour-expired RCAF fighter pilots whose valuable experiences were transmitted in part to the younger flyers. Klersy absorbed their formal lectures and informal mess chatter, combining the lessons with his own driving enthusiasm.

Even with No. 130 he was able to show dash. During one exercise he and another pilot succeeded in "scrambling" in 65 seconds flat, but the achievement was not considered a record. Klersy and his comrade had known about the alert in advance and had been crouching just inside the door of the Ready Room, waiting for the bells to be rung. More impressive was his target shooting. At this he shared top honours with Pilot Officer Donald Pieri, a Torontonian who would later destroy six enemy aircraft and win a Distinguished Flying Cross. At last, in May 1943, he was posted overseas. On July 9 he reported to No. 401 (Ram) Squadron, then flying *Spitfire V's* out of Redhill, Surrey.

No. 401, as rip-roaring a squadron as ever served in Britain, was then in a slump. The *Luftwaffe* was much more concerned with American bomber attacks on the *Reich* than with many of the pin-prick daylight raids mounted by the RAF. More fortunate squadrons like No. 402 were flying *Spitfire IX's* and escorting medium bombers against areas that at least constituted the outworks of the *Reich's* defences. No. 401, further south, and operating *Spit V's*, was escorting other bombers attacking such remote fringes of *"Festung Europa"* that it was not surprising that German fighters were seldom seen.

Nevertheless, Klersy's time was not wasted. He and other novices gained experience in station-keeping, navigation, and operational procedures. In the meantime, they listened to the "old pros" of No. 401 and its sister unit, No. 411—men like Squadron Leaders E.L. "Jeep" Neal and G.C. Semple, or Flight Lieutenants Ian Ormston and N.A. Keene—all DFC winners, though none were aces. They had flown out their tours against evasive fighters flown by the pick of the *Luftwaffe*. Soon they would be going home to OTU instructional duties. Yet before they left, by the strange mixture of constant training and seeming osmosis, they were to turn their tyros into efficient, deadly pilots. When 1944 brought the opportunities the young men—Klersy among them—were to respond as a supremely effective fighting team.

In October 1943, No. 401 moved to Biggin Hill. Its pilots became regular visitors at the famous "White Hart" Inn. While there the squadron re-equipped with *Spitfire IX's*, with vastly superior high-altitude performance over the Mark V's. Late in November, during an escort mission. Klersy first encountered enemy aircraft, and in strafing a German airfield he fired his guns in earnest for the first time.

Nevertheless, it was not a happy time for the squadron. Throughout November and December 1943 the Rams destroyed three enemy aircraft, but five pilots were shot down or lost through engine failures, three of them on December 20 alone. Perhaps in reaction to this, the squadron marked Christmas that year in rare style. On Christmas Day, amid the general celebrations, Klersy stole the Biggin Hill Station Headquarters Christmas tree, placing it in No. 401's mess. Presently he announced over the Tannoy system that Nos. 411 and 412 Squadrons were dead-beats, and asked whether or not they had received their supplies of bows and arrows. The other squadrons retaliated in kind over the same system. Thereafter the party became increasingly wild and woolly. No. 401's diarist wrote with pride (or was it amazement?) that the evening ended with all the pilots still on their feet.

The party had been a welcome break, but as 1944 began the routine went on—sweeps, escort sorties, patrols, and only an occasional brush with the enemy. One dramatic incident occured on January 24, 1944. During a fighter sweep, Flight Lieutenant Jack Sheppard's engine "packed up", forcing him to bail out over the water. Klersy and another pilot circled him for a time before setting course for base, short of fuel. As they flew westward, they met a *Walrus* coming to the rescue. Klersy banked around, guided it to the downed flyer, then headed for home. He landed at Hawkinge airfield with two gallons of fuel in his tanks. Sheppard soon rejoined the squadron, flushed with the hospitality of his benefactors.

The routine continued and the sorties piled up. By the end of February he had flown 55 and had not yet even damaged an enemy machine. His first break came on March 7, 1944 while No. 401 was escorting more than a hundred *Marauders* which were bombing a marshalling yard. Jack Sheppard spotted an *Fw 190* "on the deck" and bounced it, shooting it down with one burst. Klersy, right behind, watched the German crash, then saw another *'190* below. While Sheppard gave cover, he dived on his prey. A hail of cannon shells and machine gun bullets poured into the enemy's cowling and cockpit. The Focke-Wulf flicked over on its back and crashed into a hill in a spectacular fireball—his first "kill".

No. 401 helped in the pre-D-Day softening up of German defences by flying hundreds of sorties on sweeps and dive-bombing attacks. When the big day arrived, Klersy flew three sorties. The *Luftwaffe* did not appear that day, but on June 7 the enemy air force tried to intervene. It was a bloody attempt. No. 401 destroyed seven enemy machines that day, including an *Fw 190* shot down by Klersy. From then onwards his score mounted rapidly.

Klersy and his squadron mates were now flung into the whole range of invasion operations—fighting, patrolling, sweeping, bombing, strafing—anything to support the Allied armies as they fought their way inland. Between June 18th and 20th the squadron moved to Beny-sur-Mer to occupy a dusty, hastily constructed airfield. It was a pastoral setting, yet so close to the lines that the pilots could hear the artillery. They dug trenches as a precaution against air attacks while living under canvas. When the weather was good, they were out flying as many as four patrols a day. If, as often happened, the skies clouded over and rain washed out operations, they gathered around camp tables to write letters, read reports, swap stories and play poker.

Brushes with enemy aircraft were rare at first. The *Luftwaffe* had been caught off balance and required a week to bring up reinforcements, draining the *Reich* of much of its air defences. By mid-June, however, German fighters were appearing in strength. From then until the end of August the enemy flew some 200 to 500 sorties each day, mainly in sweeps of 30 to 50 aircraft intent upon ground attack. The *Luftwaffe* was battered to pieces by a solid wall of Allied air power. Half-trained German pilots and an inadequate system of air control blunted the enemy's air efforts. The Rams reaped a rich harvest of aircraft that summer—46 destroyed, two probably destroyed and 17 damaged for the loss of only four pilots in aerial combat. Of these, two were killed, one evaded capture, and one became a prisoner of war.

If enemy air opposition was vigourous but inept, German flak was a different story. Normandy bristled with light and medium calibre guns which turned dive-bombing and strafing passes into nightmares. Fortunately the pilots downed were frequently able to hide until advancing American and British troops reached them. Yet because it was always a threat, anti-aircraft fire imposed a serious strain on pilots. Eight members of No. 401 were shot down by flak between June 21 and August 18, including three commanding officers. One became a prisoner, two were killed, and the remaining five, including all three COs, evaded capture and were back in Allied hands by mid-September.

A lot happened to Bill Klersy that summer. By the end of July he had run his tally up to seven enemy machines destroyed, won a Distinguished Flying Cross, and had been given command of "A" Flight. High-spirited, aggressive and blessed with sharp eyesight, he had vaulted into the ranks of the squadron's outstanding pilots. Meanwhile, as the unit continued to live in tents, his shaggy mop of curly hair became even more unruly.

Klersy's victories were scored in varying circumstances. On June 28, for example, No. 401 was bounced by a dozen *Fw 190's* and the battle broke up in a wild, classical dogfight in which he shot down two of the enemy. On July 17 he and three other pilots were conducting a dusk patrol over the lines when they ran into three *Do 217* bombers—an unusual incident, as these aircraft had generally been employed at mine-laying away from the immediate land-battle area. In a well co-ordinated interception Klersy destroyed one Dornier while his companions shot down another and damaged the third.

The American breakout into Brittany early in August swung the focal point of the battles away from Caen and No. 401 Squadron. That month the Rams were primarily occupied with shooting up retreating enemy vehicles. Only a few scattered encounters with the *Luftwaffe* were recorded between the 17th and 20th when Klersy was absent on leave. The squadron then became involved in the rapid moves as they followed the Allied armies into Belgium. There, on September 10, Klersy completed his first tour. Before leaving for a ground tour he was recommended for a second award, a Bar to his DFC.

On Christmas Day Squadron Leader Hedley Everard, who had commanded No. 401 for only three weeks, was shot down and taken prisoner. Klersy was summoned back to succeed him, taking up his duties on January 3, 1945. By the end of that month he had run his total of sorties to 200 and had led his pack in shooting up a batch of *Ar 234* jets at Osnabrück. February was devoted mainly to dive-bombing, but on March 1 the *Luftwaffe* put up an unexpected show of strength, giving No. 401 a chance to score heavily.

He was leading the squadron on a mid-morning armed reconnaissance in the Dorsten area when a gaggle of some 40 enemy machines emerged from the clouds 3,000 feet above the *Spitfires.* With superiority in height as well as numbers, the Germans peeled down onto the squadron. Klersy ordered his pilots to break round and face the enemy, but the maneuver was not quite complete when the "bounce" occurred. Order vanished; a dogfight *par excellence* split the sky apart.

Klersy fired at a *Bf 109* from 500 yards. The German pilot had neglected to jettison his belly tank, which was set alight. Another burst finished the Messerschmitt; it dived away, engulfed in flames, and exploded on the ground. Another *'109* flew into his gunsight. He pressed the triggers and watched as, for three seconds, his shells tore the German fighter into flaming shreds. Klersy then climbed after an *Fw 190*. His opening burst appeared to have no effect, but another attempt scored a strike on the enemy's cockpit, evidently killing the pilot. The *Fw 190* went into a shallow dive which steepened progressively until the Focke-Wulf smashed into the ground and exploded. Three in one combat! Klersy's score stood at ten destroyed.

No. 401 Squadron had shot down four aircraft, probably destroyed one and damaged two at a cost of one *Spitfire* lost and one damaged. Klersy added another *Fw 190* to his "bag" on April 19. The following day—Hitler's birthday—witnessed a lop-sided triumph over the *Luftwaffe*.

Three armed reconnaissance patrols were flown. During the latter two the squadron encountered large numbers of enemy fighters taking off from Schwerin and Hagenow airfields. The German pilots behaved like ducks in a shooting gallery. By the end of the day one *Spitfire* was missing but 18 German fighters had been destroyed, three of them by Klersy alone and one shared with another pilot.

His last two victories were scored on May 3, 1945 when he led the squadron in strafing an airfield northeast of Kiel. There was no flak and the *Spitfires* took their time, shooting up one parked airplane after another. Eventually 15 machines were burning, including a *Ju 52* and an *He 111* on which he had fired. The next day he flew his 321st and final sortie of the war. Four days later the squadron was celebrating VE-Day.

On June 29 the *London Gazette* announced that Squadron Leader Klersy had been awarded the Distinguished Service Order. The citation mentioned his work in shooting up enemy vehicles and locomotives as well as his aerial successes, and concluded by saying:

> This officer has moulded his squadron into a powerful operational unit that, by maintaining a consistently high standard in every phase of ground or air activity has set a magnificent example to the rest of the Wing.

Klersy would have been proud, but by that time he was dead. On May 22, 1945, while flying with two other *Spitfires*, he encountered low cloud. He warned the others to climb above it, then vanished into the murk. His comrades broke out on top of the clouds but Klersy did not emerge. Two days later, the wreckage of his plane was found near Wesel. He had struck a hill and had been killed instantly. He was not yet 23 years old.

Laubman
Top Gun at Nijmegen

The _Spitfires_ were coming back. It was September 26, 1944, and the mechanics at Le Culot in Belgium already knew that the fighters had "mixed it" with the enemy. Now they stood by the runway, waiting to meet their aircraft and guide them down the bumpy strip. There was the formation leader, Flight Lieutenant R.I.A. Smith, coming in, followed by the others. The bystanders counted—one, two, five, ten, eleven—they were all back and the blown patches over the gun ports showed that most had fired their guns.

Now Flight Lieutenant Don Laubman's "Z-Zebra" was in the circuit. The nose came up just before the wheels touched and then his two mechanics were alongside, climbing onto the wings as he taxied to the dispersal area. They could not shout over the roar of the _Merlin_ but their faces were virtual question marks. One held up a finger and arched his eyebrows. Laubman glanced down the wing, grinned and held up two fingers. He could not hear their triumphant shout, but he knew how they felt. He also knew how he felt—happy, jubilant, but tired. Combat did that to a man, shooting him up with adrenalin and then momentarily draining him.

It had been a tremendous "do". They had run into two large formations of enemy aircraft near the Nijmegen bridge and the _Luftwaffe_ was now minus eight fighters. The pair Laubman had bagged were his seventh and eighth victories.

For as long as he could remember Don Laubman had been interested in airplanes. At Westlock, Alberta, where his father worked as a sales representative for a tractor firm, he witnessed flights by a barnstormer. Later, when the family moved to Edmonton, he attended all the air shows. Often, as he walked to school, he would pause to stare at the airplanes parked at Blatchford Field. The silver Lockheed aircraft of Trans-Canada Airlines were particularly fascinating. He built model airplanes, but apart from a flight with a friend, R.H. Cull, who held a private pilot's license, young Laubman had no first-hand experience with aviation until the war.

He was eighteen when the world tragedy began. Soon the Edmonton Flying Club was alive with uniformed trainees. Vaguely aware that he wanted to join the Air Force, yet uncertain as to which trade he was after, he approached the Recruiting Office in Edmonton. Hitherto he had believed that an Air Force pilot had to have a university degree. A Corporal behind the desk explained that this requirement had been dropped, so Laubman jumped at the chance. Provisionally accepted for aircrew, he was finally sworn into the RCAF on September 13, 1940.

Laubman and Cull joined at the same time, and their careers followed parallel paths through training, instructional duties, home defence flying, and finally to overseas postings. Cull would end the war with a Distinguished Flying Cross and four enemy aircraft to his credit.

Laubman's first extensive experience with flying was at No. 5 Elementary Flying Training School at Lethbridge. He was particularly impressed by one instructor, "Jock" Palmer, who, during the First World War, had won the Military Medal in France before switching to the Royal Flying Corps. Palmer had then gone into post-war barnstorming. With a reputed 10,000 flying hours behind him, this veteran was an outstanding example of the "old pros" who helped make the training scheme hum.

The young trainee was enthusiastic—almost too much so. On one occasion he tried dogfighting (which was forbidden) with another *Tiger Moth*, then learned that the "enemy" pilot had been the Chief Flying Instructor. "There was", recalls Laubman, "a period of uncertainty as to whether I was going to stay with the firm or not."

Escaping with a tongue-lashing, he went to No. 3 Service Flying Training School, Calgary, flying *Ansons*. That was a let-down, for he had already set his mind to becoming a fighter pilot and the *Ansons* appeared to indicate that he was headed for bombers. Nevertheless, he carried on and won his wings as a Sergeant pilot in May 1941. Then came another disappointment; he was posted to No. 31 EFTS at Calgary to serve as an instructor. Yet while he was doing that routine job, something happened. "I really learned to fly there," he said later, "and I got all the foolishness out of my system."

He was considered an above-average instructor, and in time he was forgiven his dog-fighting escapade and commissioned. In the meantime he and Dick Cull, who was also at No. 31 EFTS, began a campaign to get overseas. In September 1942, after much nagging and maneuvering, they obtained postings to No. 133 Squadron, a *Hurricane* outfit at Lethbridge which subsequently moved to Boundary Bay. It still wasn't combat flying but the two "gung-ho" pilots were now out of the training rut. Presently they found a way to get out of Canada itself. Laubman subsequently recounted with relish the Machiavellian ploy they used:

> After a while a policy was announced for Home Defence pilots to go overseas, one or two per month. At No. 133 we drew names out of a hat to establish priorities and I drew a high number—27, I think. So I went to Number 26 and virtually pleaded to the effect, 'Look, three weeks won't matter that much to you, but it will to me'. He traded numbers. Then I went to Number 25 and so forth. I finally got to Number 3 position. Dick Cull, using the same method, got to Number 2. No. 1 wouldn't budge.

Thus, in May 1943 he was posted to Halifax. Late in June he boarded a ship for Britain, arriving at the Personnel Reception Centre at Bournemouth on July 2. Now came another bad moment; with both *Hurricane* and *Anson* time, what sort of aircraft would he be told to fly? Dick Cull was now with No. 412 Squadron and Flying Officer Laubman wanted the same unit. He secured an interview with the unit's CO, George Keefer, and persuaded Keefer to request him. Satisfied that this would be done, he went back to Bournemouth to await posting instructions.

But when posting orders arrived, it was another shock; he was to go to No. 263 Squadron at Warmwell. That squadron's *Whirlwinds* may have been fighters, but they were far removed from being *Spitfires*. Then, abruptly, the postings mill reversed. Within two days he was ordered to report to No. 412 Squadron at Staplehurst.

His first operational sortie was on August 16, 1943 when No. 412 was part of an escort force for *Marauders*. Thereafter the routine was fairly well established. From one to three times a week, escort was provided for the *Marauders*, *Mitchells* and *Bostons* that were hammering at targets in northern France and Belgium. Occasionally a bomber would be shot down by flak and in a few rare instances enemy fighters seen. That fall, without interrupting its operations, No. 412 moved to Biggin Hill and re-equipped with *Spitfire IX's*.

On December 30, 1943 there occured one of the most embarrassing events in his life. It involved a non-victory.

The squadron was out on a Ramrod. There was a lot of cloud, and then one *Spitfire* had to go home with a mechanical fault. Laubman spotted three *Bf 109's* and dived to attack. He was overtaking one German plane, in a perfect firing position, when he pressed the button on his stick. Nothing happened; his guns were silent. He tried again without result.

He was now alone and feeling very naked. The Messerschmitts vanished into the sun, so he headed for home and safety. Over the Channel, however, a thought occured to him. Carefully he checked his switches, then pressed the trigger button. The *Spitfire* shuddered as the cannon and machine guns belched forth. There was nothing wrong with the guns; attacking the *'109's* he had pressed only the camera button!

Back at base he kept quiet about the incident. The ground crew, however, noting that the guns had been fired, unloaded the camera gun and passed it to Fighter Command Intelligence. The next thing Laubman heard was that, on the basis of the film, he had been awarded a "damaged" claim. The Intelligence officers, studying the film, had noted that cannon strikes could be seen on the *'109*. Laubman concluded that the "cannon strikes" were nothing more than the sun glinting on polished metal parts of the enemy fighter, but rather than face a storm of ridicule he remained silent about his "victory".

Another incident took place on March 16, 1944 during a Ramrod. Flying Officer T.M. Saunderson suffered engine failure and had to bail out over the Seine Estuary. Laubman circled the downed flyer until an Air/Sea rescue *Walrus* picked up Saunderson. It was only then that Laubman turned for home. He landed half an hour after the rest of the squadron with his fuel tanks almost dry.

His first victory came on March 23 when, with Flight Lieutenant W.B. Needham, he attacked a black and grey *Ju 88* near Creil. The two pilots riddled the bomber until it crashlanded in a field. Back home, Laubman discovered that a sharp-shooting German gunner had put several rounds in his tail.

The invasion of Normandy opened the way for the liberation of Europe. Soon No. 412 was following the Allied armies, leapfrogging from airfield to airfield through France. Laubman's score now began to increase. On July 2, 1944, while the squadron was escorting some dive-bombing *Mustangs*, about 30 enemy fighters were met. One *Spitfire* was shot down but four German aircraft were destroyed, including two *Fw 190's* claimed by Laubman. Three days later he destroyed another *Fw 190* after a long chase "on the deck". On August 10 he shot down a *Bf 109* and shared in the destruction of another. He was now an ace, but his greatest days were still ahead.

Once the Allies had broken out of Normandy, overrun northern France and advanced into Belgium, their drive began to slow down. Extended lines of communication and stiffening German resistance threatened to bring the armies to a halt west of the Rhine. In order to maintain the initiative, Field Marshal Montgomery decided to seize the bridges over the Maas, Waal and Neder Rijn Rivers with three parachute divisions. The attack began on September 17. The first two objectives, at Eindhoven and Nijmegen, were captured and secured, but at Arnhem the troops were dropped too far from their objective and landed in the midst of enemy troops led by two crack German generals, Student and Model. Bad weather hampered air support. In the next nine days the Germans isolated the Arnhem bridgehead. Heroic efforts by ground forces rescued some of the paratroops there, but by the 25th the Germans had cleared the pocket. The Allies, however, now stood on the Waal River, and the bridgehead at Nijmegen stood against all enemy attacks.

The skies cleared on the 24th, enabling the RAF to attack enemy strongpoints, to defend the troops trying to link up with the Arnhem pocket, and to protect the Nijmegen bridgehead. The good weather also permitted the *Luftwaffe* to intervene. Between the 25th and 30th a series of desperate air battles were fought over that corner of Holland.

No. 126 Wing, composed of Nos. 401, 411 and 412 Squadrons, accompanied by No. 127 Wing (Nos. 403, 416 and 421 Squadrons) moved up to Le Culot, Belgium, on September 21. This move put them close to the battle. On the 25th they shot down 16 enemy fighters, one of them a *Bf 109* claimed by Laubman. The big days, however, were the 26th and 27th.

The morning of the 26th was slack, but shortly after dinner large enemy formations of up to 100 fighters began intruding over the battle area. No. 412 was patrolling over Nijmegen at 3,000 feet. It was 1.00 P.M. when a mixed force of *Bf 109's* and *Fw 190's* appeared "on the deck", apparently heading for the bridge. Eleven *Spitfires* plunged to attack.

Laubman bounced an *Fw 190*, fired a long burst and saw strikes all over the enemy machine. The Focke-Wulf dived straight into the ground. He then chased another *'190* and opened up at 200 yards range. The German crash-landed and broke up. The young ace fired at three more fighters before finishing his ammunition. He headed for Le Culot, elated.

The day was not yet over. Late that afternoon, during a high level patrol, No. 412 attacked a dozen scattered *Bf 109's*. Laubman bounced one, following it through clouds and down to the deck in a three mile dive. At long range he fired a short burst. The Messerschmitt began streaming glycol. The chase went on for 20 miles while he fired repeatedly, scoring several strikes. At last the *'109* simply flew into the ground at 300 miles an hour.

That night a few German bombers attempted unsuccessfully to

destroy the Nijmegen bridge. On the 27th the *Luftwaffe* put up another major effort, flying about 300 sorties. The first *Spitfires* reported large formations of German fighter-bombers, and the pressure was maintained until the late afternoon. No. 83 Group, composed mostly of RCAF squadrons, flew 398 sorties and lost nine pilots, but the enemy paid with 46 aircraft.

No. 412 was off at dawn with twelve aircraft carrying 45 gallon drop tanks. They were to patrol north of the main battle area at 5,000 feet. No sooner had they reached their patrol area than a score of *Bf 109's* tried to sneak through at 6,000 feet, hugging the cloud base. The fight was on.

Laubman plunked himself behind a *'109* and fired two bursts at 250 to 300 yards range, scoring strikes each time. Another jab of the trigger and the German began losing glycol and started to go down. More jabs—more strikes. Finally, he fired a long burst at 100 yards range. The *'109* flicked into the ground and exploded. Glancing behind, Laubman spotted another *'109* coming in on his tail. Applying hard rudder and aileron, he broke right around and came in from astern. One long torrent of gunfire was enough. The Messerschmitt dived into the ground and blew up.

Back at base the pilots reported their kills—six in all. There was just time enough for debriefing, refuelling, re-arming and then they were off again for a similar patrol. Again there were swarms of enemy fighters around. Laubman led his section in behind a score of Germans, shooting down one *Bf 109* and damaging another before he ran out of ammunition. The squadron emerged with four confirmed kills, but three *Spitfires* were damaged and Flying Officer P.E. Hurtubise was shot down and killed.

Again the squadron debriefed and refuelled. At 3.30 P.M. they were off for their third patrol. The ground controllers reported more enemy formations approaching. Laubman climbed to 14,000 feet. He was heading east when he noticed four *Fw 190's* above in a gentle dive. Two suddenly plunged for the deck with a pair of *Spitfires* in pursuit. Laubman pulled in behind the other two, peered into the gyro gunsight and hit the trigger button.

The *Spitfire* shook as cannon shells laced into one Focke-Wulf which streamed white smoke, half-rolled, and dived vertically, damaged. Laubman immediately switched over to the other *'190*. A two-second burst produced several strikes. The German pilot dived; Laubman followed. Both fighters levelled off at 2,000 feet. More bursts, more strikes and the enemy bailed out. It was Laubman's fourth kill of the day, his eighth in three days, and victory Number 13.

No. 412 had again acquitted itself well. Four more fighters had been destroyed for the loss of a *Spitfire* piloted by Flying Officer R.

Clasper. In three days of fighting the total score for the unit was 26 enemy aircraft shot down for the loss of two pilots. It had been a veritable turkey shoot with the green *Luftwaffe* pilots for targets. Later, Laubman remarked, "I felt sorry for them. The Germans had reached the bottom. It was like shooting fish in a barrel."

Enemy air operations tapered off abruptly thereafter, partly due to the losses suffered but mainly because the ground situation had stabilized. No. 412 Squadron moved up into Holland to take part in dive-bombing operations, but scarcely a sign of the *Luftwaffe* was to be seen.

Flight Lieutenant Laubman had been awarded the Distinguished Flying Cross on September 25. Less than a month later, the squadron celebrated his receiving the Bar to the DFC. His last sortie before his tour expired was on October 28 and proved to be a bang-up show in every way. Having just finished dive-bombing a marshalling yard at Coesfeld, he discovered two *Fw 190's* "on the deck" less than a mile away. He succeeded in overtaking them and in a short, sharp combat destroyed both, making his total victory tally 15.

He left No. 412 in November 1944 for a non-operational tour in Canada, but in March he returned to Britain. On the 25th of that month Squadron Leader L.A. Moore DFC was shot down by flak and killed, leaving No. 402 Squadron without a CO. Laubman was promoted and assumed command of that unit on April 6. His tour with them lasted exactly eight days and 12 sorties.

He was leading the squadron on an armed reconnaissance on April 14 when a cloud of dust attracted his attention. A check of the dust revealed two German half-tracked vehicles. He shot up the rear one which began to burn, then shifted his attention to the lead vehicle. Just at that moment the trailing half-track blew up, catching the fighter in an oily fireball. Suddenly Laubman found he was flying an all-black *Spitfire*. He opened the canopy, noting at the time that his engine temperature was mounting. He climbed to 7,000 feet and headed west, trying to reach the Weser River. However, he could not jettison his drop tank, which made his glide excessively steep. He might still have reached safety had not his engine caught fire a mile from the river. There was nothing to do but bail out.

He hit the silk at about 800 feet. For a moment everything seemed peaceful, until a series of explosions shattered the calm. Someone was shooting at him as he floated down! Looking around, he felt a surge of mixed relief and anxiety. The detonations came from his burning *Spitfire* below, where the ammunition was being set off by the flames. Nevertheless, he was drifting towards the wreckage; indeed he landed only 30 yards from it in a ploughed field.

He crawled into some woods, but the bushes and undergrowth had been cleared away, leaving virtually no cover. Within an hour he was discovered by some frightened members of the Hitler Youth, one of them with a Luger, plus a few civilians and two or three young but mature soldiers. The civilians were irate and babbled away. Laubman knew little German but he caught one phrase—"baby killer"—and feared that he was about to be shot out of hand.

The soldiers, however, took charge, escorting him to a temporary POW camp at Pinneberg on the northern edge of Hamburg. There were about 50 others in the camp, most of them downed aircrew, and Laubman was the top-ranking officer.

He was in the camp hospital recovering from jaundice the day a British armoured car drove in the main gate. It remained just long enough for the camp commandant—a Major General—to surrender the camp formally to Laubman. The Canadian was baffled. What was he to do? Finally he suggested that all the Germans should deposit their arms in the guardhouse and remain in their quarters. Having issued these orders to his former captors, he returned to the hospital. Once he was called to the phone to find the former commandant requesting permission to leave his rooms and go to the mess for dinner. Laubman's command lasted only two or three days. Much to his relief, British troops took over the camp. Shortly afterwards he was repatriated to Canada.

He left the RCAF in September 1945. For a time he considered taking up bush flying in partnership with Dick Cull. By then, however, he was planning to marry, and a more settled existence appeared to be in order. In January 1946 he returned to the Air Force. On October 1, 1946, like most other officers in the Permanent Force, he reverted to his substantive rank, that of Flight Lieutenant.

Throughout much of his post-war career he maintained a link with fighters. In March 1949 he joined No. 410 Squadron, the RCAF's first jet-fighter unit, and was a member of the *Vampire* aerobatic team. In January 1951 he became the first CO of No. 421 Squadron, which was reformed on *Mustangs* before converting to *Sabres*. Rising with the expanding fighter arm, he made the transition from being an operational pilot to staff officer. From July 1963 to August 1966 he commanded No. 3 Fighter Wing at Zweibrücken, Germany, and in July 1969 he was made commander of the Canadian Forces No. 1 Air Division with the rank of Major General (army rank titles had been adopted with the integration of the forces in 1968). His final posting was to Canadian Forces Headquarters in August 1971, to be Deputy Chief of Personnel. In October 1972, however, he took early retirement, settling for a time in Thompson, Manitoba before moving on.

MRS. D. C. FAIRBANKS

Above: F/L D. C. Fairbanks with his Tempest damaged by an exploding V-1.

Left: Fairbanks in January 1945.

Lower left: Fumerton and Bing with the wreckage of a German aircraft they had destroyed over Alexandria, 7 April 1942.

Lower right: Fumerton's Beaufighter, 'A' of 89 Sqn. in Egypt after returning from operations on Malta.

MRS. D. C. FAIRBANKS

C.P.S. BING

C.P.S. BING

Above: W/C R. C. Fumerton DFC photographed while C.O. of 406 Squadron.

Right: S/L D. C. "Chunky" Gordon.

Below: Spitfires of 601 Squadron take off from the North African desert.

PAC PL-28742

Above: F/L R. G. Gray and his navigator F/O Frank Smith.

Right: Lt. R. H. Gray, RCNVR.

Below: This photo taken from a Royal Navy Avenger on 9 August 1945 shows Onagawa Wan — the site and date of the action in which Lt. Gray won the Victoria Cross.

PAC PA-89093

PAC C-5459

S/L George Hill, DFC

S/L A. U. Houle, DFC

S/L Houle in the cockpit of a Spitfire. Note the shattered rear view mirror!

Right: S/L G. C. Keefer, DFC, and his dog "Rommel".

Below: W/C Keefer's Spitfire IX bore his initials — a privilege extended to Wing leaders.

PAC PL-22165

RE-68-1143

S/L I. F. Kennedy, DFC

PAC PL-25867

W/C J. A. Kent, DFC, AFC

PAC PL-8578

Right: F/L R. Kipp

Below: The nose of 418 Squadron Mosquito "Black Rufe" showing marking for the squadron's 100th kill.

PAC PL-2201

This photo of 401 Squadron pilots playing cards at dispersal in October 1943 is the only photo available of F/O Klersy (right foreground).

Hurricanes of 1 OTU, Bagotville, PQ.

PAC BG-20

Above: The bridge at Nijmegen shortly after its capture in September 1944. The battle for this bridge was the focus of heavy aerial fighting.

Left: F/O Don Laubman posed in front of his Spitfire.

Below: Spitfire IX's of 412 Squadron in Normandy. The aircraft in the foreground, VZ-Z is probably the aircraft in which Laubman scored his victories in the battles over Nijmegen.

S/L J. F. McElroy, DFC

PAC PL-14179

Postwar photo of S/L S. McKay, DFC

PAC PL-90234

Messerschmitt Me262, the first jet fighter to see combat.

CAF RE-24062-2

Above: S/L D. A. MacFadyen's Mosquito NT325 HU-N.

Left: S/L D. A. MacFadyen.

Below: MacFadyen's ground crew and the kill markings on the nose of HU-N.

D. A. MacFADYEN

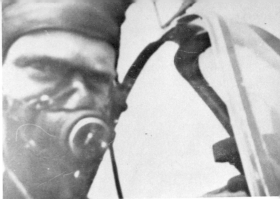

F/O W. L. McKnight with S/L D. Bader.

IWM CH 1324

D. R. MATHESO

Top: F/L W. McLeod in the cockpit of his Spitfire.

Lower: McLeod studies a map on the wing of his aircraft.

Spitfire V being rearmed in dispersal at Malta.

IWM CM323

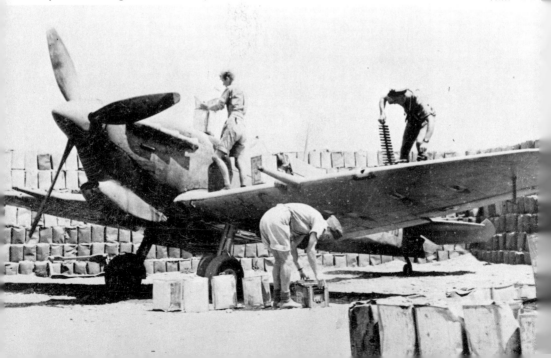

McElroy
"Mac"

Some fighter pilots went through the war with scarcely a bullet hole in their aircraft; others seemed to attract lead as a jam sandwich draws flies. In the latter category, one must count Squadron Leader J.F. "Mac" McElroy, whose aircraft was heavily damaged no fewer than four times.

He was born on November 3, 1920 in Port Arthur, Ontario. His father was employed by the CNR and so the family moved frequently, first to Vancouver, then to North Battleford, and finally, in 1936, to Kamloops, where he completed his high school education. During the summers he worked as a clerk and a labourer, but he also found time to drill and train with the North Battleford Light Infantry and the Rocky Mountain Rangers. These activities matured him as he grew up in the semi-arid heart of British Columbia.

Immediately on completing Grade XI in June 1940, he applied to join the RCAF. He impressed the Recruiting Officer, who wrote that he was "very keen to serve and well above average—typical fighter pilot." At No. 3 Initial Training School, Victoriaville, he evoked a similar reaction, being described as "mature" with "plenty of 'go' in him." Even at EFTS, his instructors considered him fighter pilot material, though he did have some trouble with spins and side-slips. He was awarded his wings at No. 9 SFTS, Summerside, and was commissioned on September 1, 1941. By November of the same year he was in

Britain.

Four months of operational training followed. In March 1942 he was posted to No. 54 Squadron, a *Spitfire* unit at Castletown. In May the youthful tyro received a bad fright. He and another pilot had been detailed to carry out a practice "Rhubarb" which took them over water. They had been briefed to fly at 200 feet. In the event, haze shrouded the horizon, making more difficult the task of gauging one's exact height at low altitude. Suddenly his *Spitfire* shuddered violently and a cloud of spray splattered the machine. He had hit the sea!

Easing back on the stick, he climbed to 7,000 feet. Fortunately, only the propellor had struck the water, but it was now slightly bent, causing the whole airplane to vibrate furiously. Pilot Officer McElroy limped to Wick airfield and landed, safe but shaken.

Shortly afterwards he left No. 54 on assignment to the Middle East. In June he reported to No. 249 Squadron in Malta. During the next six months he was to become a much battered ace in a very battered island. Among his companions were "Buck" McNair, "Screwball" Beurling, and John W. Williams.

He began by damaging a *Bf 109* on July 2, and that month claimed five enemy aircraft destroyed (including one shared), two "probables" (one shared) and four damaged. His best day was on the 10th, when he downed a *Bf 109* and an *MC.202*. He recorded no successes in August, but on September 20 he added a *Bf 109* to his tally. Curiously, he had not yet been recommended for a "gong". Then, in October, he vaulted into prominence.

The general nature of the "October blitz" has been outlined in detailing the career of Beurling; it was the *Luftwaffe's* last major effort to knock out Malta, and it was also the most feeble. The RAF itself virtually dictated how the enemy would run it, for the enemy, even as they were trying to clobber Malta, were also forced to maintain defensive shipping patrols. The German and Italian units assigned to the blitz were understrength and operating many worn-out machines. Even the Axis aircrews were suffering from "Malta fever"—demoralization brought on by fatigue and frustration.

The offensive was preceded by six probing attacks, numbering about 120 sorties, launched on October 10. So alert were the defenders that five of these minor raids were intercepted north of Malta. The next day the enemy upped its scale of operations, flying 216 sorties. On the 12th—the peak day—it was 279 sorties. At the time it was believed that the enemy was suffering 4-1 losses. The RAF successes were probably closer to 2-1, but that was only part of the story. Not only did the Axis aircraft fail in their objective, but a high proportion of their shot-down personnel fell into British hands.

McElroy downed a *Bf 109* on October 10, bringing his total to

6 1/2 destroyed. On the 12th he survived one of the most desperate battles of his life. Two months later he described the combat for a visiting newsman:

> Five of us took off in our *Spitfires* and almost immediately ran into 14 Messerschmitts. We had a general scrap and I was lucky enough to get myself a Jerry. On the way home, I saw a *Ju. 88* and got on its tail, but before 'squirting' it, I looked behind and there were six more *Me. 109's* on my tail. They were diving at me so I turned and went right into them and the resulting scrap lasted three or four minutes—although it seemed like as many hours. I got my sights on one of the kites and let him have it fair and square and then turned to engage another plane. But the Jerries had had enough and they broke off the fight and headed for home. The whole trip lasted only 50 minutes but they were pretty hectic minutes I can assure you. It was good solid scrapping all the way. When I landed, I found my *Spit* was riddled with machine gun bullet holes, so I guess I was lucky all 'round.

Three days later he was one of seven pilots who engaged ten *Ju 88's* escorted by 50 *Bf 109's*. Within minutes he had damaged one bomber so extensively that it was assessed as "probably destroyed." His own aircraft had been hit, however, and some shrapnel had wounded him slightly in one leg. Then the cockpit began to fill with smoke. Assuming that he was on fire, McElroy attempted to bail out, only to discover that the canopy was jammed. The plane dived out of control for several thousand feet. Finally he succeeded in levelling out and nursed it down for a crash-landing. Next day, the 16th, he was back in action, but before he could do any shooting he "got in the way of a Messerschmitt" and once more had to crash-land.

The Axis admitted defeat on the 18th by sending no more bombers, and the offensive ended on the 19th. After that, the *Luftwaffe* and *Regia Aeronautica* restricted their activities to isolated reconnaissance sorties and strafing attacks by fighters. McElroy shared in the destruction of one such intruder, a *Bf 109*, on October 22, and on the 27th he damaged an *MC.202*. These were his last victories in Malta. In November he was awarded the Distinguished Flying Cross, and the following month he was posted to Britain.

Following a non-operational tour as an instructor, he was sent to Canada on leave, where he used his time for a fast courtship and speedy marriage. Late in 1943 he was posted back to the United Kingdom. On January 5, 1944 he reported to No. 421 Squadron, then commanded by W.A.G. "Wally" Conrad, a veteran of both North African and European air battles. Among his exploits, Conrad had once been forced down in France but had evaded capture and returned to England. After getting oriented to the tactics and problems of the theatre, McElroy once more resumed operations, this time the offensive variety of sweeps and escort sorties. In April he was initiated to dive-bombing. Later the unit went in for ground strafing, preparing for its role in the forthcoming liberation of the continent.

At last D-Day arrived, but it seemed to herald nothing but bad luck for No. 421. In the first week of the invasion the squadron lost four pilots without seeing a trace of the *Luftwaffe*. On June 15, however, during an early evening patrol, McElroy led the squadron into a formation of twenty *Bf 109's*. In the scrap that followed, seven enemy fighters were shot down in exchange for one *Spitfire* lost with its pilot. On this occasion "Mac" just had to take it. Although he damaged one Messerschmitt, another fighter blasted his port aileron clear away and practically shot out the other controls. At 200 miles per hour the *Spitfire* stalled.

Fortunately he had 15,000 feet of height and was able to put the airplane into a steep glide. Using the elevators and rudder judiciously, he finally reached a temporary airfield to execute a landing which more closely resembled a controlled crash. The *Spitfire* was a write-off but McElroy walked away. Before the month ended he had retaliated by shooting down two German fighters.

On June 29 Squadron Leader Fred Green DFC was wounded by flak, leaving No. 416 Squadron without a CO. McElroy was promoted and given charge of this unit. On July 27 he surprised an *Fw 190* as it was coming in to land at a small strip near Alencon. Attacking with 90 degrees of deflection, McElroy simply aimed ahead of the Focke-Wulf and let it roll into a stream of lead. The enemy fighter broke in two.

He was awarded a Bar to his DFC in August, but though he flew many sorties there was little out of the ordinary to report. On September 4, however, he learned that he had become the father of a baby girl and No. 416's personnel became the recipients of cigars. The squadron diarist irreverently wrote, "I guess that leave in Canada after his last tour wasn't in vain."

On September 30, with only his starboard cannon and machine guns working, he crippled a *Bf 109* which was then polished off by Flight Lieutenant David Harling. This was his final victory, and it brought his total in air-to-air combat to 13 1/2 confirmed plus three "probables" and nine damaged. The squadron then moved to Holland, but found the Germans waiting for them. On October 2 and again on the 12th the field was bombed by *Me 262* jets which inflicted considerable damage and casualties. Orders went out that personnel were to wear their "twitch hats" (steel helmets) and many complied, for the jets struck without warning. Winds and rain added to the discomfort.

On the 22nd the squadron was pulled back to Melsbroek, Belgium. It was there that Squadron Leader McElroy finished his tour (148 sorties). He was posted back to Canada.

He spent the last year of the war at Vancouver and Victoria. In September 1945 he was released from the RCAF. For three years he kept up with aviation by working as a flying instructor in Vancouver, where he was also a member of No. 442 (Auxiliary) Squadron. Later he worked as a car rental manager and then as a security officer. He missed flying, however, and when the RCAF began its Korean War expansion period he joined on a short service commission which he was able to extend into a permanent commission. He served as an instructor and for a time flew *Sabres* with No. 421 Squadron in Europe. In November 1964 he retired from the Air Force, settling in London, Ontario.

MacFadyen
The Perfectionist

Flying Officer Harold Molyneux, the recruiting officer in Toronto, was pondering an applicant's papers. As a fighter ace from the First World War, he was keenly interested in the young men who paraded through his office. This applicant was unusual, however. He was tall, slim, played tennis, figure skated and looked it. The young man was keen; he had picked up a private pilot's license at Barker Field during the winter of 1939-40 to enhance his chances of getting into aircrew. And what references! The Right Honourable Arthur Meighen and Major General S.C. Mewburn were prepared to vouch for the applicant's character. Molyneux squared the man's forms on his desk and scribbled, "Applicant is of a very high standard. Good home atmosphere and shows it." A few hours later, the new recruit took the Oath of Allegiance. The fate of a dozen German aircraft had been sealed. At the same time, Donald MacFadyen embarked upon a strange, paradoxical conflict with authority.

MacFadyen, the son of a prominent Canadian banker, was born in Montreal on December 18, 1920 and raised in Toronto. After completing high school, he went to work as a ledger keeper in a Toronto branch of the Bank of Montreal. A serious young man, he enjoyed collecting tropical fish and stamps besides indulging in vigorous athletics. When the war broke out he carefully prepared himself for enlistment, so that even before he entered the Recruiting Centre he had

45 hours flying time to his credit.

Joining the RCAF in May 1940, he took most of his early training in the Toronto area. At Malton he learned to fly the Fleet *Finch* and, not unnaturally in view of his experience, he was the first member of his course to go solo. He graduated first in a class of 21. From there he was posted to Camp Borden where, in November 1940, he graduated at the head of a class of 37, received his wings, and was commissioned.

Already, however, he was having difficulties with the RCAF. He had come from a wealthy family, and he thus encountered a curious form of inverse snobbery whereby his "privileged" antecedents were resented. His intellectual capacity engendered fear and mistrust; at Initial Training School he was outraged when, after turning in a perfect mathematics exercise, he was accused of cheating. At Camp Borden he was asked to do excessive aerobatics in an attempt to "cut him down to size". His response was to perform faultlessly. Evidently he was a perfectionist, and the more he showed it, the more resentment he encountered, with results detrimental to his promotion and outlook.

From Camp Borden he went to the Central Flying School at Trenton, and then to No. 9 Service Flying Training School at Summerside, P.E.I. to serve as an instructor. This pattern, common to the careers of Bannock, Cleveland, Gray, Kipp, and MacFadyen, is striking, for all began as instructors and ended up as successful intruders. MacFadyen himself later concluded that, in piling up hundreds of hours in trainers, he became an instinctive pilot. Later, cruising at 500 feet over blacked-out Europe, he would be able to fly as naturally as he breathed. That left his mind and eyes free to search, plan and shoot.

Yet his combat successes would also be attributable to his approach to flying: perfectionism. He showed that by his outstanding record in training. Though he described himself as being "never a visible idiot", he honed his skills to such a degree that he could fly an aircraft between and *under* two trees. On the day after VE-Day he would fly a *Mosquito* down the narrow notch of the Dortmund-Ems Canal with such finesse that he would whip a fishing line out of a man's hand. Incredibly enough, he did not do these things for "thrills", but to demonstrate to himself how an airplane could and should be handled. It was that kind of skill that would save his life.

He was at Summerside only four months, but it was time enough for him to have some royal disagreements about what training procedures should be followed. It seems incredible that, as a mere Pilot Officer and less than one year in the service, he should have been so combative, but that was another aspect of his character—utter self-confidence. Nothing could shake him but superior arguments, and few of those were presented to him.

In May 1941 he went back to Central Flying School at Trenton where he became an A.2 instructor, virtually "teaching teachers". He was intensely proud of the fact that he was the first BCATP graduate to attain this level. Subsequently he would look back on his days at Trenton as the most productive of his Air Force career. On being raised to the level of an A.1 instructor, he toured training establishments in central Canada and the Maritimes with the CFS Visiting Flight, testing and re-categorizing other instructors. Moreover, in company with Squadron Leader A.J. Shelfoon, he helped re-write the existing training manuals.

In May 1943 he was posted overseas. Most pilots travelled to Britain by ship; MacFadyen took a *Boston* bomber over with RAF Ferry Command. The last leg of the trip was from Reykjavik, Iceland to Prestwick, Scotland. As he broke out of clouds over the UK he glimpsed the Isle of Tyree, from where his grandparents had emigrated to Canada.

Once overseas he went to No. 12 (Pilots) Advanced Flying Unit, Grantham, to fly *Blenheims*. He was there from July to September 1943, during which he was commended for his "outstanding ability and keenness". At the end of this course he went to No. 1536 Beam Approach Training Flight, to learn the complicated procedures involved in blind landings. At the end of six days it was concluded that he could probably teach his own instructors! The perfectionist in him was in the fore, as revealed by an interesting report from No. 1536 BAT Flight:

> Tell him to fly at a certain height or rate of descent, and at a certain airspeed, and his needles would glue themselves to the required figures.

Late in September 1943 he went to No. 60 Operational Training Unit at High Ercall. Between lectures in an ancient classroom, the desks left over from a boy's school, MacFadyen with his confident, talkative nature found himself drawn to and paired with Pilot Officer James D. Wright of Rosthern, Saskatchewan. Wright, the observer, appeared to be the direct opposite of MacFadyen. He may have been quiet, but he was also an achiever; at Air Observer's School in Canada he had graduated at the head of his class. On December 7, 1943 the team reported to No. 418 Squadron at Ford, Sussex.

Their first sortie was a night intruder trip to Paris on December 17. All new crews were given this sort of job as an initiation ritual and the same thing always happened—nothing. Having demonstrated that they could find their way around a chunk of blacked-out enemy territory, the new boys were allowed to take part in the squadron's main work, long range intruder sorties suppressing enemy night fighters. MacFadyen's first such flight was on December 20. Two nights later, intruding over Orléans airfield, he attacked an aircraft which he could not identify in the darkness, saw strikes, then had to break steeply to port to avoid a collision. An attempt to relocate his victim failed. Concluding that the enemy machine had landed safely, he claimed only a damaged, but later intelligence suggested that the German aircraft had been severely mauled, and the combat claim was upgraded to "probably destroyed".

The next three months were taken up with routine Flower and intruder patrols. Some flights were extremely frustrating. On one occasion he had to return to base only 18 minutes after takeoff following the failure of the "Mossie's" electrical system. On another flight he attempted to strafe Avord airfield, but had to break away when confronted with a torrent of small-calibre automatic weapons fire.

On the night of February 24, 1944, MacFadyen and Wright were on a Flower patrol inside Germany. Bomber Command was attacking Schweinfurt and enemy night fighters were active. At 2.15 A.M. the team spotted an aircraft approaching Wurzburg airfield and joined it in the landing pattern. As the German plane set itself up for its final approach, MacFadyen opened fire. The enemy machine began to glow and then, in a cataclysmic flash, it exploded.

On returning to base, he claimed one *Me 410* destroyed. His fellow pilots leaped on him gleefully a few days later when the films from his gun camera were developed. The shadowy, indistinct pictures showed his victim taking a load of lead, but they also seemed to indicate that the target had twin fins, suggesting it was a *Bf 110*. The successful pilot took a severe ribbing for his failure in aircraft recognition.

But was it a failure? More than 30 years after the event, MacFadyen remains convinced that the aircraft, which he had followed through three tight circuits, was an *Me 410*, and that the second "rudder" recorded by the camera was more likely a radio mast or radar installation. The incident would be a minor one, were it not a further indication of his character, asserting his own interpretation of events over the "official" version. Moreover, the general rejoicing within the squadron over his "error" reflected his unusual standing with other personnel.

His self-confidence was still unnerving to his associates. Moreover, he *knew* what he was doing, and freely offered advice to those whom he felt could benefit from his expertise. His outspokenness, and the fact that he usually *was* right, did not endear him to his companions, who found him a prickly character, incessantly talking shop. Superiors were describing his self-assurance as "irritating", his single-minded dedication as "fanatical". His was the problem of the individualist in conflict with "the system" which he tried to bring round to his viewpoint. Years later he wrote of himself:

> From an emotional standpoint, it was *my* war. With the
> slightest encouragement, I would prosecute it with a concen-

tration that made other people uncomfortable. A compulsive perfectionist, appallingly egocentric, I would reduce every uncertainty, every unknown, too quickly, to rational manage-ability. Operationally, I was born to be a tactician, and would have matured into a strategist.

Taken out of context, this incautious statement might appear to be a damningly conceited declaration, were it not so honest and self-critical. Moreover, it was justified by the record. His self-esteem was well-founded in his accomplishments. His later work in developing tactics for use against *V-1's* and in radar-equipped intrusions proved that.

And yet, for all that cock-sure exterior, that "Don't give a damn because I know I'm right" attitude, there was another side of him—an emotional side which he kept locked up from all but a few chosen intimates. There was his sense of outraged frustration at having done so much, and tried to do it *perfectly*, and still being no more than an Acting Flight Lieutenant. There was the Scottish romanticism that made him thrill at the sight of his ancestral island. Another incident reveals the inner man, and how he tried to hide him. It was the squadron Christmas party of 1943, subsequently described by a man who posed as a hard, brittle character:

Did you know that the 418 Christmas Party consisted of a hangar full of packages received (at such great cost) from home by sea; all of the local children who could be found; and an *Oxford*-load of ice cream from a Midlands USAAF PX, obtained in trade for an *Oxford*-load of peanut butter? You should have seen the eyes of little kids tasting *real* ice-cream for the first time. I stayed away from most of the party because it made me cry.

On March 21, 1944 he set out on his first (and only) Day Ranger. He was accompanied by another *Mosquito* flown by Lieutenant J.F. Luma, USAAF. Four hours and fifteen minutes after takeoff, they were back, having destroyed seven and damaged twelve enemy aircraft over northern France. MacFadyen's share was three destroyed and eight damaged.

Yet above all else, he was a night intruder specialist; indeed, he felt that No. 418's crews should concentrate on night work, where they were acknowledged experts. On May 2 he learned that he had been awarded the DFC. Shortly afterwards he was attached briefly to No. 29 Squadron (RAF) to advise that unit on the tactics which No. 418 was finding so successful. His score continued to rise with a giant *He 111Z* destroyed on the night of May 3. On this occasion his aircraft was hit by machine gun fire which slightly wounded Wright. The starboard engine temperature gauge soared, so the *Merlin* was shut down and the trip home was made on one engine. On his arrival he discovered that the temperature gauge alone had been damaged, not the engine itself.

The Allied invasion of France brought new opportunities. On the night of June 6/7 German reinforcements were being flown forward. Two *Mosquitos*, one piloted by MacFadyen, the other by Flight Lieutenant Stan Cotterill, exacted a dreadful toll, shooting down five enemy aircraft, four of them *Ju 52* transports. MacFadyen caught one of these north of Coulommiers airfield and sent it down on fire. As it plunged to its doom, enemy paratroopers were seen leaping out, their clothes and parachutes blazing. MacFadyen steeled himself to the horror; in his combat report he described them as "burning objects."

He was engaged on a routine Flower patrol on the night of June 12 when out in the darkness he saw a long, stabbing flame racing across the sky. He had spotted one of the first *V-1* robots aimed at Britain. Four nights later, No. 418 scrambled five "Mossies" as the Germans began launching buzzbombs in earnest. That night a total of 146 were reported by Allied radar as the enemy tried to swamp the defences.

Appropriately, MacFadyen and Wright, having been the first to see a *V-1*, were the first members of the squadron to destroy one. At 1.25 A.M., some 25 miles southeast of Beachy Head, they attacked a buzzbomb that was belting along at 340 miles per hour on a course almost due north. The target could not outfly the fighter, but it could outrun it. From a range of 300 yards, MacFadyen fired a short burst. Flashes marked the cannon strikes and the *V-1* began to burn. From 2,000 feet it plunged flaming into the sea. A little more than an hour later he attacked another *V-1*. Although he saw no strikes, it dived into the sea and exploded. However, the "Doodlebugs" were tricky customers; in three other cases he chased specimens which drew away before he could get in a good burst. He finally landed at Holmsley South at 3.20 A.M. A little more than an hour later, Flight Lieutenant Colin Evans returned, reporting that he had chased four buzzbombs and shot one down.

No. 418 enjoyed an exceptionally successful "shoot" on the night of July 6/7. The German rate of fire was down to about half of normal (only 67 were plotted from dawn of the 6th to dawn of the 7th), and by now the paths of the robots were known.

MacFadyen, knowing that his tour was drawing to a close, flew two sorties that night. Shortly after midnight he caught a *V-1* which had been fired from a site near Dieppe. From a range of 400 yards he aimed one short burst and watched the "Doodlebug" dive into the sea where it blew up. Half an hour later he pounced on another and shot its engine out from the fantastic range of 500 yards. It too exploded in the sea. He next singled out another *V-1* and scored strikes, but then another "Mossie" intervened to finish it off. Shortly afterwards, he landed at Ford, refuelled, and took off again. At 3.51 A.M. he bounced yet another *V-1*. Two short bursts did it. The robot's ramjet engine died out and the creature exploded in the sea. Back at base there was much jubilation. MacFadyen, Bannock, and Colin Evans had each destroyed three *V-1's*, and other pilots had shot down two more.

He left No. 418 later that month and was posted to No. 60 OTU, High Ercall, then to No. 54 OTU, Charter Hall, for instructional duties. As usual, he was smart, neat, and super-efficient. At Charter Hall his superior, Wing Commander M.C. Maxwell, considered him "possibly the best pilot this OTU has ever had."

Late in November he was sent to No. 406 Squadron. Initially he was there only to instruct, for No. 406 was about to unleash its radar-equipped *Mosquito XXX's* on intruder operations. However, he was able to team up with Flight Lieutenant V.G. Shail, an ex-grocery clerk from Saskatchewan who had been with the squadron since November 1943, yet had encountered no enemy aircraft. On the ground the pilot and radar operator went their separate ways; in the air they were a first-class team.

Having been given clearance for a second operational tour, Mac-Fadyen's position with No. 406 was formalized by making him the training officer. He was also appointed Deputy Commander of "B" Flight. On April 26, 1945 he would be promoted to Squadron Leader and made a full-fledged Flight Commander.

Wing Commander Bannock, the new CO, scored No. 406's first intruder victory—a *Ju 88* shot down on Christmas Eve. Pilot Officer W.G. Kirkwood bagged another on New Year's Eve, and on the night of January 1/2 Flight Lieutenant P.E. Etienne shot down a *Bf 110*. MacFadyen, preoccupied with his instructional duties, flew few sorties until the end of January 1945, but his scoring began again when, on February 21, he destroyed a *Bf 110* just as it was about to land at Stormede airfield.

His next claim was far less satisfying. On the night of February 28, MacFadyen and Shail attacked what appeared to be a *Ju 88* on Hailfingen airfield. The combat report vividly describes the frustrating events which followed:

> Five separate attacks from 800 feet down to minimum range were made, until ammunition ran out. Many strikes were seen on each attack and during the second, fire broke out in the cockpit. This fire, however, died down and although the enemy plane continued to smoke during subsequent attacks and after, no more open flames were seen. During attacks, small parts of the enemy aircraft were blasted into the air, the *Mosquito* being hit on the starboard spinner and port wing. The airfield remained alight throughout and there was no visible return fire. We were

tempted to land and hack the thing to pieces with the fire axe but 'Stubby' finally persuaded me to go home. We believe the aircraft must have contained no petrol.

The Junkers was assessed as "probably destroyed."

Throughout March and April 1945, MacFadyen piled on eleven sorties, racking up five more enemy aircraft destroyed and eight damaged. Two of these trips were Night Rangers, deep into Czechoslovakia where he wiped out an *Fw 190* (March 4) and an *He 111* (March 24) with three of the former and four of the latter types damaged.

His best trip was on the night of April 9. Bomber Command was hammering the Kiel shipyards with nearly 600 "heavies" while smaller forces were carrying out feint raids on Stade, Hamburg and Berlin. The Germans scrambled six night fighter wings but mistook the RAF's objective and sent them to Stade. No. 406 put up eight *Mosquitos* as part of Fighter Command's effort against the *Luftwaffe's* night fighter arm.

MacFadyen was assigned to the airfield at Lübeck/Blankensee. The routine was second nature to him, for he was one of the tacticians who had worked out the art of low level radar interceptions. At 11.50 P.M., while cruising near the base at 1,000 feet, Shail picked up a blip at a range of four miles. They moved in on the contact, which turned out to be a *Ju 88G*, and shot it down in flames. Twenty minutes later they picked up another *Ju 88G* and clobbered it. This machine caught fire, then exploded when the "Mossie" was scarcely 100 feet behind. Considerable debris hit the aircraft; they flew home trailing 50 feet of steel radio antennae which had cut into the starboard radiator, miraculously without fouling in the propellor.

Not all his encounters with enemy aircraft resulted in personal victories, but teamwork with other crews could still deprive the *Luftwaffe* of a fighter. On one sortie MacFadyen, reacting to airfield lights, sighted a *Bf 110* taking off from Stormede. He was out of position for a good shot, and the *'110* could outclimb his "Mossie", but he knew there was an Australian pilot patrolling higher up and away. He called this man on the radio, advising him of the Messerschmitt's speed, direction, and probable height.

Ten minutes later the other pilot reported a radar contact. This was followed by a "Bogey challenge". There was a brief silence (time enough for a burst of gunfire, though that would not go out over the air), and then a voice crackled in the Canadian's earphones, "Thanks, cobber."

In all his flying, his closest call had nothing to do with enemy aircraft. On May 3, 1945 he took a *Mosquito* out for a test flight. The main runway at Manston was temporarily blocked by a *Lancaster* which had made an emergency landing earlier. As ground crew were unloading the bombs, MacFadyen was instructed to use an adjacent grass strip.

He started his takeoff run, but suddenly the starboard propellor began to surge violently. He found himself with his wheels half-way up, one engine out, and a prop that wouldn't feather. He was also swinging straight for the *Lancaster* and its bombs!

Summoning all his considerable skills, he hauled the protesting "Mossie" over the bomber, clearing it by inches, then sagged near the ditches and wires behind the Dover cliffs. He jammed on the emergency radio switch, tersely described the technical fault (for the benefit of crash investigators) and waited for the impact. It did not come. He whistled over the edge of the cliffs and out to sea. Gradually he built up flying speed and got the malfunctioning propellor to feather. At last he was able to limp back to Manston.

Late in April Squadron Leader MacFadyen had been awarded a Bar to his DFC. Three months later news reached the squadron that "Stubby" Shail had won a DFC, so that both members of the team were rewarded. MacFadyen remained with No. 406 until it disbanded at the end of August, after which he returned to Canada. On October 19, 1945, six days before he was released from the RCAF, the *London Gazette* announced that he had been awarded the Distinguished Service Order. The citation noted his most recent victories, including the double "kill" the previous April, and concluded by saying:

> Throughout his two tours, he has displayed outstanding keenness, efficiency, courage and determination and has at all times set a fine example of loyal and devoted service.

Following his release, he attended the University of Toronto, after which he joined Kenting Aviation Limited. In 1951 he also joined the RCAF Auxiliary, serving with No. 400 Squadron in Toronto. He was still crisp, tidy, efficient, and outspoken, with the old habit, unforgiveable to many, of being perpetually right. However, in 1952 he left the Auxiliary, his job taking him to South America.

In his civil career, MacFadyen, working through a series of companies, became an expert on aerial surveys, including photography, airborne geophysics, and their application to integrated geological, soil, forest and hydrological studies. In Brazil he directed operations which led to the discovery of large ore bodies; in Peru his surveys indicated previously unknown potential hydro-electric resources; in Argentina he assisted in a national inventory of minerals. Currently he is the Executive Vice-President of the Northway Survey Corporation in Toronto, and Vice-President of Northway Consultants Limited.

Looking back on his Air Force career, he recalls events, personalities and opinions with crystal clarity. He views those days with mixed pride, sorrow and frustration, for he recognizes, with a paradoxical blend of arrogance and humility, that his virtues and skills were frequently and, on occasion understandably, misunderstood or misinterpreted by those who were offended by his perfectionism and blunt honesty. Perhaps, in a recent letter, he best summed up the war and his relation to it:

> Looking back on it, it seemed a great time of life, doing something so significant, judging oneself, exercising one's optimism and hope. The best friend a man ever had was an unknown person, a shadow moving in the cockpit of *another Mosquito* as he did his check before takeoff—only enough light to glisten off propellor blades, engines revving up to clear, turning onto the runway—he knew you were right behind him— both of us knew what we had to do. At some moments a man is a whole man.

MacKay
The First and the Last

Jets! German jets! German jet fighters! The Allied air forces were alive with talk of the new aircraft which was entering *Luftwaffe* service in the late summer and early fall of 1944. The enemy had sprung a series of new weapons on its opponents that year including the *V-1* pilotless flying bomb and the mysterious *V-2* rocket. Intelligence reports mentioned the jet fighters with increasing frequency. From the Normandy front had come the first sightings of *Me 262* fighter-bombers making occasional attacks. September 1944 had brought additional sightings. The new Messerschmitts were active and pilots of the Second Tactical Air Force were becoming more familiar with the lean, nasty jets which seemed so fast as to be invulnerable. Were they indeed so—invulnerable?

Early in the afternoon of October 5, 1944, No. 401 (Ram) Squadron was patrolling at 13,000 feet in the Nijmegen area. The twelve *Spitfires*, led by Squadron Leader R.I.A. Smith DFC, were on a northeasterly course when an *Me 262* jet fighter appeared flying head-on to them but about 500 or 1,000 feet below. At the same instant it was identified, the German pilot apparently saw the *Spitfires* and began climbing to port. The neat formation broke every which way in a scramble to get a crack at the enemy. For a moment it seemed that a massive mid-air collision must occur.

Red Section, led by Flight Lieutenant Hedley Everard DFC, got in the first shots. Everard opened fire at a range of 900 yards and followed the jet as it began to spiral. Pieces were flying off it when it crossed in front of Flying Officer A.L. Sinclair of Blue Section. Sinclair fired and saw strikes but was crowded out by other aircraft, probably Everard, Flight Lieutenant R.M. Davenport, Flying Officer John MacKay, and the CO. All of these were hanging about the Messerschmitt, firing as it twisted amid a storm of shells. For all its speed and firepower, the jet was caught like a fish in a net.

Everard was falling behind as the '262 drew away, trailing white smoke. Davenport emptied his guns into the German plane. Squadron Leader Smith could see both engine nacelles burning as he attacked. Then John MacKay came tearing in. He saw strikes about the rear fuselage. Not enough lead! He made corrections and fired again. Strikes on the wing roots—much better! At that moment Smith swooped in to administer the *coup de grace*. Burning like a torch, the "jet job" almost rammed the CO, then plunged into the ground and exploded. Here was triumph indeed! The jet *could* be brought down!

Smith, MacKay, Everard, Sinclair, and Davenport were each credited with one-fifth of the kill. Theirs was the first jet destroyed by Commonwealth air forces and only the second shot down in aerial combat (a pair of *P-47's* had forced one into the deck ten days before).

Nine years later one of the principals of this combat was again in action, this time in Korea. It was June 30, 1953. Although the RCAF had no combat units in that country, several Canadian fighter pilots were attached to American *F-86* wings to gain combat experience. Although they were limited to a short tour of fifty sorties, the Canadians had destroyed eight *MiG-15* jet fighters. Flight Lieutenant E.A. Glover alone had accounted for three, winning both a Commonwealth and an American DFC in the process.

On this day the air war reached a peak of ferocious fighting in which sixteen *MiGs* were shot down—a one-day record for the war. Early in the afternoon Squadron Leader John MacKay was leading three American-manned *Sabres* over North Korea when they spotted a lone *MiG* on the tails of four friendly aircraft. MacKay closed in on the enemy jet and opened fire, scoring strikes around the tail section. A black object rose out of the *MiG*; the pilot had bailed out and MacKay had another victory to his credit. His *MiG-15* was the last shot down by a Canadian during the Korean War, which ended a month later. Indeed, this was the last time that an RCAF pilot has fired his guns in combat. MacKay was one of the first Canadians to be involved in battle with jet aircraft; he is also probably the last to do so as well.

He was born at Arbakka, a village near Winnipeg, on February 15, 1920. His full name was John MacKay Mahachak, but he dropped the Austrian surname while attending school in Alberta. In 1940-41 he held a number of odd jobs—hard rock miner, machinist, and fireman on steamships. Finally, in September 1941, he enlisted in the RCAF.

He followed the routine training pattern, going from No. 5 Initial Training School (Belleville) to No. 21 Elementary Training School (Chatham, New Brunswick) and then to No. 9 Service Flying Training School (Summerside, Prince Edward Island). He won his wings on July 3, 1942 and was commissioned. There followed a ten week course at the Flying Instructor's School, Trenton, after which he was posted to No. 6 Service Flying Training School at Dunnville, Ontario. From September 1942 until July 1943 he taught others the whims of *Harvards*.

At length he was posted overseas, arriving in Britain on October 16, 1943. Further training followed, on *Masters* and *Spitfires*. Finally, on August 5, 1944 he joined the redoubtable No. 401 Squadron, then based at Beny-sur-Mer in Normandy. The unit was then under Squadron Leader Hugh Trainor DFC, an outstanding commander.

Four days after reporting in, MacKay was on operations. By the end of August he had flown 26 sorties, carried out dive-bombing attacks, seen his first dogfights, and known the loss of flying mates. On August 19 the squadron bumped into 40 German fighters, shooting down one and damaging two without loss. MacKay's initiation to aerial combat was followed up the next day when the Rams bounced 20 *Fw 190's* and shot down two, again without loss.

Early in September the Canadian fighter wings began moving forward, following the Allied armies which were hounding the Germans out of France and Belgium. As they advanced, the Allied airmen were able to see for themselves what their strafing and dive-bombing had accomplished. All about lay the battered wrecks of enemy vehicles.

There were a lot of changes that month. No. 401 occupied five airfields in turn before it settled down at Le Culot, Belgium, on September 21. Two days before, the CO had been shot down for the second time in a month, this time falling into enemy hands. His place was taken by R.I.A. Smith. Somehow the Rams missed most of the staggering air battles over the Nijmegen bridges. Nevertheless, they did have a few scraps with enemy aircraft, and in one of these MacKay claimed a *Bf 109* damaged.

Early in October the squadron moved to Holland, finally establishing itself at Volkel. The war in the West was grinding to a near-halt as German defences stiffened and the Allies found their supply lines stretched to the limit. The winter of 1944-45 was grim and dour, with foul weather intensifying the feeling of stalemate.

For two months, mid-October to mid-December, the air war was slack. The *Luftwaffe* needed time to refit, rearm, and retrain. It had become an on-again, off-again air force, incapable of sustaining severe losses or providing consistent cover to German troops. Canadian pilots found life a series of armed reconnaissance patrols, strafing trucks and trains, bombing bridges, and being shot at by every German infantryman, machine gunner, and anti-aircraft crew west of the Rhine.

On December 6 the squadron moved again, bedding down at Heesch, Holland. It appeared that the *Luftwaffe* was still hibernating. Ten days later the Allied front nearly collapsed when panzer troops punched into the Ardennes. With the Battle of the Bulge the air war took on new life.

That was apparent on December 17. No. 401 was taking off, its *Spitfires* loaded with 500-lb bombs, when five *Bf 109's* streaked across the field. The *Spits* unloaded their bombs as quickly as possible, but by then the Messerschmitts were gone. Henceforward, however, sightings of hostile aircraft were more frequent. On Christmas Day a real scrap ensued.

The Rams celebrated the day by bouncing two *Bf 109's*. Both exploded in mid-air, one of them falling to MacKay. The debris damaged one *Spitfire* which returned safely to base. Hedley Everard, newly appointed as CO, wasn't so lucky. A chunk of Messerschmitt damaged his *Spit* and he ended up in a POW camp.

On New Year's Day the Rams were taxiing out for a patrol when a formation of 40 German fighters swept over the field. The *Luftwaffe* was attacking! Within a minute the *Spitfires* had scrambled. There was no time to form sections, no chance to plan interceptions. It was every man for himself.

MacKay picked up an *Fw 190* and gave chase, firing short bursts all the time, but the German was jinking wildly. Gradually the *Spit's* ammunition dribbled away. At last the *'190* straightened out. MacKay fired a one-second burst and the enemy fighter exploded. Yet the battle had only started. The rest of this incredible encounter is best described in the terse language of the combat report:

Chased a *190* into enemy territory. On turning back I lost rest of the section. I started returning to base flying on the deck. On reaching Nijmegen flak opened up on me when I pulled up, so headed for the deck again and noticed two aircraft coming in from the east. Broke into the aircraft, saw *Tempest* closing on an *Fw. 190*. The *Fw. 190* started to turn sharply. In about one turn *Fw. 190* was almost on *Tempest's* tail, so I engaged *Fw. 190* on the deck. I fired short bursts but ammo was exhausted. I closed right in to 30 or 40 yards. *Fw. 190* attempted to do a sharp climbing turn to port out of a shallow dive. His port wing and nose of aircraft struck ice of lake below and blew up.

On pulling up from dive sighted *Me. 109* from above heading East. After three-quarters turn got on his tail and forced him down on the deck. After taking violent evasive action he was forced to straighten out for a second. He was in a slight dive and struck an open field. He bounced into some trees and broke in pieces.

These two victories, gained when he was alone and not firing, seemed so incredible that the Intelligence Officer at first refused to give credit for them. Subsequently, pilots of No. 401 Squadron searched for the enemy wrecks and located them exactly where MacKay had said they would be. Army observers added confirmation, although a half-share of one kill was awarded to the *Tempest* pilot. MacKay was immediately recommended for the Distinguished Flying Cross.

On January 14, 1945 he achieved a clean hat-trick, scoring three unaided victories in a single sortie. During a mid-morning sweep the squadron discovered several *Fw 190's* taking off from an airfield in Holland. The *Spitfires* put their noses down and caught the enemy cold. MacKay got close to one and set it alight. Another appeared over the treetops coming at him almost head-on. A two-second burst of cannon and machine gun shells made this one burn too. Minutes later he attempted to sneak up on two *Fw 190's*. Just as he was about to shoot he looked around for his wingman. There wasn't a *Spitfire* about; where his wingman should have been sat an evil-looking *Fw 190*. MacKay broke viciously to port. The German pilot tried to follow but lost control, went into a spin, and crashed.

It was an eventful day for No. 401. Five German fighters were shot down, but the Rams had taken losses. MacKay's wingman, Flight Lieutenant R.J. Land, never came home, a victim either of flak or of the *'190* which had almost nailed MacKay himself.

Late in January 1945 MacKay went on leave. On February 22 the commander of "A" Flight, Flight Lieutenant Freddy Murray DFC, was shot down by flak and captured. MacKay returned to the squadron to take over Murray's duties. In no time at all he was back into the swing of things. On March 1 the squadron was bounced by 40 enemy fighters, some of them obviously flown by *Luftwaffe* veterans. In a rag-tag dogfight MacKay shot down one. The Rams' tally sheet indicated the savagery of the battle—four German aircraft destroyed, one *Spitfire* missing, and another damaged beyond repair.

MacKay now had seven enemy machines downed, plus shares in two others. German aircraft were being squeezed into a shrinking *Reich*, which made hunting easier, even if there was less game. MacKay took his share of the pickings; before his tour ended at the close of April he was credited with the following:

March 28, 1945 - two *Bf 109's* destroyed
April 16, 1945 - three *Ar 234* jets damaged
April 20, 1945 - one *Bf 109* destroyed.

Each of these encounters involved something especially dangerous. In the first, MacKay attacked a small enemy formation and had to maneuver while trying unsuccessfully to jettison his long-range fuel tank. In the second, he strafed the enemy jets in the face of a virtual wall of anti-aircraft fire. The final victory was gained in one of the most memorable actions of No. 401's history.

Appropriately, it was Hitler's birthday. The squadron was on an armed reconnaissance when they discovered a group of German fighters taking off from a grass strip south of Schwerin. There were more enemy kites at 10,000 feet and still more at 20,000. Squadron Leader Bill Klersy did what was most natural for him; he attacked, and the other *Spitfires* followed him down.

It seemed as though everybody had a crack at something, and no fewer than ten pilots submitted claims totalling eleven enemy aircraft destroyed and three damaged. MacKay's contribution was a '*109* shot down in flames with a single long-range burst. The squadron was jubilant over its victory, but there was also the familiar note of sadness. Flying Officer R.W. Anderson had been shot down and killed.

In the summer of 1945 Flight Lieutenant John MacKay, now wearing the ribbon of the DFC with the rosette denoting a Bar, was with the General Support Unit of No. 83 Group, checking equipment, weapons, and tactics. In December he went to No. 412 Squadron, then part of the Occupation forces in Germany. On the 19th MacKay was taking off when his engine failed. He crashed while attempting to force-land from 150 feet. His injuries kept him hospitalized for several weeks. Finally, in March 1946, he returned to Canada.

Having chosen to make the RCAF his career, he gained a reputation as a dedicated officer who demanded and got the best from those under him. At various times he commanded three fighter squadrons—Nos. 416, 439, and 444—as well as the Central Flying School at Trenton. He reached the rank of Wing Commander on January 1, 1957.

He put in more than 3,000 flying hours with the RCAF. From the *Tiger Moths* and *Finches* of his training days he had gone to *Spitfires*, *Masters*, and *Tempests*. During his post-war career he flew the *Sabre*, *CF-100*, *Lincoln*, *Meteor*, *Vampire*, *T-33*, *Expeditor*, *Hunter*, *Athena*, *Mitchell*, and *Valetta*. Among his many ribbons was that of the American Air Medal, awarded him during his brief tour in Korea.

Wing Commander John MacKay retired from the RCAF in February 1969, having been in the force for more than 27 years. He now resides in Surrey, British Columbia.

McKnight
Napoleon in the Cockpit

In the air terminal at Calgary International Airport an impressive plaque honours the memory of Flying Officer W.L. McKnight, while one of that city's main road arteries is named for him. These memorials are fitting, for "Willie" McKnight was the most outstanding Canadian fighter pilot in the first half of the war.

In the autumn of 1939 the Royal Air Force included hundreds of Canadians among its aircrews. These were the young men who had enlisted in that force, rather than waiting for the RCAF to expand. As a dramatic gesture the RAF formed a "Canadian" squadron, No. 242, in November 1939. Subsequently, it was blooded in the Battle of France, performed admirably at Dunkirk, and touched the peaks of greatness during the Battle of Britain. Although it existed until the end of the war, its Canadian content became diluted as British pilots were posted in while the original Canucks were killed, wounded, or posted to senior positions elsewhere. By the Spring of 1941 No. 242 had ceased to be a uniquely Canadian squadron. The career of "Willie" McKnight coincided with the unit's "Canadian" period.

It is always tempting to apply superlatives to successful fighter pilots, but in his case they come more easily than in most. He was an ebullient scrapper who fought like a madman. He was very dark, very handsome, and very short. His squadron-mate, Stan Turner, described him as a man with a Napoleon complex. Squadron Leader Douglas

Bader was impressed by McKnight's incredibly keen eyesight—a characteristic which also distinguished "Buzz" Beurling. It is impossible to say whether his successes were due to psychological or physiological factors. Whatever it was, his achievement was simply this: to meet the *Luftwaffe* when it was at its peak in strength, training, equipment and morale, and to destroy more than 16 enemy aircraft in six months.

He was born in Edmonton on November 18, 1918 and educated there. He served in the militia from 1935 to 1938, and also attended medical school at the University of Alberta. Suddenly, early in 1939, he yielded to the flying bug, sailed to England, and enlisted in the RAF. He was completing his pilot training when the Germans invaded Poland.

On November 6 McKnight was posted to No. 242 Squadron. The commanding officer, Squadron Leader F.M. Gobeil, was an RCAF officer serving on exchange duties with the RAF, but all the other pilots were CAN/RAF personnel including Flight Lieutenants D.R. Miller and J.L. Sullivan, Flying Officer R. Coe, and Pilot Officers J.W. Graafstra, R.D. Grassick, L.E. Chambers, F.L. Hill, J.W. Mitchell, H.L. Niccolls, M.K. Brown, G.A. Madore, D.F. MacQueen, R.H. Weins, D.F. Jones, J.B. Smiley, A.H. Deacon, J.B. Latta, J.F. Howitt, W.A. Waterton, P.S. Turner, and McKnight. By September 29, 1941, when Grassick was posted away, virtually all of these "old originals" were gone. Half of them, including McKnight, were dead.

Initially the squadron personnel were involved with intensive training in tactics, aircraft recognition, radio procedures, signals, navigation, armament and rigging. At last, in January 1940, the first *Hurricanes* arrived. That winter was particularly fierce, however, and as much time was spent in shovelling snow as in flying training. The pilots dreamed of spending Easter in France, where the British Expeditionary Force guarded the northern borders. Nevertheless, No. 242 was not declared operational until March 24. The next day five pilots, McKnight among them, flew the squadron's first operational sorties—convoy patrols in protection of British coastal shipping.

No. 242 began moving to France early in April, but when the Germans invaded Norway the transfer was cancelled and the squadron held back in England as a reserve. Then, on May 10, the enemy launched its great offensive in the West. Holland was overrun in five days, the Belgian army was hurled back, and German armoured divisions supported by dive bombers began to outflank the French in a thrust through the Ardennes. The blitzkrieg hammered the Allies mercilessly. The Battle of France had begun.

The squadron was not committed as a unit to the battle. Instead, about half its pilots flew to France where they were attached to Nos. 85, 607 and 615 Squadrons. In the subsequent retreats many records of these three units were lost, and the actions in which No. 242's pilots participated are recorded with scant detail.

McKnight flew to Abbeville on May 14 where he was attached to No. 615 Squadron. Within six days it had changed its base three times, and by the 21st it had been withdrawn to Britain. By then, however, McKnight had drawn his and No. 242's first blood.

It happened during an evening patrol on May 19. Four *Hurricanes* were flying near Cambrai when two groups of *Bf 109's*, totalling fifteen in all, attacked the little formation. McKnight was flying in the No. 4 position when he spotted the Germans. He shouted a warning over the radio, then went into a steep climbing turn to port. This brought him up behind one Messerschmitt. At 250 yards range he pressed the trigger button and let the eight Browning .303's do the rest. The *'109* began to smoke. Three more jabs on the trigger did the trick. The enemy fighter dived into the ground.

Once No. 242's pilots had returned to their unit they were granted seven days' leave to recover from the ordeal in France. Within 48 hours this was cancelled as the situation on the continent worsened. The British armies were being isolated from the French and Belgians. They had no option but to retreat in as orderly a fashion as possible to the coast. The Canadian squadron was rushed to Manston, in the south of England. For the next few days the pilots operated from French airfields, returning to Manston in the evenings. It was a tragic time. Three pilots were lost and one wounded on the 23rd, and two more were lost on the 24th. After that, they operated only from Manston. All French airfields near the BEF had been overrun by the enemy. No. 242 was now committed to providing air cover over the port and beaches of Dunkirk, where more than 330,000 soldiers were being evacuated.

The squadron was out every day from May 27 until June 2. The pilots did not know that they were participating in a near-miraculous victory; all they saw were ships and troops and the *Luftwaffe* harassing both. Their job was to chase those air fleets away. For its part, the RAF was now operating at full strength and from secure airfields. For the first time since the battle opened the force was meeting the enemy on reasonably equal terms. It was also the first time that the German air force received a decidedly bloody nose.

The air battles over Dunkirk were, in a sense, a draw. The RAF claimed 390 enemy machines destroyed, and later scaled this down to 262, for a loss of 106 fighters. The *Luftwaffe* actually lost 132, some of which probably fell to anti-aircraft fire. Nevertheless, the enemy failed to halt the evacuation, and that was a defeat in which Fighter Command played a significant part.

McKnight did more than his share in those epic days. On May 28, during an afternoon patrol, the squadron encountered twelve *Bf 109's* over Ostend. As No. 242 climbed to attack them, some 60 Messer-schmitts emerged from the clouds and bounced the *Hurricanes* from all sides. Pilot Officer Stan Turner shot down one *'109* and McKnight sent another into the sea before the second batch of bandits hit. A storm of lead battered McKnight's machine, knocking out the oil and coolant systems. Only a spectacular dive into the clouds saved him. Back at Manston, the squadron tallied up victories and losses. Two *Hurricanes* had not returned.

On May 29 several new factors came into play. British troops in the Dunkirk perimeter had now been concentrated within strong defences, which simplified the task of the RAF. Moreover, the Air Officer Commanding Fighter Command, Air Marshal Sir Hugh Dowding, resolved to reduce the number of patrols over Dunkirk while doubling the strength of the remaining patrols. The new tactics left the beaches open to attack on several occasions, but it also resulted in RAF casualties being slashed while *Luftwaffe* losses rose sharply. That, at any rate, was what Fighter Command believed, for 65 German machines were claimed shot down against a loss of sixteen fighters. The enemy believed they had downed 68 British machines while losing fourteen of their own.

Late that afternoon No. 242 despatched nine pilots to patrol Dunkirk in company with No. 229 Squadron, also flying *Hurricanes*, while two *Spitfire* squadrons, Nos. 64 and 610, provided top cover. Near Dunkirk the leader spotted anti-aircraft fire and turned to investigate. No. 229's pilots saw the enemy first and dived to attack, followed by No. 242. At that moment 25 Messerschmitts plunged from above and the ensuing dogfight raged from 10,000 feet down to ground level.

A *Hurricane* attacking a *'109* was in turn attacked by another *'109*. McKnight bounced the second German fighter and fired a four-second burst at point-blank range. His victim rolled over on its side, then dived into the sea. Another Messerschmitt was chasing a *Hurricane*. McKnight dropped in behind and shot it down. Above him was a German bomber—a twin-engined *Do 17*. The *Hurricane* went into a steeply climbing turn. From the port rear quarter McKnight cut loose with a series of short bursts. The first disabled the enemy's port engine and the last set the bomber alight. It finally crashed nine miles east of Dunkirk. His ammunition expended, McKnight headed for home. No. 242 had done well, submitting claims for five enemy machines destroyed, three probables and two damaged without loss to them-selves.

The squadron flew two patrols the following day without encountering enemy aircraft. It was a different story on the 31st. No. 242 despatched eight *Hurricanes* to find and destroy a German observation balloon. They failed to locate their target but found instead a formation of enemy bombers heavily escorted by *Bf 110's*. Seven of the *Hurricanes* engaged the bombers but McKnight, lagging behind, found himself alone among some 25 *Bf 110's*. The overwhelming numerical odds probably favoured him, for the German escorts got in each other's way. Attacking one group of three Messerschmitts, he fired at a *'110* and saw it swerve. The German formation began to break up. Switching his fire to a second *'110*, he cut loose with devastating results. The enemy fighter collided with the first that McKnight had hit. Locked in a fatal embrace, the two Messerschmitts went down in flames.

McKnight's score was fantastic; in four days he had destroyed six enemy aircraft and his total was now seven machines. Later that day, during a second patrol, he damaged a *Bf 109*. Next day, June 1, he added two *Ju 87's* to his tally. In this engagement he and another pilot caught some fifteen of the enemy planes attacking ships off Dunkirk. His victims went straight into the sea, but during the action he expended all his ammunition. Undeterred, he continued to make feint attacks on the dive bombers until the enemy broke off the action. It was one of the *Luftwaffe's* worst days, for 29 enemy aircraft were shot down (the RAF claimed 78, then reduced that to 43). Fighter Command lost 31 aircraft. The Germans sank four destroyers and ten other vessels, but nevertheless more than 64,400 Allied soldiers escaped to fight again.

The action of June 1 virtually ended No. 242 Squadron's participation in the Dunkirk evacuation. There were still British forces operating in France, however, and between June 8 and 18th the squadron was sent back to the continent. It was to help cover the withdrawal from the Lower Seine area. Little could be done, however, and ultimately the pilots and groundcrews had to disentangle themselves from the confused retreat and evacuate to England.

Its morale shattered by the fiasco in France, No. 242 began to reassemble at Coltishall. Its members brooded over their losses. In the preceeding five weeks the unit had been credited with the destruction of more than twenty enemy aircraft, but it had lost eleven pilots. One consolation was the news that "Willie" McKnight had been awarded the Distinguished Flying Cross. Then, on June 20, a new commanding officer arrived—Squadron Leader Douglas Bader.

Bader was a remarkable man. In 1931 he had lost both legs following an air crash. Through sheer willpower he had driven himself on, refusing to accept the role of a cripple. He had been released from the RAF, but then had nagged his way back into the force. In the months ahead he would become a legend, shooting down more than twenty enemy aircraft and winning four decorations. For the moment, however, he was dedicated to whipping No. 242 back into shape. In this he was skilfully ruthless. Within a fortnight he had acquired new flight commanders, bullied the RAF supply organization into completely re-equipping the squadron, and had won the respect of every man from the lowest "erk" up.

No. 242 was back on an operational footing by mid-July. Unhappily, Coltishall was under the control of No. 12 Group in Fighter Command, the formation entrusted with the defence of the industrial Midlands. A few enemy aircraft were engaged, but for the greater part of July and August the frustrated pilots saw no action, although the Battle of Britain had begun and was then raging to the south. On August 30, however, the squadron flew to Duxford, closer to the main battle. That afternoon they became engaged in a veritable bloodbath.

The whole squadron—fourteen *Hurricanes*—was scrambled to meet a force of German aircraft that was heading for North Weald airfield. The enemy numbered between 70 and 100 machines, consisting of *He 111* bombers (erroneously identified as *Do 215's* at the time) with *Bf 110's* and a few *Bf 109's* as escorts. The action was short, sharp and savage. Led by Bader, the *Hurricanes* dived right into the middle of the German formations and started shooting. There were enough targets for everyone. McKnight bounced a *Bf 110* and with one burst shot it down in flames. He then attacked another from the port side and set it alight; it rolled over on its back and went down streaming smoke and flames. Another *'110* got on his tail but he turned steeply and came in behind the German. The chase went on from 10,000 to 1,000 feet while the enemy pilot weaved about in tight turns, McKnight all the while clinging to its tail like a burr. At last the Messerschmitt levelled off. From 30 yards range, the young Canadian opened fire. The enemy's starboard engine stopped, the port engine caught fire, and the *Bf 110* crashed in flames.

Another *Hurricane* drew up alongside. It was Bader. The CO looked at McKnight and held up two fingers. McKnight grinned and held up three fingers. Then they flew back to Duxford and a celebration. Not a single *Hurricane* had been hit, while the Germans had lost twelve aircraft. The enemy's objective, North Weald, had not been bombed. It had been a brilliant victory, and there would be many more like it in the future.

The squadron had no further contact with the enemy until September 7 and McKnight did not score again until the 9th. That day, while the Germans attacked London, No. 242 was scrambled to intercept more than 100 raiders approaching the capital from the north. This time the unit was accompanied by three other fighter squadrons, the whole formation being controlled by Bader. As the *Hurricanes* dived to attack the bombers, a number of escorting *Bf 109's* attempted to interfere. McKnight turned to face these opponents and in rapid succession shot down two Messerschmitts in flames. Another *'109* opened up from behind, however, and suddenly the *Hurricane* shook and rolled. Regaining control, McKnight dived out of the fight, one aileron having been shot away. He regained his base where he learned how lucky he had been. Two *Hurricanes* had been shot down and Pilot Officer K.M. Schlanders of St. John's, Newfoundland had been killed. On the other hand, No. 242 had claimed eleven of the enemy, and McKnight's personal score stood at fourteen destroyed plus one damaged.

The squadron was engaged in savage fighting on September 15 but McKnight had no opportunity to score. On the 18th it was a different story. That day five fighter squadrons, No. 242 among them, intercepted a formation of about 30 unescorted bombers. The result was a lopsided massacre. Practically every German plane was claimed as destroyed and Bader himself wrote that he had never before seen so many parachutes. McKnight shot down a *Do 17* and shared in the destruction of a *Ju 88*, in both instances having the satisfaction of watching the German crews bailing out. Postwar analysis has shown the overall RAF claims to have been exaggerated; possibly as few as four bombers were shot down.

McKnight's skill and daring brought new rewards. Late in September he was awarded a Bar to his DFC. No. 242 continued to score, but for a moment his personal tally ceased to grow. After the end of September enemy daylight raids petered out and combats were rare. Increasingly the *Luftwaffe* switched its bombers over to night operations while formations of *Bf 109's* carrying bombs harried the English coasts.

McKnight's final victory was scored against such a nuisance raider. On November 5, 1940 No. 242 was scrambled along with No. 19 Squadron to intercept roughly two dozen *Bf 109's* high over the Thames Estuary. Bader was leading the squadron and McKnight was leading a section when the enemy appeared some 3,000 feet above the *Hurricanes*. With the advantage of both height and performance the *'109's* proceeded to make zooming attacks, diving for a quick squirt and then climbing out of range. McKnight tried several times to attack a Messerschmitt without success.

Suddenly a *'109* passed in front of him and the hawk-eyed Canadian was on its tail. Once more he found himself in a long, screaming, diving chase which took the two aircraft from 27,000 down to 2,000 feet. From a range of 150 yards he opened fire and saw strikes. The Messerschmitt billowed smoke and waggled its wings. McKnight overhauled it and motioned to the German to land, but the enemy pilot opted to bail out. The day's action proved to be a draw between No. 242 and the *Luftwaffe*; the squadron's only victory had been McKnight's kill while on the debit side Pilot Officer Norris Hart, a Manitoban with four victories to his credit, had been shot down and killed.

No. 242 moved back to Coltishall in November, but the following month it was transferred to Martlesham Heath in anticipation of offensive action by Fighter Command. Insofar as the squadron was concerned, this began on January 10, 1941 when twelve *Hurricanes* escorted six *Blenheims* which bombed Guines airfield near Calais. Save for some moderate anti-aircraft fire, no opposition was reported.

Two days later, on January 12, low clouds hung over England and France. The squadron decided to resort to "Rhubarbs", low-level freelance strikes at enemy ground installations. Squadron Leader Bader and Flight Lieutenant Stan Turner carried out the first "Rhubarb" that morning, shooting up an E-boat and a drifter in mid-Channel. That strike fired everyone's enthusiasm so at 12.15 P.M. four more *Hurricanes* took off, piloted by Flying Officers McKnight, H.N. Tamblyn and B.A. Rogers and Pilot Officer M.K. Brown.

Near Gravelines, the fighters split up with McKnight and Brown going westwards while the others flew east. McKnight and his wingman machine-gunned an E-boat, then flew inland where they were subjected to intense and accurate anti-aircraft fire. Abruptly, a *Bf 109* appeared and Brown had to take evasive action. In the confusion he became separated from McKnight so he headed for home. Back at base he reported on the flight. Tamblyn and Rogers landed and filed an account of their sorties. McKnight never came home. Whether he fell to the flak or the German fighter was never determined. What was certain was that the "top gun" of No. 242 Squadron had passed from the scene—"gone for a Burton".

McLeod
Number Two

All the leading fighter aces of the war displayed aggressive qualities. Air fighting being an aggressive business, it was natural that top scorers would have to be so. One man, however, was driven by a personal demon. He was "Wally" McLeod and he hated to be Number Two. He was the highest-scoring RCAF pilot of the war but another flyer, Beurling of the RAF, was the top Canadian ace. McLeod's avowed goal was to surpass Beurling's record and he died in the attempt.

"Wally" McLeod was born on December 17, 1915 in Regina. When he was three years old his mother died of influenza. He and his two sisters were raised by their father, a Saskatchewan schools inspector. The boy was active in local militia units between 1930 and 1935, while he was completing his education. For one year he taught school; then for two years he worked as a bookkeeper, salesman and junior accountant. Finally, in 1937, he went into business for himself as a theatre owner and operator. He remained in this line of work until September 1940, when he enlisted in the RCAF.

He progressed rapidly through the training scheme where he showed a flair in signals and airmanship. If there was any fault to be found in him, it was that he was overconfident and excessively talkative. Nevertheless, in April 1941 he was awarded his wings at Camp Borden and immediately posted overseas with the rank of Pilot Officer.

There followed the usual advanced training in Britain. For the next few months he led a roving existence, going first to No. 132 Squadron, next to No. 485, then to No. 602 and finally, in December 1941, to No. 411. He was with that unit for five months, during which time he damaged two German fighters and pranged a *Spitfire* during a night flying exercise. In May 1942, however, he wangled a posting to Malta. For the next five months his life was tied up with Nos. 603 and 1435 Squadrons in the furious defence of that dot of land.

His introduction to air fighting on Malta was rude and to the point. On his second day on the island he was flying as wingman to his CO, Squadron Leader Lord Douglas Hamilton. They were attacking a *Z.1007* bomber when McLeod glimpsed a fighter behind him which he mistook for a *Spitfire*. The aircraft was, in fact, an *RE.2001* and the error became apparent when its pilot riddled McLeod's fuselage and almost shot the tailplane off the *Spitfire*. Fortunately he was able to limp home, greatly chastened.

McLeod's record on Malta proved to be one of near-misses and notable successes. Five times his aircraft was badly damaged and twice he was shot down—once by another *RE.2001* which hit his oil cooler and once by a *Ju 88*. On the other hand, he blasted at least eleven enemy aircraft out of the sky and his Malta score may have been as high as thirteen destroyed , though existing records are vague.

His first victory was over an *MC.202* which, he insisted, "went into the drink from sheer fright". In discussing the action, he went on to explain:

> The Eye-ties always go in for weird and wonderful aerobatics which is about the best thing they do. This chap was hit by my fire but I don't think he was out of control. He just appeared to panic and hit the sea in a steep spiral dive.

His second confirmed victim was a *Bf 109* which was hit in the fuel tank and exploded. The German pilot was thrown clear and parachuted into the sea. McLeod flew low and saw the downed flyer wave, apparently quite cheerfully. The Canadian dropped his dinghy, "to show that I had no hard feelings either", but the German made no effort to climb into it. A rescue launch crew soon discovered why. The enemy pilot had been hit in the chest by a cannon shell and died in the launch.

McLeod had to spend at least some time on the ground. During enemy raids he took refuge in the underground shelters, unlike some pilots who, in a spirit of bravado, preferred to stay on the surface. The shelters, 60 feet down and blasted out of solid rock, offered a sporting chance at catching up on some sleep.

Yet if he refused to tempt fate while on *terra firma*, McLeod showed tremendous zest for battle when he was airborne. Once, in a scrap between eight *Spitfires* and 70 enemy aircraft, his wings were holed and his flaps shot away. With only one cannon working, he closed in on a *Ju 88* and shot it down. In the fury of the Battle of Malta he was promoted to Flight Lieutenant and made a flight commander in No. 1435 Squadron. In October he was awarded the Distinguished Flying Cross.

That month proved to be the most dramatic of his stay in Malta. In three consecutive days, October 11-13, he destroyed five and damaged four enemy aircraft, and in the following eight days he added two more fighters to his bag of "kills", as well as one more damaged. He thus became the second-ranking Canadian ace in Malta.

His most brilliant feat was accomplished at dusk on the 11th. As a force of 25 *Ju 88's* approached the island from out of the sun, McLeod led four *Spitfires* down onto six of the bombers. One of the German aircraft was plastered by him and went down, but an enemy gunner put a burst into the *Spit's* engine. Nursing the motor, McLeod managed to shoot down another bomber, then led his formation into nine more Junkers. He finally crash-landed at base in the middle of another bombing raid.

His last sortie was flown on October 22, 1942, when he destroyed another *MC.202*. Following that, it was back to Britain and then to Canada for Flight Lieutenant McLeod, who by now had been awarded a Bar to his DFC. During his tour on Malta he had endured terrible hardships. "It was worth it all and a lot more", he said. "Malta is what I would call the *Spitfire* pilot's Happy Hunting Ground". Perhaps he really meant it and perhaps it was a bold cover. The truth is that McLeod emerged a physical and emotional wreck. He had lost 25 pounds, was irritable, slept fitfully, and frequently had nightmares concerning air disasters. His flying was seedy. All this flashed a warning to Air Force doctors—combat fatigue.

There was, moreover, another item which gnawed at him. Throughout his brilliant tour he had been overshadowed by the single-minded Beurling. Virtually every news release about McLeod mentioned the other man as well. What their personal attitudes to one another may have been will never be known, but when "Wally" left Malta a newsman wrote:

> He laments that he hasn't Screwball Beurling's 'shooting-eye', or he's sure he would have definitely destroyed most of his 'probables' and 'damaged'.

Two years later, the demon was still evident to McLeod's superior, Wing Commander J.E. Johnson, and throughout his second tour it manifested itself in McLeod's restlessness and his determination to see every dogfight through to the end, regardless of the circumstances.

McLeod remained in England for two months, recuperating from his Malta ordeal. In December 1942 he was repatriated to Canada, and in March 1943 he joined the staff of No. 1 Operational Training Unit, Bagotville, Quebec. He proved to be a first-rate gunnery instructor, raising the general level of accuracy by 50 percent.

Unhappily, he did not conform to the ideal picture of a hero, which usually depicts the successful warrior as a quiet, modest man. McLeod was overconfident, fully aware of his reputation, and anxious to impress all within earshot. These attitudes, coupled with excessive drinking, led to several unpleasant incidents. Only his service record prevented him from being censured, but at last his superiors took him in hand. An ultimatum was laid down—buck up or forget about another overseas tour. "Wally" McLeod bucked up. Admitting that by temperament he was more suited to operational flying than to instructing, he nevertheless pulled himself together for a two month probationary period. In November 1943, having met the terms of the ultimatum, he requested an overseas posting. On this occasion his record was reviewed with more sympathy.

In January 1944 he left Bagotville and proceeded overseas once more, this time to receive a half-stripe and to assume command of No. 443 Squadron, which was equipping with *Spitfire IX's*. Once the squadron had been whipped into shape it commenced operations on April 13, 1944. Six days later McLeod showed he was back in form by shooting down a *Do 217* bomber over Belgium. On May 5 he destroyed an *Fw 190* in an engagement that showed clearly how, once he had sunk his teeth into an opponent, he would never let go.

He was leading a section of No. 443 Squadron south of Brussels that day when a small formation of enemy fighters was spotted flying at 1,000 feet. The *Spitfires* dived in from astern. The alert Germans broke to port and the two formations dissolved in a whirling dogfight. McLeod lost his wingman and simultaneously discovered that his belly tank would not jettison. According to the rules he should have gotten out of the fight immediately. Instead, he gave chase to a *'190* which apparently was heading for home. For ten minutes he pursued the German at tree-top level until finally the enemy pilot attempted to turn. McLeod cut him off, snapped off a burst, and saw strikes. The *'190* rolled over on its back. From dead astern and only 75 yards range, McLeod fired again. The Focke-Wulf crashed in flames and exploded. The victor circled momentarily, photographing the wreck with his ciné gun camera, then flew home. He was accorded an angry welcome by Wing Commander Johnson, who pointed out that he had taken unnecessary risks.

June 1944 was a happy though hectic month, so much so that near the end it became increasingly difficult for the mechanics to keep twelve squadron aircraft serviceable at any one time. D-Day was, of course, the highlight event and on that day McLeod flew four uneventful patrols. On June 15 No. 443 Squadron moved from Ford in Sussex to the French resort area of St. Croix-sur-Mer in Normandy, but not for a holiday. That month the squadron destroyed nine enemy aircraft and lost five pilots.

McLeod's share was four destroyed—a *Do 217* shot down about 11.00 P.M. on June 14, apparently en route to the Allied beachhead with a load of glider bombs; a *Bf 109* flown by an experienced enemy pilot, whose tail he shot off on the 16th; and two *Fw 190's* which he blasted to bits with the expenditure of only 52 cannon shells on the 23rd.

Yet not all actions were so successful. On several occasions, enemy fighters escaped into clouds before they could be engaged. On July 12 McLeod was within 350 yards of an enemy formation when his engine began to act up and he could get no closer. On the other hand, during July he added two more German fighters to his growing bag. On the 20th he chased a lone *Fw 190* whose pilot finally bailed out before a shot could be fired. Ten days later, following another extended pursuit "on the deck", he shot down a *Bf 109*. It was victim No. 19 or 21 (depending on how one interpreted the records from Malta) and McLeod's last.

No. 443 saw few enemy aircraft during August, but it was particularly active in ground strafing during the Battle of Falaise, when the remnants of the German armies attempted to retreat through a narrow corridor which was mercilessly attacked from the air. On one day, August 18, No. 443 claimed to have destroyed or damaged no fewer than 78 enemy vehicles. The other side of the coin was that such low-level work resulted in frequent flak hits on the *Spitfires*. During the course of one sortie McLeod lost an old friend.

Unlike most squadron commanders, who flew first one and then another aircraft, McLeod almost always flew the same machine. It was MK 636, a *Spitfire IX*, and on its fuselage were painted the codes "2I" (identifying No. 443 Squadron) and "E" (the letter assigned to this particular aircraft). Since joining the squadron, all but one of his victories had been scored on this machine. On August 17, however, following an attack on enemy transport vehicles, he discovered that his glycol tank was leaking, probably due to ground fire, and the engine temperature was soaring. He managed to reach Allied lines near Falaise before the *Merlin* cut and he crash-landed. He was uninjured. Shortly afterwards, an artillery-spotting *Auster* delivered him back to his unit. Three days later he went on leave to England.

His fine work, notable in leading No. 443, had led to a recommendation for another decoration. Early in September it was announced that he had been awarded the Distinguished Service Order. The newspapers started a fresh round of stories about "Wally" McLeod, the RCAF's leading ace and the second-ranking Canadian fighter pilot of the war. He was still only Number Two. Determined to change that, he became even more meticulous, checking his cannons and studying his combat films.

McLeod returned to operations early in September, but almost immediately the squadron was pulled out of the line for a rest while Allied airfield construction crews attempted to catch up with the advancing armies to provide fields for the tactical air forces. When the front began to gel in Holland and Belgium, No. 443 Squadron went back into action. On September 26 McLeod led his boys into a scrap with a dozen enemy aircraft near Arnhem, but the dogfight was inconclusive and no claims were filed. Next day, the 27th, was very different.

The squadron was patrolling between Nijmegen and Venlo, led by Wing Commander Johnson, when nine *Bf 109's* were seen flying at 1,000 feet. The *Spitfires* bounced and shot down five of the enemy, but McLeod was missing when they returned to base. He had been last seen climbing after a Messerschmitt which had the advantage of position. Later he was found in the wreckage of his *Spitfire*, probably having fallen to the guns of that *'109*. The man described by his superiors as "one of the outstanding fighter pilots produced in this war" the RCAF's "Eagle of Malta" "Wally" McLeod, was dead.

McNair
He Kept Coming Back

Few fighter pilots lived through such a hazardous career as that experienced by Robert Wendell "Buck" McNair, who survived battles, ditching, fires, and near-incredible escapes. McNair was a human boomerang who kept coming back. He was not only a crack pilot; he was also one of the RCAF's most successful wing leaders. His death in 1971 followed a long, courageous struggle with cancer.

The son of a railway engineer, McNair was born in Springfield, Nova Scotia, on May 15, 1919. He was educated in Edmonton, Alberta, and Prince Albert, Saskatchewan, where he graduated from Grade XII in 1937. He had developed an interest in radio operations, and was employed by the Saskatchewan Department of Natural Resources in the summer of 1936. Following high school, he joined Canadian Airways as a radio operator and handyman, remaining with that firm until 1939.

It was natural that when war broke out he would seek to join the RCAF. There was a waiting list ahead of him, but on June 28, 1940 he was sworn into the force. He then followed a path well worn by other trainees: No. 1 Initial Training School (Toronto), No. 7 Elementary Flying Training School (Windsor), No. 31 Service Flying Training School (Kingston), with his wings parade coming in March 1941. Within three months he had joined No. 411 Squadron, then forming at Digby on *Spitfires*. The unit became operational on

August 21, and Pilot Officer McNair flew his first sortie the following day.

His career narrowly escaped an abrupt end early in September. One evening he and another pilot took off in a *Magister* training aircraft, with McNair as passenger. He was feeling sleepy, so he loosened his harness and dozed off. His friend, unaware of these actions, chose this time to practice aerobatics in the agile little "Maggie". McNair awoke with a start, just as he was thrown from the aircraft. At low altitude he pulled the ripcord of his parachute and landed safely. That was the first of many escapes.

On September 27, 1941, No. 411 Squadron suffered its first loss when a *Spitfire* was shot down, though its pilot was saved. In turn, the unit submitted its first operational claim—a *Bf 109* damaged by McNair. Then, on October 13, he claimed the first "destroyed" for No. 411, and in the process he was shot down himself.

The Digby Wing (Nos. 266, 411 and 412 Squadrons) had covered the withdrawal of a bomber force from France and was en route home when someone reported *Bf 109's* near Boulogne. Peering down, McNair spotted them almost three miles below. He rashly dived to attack. Presently his lone *Spitfire* was closing in on seven enemy fighters which were circling a pilot in the Channel. He got on the tail of one and fired a burst at a range of 250 yards. The German went into a steep diving turn to the left. Another "squirt" from 60 yards finished the job; the *'109* went straight into the sea. Satisfied, McNair set course for home.

He was still a green pilot, however, and failed to keep a proper lookout. Without warning he was attacked by a *Bf 109* whose pilot scored strikes on McNair's engine with the first burst. Evasive action did not help; the German remained glued to his tail and knocked more holes in the *Spit* before overshooting. With his cockpit full of smoke McNair fired at his assailant, saw his bullets hitting home, and noted that the hood had flown off the Messerschmitt. Now, however, flames were beginning to lick around the *Spitfire's* fuselage, so McNair pulled up to 400 feet and bailed out. Fifteen minutes later an Air/Sea Rescue launch picked him up from his dinghy.

Thereafter No. 411 was engaged mainly in routine sweeps and in converting from *Spitfire II's* to *Spitfire V's*. In December 1941 the squadron was advised that volunteers were needed for "overseas" duty (i.e. Asia and the Middle East). Virtually everyone wanted to go, but initially only two were chosen. In the meantime McNair's luck held up. On January 17, 1942 he strafed troops and a freight train, then flew back to base despite flak hits in the port wing and radiator. Early in February came welcome news; he was going to No. 249 Squadron in Malta.

The island fortress had been under siege for nearly two years.

The scale of enemy attacks had varied over that period, with an exceptionally heavy blitz having been launched in the Spring of 1941. *Luftwaffe* operations were particularly subject to change as enemy aircraft were switched about from Sicily to Africa to Russia. Early in 1942 the raids had been stepped up again, with 669 tons of bombs being dropped in January and 1,020 tons in February. The appearance of the *Bf 109F* had made life particularly hard for the *Hurricanes* defending Malta; by March 6 there were only 32 available. The island was valued as a base for submarines, destroyers, reconnaissance aircraft, and torpedo bombers, but the mounting attacks were neutralizing Malta, forcing the curtailment of offensive operations and even the withdrawal of strike forces.

McNair's arrival coincided with the delivery of the first *Spitfires* to Malta. Fifteen of these were flown off the carrier HMS *Eagle* on March 7, and a further 16 arrived on the 21st and 29th. For its part, the *Luftwaffe* was not going to allow a build-up on the island. Beginning on March 20 they launched a four-day blitz which reduced the airfields to shambles.

The aggressive Canadian shot down a *Bf 109* on the 20th. Six days later he destroyed at least one *Ju 88* as the enemy blasted away at three freighters in the harbour. Unfortunately the ships were sunk and scarcely one-quarter of their cargoes was salvaged. Suddenly, Malta faced its most serious shortages as the enemy hit the island with its heaviest bombardment of the war. Between March 24 and April 12 nearly 1,900 tons of bombs were delivered, and the figure for the whole of April was 6,700 tons.

By mid-April there were only about six fighters operational at any one time. Anti-aircraft guns were rationed to 15 rounds per day. The airfields were pitted with craters. Worst of all, rations were cut and then cut again. For the next few months the progress of the siege was measured by the number of holes that had to be taken in on belts. In the fury of the bombardment officers and men slept jammed together in underground shelters, quarries, caves and tunnels. The lives of everyone, servicemen and civilians, began to resemble those of rats.

The confusion of the air battles frequently increased the dangers and frustrations inherent in the situation. On one occasion McNair and another pilot were ordered to fly to Halfar airfield, where some *Hurricanes* attempting to land were being beaten up by *Bf 109's*. As the two *Spits* approached, the enemy fighters climbed away, but the *Hurricanes* kept getting in each other's way as they tried to pick out a landing run on the bomb-pitted field, and even shied at the *Spitfires* which they mistook for Messerschmitts. With his own fuel running low and some *'109's* sitting above watching, McNair finally radioed the

Hurricanes. In lurid language he ordered them to land or he would personally shoot the lot of them down.

During the fearful siege, disasters and triumphs followed rapidly upon each other. On April 24 the USS *Wasp* flew off 47 *Spitfires*, of which 46 reached Malta. However, the new fighters had to have their guns and radios made ready. Ninety minutes after their arrival the *Luftwaffe* mounted a new series of raids. Within 24 hours 17 *Spitfires* had been destroyed and 29 damaged on the ground. Short of every essential item, Malta appeared doomed to fall through starvation of food and fighting material.

Yet events soon showed that the island would not be destroyed. From April 29 onwards the Germans slackened their bombing and switched many aircraft to Cyrenaica, Russia and France. On May 9 some 60 *Spitfires* arrived. This time the RAF was ready to receive them quickly, and the *Spits* were operational within 90 minutes of touchdown. On the 10th the fast minelayer HMS *Welshman* broke the blockade to deliver ammunition. Finally, on June 15, two freighters reached Grand Harbour, after being fought through at the terrible cost of one cruiser, five destroyers, two minesweepers, six merchant ships and twenty aircraft lost, plus thirteen ships damaged. The enormous casualties give some indication of the closeness of the siege and the desperation of the defenders.

Late in June McNair was posted back to England. During his tour he had destroyed five, possibly seven, enemy aircraft and damaged many more. Of all his combats, however, one in particular stood out in his memory. Shortly after his return to Britain he recounted this particular action:

There was a reconnaissance aircraft which came over at about 20,000 feet after every raid. This day I stooged around upstairs waiting for him because with his height he was always able to escape when we scrambled after him. There were two *Me. 109's* with him and when they saw us calling they got out of town and the recce plane, a *Ju. 88*, started back to Sicily as hard as it could go. I caught up to him as he passed over the Sicilian coast and in a stern attack I saw him burn and spin earthwards.

McNair had landed back at Takali airfield with "barely a quiver left in my petrol guage . . . a lot of satisfaction."

He returned to No. 411 Squadron as a Flight Lieutenant and wearing the blue-and-white ribbon of the Distinguished Flying Cross which had been awarded him in May. He was now made a flight commander with No. 411, then flying in a quiet sector. Clearly he had an insatiable appetite for combat, for one of his superiors wrote:

Flight Lieutenant McNair required almost continuous action, even though such action had an adverse effect on his health.

August 19, 1942 saw No. 411 in combat over Dieppe, and McNair had the battle he wanted. He flew four sorties that day. In the first of these the squadron tangled with a force of *Fw 190's* which out-numbered the *Spitfires* by three to one. No. 411 lost three aircraft, but one German fighter was probably destroyed by McNair. Next day he damaged another Focke-Wulf. That was his last victory before his tour expired in September, and he was repatriated to Canada.

In Canada he was assigned to publicity duties connected with War Bond sales. In December 1942 he was posted to Western Air Command for service with No. 133 Squadron. He immediately began to protest his relegation to such a backwater. Fortunately this was slated to be only a temporary appointment. On January 22, 1943 he was sent to Halifax and thence overseas once more.

He started out with No. 403 Squadron, but on May 17 he was promoted and given command of No. 416 Squadron, whose redoubtable CO, Squadron Leader Foss Boulton, had been shot down and taken prisoner. A month later he handed over the unit to Squadron Leader F.H. Grant and was switched to lead No. 421 Squadron, whose commander-designate had been shot down before he could assume the post. It was with No. 421 that McNair experienced a new round of brilliant successes and terrifying escapes.

He renewed his scoring on June 20, 1943 by destroying an *Fw 190*, added another to his bag four days later, then shot down a *Bf 109* on July 6. On the 9th he damaged another Messerschmitt, but this time he was hampered by his windscreen frosting over. Next day, however, he destroyed a *Bf 109* in a combat which provided a copybook example of fighting tactics.

Squadron Leader McNair was at the head of No. 421, while No. 403 was flying about 2,000 feet below and ahead. A dozen German fighters were spotted flying level with No. 421 while a dozen more appeared ahead. No. 403 turned after the second enemy formation. The original dozen, reinforced by eight *Bf 109's* which had emerged from the clouds, attacked No. 403. At this point McNair ordered one section of No. 421's *Spitfires* to jump the Messerschmitts. This they did, but they had no sooner dived into the fight than more *'109's* attacked No. 403. McNair now took the remainder of his squadron down onto the last group of Germans. Most of the enemy vanished into clouds, but he was able to close on one from dead astern and blow it to pieces with one long burst. Other pilots in the damaged three of the enemy. Neither No. 403 nor No. 421 lost any aircraft.

"Buck" McNair had had more than his share of close shaves, but on July 20, 1943 it appeared that he was living on borrowed time. While leading a patrol along the Dutch coast, his engine began to lose power. He turned for home, accompanied by Pilot Officer Thurne Parks, while the remainder of the squadron continued the patrol.

His *Spitfire* lost height rapidly, and soon he was down to 12,000 feet. Twelve miles from the French coast, near Dunkirk, the *Merlin* burst into flames and the *Spitfire* dived out of control. The fire, fed by petrol, licked back into the cockpit. It is probable that only McNair's goggles saved his eyes. As it was, his eyebrows and eyelashes were singed and his face badly burned. At 5,000 feet he struggled free and hit the silk.

The bailout was hazardous in itself. Once in space he discovered that the wire handle which released the parachute had been burned away while the cords holding the 'chute to the harness were badly charred and might break from the shock of the "brolly" opening. With one hand he seized the cords to take some shock off them; with the other he gripped some unburned wire (but no handle) that pulled the release pin. He had fallen almost 3,000 feet before the parachute blossomed above him.

As he neared the water he found that the heat of the fire had fused the metal catch on his release mechanism. If he could not get rid of the 'chute he would either be entangled in the lines or dragged through the water by the wind. With his remaining strength he tore himself loose of the cords, and from a height of 75 feet dropped free-fall into the Channel. The impact dazed him. When he recovered his senses he found himself bobbing about, supported only by the Mae West life preserver; he had lost his dinghy in the fall. Nevertheless, he gave the "thumbs up" sign to the faithful Pilot Officer Parks, who had followed his leader down to the sea and who orbited McNair for more than an hour before an Air/Sea rescue *Walrus* picked up the downed flyer and spirited him away to safety. Two weeks later he was back in action. The level-headed Parks was later mentioned in despatches.

McNair's work was winning him added recognition. On July 30, 1943 he was awarded a Bar to his DFC. On the last day of August he shot down a *Bf 109* with a minimum expenditure of ammunition—40 rounds of cannon and 84 rounds from his machine guns—and was able to fly alongside the enemy plane momentarily to observe that the pilot was slumped over the controls. In September he destroyed two more fighters, one a curious all-blue *Fw 190* which he shot down southeast of Beaumont-le-Roger airfield on the 6th. His last victory was on October 3, 1943. In the McNair tradition, it was a spectacular show.

Escorting *Marauders* over Holland, McNair chased eleven *Fw 190's* and eventually caught up with them. He attacked one, fired a two-second burst, but then received a load of lead in his engine from another Focke-Wulf. With the *Merlin* almost lifeless he spun down, followed by the rest of his squadron. At 13,000 feet the engine picked up again, and he managed to limp home. He had not seen the result of his attack, but two pilots of No. 403, which had been flying lower down, reported a '190 spinning in flames. It could only have been the machine at which McNair had fired.

Four days later it was announced that Squadron Leader McNair had been awarded a second Bar to the DFC. On October 17 he was promoted once more, being made Wing Commander (Flying) for No. 126 (RCAF) Wing. Over the next six months he directed the training of the wing and on several occasions led it into battle.

He applied the same leadership methods that he had employed as a flight and squadron commander. After each sortie, whether it was a sweep or an exercise, he would call the pilots together for a bull session. After commenting on the operation in general, he would invite them to criticise their own flying and that of their fellows. Even his own actions were open to comment, and on one occasion he accepted as valid the complaint by an NCO wingman that his steep turns were so tight that the wingman could scarcely follow. The system did more than keep the pilots on their toes; it enabled McNair to evaluate flyers prior to selection of flight and squadron commanders.

On April 12, 1944 Wing Commander McNair relinquished his post, but two days later the *London Gazette* published the news of his being awarded the Distinguished Service Order. The citation to the award read:

> Since being awarded a second Bar to the Distinguished Flying Cross Wing Commander McNair has completed many further operational sorties and destroyed another enemy aircraft, bringing his total victories to at least sixteen enemy aircraft destroyed and many others damaged. As officer commanding the wing he has been responsible for supervising intensive training in tactics. The results achieved have been most satisfactory. The wing, under his leadership, destroyed at least thirteen enemy aircraft. Throughout, Wing Commander McNair has set a magnificent example by his fine fighting spirit, courage, and devotion to duty both in the air and on the ground. He has inspired his pilots with confidence and enthusiasm.

McNair was repatriated to Canada for a rest, then returned overseas to a staff posting with RCAF Overseas Headquarters. He was still there when the war ended in Europe.

Electing to remain in the peacetime RCAF, he reverted to Squadron Leader on October 1, 1946. There followed many postings as he served in staff positions at Air Force Headquarters, Lachine, Tokyo, Lac St. Denis, and Washington. He also commanded No. 4

Fighter Wing at Baden-Söllingen from August 1957 to September 1961. Along the way came promotions—to Wing Commander in January 1949, to Acting Group Captain in the period 1951-53, and finally became substantive Group Captain in January 1956.

It was a career still marked by courage. On December 30, 1953 he was aboard a *North Star* which crash-landed at Vancouver. He personally conducted the evacuation of all passengers, then returned to the wreckage to check for anyone who might have been left behind. He did so in spite of the danger of fire and the fact that his clothes were soaked in gasoline. For this he was honoured with the Queen's Commendation for Brave Conduct.

His long ordeal with cancer began in 1966, when the disease was diagnosed. McNair fought it through five years and many blood transfusions. As the killer advanced, he accepted a post with the Canadian Joint Staff in London. He remained in harness, however, performing his duties almost to the last, even from the last hospital bed. He died on January 15, 1971, and was buried in Brookwood Cemetery, where many of his RCAF comrades had been interred nearly 30 years before.

Mitchner
Strafer and Scrapper

It was 7.30 P.M., July 27, 1943, as nine *Mitchell* bombers linked up with their escort of 74 *Spitfires* near Coltishall. At sea level they thundered towards Holland until, as the enemy coast drew near, they began to climb. The bombers were at 11,000 feet when they began dropping their loads on Schipol airfield, near Amsterdam. It was then that large formations of enemy fighters, totalling as many as 45, began swinging down on the escorts.

As the formations dissolved, Pilot Officer John Mitchner found himself dogfighting with a *Bf 109*. The two aircraft twisted about at more than 350 miles per hour until another *'109* presented its tail to Mitchner. He jabbed his triggers for two seconds and saw strikes on the enemy's fuselage and tail unit. He then selected another Messerschmitt and peppered it. Rolling over into a dive, this victim plunged away, trailing white smoke and glycol.

Mitchner followed it down. The *'109* levelled off at 1,500 feet. Minutes later, the *Spitfire* caught up with its fleet adversary. From a range of 300 yards Mitchner opened fire. The hood flew off the Messerschmitt and then something else whipped away, possibly a flying helmet. Crippled by the attack, the German fighter ploughed onto the beach of the Dutch coastline. It was Mitchner's first "kill".

Born in Saskatoon on July 3, 1914, he had been educated in his home town where he was active in Boy Scouts and the YMCA. On completing his schooling he took up bookkeeping and was in the employ of a Vancouver fuel oil company when the war broke out.

There was a long line of applicants ahead of him, many of them younger, but at last, in October 1940, he was sworn in. His first posting after Manning Depot at Brandon was to Saskatoon for one month's guard duty—the strange, pointless ritual for so many trainees while waiting a turn in the BCATP schools. Then he was sent to Regina, attending No. 2 Initial Training School before being posted to No. 8 Elementary Flying Training School at Dauphin, Manitoba. His training was routine; the only untoward incident occured on March 26, 1941 when, to avoid hitting another aircraft while taxiing, he applied the brakes too hard and stood his *Tiger Moth* on its nose. An average student, he stood well down the list in his class, and when he won his wings in June 1941 he was graduated as a Sergeant pilot.

He was sent overseas immediately, but it was more than a year before he reached the front line, the intervening period being taken up with operational training and flying uneventful convoy patrols with RAF squadrons. He had a minor prang on July 30, 1942, when, returning from a convoy patrol in a *Hurricane* of No. 247 Squadron, he overshot his field and ran into a fence. Finally, on November 17, 1942, he joined No. 402 Squadron at Kenley.

His tour with No. 402 consisted of three distinct phases. The first lasted until mid-March 1943. During that time he was scrambled occasionally in futile attempts to catch German fighter-bombers which were making low-level hit-and-run raids along the English coast. Mostly, however, No. 402 was involved in Circus operations, escorting small formations of light bombers to targets in France and the Low Countries. German fighters were seldom seen during these raids. When they did appear, they were in small batches which hung around above the *Spitfires*, watching for an opening.

Sometimes the Germans found one. On January 17, 1943, for example, No. 402 was strafing locomotives a few miles east of Le Havre when nine *Fw 190's* flying in line abreast formation took them by surprise. In a short, sharp action, Mitchner climbed away from a Focke-Wulf which had sneaked up on him, then turned the tables and knocked a few holes in his tormentor. The squadron that day claimed one enemy aircraft destroyed and five damaged, but three *Spitfires* were shot down.

The second phase lasted from mid-March 1943, when the squadron moved to Digby, until early November. In that eight-month period the intensity of the air war was heightened on both sides. Previously, the *Luftwaffe* had allocated only two fighter wings, *JG 2* and *JG 26*, to the Western Front. After all, the small scale RAF and USAAF daylight raids had posed no serious threat to German security, particularly as the raids were normally on targets in Occupied territory. When the Allies launched more and heavier attacks, including American Eighth Air Force raids on Germany itself, the enemy had to switch fighters from other fronts. Even the modest RAF day raids now had to be taken more seriously, directed as they frequently were at airfields which now constituted the forward defences of the *Reich*. In consequence, enemy interceptions were more frequent and by larger formations of up to 80 aircraft. During this phase No. 402 was commanded by Squadron Leader Lloyd Chadburn and then, when "Chad" took over the Digby Wing, by Squadron Leader Geoff Northcott, a pipe-smoking tactician from Minnedosa, Manitoba.

It was in this period that Mitchner suddenly blossomed as a fighter pilot. In March he was commissioned and in August, having shot down his first victim, he was jumped to Flight Lieutenant and made the senior flight commander in No. 402. Although his score in aerial combat was still relatively modest (one destroyed, two damaged), he had been able to demonstrate his aggressiveness in other ways. In June he and another pilot had carried out a shipping reconnaissance off the Dutch coast. Not content with simply reporting what they saw, they had proceeded to strafe a barge, a 2,000 ton steamer and a large ferry. Then, in the Fall of 1943, he began to take the *Luftwaffe* apart. Between September 5 and November 3 he shot down three German fighters, shared another with Chadburn, assisted in the probable destruction of two more, and damaged one, achievements that brought him a Distinguished Flying Cross.

Typical of these actions was a battle waged on September 27. The Digby Wing (Nos. 402 and 416 Squadrons) was providing close escort to 36 *Marauders* which were bombing German airfields in northern France. Two enemy fighters appeared, acting as bait, but departed when it became obvious that the *Spitfires* were not being fooled. Then ten *Bf 109G's* dived out of the sun. No. 402 turned sharply to meet them and the Germans broke downwards and away. No further incidents occurred until the bombers were over the target when about ten or twelve *Fw 190's* appeared and began making firing passes at the *Spits*.

The next few minutes were pandemonium. Seeing five Focke-Wulfs coming up behind his section, Mitchner yanked his fighter about to face them. That spoiled their aim, but now he saw a *'190* creeping up on Chadburn. Along with Pilot Officer B.E. Innes he attacked this "bandit". Both pilots saw their cannon shells chewing up the enemy's fuselage, but the *'190* disappeared into clouds before its fate could be observed. It was credited jointly to Mitchner and Innes as a "probable".

While reforming his section, Mitchner was warned by Chadburn that two *Fw 190's* were trying to overhaul him. The Wing Commander instructed him to fly straight and level, not letting on that the *'190's* had been seen. Moments later, Chadburn "bounced" the pair, shooting down one and probably destroying the other.

Throughout the battle, despite the confusion of the dogfights, the *Spitfires* fought as a team—and the teamwork paid off. Cold print barely conveys the skill required to keep leaders and wingmen together, or to reform scattered sections. Moreover, the mutual confidence of all concerned is underlined by Mitchner willingly playing the sitting duck while trusting that Chadburn would keep him covered. On this occasion the only bomber lost was a victim of flak. One *Spitfire* was shot down, but the Germans took more than they dished out.

The third phase of Mitchner's tour with No. 402 lasted from mid-November 1943 until the end of January 1944, when he was posted to non-operational duties after completing 127 sorties. Although the *Marauders* and *Mitchells* continued to pound at the fringes of the German empire, the *Luftwaffe* was content to pull back major fighter units into the *Reich* itself, partly to avoid clashes with superior numbers of Allied fighters, partly to make more German aircraft available for night work using "*Wilde Sau*" (Wild Boar) tactics. Air action for the *Spitfires* evaporated and the pilots found themselves with nothing more exciting than moustache-growing contests.

From February through until August 1944, Mitchner was on staff duties at RAF Station Tealing. In the latter month he was posted to No. 421 Squadron, then involved in the Battle of Falaise. The *Luftwaffe*, badly mauled in the Normandy campaign, had virtually pulled out of the fight. Mitchner was presently wrapped up with the important and highly dangerous job of tactical interdiction. Day after day he and his comrades roared low over the roads of northern France strafing German trucks, staff cars, tanks and armoured vehicles. Such targets were classified as "flamers" (set on fire), "smokers" (seen to be smoking but not alight) and "damaged" (known to be hit but with no observable results). Occasionally the *Spitfires* carried 500-lb bombs to smash bridges or targets of opportunity. In one attack he helped riddle a column of enemy horse-drawn heavy artillery. This work came to a halt early in September when the Allied armies virtually outdistanced their air support. It was not until the Battle of Nijmegen that the *Spitfire* wings caught up with the ground forces.

Mitchner's contribution to the Nijmegen air battle was impressive. During an early afternoon patrol on September 25, No. 421 encountered a dozen enemy fighters which apparently were attempting to reach the Allied lines for a strafing attack. Mitchner got on the tail of a *Bf 109*, followed it through a screaming dive from 7,000 to 3,000 feet, out-turned it and put a burst of cannon fire into its cockpit. The German pilot bailed out. Mitchner climbed back to 12,000 feet. Ten minutes after the first combat he saw an *Fw 190* below and dived on it. The *'190* plunged into clouds. The Canadian followed but, fearing a trap, he throttled back before entering the woolly mists. As he emerged, he found himself flying alongside the Focke-Wulf. The German, too, had cut his power, hoping that the *Spitfire* would overshoot and present a target. Instead, Mitchner was able to swing in behind his prey. One long burst did the trick; the *'190* caught fire, then exploded with a satisfying roar.

Two days later he shot down another *Bf 109*, his last victory with No. 421. On September 26, No. 416 had lost Flight Lieutenant G.R. Patterson in a dogfight. On the 29th Mitchner was posted to that unit to take over Patterson's flight. He promptly left his mark on No. 416's records by destroying two *Fw 190's* in one sortie.

Abruptly the *Luftwaffe* stopped coming over. The *Spitfires* reverted to patrolling the lines and escorting medium bombers, looking for an enemy who had gone into hibernation. Throughout October about the only German aircraft that No. 416 encountered were *Me 262* jets which streaked over Grave airfield, making life miserable with anti-personnel bombs. The jets, coupled with foul weather in Holland, eventually forced the squadron to switch its base to Evere, Belgium. On October 29 Mitchner was promoted to Squadron Leader and given command of No. 416, succeeding another ace, J.F. McElroy.

His last aerial victory was on December 8, 1944 when, in the course of a fighter sweep near Münster, he shot down a *Bf 109* flown by a particularly loutish pilot. Thereafter he was invariably involved in uneventful escort sorties, dive bombing attacks, and armed reconnaissance flights in quest of ground targets. Although many pilots were killed in this dicey low-level work, Mitchner was never once hit by enemy fire. On the other hand, he showed considerable flair in strafing. In one operation, the squadron shot up a whole enemy train and on another occasion, following his lead, they plastered nine vehicles, including three staff cars.

Squadron Leader Mitchner was on leave in southern France when the Germans capitulated. Hastening back to his unit, he joined in the celebrations. Shortly after the close of hostilities, he was awarded a Bar to his DFC. The citation is worth quoting, for it illustrates that his superiors respected him at least as much for his interdiction expertise as for his aerial combat skills:

> This officer has completed many sorties against the enemy since being awarded the Distinguished Flying Cross. He has consistently displayed a high degree of skill and determination and has been responsible for the destruction of ten enemy aircraft. One day in April 1945, Squadron Leader Mitchner led two armed reconnaissances, resulting in the destruction of

45 motor transports, whilst more than 100 were damaged. His devotion to duty has been most commendable.

During his two tours of duty, Mitchner had flown some 250 sorties. In addition to his victories in air-to-air combat, he claimed to have destroyed or damaged more than 100 vehicles. His honours included a Netherlands' Flying Cross awarded to him in January 1946.

Returning to Canada in March 1946, he opted to join the post-war RCAF. His postings included the command of No. 417 (Fighter Reconnaissance) Squadron at Rivers in 1947-48. Promoted to Wing Commander in 1951, he formed and led No. 434 Squadron at Uplands in 1952-53. In the latter year, following the discovery that he had diabetes, he was taken off flying duties. The disease was checked and he continued to serve as CO of such non-flying stations as St. Sylvestre and Lac St. Denis, both radar bases. In 1960, however, his health suddenly deteriorated and he was given a medical discharge. Retiring to central British Columbia, he died at Penticton on December 2, 1964, leaving a widow and three children to cherish his memory.

Schwab
Biplane Ace

Some of the most bitter fighting conducted by the RAF during the first two years of the war was carried out with Gloster *Gladiators*, the last biplane fighter to serve with that force. By the mid-thirties the biplane, which had dominated the world's air forces for nearly 30 years, had begun to give way to the monoplane, but the *Gladiator* soldiered on until 1942. Despite its low speed, it proved to be effective in the stop-gap situations into which it was hurled. Pilots with determination and initiative frequently overcame the obsolescence of their aircraft. From Norway to Ethiopia they strafed enemy troops and accounted for scores of enemy aircraft. Among the *Gladiator* aces— the last biplane aces in history—was Lloyd Schwab of Niagara Falls, Ontario.

Schwab was born on January 22, 1915 and enlisted in the RAF at the age of 21. In 1938 he was posted to the Middle East. The following year he joined No. 112 Squadron which was forming at Helwan as part of the defences of Cairo and the Nile Delta. When Italy entered the war in June 1940 the three front-line squadrons in the area, Nos. 33, 80 and 112, were all equipped with *Gladiators*, *backed* up by a few aging *Gauntlet* biplanes which were used in training, thus keeping down the flying hours on the "Glads".

The RAF, although outnumbered and for the most part outclassed technically, took the offensive at the very beginning of the Mediterranean campaign. As a result, the Italian air force was compelled to think defensively, which blunted the edge of the *Regia Aeronautica*. *Blenheims* and *Gladiators*, supported by a handful of *Hurricanes*, soon secured for themselves the airspace over the British lines and struck deep into enemy territory. During that eventful summer of 1940, No. 112 Squadron moved up to Maaten Gerawla airfield. Flight Lieutenant Schwab, commanding "A" Flight, soon began to run up a formidable string of victories.

His first victim was an *SM.79* tri-motored bomber which he shot down in flames on August 17. Soon afterwards, No. 112 shifted its base to Sidi Heneish, further back, from where it harried the Italian army which had begun a slow, painful advance into Egypt. Then, on October 31, the *Gladiators* were involved in one of the most savage air battles up to that time.

Five *Gladiators* were patrolling near Mersa Matruh when they spotted 15 *SM.79*'s attempting to bomb British forward positions. The fighters gave chase but were in turn jumped by half a dozen *CR.42*'s, an Italian biplane fighter of more recent vintage than the *Gladiator*. Indeed, the total number of escorts was 18 *CR.42*'s, and for a moment they appeared to be in a position to wipe out the defenders. One *Gladiator* was shot down, its pilot bailing out after suffering minor burns.

At that instant Schwab, who had taken off with another pilot later than the original patrol, engaged the *CR.42*'s with two companions. In the swirling dogfight, which more closely resembled a combat of 1918 than one of 1940, he shot down two Italian fighters. Then his engine failed and he force-landed in the desert. In the confusion of the battle two other *Gladiators* collided and only one of the pilots was saved. The final tally was four *Gladiators* and one British pilot lost, but the enemy paid dearly: four Italian bombers and four fighters were shot down. Hundreds of British troops witnessed the battle and one army officer declared, "If the stage had been specially arranged for us to see the RAF in action, it could not have been better. I saw two Italian bombers burning in the air." One *Gladiator* pilot, swooping low over the burning wrecks of three *CR.42*'s, was cheered by the troops who had gathered around the downed fighters. Such was the rapport which existed between the small land and air forces.

Already, however, the complexion of the war had begun to change. Late in October, Italian troops had invaded Greece. Almost immediately they ran into trouble, for the Greeks put up savage resistance and soon stopped the enemy's offensive in its tracks. Britain offered aid to her new ally, but the Greeks declined any additional troops for fear of provoking a German reaction. However, air support was another matter. Presently five RAF squadrons were despatched to the Balkans. Thus began the division of British air strength in the Middle East which eventually would result in fatal weaknesses both in Greece and North Africa. Nevertheless, at the time support for Greece was a political necessity.

No. 112 Squadron was not immediately involved in the Balkan campaign. Flight Lieutenant Schwab remained in Egypt and on November 18, while covering a visit by Field Marshal Wavell to the troops, he shot down another *SM.79* bomber. Two weeks later, however, he was ferrying aircraft to Greece, and in January 1941 the whole squadron was sent to bolster those RAF units already there.

The situation in Greece was far from satisfactory. The Royal Hellenic Air Force, equipped for the most part with obsolete French and Polish aircraft, had suffered heavy casualties in ground support operations at the beginning of the campaign. All-weather airfields were rare. British bombers had to be based near Athens, 200 miles from the front, while the fighters were accommodated at such fields as could be improvised near the battle. There they operated under most difficult conditions, with rains on occasion flooding the landing grounds. Moreover, in order to maintain the morale of the Greek troops, the aircraft were frequently employed in direct support operations in full view of the front lines. The British air commander pointed out that, while this served the purpose of invigorating our allies, it nevertheless constituted a misemployment of the air force.

For its part, the *Regia Aeronautica* became increasingly effective. Growing numbers of *MC.200* and *G.50* monoplane fighters made life harder than ever for the *Gladiators*. In February, however, the first *Hurricanes* began to appear in Greece, and with these the Allied air forces continued to hold their Italian opponents in check.

On February 20, the RAF had a particularly hectic but satisfying day. While the *Hurricanes* of No. 80 Squadron escorted 20 *Blenheims* on a raid, No. 112's *Gladiators* protected some *Wellingtons* and a Greek *Ju 52* which were dropping food supplies to Greek troops. Shortly after these forces had taken off, a dozen Greek PZL *P.24* fighters followed. Thus, there was no shortage of fighters around when the Italians attempted an interception with about 50 aircraft.

The *Gladiators* followed their charges until the supplies had been dropped and the transports had turned back. Then Schwab and his fellows set off looking for trouble. They found it. In a swirling dogfight over Tepelene, the *Gladiators* shot down four *G.50's*, one of which was credited to the Canadian flight commander. That day a total of twelve Italian aircraft were downed—four by the *Gladiators*, four by the *Hurricanes*, and four by the *P.24's*. One week later, the *Gladiators* and *Hurricanes* fought another epic battle, shooting down 27 enemy aircraft, of which No. 112 scored six destroyed, although none by Schwab.

The end of the Greek campaign was not far off. Although the opposing land forces were virtually dead-locked, German influence in the Balkans was increasing, and with it the likelihood that Hitler would soon come to the rescue of Mussolini. A small British expeditionary force was now sent to Greece, arriving just in time to be swallowed up in the German onslaught.

Schwab gained another victory in March—a *G.50* probably destroyed over Paramythia on the 26th. On April 4, 1941 he took command of No. 112 Squadron, succeeding Squadron Leader H.L.I. Brown. Two days later the long-expected blow fell; German forces invaded Greece and Yugoslavia, bringing to bear overwhelming air power. By that time the RAF could muster barely 80 serviceable aircraft as opposed to some 800 German and 300 Italian aircraft. The campaign was swift, and its tragic outcome virtually inevitable. Schwab himself destroyed a *G.50* on April 13, but on the 15th the RAF was down to 46 aircraft, including the twelve *Gladiators* of No. 112. That day the squadron pulled back from Yannina to Agrinion. Soon after, it was evacuated to Crete.

The pilots and groundcrew became separated in the retreat, and the operational effectiveness of No. 112 evaporated. An attempt to base the squadron on Crete failed in the face of *Luftwaffe* raids. By the time the unit was withdrawn to Egypt it was down to three *Gladiators*; the bulk of all personnel were flown out in *Sunderlands*.

The last stages of the Greek campaign and the Battle for Crete were carried out amid great confusion. In the withdrawal, the records of No. 112 Squadron were destroyed. Thus, details of its combats are incomplete. The British air commander subsequently reported that during the campaign his fighters destroyed 232 enemy aircraft confirmed and 112 unconfirmed; there can be little doubt that the majority of these were gained by the gallant but outclassed *Gladiators*. No. 112 Squadron's share was at least 75 machines shot down.

Late in June Squadron Leader Schwab was posted away for a rest, much to the disappointment of his colleagues. In July he was awarded the DFC with the following citation:

> This officer has led his squadron in combat against the enemy with considerable skill and has personally destroyed eleven of their aircraft. He has displayed great courage and determination.

Eighteen months later, he was awarded the Greek Flying Cross. By then he was serving as an instructor, first in Britain and later in Canada. In September 1943 he was promoted to Wing Commander and returned to Britain once more, this time to take charge of an advanced flying unit. He remained in the RAF after the war, retiring in March 1958.

Smith
Double Trouble

Malta: July 24, 1942. Another raid is about to begin. A small clutch of bombers covered by a swarm of *Bf 109's* flying behind and above the raiders converge on the island. While the sirens wail their mournful warning, *Spitfires* are clawing for altitude, racing to reach the enemy's height.

At 18,000 feet, just over the island, two *Spitfires* come roaring in on five *Ju 88's*. Flying Officer Rod Smith selects the left-hand bomber and delivers an attack on the port quarter, opening fire at 250 yards and keeping it up until he is 100 yards away. His six-second burst does the trick. The Junkers' port engine begins to burn and the flames lick into the fuselage. One of the crew bails out and the bomber begins a death plunge, crashing just south of Luqa airfield.

But here come the escorts and there goes Smith's partner, trailing white smoke after being hit in the glycol tank by an enemy gunner. Time to get out of here! Covered by Smith, the crippled *Spitfire* glides back to Luqa, lowers its undercarriage, and without power makes a beautiful landing. Each pilot has destroyed a bomber, making it a very successful family affair. Flying Officer Smith's wingman is his brother Jerry.

Born in Regina in March 1920, Rod Smith was fascinated by airplanes for as far back as he could remember. He loved to go to the local airport and watch them landing and taking off. When he wasn't going to school or delivering newspapers, he was devouring aviation magazines and building model aircraft. Even then he wanted to fly fighter planes and his whole life was planned around them. First he was going to finish high school, then he was going to England to join the RAF, and then . . .

And then came the war, making a trip to Britain unnecessary. In September 1940 he enlisted in the RCAF (Jerry followed a month later). Almost immediately he was funneled into the aircrew training scheme. After square bashing and indoctrination at No. 2 Initial Training School in Regina he was whistled off to Fort William for elementary flying training on *Tiger Moths*. From there he went to No. 2 Service Flying Training School at Uplands. In March 1941 he graduated eighth in a class of 44, received his wings, was granted a commission, and immediately received posting instructions for overseas.

In May he reported to No. 58 Operational Training Unit, Grangemouth, to learn the ins and outs of combat flying under the watchful eye of another Canadian, Squadron Leader M.H. "Hilly" Brown, veteran of the Battle of France and the Battle of Britain. Finally, in June 1941, the eager young Smith was posted to No. 412 Squadron to begin his first tour on *Spitfires*.

No. 412 was then working up to operational standards and it was not until September 17 that Smith flew his first "combat" sortie, a convoy patrol. Later that month the squadron began taking part in sweeps over northern France. Convoy patrols were always a bore but the infrequent sweeps were fraught with excitement and danger. On October 13, for example, Sergeant E.H. MacDonnell shot down the squadron's first victim, a *Bf 109*. On the other side of the coin, when, on November 8, the unit became hotly involved with enemy fighters, three *Spitfires* were lost with their pilots.

One memorable flight took place on February 12, 1942. That was the day the German battleships *Scharnhorst* and *Gneisenau* made their famous "Channel dash". Nine aircraft from No. 412 went off looking for the warships, the intention being that they attack the enemy fighter cover and thus give respite to *Beaufort* torpedo bombers. Visibility was poor, especially looking downwards, and although the pilots were airborne for more than an hour, they saw nothing.

On May 30, 1942 Smith flew his last patrol with No. 412 before being posted to No. 126 Squadron in Malta. He reported to his new unit on July 15, to discover that Jerry had been assigned to the same outfit two weeks previously. It was pure coincidence, but in the next few weeks the Smith brothers were to make a magnificent showing. Their story would a mixture of triumph and tragedy.

Jerry was already a seasoned "pro". In June, during a bloody attempt by the Royal Navy to run a convoy to Malta, he had destroyed one enemy aircraft, probably destroyed another, and damaged two more, all in the course of a single day. That had been while he was serving with No. 601 Squadron. He had added one more destroyed plus one damaged to his score before his brother arrived to serve in No. 126, and by happy chance Rod's first taste of Malta combat was experienced with Jerry as his leader.

It happened on July 18. The two men bounced a lone *Ju 88* over the sea as it was heading back to Sicily. Jerry delivered the first burst, then broke away while Rod opened up. The enemy's starboard engine began streaming glycol, but at this moment Rod's cannons packed up. With fuel running low there was no time to finish off the cripple, so the *Spitfires* headed for home. When last seen, the Junkers was limping along just above the water with its tail down. It was jointly credited to the boys as a "probable".

Rod and Jerry teamed up again on the 24th in the action earlier described in which each shot down a *Ju 88*. Rod's first confirmed victory and Jerry's third. Two days later they were in action again, this time diving through a swarm of *Bf 109's* to get at eight Junkers. So great was their speed that before a proper attack could be set up they were in among the bombers. Rod snapped a burst at a *'109* on the way down, then had to fight to bring his *Spitfire* back under control. He emerged without claiming anything, but Jerry knocked a few holes in one bomber and was credited with a damaged.

Once again, Jerry had been hit. He broke away trailing white smoke while Rod covered him back to base. Luqa was uninhabitable at that moment—it was being pounded by more bombers—so Jerry settled for Halfar airfield and landed wheels down.

Another savage air battle took place on the 28th. This time seven *Spitfires* piled into a trio of Junkers and shot them all down. Rod tackled one, firing a series of bursts from 250 to 150 yards range. The enemy's port engine was set alight and then the whole bomber became engulfed in flames. In a spectacular show of gradual disintegration the *'88* lost both engines before the wings finally dropped off. Jerry took another bullet through the glycol system and had to force-land, the third time in six days.

On August 10 the two brothers were on 30 minutes readiness, dressed to scramble. They both needed silk gloves to line their leather flying gauntlets. Rod was despatched on a motorcycle to the supply section, a half-mile distant. On his return he found that the section had been called to "immediate readiness"—pilots in cockpits, with another man taking Rod's place. There was no time to switch round again before the scramble order came through, and while Rod watched, Jerry and the other pilot took off to meet another raid.

Jerry never came back. Climbing away, he outdistanced his

wingman. There were vague reports that he intercepted the Germans single-handed and that a parachute was seen, but for all that he might just as well have been swallowed by the sky. His body was never recovered. The spell was broken; the team had been disbanded by death.

It would be simple to regard Rod Smith's subsequent combat career as one springing from that day's tragedy, to view his remaining tours as a quest for vengence. It would be dramatic to think of his future victims as the price exacted from the *Luftwaffe* by one brother for another. It would also be grossly inaccurate. Rod was grieved by Jerry's death, but he had seen enough of the war to realize that it was not men but the war itself, huge and impersonal, which lay at the root of his loss. He knew, too, that allowing passion in himself would only be an indulgence. Like the war, he had to fight impersonally; otherwise he might break or commit fatal mistakes.

Malta was important to the war effort and Malta had to be supplied. He was on business, not a vendetta, on August 13 when he shot down an *SM.79* bomber which had been near the tanker *Ohio*, a vital ship in a crucial convoy. Smith was knocked out of action in September by sandfly fever and sinusitus, but he was back to near-normal when the Axis opened the October blitz of Malta. On the morning of October 11 he was scrambled to meet nine *Ju 88's* flying in "V" formation and escorted by 60 *Bf 109's*. Climbing in behind the left-hand bomber, he opened fire from 250 yards. First one and then the other of the Junkers' engines caught fire and it dived away. One crewman bailed out just in time; the bomber then exploded and crashed into the Mediterranean. Two days later, on the 13th, he raised his score to five destroyed by shooting down a *Bf 109* over Luqa airfield.

Smith was also on the receiving end of the bullets. On October 14 a German gunner put a hole in his aileron. It was even closer on the 15th. While attacking a Messerschmitt, another *'109* blasted his *Spitfire* with cannon and machine gun fire. Miraculously, Smith was unhurt, but his aircraft was a shambles. He attempted to fly back to base, found that to be impossible, and bailed out. He landed in the sea about a mile north of St. Julien's Bay where he was promptly picked up by a launch.

His sixth and last confirmed victory over Malta was scored on October 25, 1942 when he dived on four *Bf 109's* and put a four-second burst into the cockpit of one, using almost no deflection. The stricken enemy fighter dived smoking through four miles of sky before plunging into the ocean.

Rod Smith was finally stopped, not by enemy bullets, but by jaundice. In mid-November he was hospitalized, then sent back to Britain where he learned that he had been awarded the DFC. In

January 1943 he took up instructional duties at No. 53 Operational Training Unit in Wales. Late in March he assumed similar duties at No. 55 OTU, Scotland. While at the latter unit he was detached briefly to attend a Fighter Leader Course at Acton Down. Those in authority had their eyes on him.

In October 1943 he was sent home to Canada on leave, but two months later he returned to the United Kingdom. On January 6, 1944 he began his second tour, starting with the crack No. 401 (Ram) Squadron commanded by Lorne Cameron, who already had three aircraft to his credit. The unit included several other top-notch pilots, notably Bill Klersy; a Newfoundlander, Bob Hayward; and an American, R.M. Davenport. No. 401 formed part of No. 126 Wing, along with Nos. 411 and 412 Squadrons.

His first sortie of his second tour was on February 25, when the squadron was part of a force covering the withdrawal of 600 American heavy bombers from a raid on Germany. Over the next six weeks most of his flights were escort sorties to American medium and heavy bombers. The Rams rarely tangled with enemy fighters and Smith had little opportunity to raise his score. Early in April he was posted to No. 412 Squadron. About this time the *Spitfires* went over to dive-bombing with 500-pounders slung under their bellies. In April and May alone Smith flew 41 sorties of which 18 were bombing trips. The squadron diary recorded these operations in stark prose:

> 7 May 1944. Dive bombing, 1950-2100. This evening a dive bombing attack was carried out against a Noball [*V-1* launching site] target approximately 15 miles north of Rouen. This operation was uneventful and all aircraft returned to base.

> 28 May 1944. Ramrod 938, 1525-1645. With the other two squadrons of the wing, the squadron took off on a bombing show, attacking Forêt d'Arques. Ten 500-lb bombs dropped in target area with three falling on what appeared to be buildings. Flak was medium, meagre, and inaccurate. Weather was hazy and visibility was ten miles. All aircraft returned to base.

D-Day hurled Smith and his companions into a new swirl of activity—beachhead patrols, interdiction, and the moves which took them from Tangmere, England, to Beny-sur-Mer to Cristot to St. André to Illiers to Poix, all in France, to Evere and Le Cullot in Belgium, all in the space of three months. They were hectic times, too. In June, July and August No. 412 shot down 25 enemy aircraft and lost eight pilots. Smith himself flew 111 combat sorties during that period and shot down an *Fw 190* on July 7, raising his total to seven confirmed victories. It was a summer of endless flights, dust, tents, and living out of doors. It was the summer when friends like Don Laubman and John

Banks vaulted into the list of aces (Banks, a crack shot from Saskatchewan, picked off six German fighters between June 28 and July 24). It
was the summer when Smith narrowly missed death after his *Spitfire*
blew a tire during take off from a French strip. Most of all, it was the
summer of the armed reconnaissance.

Almost daily, and often two or three times a day, Smith was out
with the squadron, prowling behind enemy lines, shooting up everything that moved. German vehicles of all types were bombed and
strafed until the *Wehrmacht* was reduced to half-mobile divisions short
of guns, men, gasoline and ammunition. But again, let the squadron
diary recount some of these flights:

22 June 1944. Armed reconnaissance, 2100-2230. The
squadron swept Caen, Lisieux, Largle, Argentan areas on this
operation. The formation shot up two bases, seven trucks, and
one half-track containing 25 troops. Enemy reaction nil. Flak
nil. All aircraft returned to base.

18 July 1944. Armed reconnaissance, 1530-1650. One tank
was damaged by the squadron on this operation, also one MET
flamer [mechanical enemy transport set on fire] and eight
MET damaged were scored. Ten troops were also strafed in the
Taluise area. All aircraft returned.

25 August 1944. Armed reconnaissance, 1215-1335. This
armed recce was carried out in the Fleury-Forges-Beauvais area.
Scattered MET was sighted and resulted in 11 flamers, 11
smokers, and 6 damaged. All aircraft returned.

Yet all that summer, active as it was, paled by comparison with
the last week of September 1944, when the *Luftwaffe* was butchered
over Nijmegen. That was the battle which saw Smith destroy six enemy
aircraft in four days, running his tally to 13 enemy aircraft, and it
brought him a Bar to his DFC. Only one Canadian, Don Laubman,
exceeded his record in that period.

No. 412's Commanding Officer, Squadron Leader D.H. Dover
DFC, was on leave at the time and Smith was acting as the unit's
leader. He was in charge in the mid-afternoon of September 25 when
the squadron tangled with three German fighters and shot down two.
He submitted no claim that day, but on the 26th it was different.

He was leading twelve *Spitfires* near Nijmegen at 2,000 feet when
he spotted two dozen *Bf 109*'s "on the deck" just east of the vital
bridge. No. 412 carried out a perfect bounce. Smith glued himself to
the tail of one German fighter and after chasing it for two minutes he
jabbed the trigger button. From 350 yards range he scored strikes in
the enemy's wing roots and fuselage. The *'109* streamed glycol, tipped
over and crashed. Hauling the *Spit* round to face a half-score more
enemy fighters, Smith dropped behind one Messerschmitt and let him

have it. Just then his port cannon jammed. Instead of breaking off the action he closed the range to 30 yards and tried again. The '109 blew up and crashed.

The pilots landed back at base to submit a fantastic score—eight German fighters destroyed without loss. There was no immediate celebration, however, for an hour later they were refuelled, rearmed and off again for another scrap.

Early on the morning of September 27 Smith led the squadron through another successful shoot. Again they downed eight "bandits", and again he personally accounted for two. These, however, were his last victories with No. 412, for on September 28 he was promoted to Squadron Leader and given command of No. 401 which had lost its CO, Hugh Trainor DFC, more than a week before. His new start with the Rams could not have been more auspicious. On his first morning in command, he led the unit into a fight with 30 Messerschmitts which were attacking some *Typhoons*. The result was utter mayhem with nine German fighters destroyed, two of them by Smith. His victims crashed within sight of each other southeast of Nijmegen.

Suddenly it was all over. The Battle of Nijmegen terminated abruptly as the Allies consolidated their gains and the *Luftwaffe* retired to lick its wounds while preparing for its next great battle three months hence. Smith saw little more of the German air arm, but on October 5, 1944 he participated with four other pilots in the destruction of an *Me 262* jet fighter, the first one to be shot down by Commonwealth pilots. This historic action is described in detail in the chapter relating to John MacKay.

Squadron Leader Smith completed his tour in November 1944, having flown 225 sorties since January. By New Year's Day he was back in Canada. He left the RCAF in June 1945. Flying continued to haunt him, though, and in 1946 he joined the RCAF Auxiliary. This led him back to No. 401 Squadron, the postwar reserve unit in Montreal, and then to No. 411 Squadron in Toronto. This happy association ended when he moved to Vancouver to practice law. He lives there today, still keenly interested in aviation.

Turnbull
The Reluctant Ace

For the men who fought on land and at sea the Second World War was a dirty business. Even when the enemy was absent, dreary mud or fierce Atlantic storms frequently made life miserable. For the airmen it was different. Combat flying had its dangers, and death could strike in horrifying fashion, through wounds, drowning, or fire in the air. Yet most flyers lived apart from the war; it was something far across an expanse of sea or on the other side of a front line. Men might disappear, but death was strangely remote. Those who were killed died privately in their aircraft, and their fellows were shielded from their agonies. In these circumstances it was possible to regard combat as a sport with machines for targets. The fact that these machines were flown by men was forgotten or suppressed.

John Turnbull was an exception. An individualist and, after "Moose" Fumerton, Canada's greatest night fighter pilot, he nevertheless retained his sense of humanity throughout the war. Flying he loved, but combat was always ultimately distasteful. He knew what he was—a successful killer doing a necessary job. That it had to be done did not make it any less ugly.

He was born in St. Thomas, Ontario, a quiet farming community south of London, on December 30, 1915. In pre-war days he swam, played golf, and indulged in badminton. He was also greatly interested in photography, a hobby which eventually he was to turn to his profit.

Having achieved junior matriculation, he took an extension course in banking from Queen's University. Between 1935 and 1940 he was employed as a bank teller at St. Thomas, Niagara Falls, and Orangeville, north of Toronto.

The war brought this tranquil life to an end. By the Spring of 1940 Turnbull had decided that he must serve. He had never flown, had never even shown any particular interest in aviation, but now he sensed vaguely that the Air Force would be the best choice. He journeyed to Toronto where he was examined and interviewed. The recruiting officer there described him as "above average in appearance and personality. . . has a pleasant and willing attitude". There were, however, many such men in those days and Turnbull sat out the summer in Orangeville, awaiting his call-up. Finally, in September 1940, he was summoned back to Toronto and sworn into the RCAF. The great adventure was about to begin.

The first five months were spent following a trail beaten by thousands of recruits—outfitting, elementary drill and calisthenics at Brandon, three months of guard duty at Patricia Bay on Vancouver Island, then on to No. 2 Initial Training School at Regina for ground training. In mid-February 1941 he was posted to No. 15 Elementary Flying Training School, also at Regina, where he was introduced to flying via the delightful *Tiger Moth* biplane. Being new at the business of aviation, he took a little longer to solo than most other students, and on his first solo flight he was so determined to make a good landing that he overshot on the first approach, went round the circuit again, then made a near-perfect touchdown. By then the flying bug had truly bitten him; the freedom it gave him was matchless.

Having mastered the *Tiger Moth*, he was posted to Moose Jaw for advanced training on *Harvards*. His first impression of these machines was that they were massive and he climbed into them with considerable misgivings. Nevertheless, he enjoyed every minute he spent in them. It was great fun to indulge in unauthorized low flying, roaring down the coulees which riddled southern Saskatchewan and Alberta, and he was fortunate enough never to be caught at this forbidden sport. In July 1941 he won his wings and graduated 6th in a class of 61. Immediately upon passing out of Moose Jaw he was commissioned and posted overseas. He thus avoided the long stretch of instructional duties which delayed the combat appearances of so many pilots.

The convoy which took him to Britain was three weeks in passage, including a stop in Iceland. Turnbull was sea-sick for the first week. His most vivid recollection of the trip, however, was that of the battleship *Prince of Wales* ploughing at full speed through the convoy, bearing Prime Minister Churchill back to Britain from the historic Atlantic Conference and flying signal flags which spelled "V for Victory". The whole drama of the war loomed up before him.

He landed at Glasgow in August and immediately took a train through blacked-out Britain to Bournemouth. Soon afterwards he was posted to No. 60 Operational Training Unit to begin flying on night fighters. His first operational aircraft was the *Defiant*. It was a monument to misguided ingenuity—a two-seater fighter with a four-gun power turret but no forward armament and, being underpowered, possessing the flying characteristics of a truck. Once he had been broken in on this most unlovely aircraft he was posted to No. 125 (Newfoundland) Squadron at Fairwood Common in the north of England for night flying duties.

Although the *Defiant* was heavy to fly, and despite the fact that most of the work consisted of exercises in co-operation with searchlights, Turnbull found night work appealing. There was no problem of formation flying and he enjoyed the sense of isolation which came with the darkness and radio silence. He was strictly on his own.

In January 1942 No. 125 established a detachment at Colerne where crews went to convert from *Defiants* to *Beaufighter II's*, and in April he began training on the newer aircraft. The "Beau" was a different animal altogether—bigger, faster, more maneuverable, although the *Merlin*-engined Mark II was still underpowered. It was not until the squadron received Mark VI's with *Hercules* radial engines late in 1942 that Turnbull found himself flying a top-notch night fighter capable of aerobatics.

It was while he was at Colerne that two important events occured. The first was Turnbull's being paired off with Sergeant Cyril Fowler, a dark, quiet, immensely capable radar operator from Birmingham. The second was his first crash. On May 2 his aircraft developed a hydraulic leak and he had to make a wheels-up landing, fortunately without bending either himself or the *Beaufighter*.

Three weeks later, on May 25, 1942, death came within a whisker of claiming the team. This time they were back at Fairwood Common. A glycol leak developed in one engine while they were at 10,000 feet over the Bristol Channel. The temperature soared so the engine was shut down and the *Beaufighter* turned for home. It was rapidly losing altitude, but so certain was Turnbull that he could reach the field that he and Fowler did not even discuss the possibility of bailing out. By the time that it appeared that they might not make it, they were over the village near the base and abandoning the "Beau" was out of the question. Suddenly a row of houses seemed to rear up in front of the fighter. Twenty-five years later Turnbull was able to recall the next few moments with vivid clarity:

> I had just enough speed to 'balloon' a bit, knock some tiles
> off a house, and pass over it. If there had been another row of

houses on the other side of the road we'd have gone into them for sure. As it was, we hit a downward slope—a wooded ravine—and skidded through the trees. One wing folded back, the *Beaufighter* groundlooped, and then the other wing was almost torn off. Cyril's seat snapped off and went rolling down the fuselage with him still strapped to it. My own seat broke off too, and finally the aircraft came to rest. There was a huge rock the size of a football between my knees, but I wasn't scratched.

Everything was quiet except for the drip, drip, drip of gasoline. I scrambled out onto the wing and yelled at Cyril to get out. He shouted back that he needed help. I found him and piggybacked him until we were about 50 feet from the plane. It still had not caught fire, so I went back and radioed the base, telling them where we were—inside the airfield perimeter and about 100 yards short of the WAAF quarters.

Fowler had suffered a broken arm with severed nerves. In a series of pioneering operations doctors were able to save the arm and reconnect the nerves. Fowler helped things along by regular exercises, and late in 1942 he rejoined No. 125 Squadron to become Turnbull's radar operator once more. Turnbull himself was commended for his cool reactions that night. The incident stands out in his own mind as the most frightening and yet the most satisfying episode in his service career.

Although No. 125 was primarily a night fighter unit, its long-range *Beaufighters* were also useful for extended patrols over the sea, looking for German reconnaissance aircraft. During one such patrol late in 1942 Turnbull briefly played tag with a *Ju 88* but the enemy aircraft escaped into clouds. Then, on November 4, 1942 he gained his first "kill".

There were two "Beaus" out over the North Sea that day, one piloted by Turnbull and the other by Flight Lieutenant Desmond Hughes DFC, a tough Irishman with six victories behind him. They were at 18,000 feet and 100 miles out to sea when, down on the deck, they spotted a lone *Ju 88*. Down they plunged. Tearing along, barely skimming the water, the two fighters closed in for a certain victory.

Hughes made the first pass. His cannon fire set the enemy's port engine smoking. Then it was Turnbull's baby. From 300 yards he cut loose with two bursts, ending when he was 100 yards astern. There was no fire or explosion in the Junkers. It simply dipped a bit and plunged into the sea. There was no sign of a dinghy. Turnbull later recalled feeling "wildly excited and very sad". Even in victory there was compassion.

In December 1942 the squadron's CO, Wing Commander C.P. "Paddy" Green, was posted to North Africa to take command of No. 600 Squadron, another *Beaufighter* unit, and gradually some of the more experienced crews from No. 125 followed him. In March 1943 it came the turn of Turnbull and Fowler. They left the relative peace of northern England for the battlefields and steaming heat of Algeria. For the next eleven months he and No. 600 Squadron followed the Allied armies from North Africa through Sicily to Italy. It was during this period that Turnbull blossomed as a night fighter pilot.

His first successful night action was fought on April 23, 1943. He had taken off at 3.00 A.M. and had been ·patrolling over Tunisia for more than an hour when ground controllers began directing him towards a target. The first rosy tints of dawn were beginning to appear when he spotted his quarry silhouetted against the sky, apparently heading back to Sicily. He fell in behind, identified it as a *Z.1007* tri-motored bomber, and fired one long burst. There was no return fire and no evasive action by the enemy. The bomber spun down through 10,000 feet before vanishing into clouds. It was reported as having crashed north of Bone, and Turnbull received credit for one destroyed.

It was during the Sicilian campaign (July 10-August 17, 1943) when Turnbull really vaulted into the list of aces. Indeed, Sicily was to be the graveyard of the *Luftwaffe* in the Mediterranean. Crippled but still fighting after North Africa, the German Air Force was to suffer complete ruin on that island. Night after night enemy bombers attempted to break through Allied guns and fighters to harass the invasion fleets, and night after night the skies were lit by burning aircraft. No. 600 Squadron, now based at Luqa airfield in Malta, was in the forefront of the battle, destroying 42 enemy aircraft during the campaign. Turnbull's share was eight German bombers knocked down between July 11 and August 9, all but one of them in multiple victories.

The most spectacular of these combats occurred on the night of July 15 which, to add another superlative, was also No. 600's best hunting night with eight bombers being knocked down. Turnbull and Fowler took off just in time to meet a major enemy raid. Turnbull spotted flak bursts which indicated that enemy aircraft were about and called up ground control to ask for a vector. He was directed northwards to intercept German bombers which were flying low over Sicily. Then Fowler got a radar contact. Hunter and hunted converged roughly head-on, though with the *Beaufighter* lower down. As the raider passed overhead Turnbull made visual contact in bright moonlight and carried out a medium turn, coming in behind and slightly below a *Ju 88*. He opened fire and the Junkers slowed. Just as the *Beaufighter* overhauled its victim the bomber exploded. A maelstrom of flame threatened to engulf the fighter and the enemy's fuselage barely missed Turnbull's machine. The close call sobered him and he became more cautious.

By now there was another contact on Fowler's radar set. The pattern was repeated—collision course, medium turn, get behind and open fire. The second victim, another *Ju 88*, blew up like the first. Then came a third contact! Once more Turnbull maneuvered to get on its tail. This time it was tougher. The enemy bomber was zig-zagging furiously, its crew undoubtedly aware that night fighters were about. The Germans sighted the *Beaufighter*, opened fire, and dropped lower down. There followed several tortuous minutes as the two planes weaved back and forth through the Sicilian mountain passes. At last Turnbull was able to get in a short, accurate burst. The enemy's port engine began to burn and one by one the Germans bailed out. Three in one sortie! Only two other RCAF night fighter pilots, Flying Officer R.D. Schultz of No. 410 Squadron and Flying Officer E.E. Hermanson of No. 409 Squadron, ever duplicated the feat.

Nor was this a mere fluke. Two nights later Turnbull and Fowler destroyed a *Ju 88* and an *He 111* in a single sortie, and on August 9 they knocked down a pair of *Ju 88's*. Yet despite his success Turnbull was not jubilant. He later recalled:

> I was young and seeing a lot of the world. In Algeria I had been based in the middle of some Roman ruins and had even been able to use an ancient Roman bath. In Sicily I pitched my tent in an orange grove and had fruit for breakfast every morning. But as to the war itself, it was a job I had to do, and I didn't enjoy it. I liked the flying and the excitement, but I didn't like shooting down people. I never gloated over the fact that I had knocked some down. Flying those big machines was a thrill, but it wasn't what I had expected to be doing. I was simply a bank clerk, and the role of killer was completely out of character.

In or out of character, Turnbull was undoubtedly a master of his trade, and in August 1943 he was awarded a Distinguished Flying Cross for "skill and tenacity". Fowler, the vital second half of the team, received a Distinguished Flying Medal.

On two successive nights, September 9 and 10, the Turnbull-Fowler combination shot down single *Ju 88's*. On one of these sorties they witnessed an inspiring spectacle—the Allied invasion fleet off Salerno as British, American, Canadian, French and Polish troops struck into Italy. Turnbull remembered the shells of the supporting warships as they arched, red-hot, across the sky and crashed into the German positions.

Late in 1943 he was pulled off operations with jaundice, and for a time he was attached to a South African squadron at Foggia, in southern Italy. At last he returned to No. 600 Squadron and on the night of January 24, 1944 he gained his final victory, a *Ju 88* shot down near Anzio. Within a month he had been posted back to Britain for a non-operational tour.

While in England, Turnbull was summoned to Buckingham Palace to be invested with the DFC and Bar. In a quiet, dignified ceremony King George VI, wearing the uniform of an Admiral of the Fleet, pinned the decorations on the young Canadian's uniform. "He muttered something I couldn't make out", Turnbull later recounted, "so I said, 'Yes sir'."

Turnbull's war was virtually over. In April 1944 he sailed for Canada where he was assigned to instructional duties at Greenwood, Nova Scotia. He spent an enjoyable year there, flying *Mosquitos* and eating choice Maritime lobsters. Nevertheless, it was boring too. Several times he wrote to Des Hughes, who was now leading a *Mosquito* squadron in the Second Tactical Air Force, asking if an overseas posting could be arranged. When none was forthcoming he volunteered for "Tiger Force"—the RCAF fleet which was intended to participate in Pacific theatre operations against the Japanese. In response to this he was posted to Patricia Bay. He was en route to the Pacific coast when Japan surrendered.

Released from the RCAF in October 1945, Turnbull spent two years catching up on his studies. Flying still appealed to him, however. Late in 1947 he was recruited by "Moose" Fumerton to go to China, assisting the Nationalists in forming *Mosquito* squadrons. From January until December 1948 he was in Hankow indoctrinating capable students in the tricky handling qualities of the "Mossie". For his work he was awarded a set of Chinese Air Force wings. The approach of the Communists, however, forced the evacuation of Hankow. He took a crowded train to Hong Kong, sailing from there to Canada.

The China adventure ended his association with aviation. Subsequently he became a salesman of photographic equipment. In 1958 he bought a farm near King City, north of Toronto, where he could peacefully raise a family of five children. He lives there today, dividing his time between sales trips, horses, and Newfoundland dogs. He seldom looks back on his wartime career, content to leave buried in the past the frightful days when he fought and killed in the night skies over Europe.

Turner
The Bull

No one knows exactly how many aircraft Stan Turner shot down, least of all himself. After a while he simply stopped counting his victories, and as he twice lost his logbook there are few records to remind him. One thing is certain; he undoubtedly logged more combat hours than any other Canadian flyer of the war; a report compiled early in 1946 credited him with 2,150 hours of flying time, of which 1,125 hours and 35 minutes was operational. Turner's record was remarkable on other counts. He virtually never took an extended "rest tour" throughout the war. He probably set something of a record for the number of ways that the enemy was able to get at him, for he was shot up, shot down, blasted by a land mine, and once had a ship sunk from under him.

They called him "The Bull" for his stocky build, but it was equally apt for his aggressive nature. On the ground and in the mess he was gruff and genial; in the air he was tough and authoritative. It paid off in more ways than one, for besides being a crack pilot, Turner was a magnificent leader who inspired his men with his sense of discipline and confidence. He proved that, in 1943, by taking over a haphazard No. 417 Squadron and changing it from the step-child of No. 244 Wing into the leading unit in that formation.

He was born on September 3, 1913 at Ivybridge, Devon, England, but his parents moved to Canada when he was still a child and he was raised in Toronto. He became associated with flying by serving as an airman in No. 110 (Auxiliary) Squadron. In 1937-38 he attended the University of Toronto, taking engineering, but aviation held greater attractions. Late in 1938 he enlisted in the Royal Air Force. He was just completing his aircrew training when the war began.

The beginning of his RAF career was hardly auspicious. In September 1939, while practising night flying, he flew a *Mentor* into a tree; the glide path indicator had been improperly set. Nevertheless, on November 20 he reported to No. 242 Squadron, the all-Canadian unit then forming at Church Fenton.

The squadron spent several months working up to operational standards. Early in January six pilots, Turner among them, were despatched to St. Athen, South Wales, to pick up the first *Hurricanes* for No. 242. On the return flight they ran into a blizzard which forced them to split up. The CO, Squadron Leader F.M. Gobeil, crashed on landing but was unhurt. Flying Officer Richard Coe of Winfield, British Columbia, was killed in the crash of his machine. All the other pilots put down safely, although Turner's *Hurricane* was slightly damaged when he landed with one wing low at an emergency airfield.

By March the squadron had been cleared for operations, and on the 28th Turner flew his first front-line sorties—two uneventful convoy patrols. No. 242 was to have gone to France early in April, but this move was cancelled when the Germans invaded Norway.

For Stan Turner the real world of combat did not open up until May 13. On that day, with the French armies beginning to crumble and Belgian forces reeling from the German *blitzkrieg*, No. 242 was ordered to provide pilots to reinforce RAF units already on the continent. Every member volunteered, so a selection was made which included Turner and "Willie" McKnight, who were attached to No. 615 Squadron. Between the 13th and 16th half of No. 242's pilots were rushed to the continent where they were spread among Nos. 85, 607, and 615 Squadrons. These were caught up in vicious fighting against odds, were forced back with the Allied retreat, and had to return to England on the 19th and 20th. By then McKnight had scored his first victory and Flight Lieutenant J.L. Sullivan of Guelph had become the first of No. 242's pilots to die in action.

The squadron was pulled together, then thrown back into the battle, covering the retreat of the British Expeditionary Force to Dunkirk and the subsequent evacuation from that port. The story of that famous operation has been outlined in relating the career of "Willie" McKnight. Turner's part in the campaign consisted of daily patrols from May 25 until June 1. His scoring was impressive. On May 25 he shot down two *Bf 109's* and probably destroyed a third. On the 28th he sent a *'109* down in flames over Ostend, then escaped from a swarm of German fighters by diving into clouds. The next day he claimed a *'109* as probably destroyed and another damaged, in the process chasing a Messerschmitt off a *Hurricane's* tail and having one in turn driven off his tail. On May 31 he shot down yet another *'109* which crashed into the sea. Finally, on June 1 he clobbered two *Bf 109's*, one of which was destroyed and the other probably destroyed, returning to base with his ammunition exhausted.

The Dunkirk evacuation virtually ended at dawn on June 4, but British troops who had been separated from the main body of the BEF were still in France, and the next job was to get them out through Le Havre. To support these operations, No. 242 was sent back to the continent on June 8, flying from fields south of the Seine River. The situation was too confused for anything meaningful to be accomplished, although Turner was able to destroy two more *Bf 109's*. The squadron's effectiveness was hampered by a fire on the 13th which wiped out much of their equipment including clothing stores. By the 18th No. 242 was back in Britain. It had virtually disintegrated through exhaustion and frustration.

The losses suffered in the past month had been frightful—Pilot Officer M.K. Brown wounded on May 16, Flight Lieutenant John Sullivan killed on May 17, Pilot Officer Lorne Chambers shot down and taken prisoner on May 18, Flying Officer John Graafstra and Pilot Officer Garfield Madore killed on May 23, the same day that Pilot Officer Joseph Smiley was captured and Pilot Officer John Benzie was wounded, Pilot Officers Robert Hill and J.W. Mitchell killed on May 24, Pilot Officers Dale Jones and Arthur Deacon missing on May 28—the former killed, the latter captured—Pilot Officer James Howitt injured on May 29, Pilot Officer Gordon Stewart killed on May 31, and Pilot Officer Donald McQueen, a promising pilot with two and one-half aircraft to his credit, killed on June 9.

To this battered, dispirited band came Squadron Leader Douglas Bader, who assumed command on June 20 and began by bullying everyone in sight—the pilots, the ground crews, the supply officers, and himself. Bader later recounted, many times over, his first encounter with Turner. He had called the pilots together to lecture them straight off about what sort of squadron he wanted and how he was going to get it. Having finished his discourse, the new CO waited for a response. Turner provided it. "Horseshit," he boomed, and then added, "Sir." It was the beginning of a lifelong friendship.

By July 9, 1940 No. 242 was a front-line unit again, and it was soon picking away at the *Luftwaffe*. Coltishall airfield itself was on the fringe of the Battle of Britain, but No. 242 regularly flew to Duxford for daylight operations. Nevertheless, the unit had destroyed only four enemy aircraft until August 30, when it had its first encounter with large enemy formations. Thereafter the squadron regularly met enough German aircraft to provide targets for everyone.

Turner was able to damage a *Bf 109* on September 7, but numerous enemy fighters disrupted his attacks, preventing him from concentrating on any one German machine for more than a few seconds. It was different on the 15th.

September 15 witnessed one of the most important actions in the Battle of Britain. The Germans were planning to batter London using 220 bombers of *Luftflotte 2*, backed up by 700 fighters. The attacks, however, were divided into two strikes with about two hours between, a scheme intended to provide maximum fighter cover to the bombers but which also enabled Fighter Command to rally all its strength on each occasion. Bader had managed to have three *Hurricane* and two *Spitfire* squadrons brought under his control for deployment as one huge hunting pack, known as the 12 Group Wing. When British radar detected the German formations assembling over France, this pack was switched southwards to meet them.

The first raid that day was launched shortly before noon. As the enemy arrived over East Kent, they were assaulted by one RAF squadron after another. By the time the attackers had reached London they had been whittled down and their formations disrupted. Most important, the *Bf 109* escorts were dangerously low on fuel. At the crucial moment, 160 fresh British fighters including Bader's wing hit the Germans like a thunderbolt. It was 12.15 P.M.

No. 242 was at 24,000 feet when the bombers appeared below them. The escorting Messerschmitts were then in the process of turning for home when the *Hurricanes* pounced. Turner selected a straggling *Do 17* and closed to 100 yards range. The enemy rear gunner opened fire. One burst from the eight Browning machine guns silenced him. Two more jabs on the trigger brought oil and black smoke pouring from the bomber. Three Germans bailed out and the Dornier crashed in a field, exploding as it hit.

The next and heavier raid crossed the coast at about 2.20 P.M. Forty-five minutes later, No. 242 intercepted the battered *Luftwaffe* formations near Maidstone. This time the Messerschmitts stuck around for the fight. Turner's combat report describes a portion of the action that followed:

> Sighted enemy aircraft and approached to attack when we were attacked by a large formation of enemy fighters. I turned and attacked a *'109*, delivered a short burst, observed hits. The *'109* slowly turned over and went into an uncontrollable spin. Was unable to be definite as I was attacked by a section of *'109's* but believe enemy pilot dead. [It was later assessed as probably destroyed.] A shell gun cartridge exploding in the

side of my aircraft under tail threw me into a spin. On recovery was below cloud, observed a *Do 215*, attacked from abeam using full deflection. His starboard engine started to smoke, the *'215* then slid into a gentle dive. It hit the ground and exploded between some houses on the north bank of the Thames east of Hornchurch. No people left the aircraft. I then returned to base.

It had been a very satisfying day; six enemy aircraft had been shot down by the squadron in the first engagement and six more in the second. Turner's second bomber was possibly a *Do 17Z* of *8./KG 2*, a formation known to have lost two machines to No. 242. The RAF lost 26 fighters and eleven pilots but shot down 60 enemy machines, conclusive proof that German air superiority could not be established over Britain. Without that, the enemy could not dare to invade the island.

Stan Turner flew more patrols but he gained no more victories that day. On September 27, however, he was awarded the Distinguished Flying Cross. Three days later he was promoted directly from Pilot Officer to Flight Lieutenant.

When the RAF began carrying the offensive back over Occupied Europe early in January 1941, Turner was in the forefront of the action. On the 10th he was among those escorting six *Blenheims* which bombed Guines airfield, near Calais, meeting no opposition. Two days later, under cloud cover, he and Bader carried out the squadron's first "Rhubarb" operation, machine-gunning a German E-boat and a drifter in the Channel. His next major piece of action was on February 8 when, with two other pilots, he harried a *Do 17* in and out of clouds until it was shot down in flames. There was a price to pay this time, however; Pilot Officer Lawrence Cryderman of Toronto had to ditch in the sea and was never seen again.

In mid-March Bader was promoted and posted to Tangmere to lead the *Spitfire* wing there. He knew leader potential when he saw it, and in the thick, imperturbable, pipe-smoking Turner he felt there was a natural squadron commander. Turner accordingly was posted to Tangmere to lead No. 145 Squadron. Throughout the summer of 1941 he and Bader argued, joked, and commented rudely on one another over the high frequency radios as they led their units into action. It was absolutely unheard of, and it provided an enormous tonic for the newer pilots behind them. The strange partnership ended abruptly on August 9 when Bader collided with a *Bf 109* over France, bailed out, and was captured.

Bader's loss resulted in one of Turner's more unusual operations, for in escaping from his aircraft Bader, a double amputee, had lost one of his tin legs. The Germans promptly radioed Britain, offering free .

passage for any aircraft which might be sent to air-drop a new leg. The RAF was unwilling to provide the enemy with a propaganda coup. It was decided to send a leg the way everything was delivered to France—in a bomber, accompanied by real bombs. Accordingly, Turner was one of the *Spitfire* pilots who escorted *Blenheims* when this unique cargo was parachuted into enemy territory.

Enemy air opposition throughout the summer of 1941 had been slight; the *Luftwaffe* was very busy in Russia. German fighters wisely kept out of range unless they clearly had the advantage in height and tactical position. Not surprisingly, Turner added very little to his score that year—two *Bf 109's* damaged on June 26 and July 14 plus a *Bf 109* destroyed on July 23. It was dull compared to the previous year, but his few successes proved he had not lost his touch. In August he was awarded a Bar to his DFC.

In October 1941 he was posted to staff duties with No. 82 Group Headquarters in Northern Ireland, but two months later he went to No. 411 Squadron. Although little of operational importance happened during his service with that unit, his impact on the outfit was immense, as the squadron diarist indicated when he wrote on February 8, 1942:

> Information received that Squadron Leader Turner, DFC and Bar, is to be posted Overseas shortly. The squadron are feeling extremely 'blue' as a result and a rush of applications was received from the pilots as well as the Adjutant and M.O., to proceed overseas. 'The powers that be' only laughed. However, one pilot, Pilot Officer McNair, is now extremely jubilant as he was [s]elected to go along. The rest of the lads are more down at the heel than ever. Being with us for only two months, Squadron Leader Turner has managed to prove his capabilities as a Squadron Commander in every way and a great improvement in efficiency and discipline, both on the ground and in the air has resulted.

It is at this point that records of Turner's operational career become cloudy. "Overseas" in this case meant Malta. On February 22, 1942 he took command of No. 249 Squadron, then at Takali and flying *Hurricanes*. He arrived when the German blitz of Malta was at its worst. and the enemy were taking a keen interest in the airfields themselves.

His Malta tour was crowded with major events. On the day that he took charge of No. 249 he piloted one of the eight *Hurricanes* which intercepted a raiding force. He saw strikes on a *Bf 109's* engine and either destroyed or damaged it. On March 18, in company with McNair, he damaged or destroyed another *'109*; the records are very vague. In between, on February 23, he had an eerie brush with death.

He and another pilot had been scrambled on *Hurricanes* to intercept four aircraft which radar had detected approaching the island. Climbing to the enemy's height, the two pilots were vectored off and about on an intricate series of courses. There was no sign of the "bandits", but the ground controller kept giving vectors. At length, his patience at an end, Turner asked exactly where the enemy were. "You should see them now; they're dead ahead of you," came the reply. He could see nothing in front. Suddenly he had a horrible feeling. Had the controller confused the two plots, mistaking the German aircraft for British and vice-versa? He twisted around just as four *Bf 109's* opened fire from astern. His goggles were blasted off his face and the *Hurricane* caught fire momentarily. The flames died out as Turner screamed away in a wingover. He would have bailed out if he could, but German shells had sealed his hood closed. He managed to reach Luqa airfield where he landed. He had been cut and singed, but he was alive. His No. 2 never came back.

Early in March Turner supervised No. 249's conversion to *Spitfires*. About that time the RAF painted two *Hurricanes* black for night operations over Sicily, shooting up targets of opportunity and dropping supplies to agents near Mount Etna. Turner participated in these sorties. On another occasion he took a *Spitfire* up for a high altitude test. He struggled up to more than 40,000 feet when his oxygen failed and he passed out. Subsequent examination of the barograph he carried showed a vertical line as the aircraft plunged straight down. When he recovered consciousness he had to use all his strength to pull out at 7,000 feet. It was a miracle that he did not tear off the wings; as it was, the aircraft was unfit to fly again.

In April 1942 he was given the local rank of Wing Commander and assigned to staff duties, first in Malta and then at Middle East Headquarters. Following that came duty afloat. Early in September the British planned a daring raid on Tobruk. An RAF officer would be needed aboard one of the ships to coordinate the air and sea aspects. Reverting to the rank of Squadron Leader, "The Bull" was assigned to HMS *Coventry*, a light cruiser. The raid, conducted on the night of September 13/14, proved to be a fiasco. Enemy gunfire sank a destroyer. Other ships moved in to support this cripple, whereupon *Coventry* and another destroyer were bombed and sunk. Turner dived off the cruiser. He was rescued by another ship in the assault force.

He was given another assignment as seaborne air controller in November 1942. Aboard HMS *Orion* he sailed with a convoy which was running supplies from Alexandria to Malta. About 6.00 P.M. on the 18th he watched as Italian torpedo bombers—the very best of the *Regia Aeronautica*—torpedoed HMS *Arethusa* and just missed his own ship. The *Arethusa* limped back to base with 155 of her crew dead.

In January 1943 he took command of No. 134 Squadron, a *Hurricane* unit which was experimenting in ground attack duties with crude napalm bombs. Flying over Tunisia with another *Hurricane*, Turner spotted a lone German tank. He swept in, placing his bombs squarely on target, but he grazed the tank and crash-landed. Looking around, he saw the tank burning fiercely, apparently with no survivors. The other pilots did not seem to see him, possibly because of dust and haze. Turner waited for several hours, intending to walk out at night. He was saved the trouble by the appearance of a British armoured car which had been directed to look for the knocked-out tank.

From No. 134 he went to No. 417 Squadron in June 1943. This Canadian fighter unit had not had a particularly glorious record. Recognizing the need for strong leadership, Turner set about his task with enthusiasm and bulldog tenacity. Perhaps he was drawing upon his experience with Bader in No. 242. Within six weeks the shake-up had paid off. No. 417 showed a dramatic improvement in airmanship and discipline, and higher-ups warmly praised the rejuvenated squadron.

He flew almost constantly with No. 417 over Sicily and Italy, but the *Luftwaffe* had already taken a beating. Consequently he reported no combats. On August 3, however, while driving with Flight Lieutenant "Bert" Houle in a truck, he ran over a land mine. Houle was blown out of the vehicle while Turner was trapped in the cab. He was out of action for ten days, but by the 13th he was back with his unit. In November 1943 he was promoted to Wing Commander once more, took over as operational leader of No. 244 Wing, and left Houle in charge of No. 417.

Leading his new formation, Turner had several brushes with enemy fighters, but by now the war was becoming a blur. He was credited with damaging two German machines, but in fact he probably destroyed a pair for which he never submitted claims; to this day he cannot explain why he failed to do so. In May 1944 he was posted again, this time to staff duties with the RAF's Desert Air Force. He was also awarded the Distinguished Service Order. The citation to this decoration tersely summarized his combat career to that date:

> This distinguished fighter pilot has flown nearly 900 operational hours in single-engined fighters. Since November 1943 he has taken part in all the more important air operations during the invasion of Sicily and Italy and in the Sangro and Anzio battles. He has destroyed fourteen enemy aircraft and has always shown the utmost gallantry, enthusiasm and leadership.

Wing Commander Turner was sent back to England in November 1944. In January of the following year he took command of No. 127 (RCAF) Wing with the rank of Group Captain; his Wing Commander (Flying) was J.E. Johnson. Turner supervised as the wing was retrained in ground attack duties, flew with it on important strikes, and remained in charge until it disbanded in July 1945.

With the end of the war in Europe he transferred to the RCAF, remaining in the force until his retirement in 1965. Among his many duties were command of flying at the Canadian Joint Air Training Centre, Rivers, Manitoba (1949-51), Canadian Air Attaché in Moscow (1954-57), and Commanding Officer of RCAF Station Lachine (1957-59), together with staff duties in Northwest Air Command and RCAF Headquarters. Upon his retirement he became an executive with the planning staff of Expo 67. Subsequently he was involved with "Son of Expo", Man and his World. Today he lives quietly at Chambly, Quebec. He still smokes a pipe, but he is reluctant to discuss his wartime experiences. Yet when Sir Douglas Bader visited Canada in September 1976, an emotional reunion took place between the two men.

Right: P/O R. W. McNair, 1941.

Below: Spitfire IIA P7923, DB-R of 411 Squadron at Digby, summer 1941.

PAC PL 4988

PAC PL-4918

Left: S/L J. D. Mitchner.

Right: S/L L. G. Schwab when he was serving at 1 OTU in Bagotville, Quebec.

Below: Gladiators of 112 Squadron at Paramythia, Greece.

L. L. BARTLEY

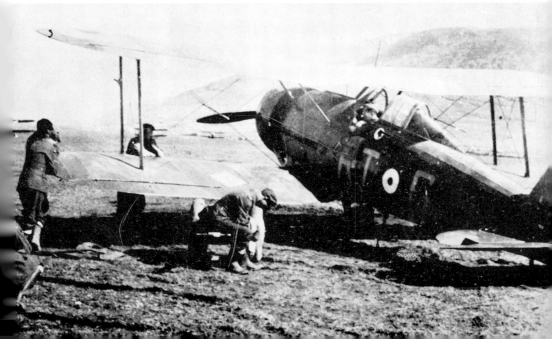

PAC PL-19465

Above: F/L P. S. Turner by his 242 Squadron Hurricane.

Above left: F/L R. I. A. Smith.

Left: F/L J. H. Turnbull.

Spitfire V of 417 Squadron in Sicily at the
time of Turner's command.

Above right: Hurricanes of the RAF Wing
in North Russia.

Right: S/L J. E. Walker.

L. L. BARTLEY

Above: Gloster Gladiator of 3 Squadron in Egypt, 1940.

Left: S/L V. C. Woodward C.O. 213 Squadron, at Edku Egypt in 1943.

Walker
Ace of Sun and Snow

The four *Hurricanes* were patrolling over enemy lines at 3,500 feet. It was mid-afternoon but the light was fading when four or five *Bf 109's* and a single *Hs 126* observation machine were seen 500 feet above. As the British fighters climbed, the German escorts turned into the attack. Suddenly the two formations were roaring towards each other on a collison course.

Flying Officer J.E. Walker saw a *'109* burst into flames, then spotted another on the tail of a *Hurricane*. He pounced on the German, fired two short bursts, and saw his opponent break away pouring black smoke. Walker followed him down, watching as the Messerschmitt rolled over, righted itself, and then became wrapped in flames before crashing west of Murmansk.

Murmansk: the ice-free Russian port within the Arctic Circle. Here was based No. 151 Wing, RAF, two *Hurricane* squadrons which had been despatched to Russia, partly to demonstrate Allied solidarity and partly to instruct the Russians in the erection, servicing and flying of *Hurricanes* which were soon to be flowing into the Soviet Union. It was September 12, 1941, the second day that the wing had been operational, and on this day three of the enemy fighters had been destroyed and the *Hs 126* damaged in exchange for one *Hurricane* whose pilot had been killed. One of the victorious pilots, Flying Officer Walker, had been launched on a spectacular combat career. He could hardly have dreamed back in Edmonton that it would begin this way.

Born in Claresholm, Alberta, on April 4, 1919, Walker had been educated in Edmonton where he eventually took a business course. He worked as a teller and ledger-keeper for the Canadian Bank of Commerce from 1936 to 1940. He was tall, fair-haired and heavy-set, and played a wide variety of sports: rugby, cricket, badminton, golf, tennis and hockey. He was generally interested in aviation, and, although he had only two short flights before enlisting, he did get to know one famous pilot, Captain W.R. "Wop" May, sufficiently well that May later recommended him to the RCAF.

Immediately upon the outbreak of war, he attempted to join the air force, but his applications were twice deferred. Nevertheless, he impressed the recruiting officers who described him as "dapper", "bright" and "alert". At last he was accepted for aircrew duties. In May 1940 Aircraftsman Second Class Walker headed for Toronto to begin training. There could be no doubt about his ambitions; at Initial Training School an instructor wrote of him, "Determined to be a fighter pilot—considerable dash—dependable—clean cut—very athletic." In December he emerged from the training pipeline at Uplands wearing his wings and the single thin stripe of a Pilot Officer. Soon afterwards he was in England and in August 1941 he joined No. 81 Squadron which, along with No. 134 Squadron, was preparing for its trip to northern Russia. One other Canadian was in the wing—Flying Officer David Ramsey of Calgary.

No. 151 Wing travelled to Murmansk by sea, the voyage lasting some two weeks, and then its aircrew, maintenance staff and administrative personnel converged on Vaenga airfield. Some had come via Archangel by means of steamers and railways. Twenty-four *Hurricanes*, including one piloted by Walker, were flown from the carrier HMS *Argus*, while 15 crated machines came through Archangel. Although conditions were relatively harsh—sanitation was primitive to the point of being disgusting—the aircrews were surprised to find the situation more comfortable than they had expected, and the Russians themselves were exceptionally helpful.

The first snow fell on September 22 and soon the wing was operating under Arctic winter conditions. Walker and Ramsey acted as ski instructors for the other members of the expedition when they were not patrolling near the port or escorting *Pe-2* bombers. At times it appeared that the bombers needed no escort at all, for they were so fast that the *Hurricanes* had to fly at full throttle. During the Russian adventure the wing destroyed sixteen enemy aircraft, probably destroyed another four, and damaged seven, all for the loss of only one fighter. Walker's contribution was one destroyed and one "probable"—the latter a *Ju 88* engaged on September 27.

By the end of November 1941 the program of training had been completed. The *Hurricanes* were turned over to the Russians while the RAF personnel went back to England by sea. After converting to *Spitfires*, No. 81 Squadron resumed operations. On June 2, 1942, Walker chalked up his second confirmed victory—an *Fw 190* over Le Touquet.

His record now brought him his first decoration, the Distinguished Flying Cross. The citation to this award noted that he was a "determined and skilful pilot" and added that he had "at all times shown a keen desire to engage the enemy".

In October 1942, No. 81 was pulled out of the line, issued with new *Spitfires* and tropical kit, then bundled aboard ship for "Torch"— the Allied invasion of North Africa. On November 8 the squadron flew from Gibraltar to Maison Blanche, Algeria. Their first night in Africa was miserable, for they had arrived ahead of their food, supplies and bedding. On the 9th the compensations were obvious; in bitter fighting No. 81 downed five *Ju 88's*, one of which Walker nailed.

Before the year was out, he had added at least two enemy fighters to his score, including one shared, and had registered a "probable" with four damaged. Somehow, during the campaign, he and his fellows secured three turkeys and three geese which were penned up behind their quarters until Christmas, when they were converted into dinners.

On New Year's Day 1943 the *Luftwaffe* despatched several waves of *Ju 87's* with fighter escort to attack the port of Bone. Three of No. 81's aircraft were shot down with the loss of two pilots. Walker was the most successful member of the unit that day, destroying one (possibly two) *Fw 190's*.

On February 13, 1943 he was promoted to Squadron Leader and given charge of No. 243 Squadron, assuming his new duties on the 19th. Shortly afterwards, on the 26th, he had a narrow escape. Six *Spitfires* from No. 243 were escorting two tactical reconnaissance *Spits* over northern Tunisia when three gun positions on the ground opened up. Walker had to crash-land inside Allied lines after his oil cooling system had been shattered.

He claimed two *Bf 109's* damaged in March, with his own aircraft being slightly damaged in one encounter while his guns jammed on the other occasion. Offsetting the disappointment was the news that he had been awarded a Bar to his DFC.

The final crunch in the Tunisian campaign came in April 1943, during which he destroyed at least four enemy aircraft, probably destroyed one, and damaged seven. In the process he suffered the humiliation of being shot down and having to take to his parachute.

On April 7 he led twelve *Spitfires* into a formation of fifteen *Ju 87's* with only three '*109's* as escorts. The dive-bombers jettisoned their loads at the approach of the *Spits*, but that did them little good. Walker claimed one destroyed, one probably destroyed, one damaged, and had the satisfaction of seeing four *Stukas* burning on the ground within sight of each other.

His next confirmed victory came on the 10th. He was leading No. 243 Squadron when anti-aircraft fire directed him to four '*109's.* As his unit dived on these, a dozen more attacked from above. Four of the enemy went down, including a Messerschmitt which exploded under Walker's fire.

The following day, during an early morning sweep at 19,000 feet, No. 243 spotted 18 *Stukas* at 8,000 feet with a dozen *Bf 109's* flying escort. Squadron Leader Walker shot down one *Ju 87* and damaged a second in a battle best described in his own words:

> I saw them get in line-abreast and prepare to peel off and start to dive. I went right across them, giving each one a squirt and definitely scoring strikes on the first. Sometime during the maneuver, my *Spit* was hit and my kite burst into flames. I decided that it was no time to linger so I dove out and pulled my ripcord. It was some relief when I saw the pilot 'chute open and then felt a tug, which meant that the main 'chute had opened. It was my first jump and, although it was awfully pleasant, my last, I hope. That 'chute seems awfully small against the big sky. Funniest thing of the whole day was when I landed and was pulling in my 'chute. Soldiers came running up with fixed bayonets and stopped disgustedly, saying, 'Dammit, sir, we thought you were a Hun.'

Walker was back with his unit and flying again that afternoon. His last "kill" of the campaign was on the 18th, when the squadron forced sixteen *Bf 109's* to dump their bombs over the desert. He shot down one of the raiders.

In June 1943 he left the squadron and emplaned for Britain. It was announced that month that he had been awarded a second Bar to the DFC. In July he was promoted to Wing Commander and took administrative control of No. 126 (RCAF) Wing until the following month, when he handed over to Wing Commander Keith Hodson. By coincidence, Hodson had once instructed Walker during the latter's training at Uplands.

Wing Commander Walker was given leave in Canada on the understanding that he would return to England within 60 days. He, however, had other plans. On October 7 he wired the RCAF Repatriation Depot, "Request extension of leave if at all possible. Am getting married". A superior officer wryly despatched a collect telegram: "Congratulations. Do it now. Imperative you return to UK expiration of leave as you are attending RAF Staff College War Course. Sorry no possibility extension".

He rapidly adjusted his plans and on October 16 married Barbara Joan Whitley of Edmonton. The following month he was back in Britain.

He had been selected to lead a new RCAF fighter wing, and in preparation for this he took the three-month RAF Staff Officer's course at Cranwell. Then, in March 1944, he was posted to No. 144 Wing. There was, however, one small item of business that needed attention. At a Buckingham Palace investiture he received the DFC and two Bars. At the same ceremony a short, cheerful Nova Scotian also had the DFC and two Bars pinned to his tunic. Outside again, Wing Commander Walker and Squadron Leader George Hill posed for photographers, then set out to assume their different commands.

On April 25, 1944, a small Auster aircraft buzzed over the English countryside, turning in towards Tangmere airfield. On this occasion, however, the pilot misjudged and a wing-tip hit a tree. The Auster smashed into the ground. Rescuers found one occupant, an RAF Sergeant, already dead and the pilot unconscious. He was rushed to hospital but was beyond all help. He died on the night of April 26. Wing Commander James Walker, victor of a dozen air battles, had been killed in a low-flying accident.

The Tumbling Sky

Woodward
Fighter in the Shadows

On August 6, 1943 the *London Gazette* published the announcement that Squadron Leader V.C. Woodward, No. 213 Squadron, had been awarded a Bar to the DFC. The citation to this honour was brief yet vague, reading simply:

> Since the award of the Distinguished Flying Cross in April, 1941, this officer has destroyed nine enemy aircraft, bringing his total victories to twenty. Squadron Leader Woodward has a fine record of achievement, displaying at all times outstanding courage and devotion to duty.

There appears to be no doubt that Woodward was one of Canada's leading fighter aces, but his exact score may never be determined with any degree of certainty, for he fought in the shadows—in North Africa, Greece and Crete—campaigns where rapid retreats forced units to destroy records which had been poorly maintained. The figure of 20 enemy aircraft is difficult either to substantiate or modify; his score and that of "Wally" McLeod are so close yet so indefinite that their exact juxtaposition on any scale would be impossible to determine.

Woodward was born in Victoria, British Columbia in December 1916. He was educated there and worked as a lumberman before enlisting in the RAF in 1938. Following pilot training in England he was commissioned in June 1939. Shortly afterwards Woodward was posted to Egypt, where he joined No. 33 Squadron, flying *Audax* and *Gladiator* biplanes.

When Germany declared war, No. 33 was well on the way to being an all-*Gladiator* outfit. For nine months the pilots practiced aerobatics, gunnery, formations, and army co-operation. By mid-May it was obvious that Italy was preparing to enter the war, and on June 10 the junior Axis power finally jumped into the fray. No. 33 was immediately despatched to Sidi Barrani on the Egyptian-Libyan frontier. Within two days the *Gladiators* were patrolling over Italian positions, taking the initiative away from the *Regia Aeronautica*.

On June 14 seven *Gladiators* led by Squadron Leader D.V. Johnson discovered a Caproni *CA.310* twin-engined bomber escorted by three Fiat *CR.32* biplane fighters over Fort Capuzzo. In the ensuing combat Woodward, assisted by a Sergeant Craig, shot down the bomber and damaged a Fiat. One other *CR.32* was destroyed before the dogfight ended. Woodward's aircraft had one bullet hole through a mainplane, but was otherwise undamaged. He had participated in the first aerial battle of the North African campaign, a fact that gave him much pleasure and pride. There would be more to follow.

Woodward enjoyed this early fighting when it was biplane against biplane in combats that resembled old Great War flying movies rather than modern warfare. In particular he loved the nimble *Gladiator*. He later recalled:

> Our kites could easily do 250 miles an hour, could turn on a dime and were generally a wizard aircraft. The Eye-ties were good pilots but lousy shots and we used to have some rare old dogfights in that clear blue sky, with never a cloud for cover. They were clean fighters, those Wops, and quite the equal of any Hun in skill at combat flying.

Yet the Italian Air Force, with combat experience from the Spanish Civil War, proved to be ineffective. The *Regia Aeronautica* was tied to the slow-moving army and was ordered to conduct standing patrols over Italian troops. This meant that the force was employed in a passive role—a mistake when air power is involved. Enemy aircrews were left open to free-ranging *Gladiators*, and RAF pilots slowly but steadily proceeded to sting the opposing air arm to death. By the end of July, No. 33 had shot down 38 enemy aircraft and destroyed about 20 more in ground strafing. Eight *Gladiators* and four RAF pilots had been lost.

Woodward was in the forefront of the action, and his coolness in battle soon won him the title of "Imperturbable Woody". On June 29, 1940 he shot down two *CR.32's*, and in July he added three more fighters, including one shared "kill", to his tally. In one combat he and another pilot were jumped by a dozen *CR.42's*. Three of the Fiats were shot down, but so was Woodward's companion. It was several minutes before he was able to shake off the remaining nine fighters and return to base.

At the end of July No. 33 was relieved by No. 80 Squadron and moved back to Helwan to refit with *Hurricanes*. After this, his achievements became less well documented, for the squadron's records of December 1940 through March 1941 were all lost and the diary for April and May was reconstructed from the recollections of various personnel. It appears, however, that during December 1940, while the unit covered General Wavell's offensive into Libya, he destroyed as many as five *CR.42's*, including two shot down on the 19th. In February 1941 the squadron moved to Greece. Presently it was caught up in the whirlwind of disaster which constituted the latter part of that campaign.

By now a Flight Lieutenant, Woodward's total of aircraft destroyed mounted. Between March 23 and April 20 he shot down eight, possibly ten, enemy aircraft and was recommended for the DFC. In that period he served alongside and then under the inspiring South African ace, Squadron Leader M.St.J. "Pat" Pattle, whose final score may have been more than 40. "Woody" had plenty of opportunities to inflict casualties on the enemy; on April 6 he sent down two (one source says three) *Z.1007* trimotor bombers in flames over the Gulf of Corinth, and on April 14 he destroyed a brace of *Ju 87's* that were dive-bombing Anzac troops.

By now the situation was deteriorating. The RAF squadrons had been helped by forward Greek observation posts which gave notice by telephone of enemy formations. The constant bombing broke this system, enabling the *Luftwaffe* to destroy 16 *Blenheims* and 14 *Hurricanes* on the ground on the 15th. Two days later the British squadrons had to abandon Larissa airfield, withdrawing to Eleusis, near Athens.

The fighting now reached a tragic climax. By April 19 the three *Hurricane* squadrons in Greece could muster only 22 machines. That day they destroyed eight enemy aircraft, including a *Bf 109* shot down by Woodward and an *Hs 126* shared among Woodward, Pattle, and Flight Lieutenant Littler. The next day, an avalance of enemy machines poured down on the *Hurricanes*.

That afternoon more than 100 German planes—*Ju 88's*, *Bf 109's*, and *Bf 110's*—attacked the RAF bases. The surviving 15 *Hurricanes* rose to intercept them. As the pilots ran out of fuel and ammunition they landed, restocked, then returned to the battle. Woodward destroyed one *Bf 110*, damaged two more, and also heavily damaged a *Ju 88*. By nightfall it was all over. The *Hurricanes* had claimed 22 enemy aircraft plus eight "probables" (*Luftwaffe* records admit the destruction of eight aircraft). Five precious *Hurricanes* had been lost, and among the dead was "Pat" Pattle.

The survivors were pulled back to the island of Argos, but when reinforcements arrived on the 23rd they were promptly set upon by raiders which destroyed between nine and 20 aircraft on the ground; figures by this time varied widely with those reporting them. There were, in any case, no more than seven *Hurricanes* left, and on the 27th, in total darkness, they were flown to Maleme, Crete. .

Shortly afterwards, the Germans turned on that island. Never were the odds so unequal. Against 650 enemy combat aircraft the RAF could muster only 24 machines. By May 19 these had dwindled to seven aircraft, and so they were evacuated that day.

Woodward remained behind to assist in the withdrawal of the ground crews. On May 20 the German onslaught reached its climax. Woodward fought in the subsequent battle with a pistol in his hand. He later recounted his experience:

> Then came the blitz. First, there were literally hundreds of aircraft, setting up a most terrific noise with sirens and in great and continuous waves, bombing our airdromes. Suddenly, the tremendous uproar stopped and was followed by an ominous silence, while we waited with our eyes on the sky. With our aircraft destroyed on the ground and our runways blasted by bombs, all we pilots could do was grab the handiest weapon and join the ground troops.
>
> Then they came—dozens of *Ju 52's*, troop carriers, crammed to the doors with paratroops, who floated down as thick as flies and armed to the teeth.
>
> The CO and I had charge of a party of 30 airmen and our only hope was to battle our way to a hillside position held by some New Zealand troops. So we went up, each with fifteen men, and started off by different routes. My men had only rifles and I had my revolver and a few rounds of ammunition. However, we managed to make it with the loss of only one man, despite a hail of fire from Tommy gunners and snipers along the route.
>
> After a three-day battle, the New Zealanders were pushed back by the Huns, who used captured British airmen as a screen when they advanced. All our men could do was hold their fire until they could see a gap through the prisoner's ranks. We finally fell back to the coast, where we joined a force of Royal Marines and were evacuated by a warship.

In the Battle of Crete No. 33 Squadron had lost six officers and 55 men, and even aboard ship they continued to be subjected to enemy air attacks. It was with a great feeling of relief that they finally docked at Alexandria on May 29.

It should be noted in passing that some controversy has arisen since the war about the incident involving the use of prisoners as a screen. The official British history of the campaign (I.S.O. Playfair,

The Mediterranean and the Middle East, Vol. II) makes no reference to it. Christopher Buckley (*Greece and Crete, 1941*) has written that such reports are unproven. On the other hand, Denis Richards (*Royal Air Force 1939-1945*, Vol. I) quotes an account by another RAF officer who was present which is almost identical to that of Woodward's. In the heat of battle many mistakes may be made, but at the same time hard-pressed junior commanders may resort to desperate methods which do not comply with the rules.

Once back in Egypt, Woodward was despatched to the Western Desert with a detachment of No. 33 Squadron (virtually all that was left of the unit) operating in conjunction with No. 274 Squadron. On June 17, while leading six *Hurricanes* on vehicle strafing, he encountered a formation of *Ju 87's* with twelve escorting fighters. In a royal scrap he destroyed a *G.50* while his companions claimed seven more machines, including three *Stukas*. His final victory was on July 12, 1941, when he was scrambled onto a *Ju 88* which he shot down in flames.

In September 1941 he was posted to Rhodesia to serve as an instructor, but in January 1943 he returned to North Africa to command No. 213 Squadron, flying *Hurricanes*. It was not a very active unit, being held back to protect the rear area of Libya. From March 1943 onwards it was assigned to the eastern Mediterranean, performing convoy patrols while waiting for bombers that never came. During this tour, which ended in August, Woodward received the belated Bar to his DFC.

From No. 213 "Woody" took up staff duties with the RAF's Middle East Air Force Headquarters. Later he commanded a communications squadron. In 1946 he returned to England for the first time in six years and elected to take a Permanent Commission in the RAF. Among his post-war duties was the command of No. 19 Squadron, a *Hornet* fighter unit in the United Kingdom. In 1963 he retired from the RAF with the rank of Wing Commander. Subsequently he moved to Australia and later returned to Canada, settling in Victoria, British Columbia.

The Tumbling Sky

Honourable Mention

Approximately 150 Canadian fighter pilots qualified during the Second World War for the unofficial title of "ace". The figure can be approximate only, for the records of some combat careers are incomplete, while in other instances a pilot may have taken one or two enemy aircraft with him on a last fatal flight. Such an occurrence has been recorded, and the manner of its discovery involved both chance and detective work.

William R. Breithaupt of Toronto was a night fighter pilot in No. 239 Squadron, flying *Mosquitos* on Serrate patrols. When Bomber Command was conducting major raids, his job was to seek out enemy night fighters and destroy them. Breithaupt was teamed with an English navigator, Flying Officer J.A. Kennedy. Between April and June 1944 they shot down four German aircraft. For this work they were both awarded the DFC. On the night of September 12th they took off to patrol near Cologne and never came back. Like thousands of other young men, they were written off as "Missing: Presumed Dead."

In January 1947 an RAF Casualty Officer discovered a grave in the churchyard of Ranschback, a village just west of Cologne, with a cross marked "Two Unknown English Flyers Shot Down 12.9.44". Further investigation resulted in testimony from German witnesses stating that the men had been the crew of a wooden twin-engined machine (obviously a *Mosquito*). On the night in question this aircraft had been attacked and set on fire by a *Bf 110* night fighter. At that point the German aircraft had overshot and the *Mosquito* delivered a short, accurate burst before crashing. The German crew had bailed out safely and were able to tell the villagers the story of the dramatic combat.

The remains of the two flyers were exhumed for re-burial in a British military cemetery. In the grave was found Flying Officer Kennedy's identity disc. The gallant crew had claimed their fifth victim in the last seconds of their lives.

First Canadian Aces

The first Canadian ace was Flying Officer Allen B. Angus of McCreary, Manitoba. He had joined the Royal Air Force in September 1937, and was serving in No. 85 Squadron, a *Hurricane* unit, when the German *blitzkrieg* smashed into France and the Low Countries.

No. 85 was assigned to patrol over elements of the British Expeditionary Force which were advancing into Belgium to meet the German thrust. On May 10, 1940, the opening day of the battle, Angus intercepted a *Ju 88* and shot it down. The enemy's return fire was accurate, however, and the determined Canadian had to force-land in friendly territory. Within hours he was flying again.

Flying Officer Angus destroyed two more enemy machines on May 12 and another pair on the 14th. Two days later he was shot down and killed. On May 31 the *London Gazette* announced that he had been awarded the DFC.

Angus is doubly deserving of mention because the credit for being the first "ace" is occasionally and wrongly given to Mark Henry Brown of Portage la Prairie, Manitoba. Brown enlisted in the RAF in May 1936, trained as a fighter pilot, and joined No. 1 Squadron in February 1937. When the war broke out he was still with No. 1, now flying *Hurricanes* in the RAF's Advanced Air Striking Force in France.

Brown's first victory was on November 23, 1939 when he shared in the destruction of a *Do 17*. Although he experienced several brushes with the *Luftwaffe* in March and April 1940, he claimed no more confirmed kills until May 10, when he and another pilot shot down a *Do 215*. Thereafter the Battle of France swallowed No. 1 Squadron. Fierce combats decimated the unit, but the *Luftwaffe* paid a price. Brown was in action almost every day. On May 19 he shot down his fifth enemy machine, an *He 111*, and probably destroyed another Heinkel.

"Hilly" Brown survived both the Battle of France and the Battle of Britain; eventually his score ran to six confirmed victories plus three shared kills, with nine other aircraft listed as "probables" or "damaged". He was awarded the DFC and Bar, plus the Czech Military Cross. Promoted to Wing Commander in July 1941, he was killed in action over Sicily in November of the same year.

First RCAF Aces

Credit for being the first RCAF ace must go to Squadron Leader (later Group Captain) Ernest Archibald "Ernie" McNab, who joined the force as a provisional Pilot Officer in 1926. McNab was one of the fortunate pilots who flew aerobatic *Siskins* in the late '20s and early '30s. In November 1939 he took command of No. 1 (RCAF) Squadron at St. Hubert. Subsequently the unit moved to Great Britain.

As no one in the squadron had flown in combat, McNab was attached to No. 111 Squadron (RAF) to get some operational experience. He got it; on August 15, 1940 he downed a *Do 215*. Soon afterwards he was leading his own outfit in the Battle of Britain.

At 3.25 P.M. on August 26 McNab led No. 1 (Can) down onto the *Do 17Z's* of *7./KG 3*. In the ensuing scrap he claimed one bomber shot down; other pilots claimed one destroyed and three damaged. By the evening of September 15 his score stood at three destroyed, one probably destroyed, and three damaged.

No. 1 (Can) frequently operated with No. 303 Squadron, and on September 27 McNab led both units in a mid-morning interception. With his section he attacked a *Ju 88* which was shot down, only two crewmen bailing out. He then caught a fleeing *Bf 110* and sent it down in flames, thus becoming an ace.

His own modesty might have deprived him of that honour. In his combat report McNab assigned the Junkers to his flight as a whole, which would have split it three ways. A close reading of the report and the squadron diary suggests that he was entitled to the whole claim, his two wingmen being important mainly to the degree that they protected his tail and shepherded the bomber into his line of fire.

"Ernie" McNab was awarded the DFC on October 22, the first member of the RCAF to be decorated for gallantry in action. He was later promoted and given non-combat duties in the expanding RCAF. In 1946 he was made an Officer of the Order of the British Empire and also received the Czech War Cross. He remained in the RCAF until his retirement in October 1957. He then settled in Vancouver where he died on January 10, 1977, aged 71.

In mentioning McNab, one must also remember Flight Lieutenant (later Group Captain) Gordon R. McGregor, the oldest Canadian fighter pilot to see action in the war. Born in Montreal in 1901, he had made a name for himself in pre-war sports flying and was associated with the RCAF Auxiliary. He accompanied No. 1 (Can) Squadron overseas in 1940, and flew in the Battle of Britain at the grandfatherly age of 39.

During the battle he was credited with four enemy aircraft destroyed, three probably destroyed, and five damaged. One of the "probables" was a *Ju 88* which he mauled on September 27, 1940. On that occasion the intervention of enemy fighters prevented him from observing its fate. In 1977, however, the Sussex and Surrey Aviation Historical Society recovered the wreckage of a Junkers which had been brought down on that date. The society checked German and British records, which led them to conclude that this was almost certainly the aircraft which McGregor had engaged. Thus, 37 years after the event, a new ace was recognized.

Like McNab, McGregor was awarded the DFC and given positions of increasing responsibility in the wartime RCAF. Interestingly, he was still associated with fighters when the war ended, being in overall command of No. 126 Wing. During the war he was awarded the OBE and mentioned in despatches on three occasions. Additional decorations were bestowed on him by France (*Croix de Guerre* with Silver Star), Czechoslovakia (War Cross), and the Netherlands (Commander of the Order of Orange-Nassau with Swords). Following the war he served as President of Trans-Canada Air Lines and Air Canada (1948-1969). He died in Montreal on March 8, 1971. His medals and many of his momentos are now held by the Canadian War Museum while his papers are in the Public Archives.

Day Fighters in the RAF

Some highly successful fighter pilots won no decorations whatsoever. One of these was Pilot Officer J.E.P. Larichelière of Montreal, who enlisted in the Royal Air Force in 1939 at the age of 27. Larichelière completed his training in the Spring of 1940 and then went to No. 213 Squadron, a *Hurricane* unit.

During the Battle of Britain No. 213 was guarding the coastal area around Portland. On August 13 the expatriate French-Canadian shot down a *Ju 88* but was in turn attacked by a *Bf 109*. He escaped into the clouds for a few minutes. On dropping into the clear again he discovered the '*109* circling the wreckage of the bomber. Larichelière pounced like a hawk and blasted the Messerschmitt into a flaming wreck. It crashed about 500 yards from his first victim.

Later the same day he engaged a formation of *Bf 110's* and against odds of 40 to 1 succeeded in shooting down one. His wildest combat, however, occurred on August 15 when, in rapid succession, he destroyed two *Bf 110's* and a *Ju 87*. This raised his total to six enemy machines in three days. His spectacular career was cut short the next day when he was killed in action before he could be recommended for any award.

Two brothers, Squadron Leader Homer P. Cochrane and Flight

Lieutenant Arthur C. Cochrane of Vernon, B.C. both joined the RAF and became aces. The former flew *Gladiators* with No. 112 Squadron in Greece and was awarded the DFC for having destroyed nine enemy aircraft. He was released from the force in 1946. The latter served with No. 257 Squadron during the Battle of Britain. He shot down three aircraft outright and had half-shares in two others. He was also credited with a "probable" *Do 17*. In 1942-43 he saw action with No. 87 Squadron in the Middle East. On January 22, 1943 he intercepted and destroyed an *SM.79* tri-motored bomber. On the side of his aircraft he painted six swastikas (counting his "probable" and two shared victories) and an ice cream cone. Arthur Cochrane, who was awarded the DFC for "high courage and great devotion to duty", was killed in action on March 31, 1943.

Robert Tremayne Pillsbury Davidson of Vancouver, another CAN/RAF pilot, was the only Canadian ace to destroy aircraft of all three Axis powers. He enlisted in the RCAF in 1937, and went on to fly in Syria, Greece, North Africa, Ceylon, and Northwest Europe. His score was one *CANT 506B* destroyed in Greece (November 1940), one unidentified Italian torpedo bomber near Sidi Barrani (January 1942), one *Ju 52* transport near Halfaya Pass (January 1942) an *A6M* "Zero" and a *D3A* "Val" over Colombo, Ceylon (April 5, 1942), and a *LeO 45* bomber-transport shot down over France in December 1943. Throughout the war he flew four tours totalling 600 operational hours, and claimed six enemy machines destroyed, three probably destroyed, and ten damaged.

Davidson was awarded the DFC for his aerial exploits, but equally significant was a *Croix de Guerre* with Gold Star which the French government bestowed upon him. Behind this was an amazing story of derring-do.

In January 1944 he had been given command of No. 22 Wing, in which three RCAF *Typhoon* squadrons (Nos. 438, 439 and 440) operated. On May 8, while on a sortie near Douai, his engine failed and he effected a crash-landing. He soon linked up with Free French forces. They would have willingly hidden him or passed him along the well-known escape route for evaders. Davidson chose to join the Maquis as a common soldier. Much of the time he spent hiding in a hole under a stable, emerging to trap German despatch riders, ambush enemy patrols, and blow up vehicles. This work stripped him of the protection offered him by the Geneva Conventions; had he been captured the Germans could have shot him with a clear conscience. He finally linked up with advancing Allied forces in September 1944.

Following the war Davidson transferred to the RCAF. He had a distinguished career with that force, retiring in August 1967. He subsequently settled in Kempville, near Ottawa, where he died on November 22, 1976.

"The Lost Legion"

Mention has been made of many RCAF aces whose careers were spent partly or wholly with RAF units. Thousands of aircrew in all trades were scattered through RAF squadrons, and in RCAF parlance they were called the "Lost Legion". Canadian Public Relations Officers seldom had the opportunity to do them justice for the home town papers, and RAF PROs did not fill the gap.

A case in point was Squadron Leader Alan F. Aikman of Toronto. He is occasionally mentioned in RAF histories because he was flying as wingman to the great Irish ace, Paddy Finucane, when the latter was shot down and killed by enemy ground fire near the French coast.

Late in October 1942 Aikman's squadron, No. 154, was loaded aboard a ship, complete with knocked-down *Spitfires*, and moved to Gibraltar. They became part of No. 322 Wing, assigned to Operation "Torch", the Allied invasion of northwest Africa, which opened on November 8. On the 12th his squadron flew to Djidjelli, Algeria, an airfield which had not yet been secured by the army. There was no fuel on hand; the first six *Spitfire* sorties were flown with gasoline drained from the other aircraft. That evening the *Spits* of No. 154 intercepted an enemy raid and shot down three bombers. Aikman claimed a *Ju 88*. The following day six trucks loaded with fuel arrived, and the unit was able to operate at peak efficiency.

Considering that the *Luftwaffe* was stretched thinly over many fronts, the enemy's reaction in the air was surprisingly strong. Aikman and his colleagues had many opportunities to score. By the end of November he had shot down three bombers, shared in the destruction of two more, and had run up a "probable" and a "damaged".

Throughout the Tunisian campaign Aikman picked away at the *Luftwaffe*. Although his "bag" included a *Ju 87* shot down on April 5, 1943, most of the opposition was in the form of single-engined fighters. Between January 13 and April 25 he shot down an *Fw 190* and two *Bf 109G's*. His final victory was scored over Sicily on July 17, 1943, when he downed an *MC.202* fighter.

Aikman was awarded the DFC in February 1943 and the Bar in October of the same year. He later flew a tour in Burma with No. 436 (Transport) Squadron.

At the other end of North Africa was Flight Lieutenant Joseph Jean Paul Sabourin who came from the village of St. Isidore in eastern Ontario. Sabourin, a university graduate, was 25 when he joined the RCAF in 1940. Having won his wings at Camp Borden in January 1941, he was posted to Britain for operational training. From there he went to Egypt, joining No. 112 Squadron (*Tomahawks*) on November 12, 1941.

On the 22nd of that month he was shot down by flak while

strafing targets near El Adem. He bailed out successfully, landed within the Indian lines, and returned to his unit. Shortly afterwards he registered his first victory.

It happened on December 5, when ten aircraft from No. 112 were acting as top cover to twelve *Tomahawks* of No. 250 Squadron. South of El Adem they met 40 *Stukas* with 30 German and Italian fighters. A vicious dogfight ensued in which four *Tomahawks* were shot down, although two of the pilots subsequently reported back safe. On the credit side, the *Tomahawks* claimed 18 enemy aircraft destroyed. Sabourin was credited with one *Bf 109E*, one *G.50* and a *Ju 87*, plus damage to a *G.50* and two *'109's*.

Late in December he was posted to instructional duties in Egypt. He chafed at this, for he was anxious to see more action. Finally, in May 1942, he went to No. 145 Squadron, the first *Spitfire* unit in the Middle East. On June 1 he and a Sergeant James damaged a *Ju 88*, and on the 8th, again with James, he downed a *Bf 109*. These were the first claims submitted by No. 145 in that theatre.

Intensely patriotic, Sabourin once wrote his sister that, although his tour was due to end shortly, he believed that he could best serve his country in action. Indeed, he was exceptionally aggressive, shooting down *'109's* on June 12 and September 8, 1942. On the morning of September 16 he added another *'109* to his "bag". That afternoon he was scrambled again, this time to intercept some *Stukas* with an escort of twelve *'109's*. In the dogfight he was hit. His *Spitfire* dived into the ground and exploded. Three weeks later the *London Gazette* announced that he had been awarded the DFC.

More fortunate was Flight Lieutenant Joseph Guillaume Robillard of Ottawa. When Robillard first tried to enlist in the RCAF in 1940 he was turned down for being underweight. Determined to get into the service, he went on a special diet and gained 14 pounds in one month. He won his wings in February 1941 and went overseas as an NCO pilot.

"Larry" Robillard joined No. 145 Squadron in England in June 1941. Soon he was flying regular sweeps over France. He downed a *Bf 109* on June 22, but the exploit which distinguished his career arose from an action on July 2. Following a brush between his squadron and some *'109's* he saw a flyer descending by parachute. Robillard believed, mistakenly as it turned out, that his commanding officer had been hit, so he circled to cover the parachute. Nine Messerschmitts pounced on him. In the ensuing dogfight he shot down two, then had to bail out when his own aircraft was clobbered.

He managed to link up with friendly French civilians who passed him from one place to another. Walking across France and Spain, he finally reached Gibraltar, from whence he was sent back to England.

Robillard became the first RCAF flyer to evade capture after coming down in enemy-held territory. In November 1941 he was awarded the Distinguished Flying Medal, and thus became the first French-Canadian airman to be decorated during the war.

He completed his tour with No. 72 Squadron, with which unit he shot down an *Fw 190* (April 4, 1942). He then returned to Canada for a publicity and instructional tour. In 1943-44, this time as a commissioned officer and flight commander, he flew a second operational tour with Nos. 402, 411, 442 and 443 Squadrons. In the summer of 1944 he destroyed three enemy fighters, raising his total score to seven. Characteristically, he tried to wangle a third tour immediately on top of his second one, but in this he failed.

He left the RCAF in 1945, but the following year he joined the Royal Canadian Navy, with which he flew until his retirement in 1955. At that time he held the rank of Lieutenant Commander. From there he joined Canadair in Montreal. Today he lives in Ottawa.

Another highly successful fighter pilot was Flight Lieutenant James Henry Whalen of Vancouver. Athletic and ambitious, Whalen had planned to join the RCAF Permanent Force even before the war. His initial effort to enlist, in October 1939, was deferred, but in June 1940 he was accepted. Seven months later he won his wings at Uplands. He was posted overseas almost immediately. On August 1, 1941 he was sent to No. 129 Squadron in England. While flying with that unit he destroyed three *Bf 109's*, two on September 17 and one on the 21st.

When the Japanese opened the war in the Pacific, Whalen was transferred to Ceylon, flying *Hurricanes* with No. 30 Squadron. On April 5, 1942, Japanese carrier-borne aircraft attacked Colombo, intent on knocking out one of the Royal Navy's main bases in the Bay of Bengal. Forewarned by a *Catalina* whose crew had signalled the approach of the enemy fleet before being shot down, the defenders of the island were alert and waiting. That day Whalen destroyed three *D3A* "Val" dive-bombers from a force of 50. The feat resulted in his being recommended for the DFC, but the award was not formally granted until December 1945, at which time it was backdated to April 17, 1944.

The reason for this juggling lay in the fact that DFCs cannot be awarded posthumously. On April 18, 1944, Whalen had been shot down and killed by small-calibre anti-aircraft fire while strafing ground targets in northern Burma.

Aces in the Orient

Mention of "Jimmy" Whalen leads to consideration of others of the "Lost Legion" who served in the Far East. Although many RCAF fighter pilots served in that theatre, only two—one a Canadian, the other an American in the RCAF—became aces solely at the expense of the Japanese.

Squadron Leader Robert Day of Victoria, B.C. was an insurance agent before the war. He flew one tour with RCAF units in Britain before being posted to India in December 1943. His first Asian tour was with No. 81 Squadron, flying *Spitfire VIII's* with red spinners. He destroyed an *A6M* "Zero" on February 15, 1944, and followed through with two *Ki 43* "Oscar" fighters, one on March 13 and the other on the 28th of that month. In August he was posted to staff duties, but in December he took command of No. 67 Squadron, another *Spitfire* outfit.

Day's most successful action was fought on January 9, 1945 when he and three other pilots bounced six *Ki 43's* over Akyab Island. Five of the Japanese machines were shot down, two of them by Day. The incident brought him a DFC.

Sergeant John F. "Tex" Barrick had won his wings at No. 10 Service Flying Training School, Dauphin, Manitoba and wound up flying *Hurricanes* with No. 17 Squadron during the retreat from Burma early in 1942. During this campaign he shot down five enemy aircraft, for which he was awarded the Distinguished Flying Medal. In one combat he downed a fighter but was then hit by two others. Although almost blinded by oil and with his flaps useless, he crash landed, only to be strafed by his opponents. He survived that with shrapnel splinter wounds, then walked for two hours before contacting Chinese troops. He went on to earn a commission and complete a second tour in Burma.

The only other Canadian to become an ace purely on the basis of action in the Far East was Sub-Lieutenant William Henry Isaac Atkinson of Minnedosa, Manitoba. In January 1943, at the age of 19, he joined the Royal Navy, intent on becoming a pilot. His basic training was in the United Kingdom, but in September he returned to Canada for flying instruction, first at No. 12 Elementary Flying Training School, Goderich, and then at No. 14 Service Flying Training School, Aylmer, Ontario. Atkinson then went back to Britain where he was commissioned in April 1944.

He moved on to the Naval Air Flying School, Henstradge, where he flew *Seafires*. His next posting was to the Royal Naval Air Station at Puttalam, Ceylon, for operational training and conversion to *Hellcats*. Finally, in December 1944, he was assigned to No. 1844 Squadron aboard HMS *Indomitable*.

"*Indom*", in company with two other carriers, left Trincomalee on December 31. The force attacked oil refineries in Sumatra on January 24 and again on the 29th, then continued to Fremantle,

Australia. There the British Pacific Fleet (BPF) was being organized to fight alongside American naval forces in the final campaigns against Japan. On February 25, 1945 the BPF, now having four carriers, two battleships, five cruisers, and eleven destroyers, sailed from Australia, proceeding in stages to the main battle zone. Aboard was a bewildering array of aircraft—73 *Corsairs*, 40 *Seafires*, 29 *Hellcats*, 65 *Avengers*, nine *Fireflies*, and two *Walrus* amphibians.

In preparation for the American assault on Okinawa, due to begin on April 1, the BPF was assigned the task of neutralizing the Sakishima Gunto, a group of islands between Formosa and Okinawa through which the enemy might try to stage reinforcements. Over the next two months, March 26 to May 25, the fleet was to devote most of its attention to these islands, with occasional attacks on airfields in northern Formosa. The routine generally consisted of two days of air strikes followed by two days of fleet refuelling and replenishing supplies.

In the first strike at Sakishima, on March 26, *Avengers* bombed Miyako airfield while the fighters strafed anything in sight. Atkinson probably destroyed a *G4M* "Betty", although this may have been a dummy, one of several the Japanese had deployed setting up "flak traps."

On April 6, 1945 the enemy hurled more than 700 aircraft at the Allied ships. About half of these were *kamikaze* flyers. That day Atkinson scored his first confirmed kill—a *D4Y* "Judy" dive-bomber. Six days later, during an attack on Formosan airfields, he shot down an *A6M* "Zero" and claimed a "probable" *Ki 61* "Tony". On the 13th it was another "probable", this one another "Betty".

Japanese repair crews proved industrious in repairing the Sakishima airfields, warranting their repeated pounding by the BPF. On April 16 and May 21 Atkinson participated in the destruction of *C6N* "Myrt" reconnaissance machines; in both instances the claim was submitted by his flight as a whole.

Nevertheless, the enemy could dish it out as well. *"Indom"* escaped the hammer blows of the *kamikaze* pilots, but the other carriers received hits which would have been fatal had it not been for their heavily armoured flight decks. Flak remained a menace throughout the Sakishima campaign; on May 13 the commander of No. 1844 Squadron was shot down and killed while Atkinson's *Hellcat* was severely damaged. Throughout these two months the BPF lost 98 aircraft to operational causes and 62 more to accidents, most of the latter involving deck landings. On the credit side, they dropped 958 tons of bombs, claimed 96 enemy aircraft, and succeeded in rescuing two-thirds of all aircrew shot down.

The British Pacific Fleet withdrew to Sydney to refit, but late in

June 1945 it sailed again, this time to take part in the air assault on the Japanese home islands. Atkinson had been assigned to HMS *Formidable*; his primary duties were night defensive patrols. On July 25 his flight intercepted several *B7A* "Grace" torpedo bombers. They never got near the ships. Atkinson claimed three of them destroyed.

For his work the youthful Canadian was awarded the Distinguished Service Cross and was mentioned in despatches. His commanding officer described him as "cheerful and spirited . . . alert and quick in the air . . . an excellent fighter pilot." By the end of the war he had logged over 140 hours on *Hellcats* with 56 deck landings, eight of them at night.

Following the war he joined the Royal Canadian Navy, with which force he rose to the rank of Commander. While much of his career was related to aviation, he also held staff appointments in Naval Headquarters, the Canadian Joint Air Training Centre at Rivers, Manitoba, and with the Canadian Defence Liaison Staff in Washington. He retired from the RCN in 1973 and now lives in British Columbia.

Twin Engined Work

Although "Moose" Fumerton scored the RCAF's first radar directed night victory, the first *Canadian* to claim such a kill was Flight Lieutenant (later Group Captain) Gordon Learmouth Raphael of Brantford, Ontario. Enlisting in the RAF in 1935, he began the war as a *Whitley* bomber pilot and was awarded the DFC in May 1940. He was later switched to night fighter work. Early in May 1941 he joined No. 85 Squadron, flying *Havocs*. On the night of May 10/11 he shot down an *He 111* under radar ground control, the first of many victories in his distinguished career.

In July 1942 Raphael was given command of No. 85 Squadron. One of his proudest moments was a visit to the squadron by Air Marshal W.A. "Billy" Bishop, who had commanded the unit during the First World War. Raphael was respected by his men, but his strict views on drinking and smoking precluded his being a popular leader.

In discussing the career of John Turnbull it was mentioned that only two other RCAF night fighters achieved three victories in one sortie. One of these was Flying Officer Rayne Dennis Schultz from Bashaw, Alberta. Schultz joined the Air Force in 1941 immediately after completing high school. Subsequently he flew two tours with No. 410 Squadron, December 1942 to June 1944 and December 1944 to May 1945. In the course of the war he destroyed eight enemy bombers, for which he was awarded the DFC and Bar.

On the night of December 10/11, 1943, Schultz and his radar operator, Flying Officer V.A. Williams, were scrambled to meet raiders who were heading for Chelmsford. A third partner in the forthcoming action was the RAF ground controller, identified in the combat report as one Flying Officer Hummell.

They had been airborne for 70 minutes when they finally made contact with a *Do 217* which took violent evasive action. The *Mosquito* caught its quarry, however, and the Dornier crashed in flames. Schultz climbed back to 15,000 feet and was vectored onto another contact. This turned into a *Do 217* which blew up when the "Mossie" was barely 50 feet away. The fighter passed through a cloud of debris and immediately latched onto a third *Do 217*. This one proved to be the toughest of all; not only did it take skilful evasive action but its gunners hit the *Mosquito* several times. One cannon shell entered the cockpit, missed Schultz by three inches, and shattered his instrument panel. Nevertheless, the Canadian team finally set both the bomber's engines alight and it crashed in the Channel. Moments later the port *Merlin* caught fire, and the fighter came home on one engine.

Schultz remained in the postwar RCAF. Understandably, he was closely associated with All-Weather operations including command of No. 425 Squadron (*CF-100's*) from October 1961 to August 1962. He was with the Directorate of Flight Safety from 1966 until his retirement in 1977.

Flying Officer Evert Emanual Hermanson of Buchanan, Saskatchewan was the other RCAF pilot to score a "hat trick" under radar direction. A student of dentistry before he enlisted, he won his wings at No. 12 Service Flying Training School, Brandon, Manitoba in December 1941.

His posting overseas came near to being an operational dead-end. At the mandatory Advanced Flying Unit he was graded as being good enough to instruct. From April 1942 until June 1944 he piled up more than 1,000 hours on *Oxfords*, and watched as his students went on to service units. Finally he was sent to No. 54 Operational Training Unit, where he was paired with Flight Lieutenant Douglas James Thomas Hamm. On September 24, 1944 they were posted to No. 409 Squadron.

At 9.00 P.M. on the night of April 23, 1945 they took off to patrol the Ludwigslurt/Wittenberge area. While orbiting at 10,000 feet they were instructed to drop down to 4,000 feet. This brought a radar contact which turned out to be an *Fw 190*. A single two-second burst blasted it into a flaming wreck.

Hamm reported several more "bogey" contacts, one of which was flying so slowly that Hermanson had to lower his undercarriage and flaps to bring his own speed down to 150 miles per hour. At a range of 1,500 feet the two men sighted their prey—a *Ju 87* which was promptly shot down. Ten minutes later they added a second *Ju 87* to their score.

These three kills were the only ones achieved by Hermanson and Hamm. Both men received the DFC. Following the war Hermanson completed his studies in dentistry. He served briefly (1949-50) in the RCAF Auxiliary. Unable to resist the tug of flying, he accepted a permanent commission in 1951. His career included instructional duties and a three-year posting with No. 433 Squadron, flying *CF-100's*. In 1964 he retired with the rank of Flight Lieutenant and settled in Calgary.

Two other instances of triple night kills under radar conditions are worth noting—one involving an American, the other a Canadian, neither of whom was a member of the RCAF.

Archibald Harrington was almost a borderline case. A native of Atlantic City, New Jersey, he enlisted in the RCAF while his homeland was still neutral. He won his wings at Uplands, just outside of Ottawa, and further cemented his ties with Canada by marrying the mayor of Ottawa's daughter. On arriving overseas he applied for a transfer to the USAAF, the United States having now entered the war. This went through just as he joined No. 410 Squadron, and he thus flew with a Canadian unit while wearing a USAAF uniform. To round out the international aspect, his radar operator was an Englishman, Pilot Officer Dennis Tongue. Together they destroyed seven enemy aircraft.

Their most brilliant feat was accomplished on the night of November 25/26, 1944. In quick succession they encountered three *Ju 88G* night fighters. In the combat which followed the *Mosquito* crew were both hunters and hunted. They shot down all three opponents, then had to take evasive action to escape another German night fighter which was stalking them!

Flying Officer George Pepper of Belleville, Ontario was a "CAN/RAF" pilot, having enlisted in 1940. In December 1941 he joined No. 29 Squadron, a *Beaufighter* unit at West Malling. His radar operator was Sergeant Joseph Henry Toone, and inevitably the team was dubbed "Salt and Pepper".

In September 1942 Pepper was awarded the DFC and Toone the DFM, the joint citation describing them as having displayed "perfect teamwork and initiative". By then they had destroyed three enemy aircraft, including a giant *He 177* shot down on the night of August 21.

Their greatest triumph was on the night of October 31 when the *Luftwaffe* attacked Canterbury. The raid was largely ineffective; a country haystack which had accidently been set on fire attracted most of the bombs. Seven enemy aircraft were destroyed, including three *Do 217's* which fell to Pepper and Toone. The first two exploded and crashed; the third, a tougher customer, was chased well out to sea before it went into the drink.

The remarkable team were recommended for fresh awards: a DFC for Toone (who had been commissioned since his DFM) and a Bar to the DFC for Pepper. The decorations were approved, but their recipients never knew of it. On November 17, 1942 their *Beaufighter* crashed in a wood near Rochester, killing both men. Pepper's remains were subsequently cremated and returned to Belleville.

Intruders and night fighters were not the only ones flying *Beaufighters* and *Mosquitos*. Some of the most disagreeable work of the war was performed by crews flying interdiction duties, particularly in the Mediterranean. The objective was simple enough—shoot up every means of transport available to the enemy, airborne, seaborne, and landbound, all to the end of strangling Axis forces through their supply lines. The trouble was that this work was invariably performed at low level and in the face of some of the hottest flak in Europe. Interdiction was not habit forming.

Flight Lieutenant Rodney T. Phipps was one such pilot. A native of Strome, Alberta, Phipps had been intent on becoming a mining engineer before the war. Enlisting in the RCAF in May 1941, he took all his training in Western Canada. Following operational training in the United Kingdom he was posted to No. 272 Squadron in October 1942. It was a *Beaufighter* unit operating in Egypt, but early in November it moved to Malta in support of the "Torch" operations. From then until March 1944 Phipps was involved in interdiction over the central Mediterranean and up the Italian boot, flying 84 sorties for a total of almost 323 combat hours, and winning the DFC for attacks on shipping, airfields, and railway installations.

His first victory was on April 17, 1943 when he and another pilot intercepted five *Ju 88's* off Cape Bon, Tunisia. He set the starboard engine of one alight, then broke away to deal with others, and was credited with a "probable". The most spectacular of his sorties was one flown on September 24, 1943, during the Allied seizure of Corsica. As in other situations where the sea routes were closed to them, the Germans were relying on air transports to succor their troops, with disastrous losses for the *Luftwaffe*. Phipps was one of several pilots who intercepted formations of *Ju 52's* near Elba. Attacking five Junkers he shot down two but was hit in the face by return fire. Nevertheless, he attacked a second formation of *Ju 52's* and destroyed two more.

Subsequently he flew an instructional tour in Cyprus, returning to Canada in January 1945. Two months later he was released from the RCAF. He died in Calgary in September 1965.

Hot Pilots: Non-Aces

Yet it should be remembered that not all outstanding fighter pilots were aces, a fact that the leading scorers would freely acknowledge. A striking example was Flying Officer Alexander Hugh Fraser of Como, Quebec. Enlisting in the RCAF in 1942 at the age of 20, he won his wings at No. 6 Service Flying Training School, Dunneville, Ontario in June 1943. However, it was not until December 1944 that he joined an operational unit, No. 439 Squadron, flying *Typhoon* fighter-bombers in Holland.

Fraser had no business getting involved in aerial combat. His job was that of ground attack, blasting bridges and vehicles, leaving the task of mixing with enemy aircraft to the sleek, maneuverable *Spitfires* and *Tempests*. Nevertheless, when an opportunity presented itself, he took advantage of it. On New Year's Day 1945 he was one of four "Tiffie" pilots returning form a weather reconnaissance flight when they encountered a score of German fighters beating up ground targets. In a savage low-level dogfight one of the *Typhoons* was shot down, but three and possibly four *Fw 190's* were destroyed. Fraser returned to base with his aircraft riddled by machine gun fire and two enemy fighters to his credit.

As if to prove that it was no fluke, the eager young pilot bagged another victim on February 14. He and Flying Officer L.C. Shaver bounced two *Me 262* jets and shot them both down in flames. Such a feat was rare enough, but for a pair of rookie *Typhoon* pilots it was almost unheard of. Fraser was released from the RCAF in November 1945. Curiously, he received no award whatsoever, not even a mention in despatches.

Another hot non-ace was Flight Lieutenant Alvin Thomas Williams of Toronto who fought in one of the earliest and least-known campaigns of the war. He had joined the RAF directly in 1937 and was posted to No. 263 Squadron in May 1940. That month he sailed with the unit to Norway where the RAF was covering Allied forces attempting to recapture the port of Narvik.

The Germans were supported by modern bombers and *Bf 110* fighters, but owing to the ranges involved and the enemy's preoccupation with the Battle of France, no *Bf 109's* were present. That was fortunate, for No. 263 was flying obsolete *Gladiator* biplanes. Their armament of four machine guns was relatively weak, and they could not catch German bombers except by diving on them. To overcome these problems the *Gladiator* pilots worked in pairs which executed co-ordinated firing passes, diving under the enemy formations and then using their momentum to zoom upwards again.

Williams proved to be adept at these tactics. On May 26, 1940 he and another pilot practically shot a *Ju 88* to bits, and two days later he downed an *He 111*. His greatest day was June 2 when he and an English pilot jumped four *He 111's*. Diving and climbing in and out of the enemy formation, taking turns at pumping lead into the bombers, the team succeeded in shooting down three Heinkels. Having dealt with them, the *Gladiators* ganged up on a *Ju 87*, set it alight, and sent it down to crash into a mountainside.

The Narvik operation was successful. Allied troops captured the port and destroyed it before departing by sea. No. 263 Squadron flew its aircraft aboard the carrier HMS *Glorious* on June 8, although none of the pilots had ever before made a deck landing, and the *Gladiators* were not even equipped with arrester gear. This gallant story had a tragic ending. Later that day the ship was sunk by German surface units. All the *Gladiator* pilots were killed, and Williams never knew that he had been awarded the DFC.

Squadron Leader Fowler Morgan Gobeil, though not an ace, won two distinctions. A former *Siskin* pilot with the RCAF, he was attached to the RAF when No. 242 Squadron was formed in November 1939. It was fitting that he should be given command of the unit, and he subsequently flew with No. 242 during the Battle of France.

On May 23, 1940, while leading the squadron on a patrol inland from Boulogne, he dived on a *Bf 109* and delivered a good burst. He was then subjected to anti-aircraft fire and was unable to observe its fate, so he claimed only a "probable". Two days later, during an afternoon patrol northwest of Courtrai, Gobeil led a section which bounced a *Bf 110*. With the Messerschmitt filling his sights he gave it a five-second burst. The *'110* went down trailing smoke from one engine and crash-landed in a field. These two claims were the first submitted by an RCAF fighter pilot during the war.

Subsequently Gobeil returned to Canada where he held appointments in training and ferry units. His second major distinction was that of being the co-pilot of a Waco *CG-4A* glider which was towed across the Atlantic in stages between June 23 and July 1, 1943—the only such crossing in history. The full story of that madcap flight has been told elsewhere; it brought him the Air Force Cross. Gobeil remained in the RCAF until 1956 and retired with the rank of Wing Commander.

Recessional

The overwhelming majority of Canadian fighter pilots, of course, had less spectacular careers than those related here. For them it is best to recall the proverb, "They also serve who stand and wait." They may have destroyed few aircraft, or none at all, but they shared the same dangers as their illustrious comrades. Their achievements were no less commendable for being modest. They shared in the strafing, covered the tails of their friends, and contributed their share to the final victory.

Wherever they fought, whatever their tallies, the Canadian fighter pilots left their mark on the formal records of their units and on the minds of those who knew them. They shared the qualities of aggressiveness, determination, a sense of adventure, and a team instinct fostered in their youth and developed through training. Some were devoted to flying, while others took it up "for the duration" and no longer. Grim or gay, they represented all national origins—English, French, Scots, Slovaks, even Germans—yet all were distinctly Canadian. Even those men who enlisted in the RAF and served far from RCAF units were marked out as being different, for they had come so far to fight, and they wore their "Canada" badges with pride. Along with their compatriots who served in bombers, transports, torpedo planes, and flying boats, they carried the name of their homeland through many a tumbling sky.

Canadian and R.C.A.F. Fighter Aces 1939-45

This list covers persons of all nationalities who were members of the RCAF as well as Canadians enrolled in the RAF. The former category includes two Americans who originally enlisted in the RCAF and who flew operational tours with RCAF units following their transfer to the USAAF. Excluded are members of other Commonwealth air forces who were never members of the RCAF, even though their combat careers were associated with RCAF units. Thus such names as J.E. Johnson (RAF) and C.C. Scherf (RAAF) are omitted.

Ranks are those held as of date of death during the war or at VJ-Day.

Scores listed are "destroyed - probably destroyed - damaged". A notation "5 - 2 - 7", for example, indicates five destroyed, two probably destroyed, and seven damaged. These figures are as accurate as this writer has been able to determine from available records, although some pilots and other writers may differ with these conclusions.

Abbreviations: CAN/RAF - Canadian in the RAF; KIA - Killed in action; KFA - Killed in flying accident; POW - Prisoner of War.

Name-Rank-Awards-Hometown	*Score*	*Remarks*
Alan Frederick AIKMAN Flight Lieutenant DFC and Bar Toronto, Ont.	9 1/2 - 1 - 3	No. 154 Sqn. See Ch. 38, pg. 284.
Allen Benjamin ANGUS Flying Officer DFC McCreary, Man.	5 - 0 - 0	CAN/RAF. KIA 16 May 1940. See Ch. 38, pg. 280.
Michael William Hamilton ASKEY Pilot Officer · Nil Saskatoon, Sask.	5 - 0 - 1	No. 92 Sqn. in North Africa, Sicily and Italy. KIA 28 Oct 1943.

Name-Rank-Awards-Hometown	Score	Remarks
Philip Leslie Irving ARCHER Squadron Leader DFC Bridgetown, Barbados	6 - 0 - 1	KIA 17 Jun 1943.
William Henry Isaac ATKINSON Sub-Lieutenant DSC Minnedosa, Man.	5 1/4 - 3 - 0	Only Canadian naval ace of the war. See Ch. 38, pp. 287.
Richard Joseph AUDET Flight Lieutenant DFC and Bar Lethbridge, Alta.	11 1/2 - 0 - 1	No. 411 Sqn. KIA 3 Mar 1945. See Ch. 3.
James Hamilton BALLANTYNE Flying Officer DFC Toronto, Ont.	7 3/4 - 1 1/2 - 2	Nos. 229 and 603 Sqns., Malta. KIA with No. 403 Sqn., 8 Mar 1944.
Wilfred John BANKS Flight Lieutenant DFC and Bar Hazenmore, Sask.	9 - 3 - 1	No. 412 Sqn.
Russell BANNOCK Wing Commander DSO, DFC and Bar Edmonton, Alta.	11 - 0 - 4 plus 19 V-1 flying bombs	Nos. 418 and 406 Sqns. See Ch. 4.
John Frederick BARRICK Flight Lieutenant DFM Sweetwater, Texas	5 - 1 - 1	No. 17 Sqn. in Burma. American member of the RCAF. See Ch. 38, pg. 287.
Robert Alexander BARTON Wing Commander OBE, DFC and Bar Kamloops, B.C.	13 - 4 1/2 - 9	CAN/RAF. See Ch. 5.
George Frederick BEURLING Flight Lieutenant DSO, DFC, DFM and Bar Montreal, P.Q.	29 1/3 - 2 - 9	The top Canadian fighter ace of the war. See Ch. 6.
Howard Peter BLATCHFORD Wing Commander DFC Edmonton, Alta.	6 - 3 - 2	CAN/RAF. KIA 3 May 1943.

Name-Rank-Awards-Hometown	Score	Remarks
Foss Henry BOULTON Wing Commander DFC Coleman, Alta.	5 - 1 - 4	Nos. 416 and 402 Sqns. POW 13 May 1943.
Russell Reginald BOUSKILL Flight Lieutenant DFC Trout Creek, Ont.	5 - 0 - 3	No. 401 Sqn. KIA 2 Oct 1944.
Harlow Wilber BOWKER Flying Officer Nil Granby, P.Q.	5 - 1 - 1	No. 412 Sqn. 4-1-0 in air-to-air combat, 1-0-1 on ground. KIA 2 Jul 1944.
John Green BOYLE Flying Officer Nil Castleman, Ont.	5 1/5 - 0 - 0	CAN/RAF. No. 41 Sqn. KIA 28 Sep 1940.
John Joseph BOYLE Flight Lieutenant DFC Toronto, Ont.	7 1/2 - 0 - 2	No. 411 Sqn. Score includes 2-0-1 on ground.
Thomas Anthony BRANNAGAN Squadron Leader DFC Windsor, Ont.	6 - 0 - 1	Nos. 403 and 441 Sqns. POW 15 Aug 1944.
William Ransom BREITHAUPT Flying Officer DFC Toronto, Ont.	5 - 0 - 1	No. 239 Sqn. KIA 13 Sep 1944. See Ch. 38, pp. 279.
Ralph Isaac Edward BRITTEN Flight Lieutenant DFC Depcousse, N.S.	5 - 0 - 1	No. 409 Sqn.
Philip Ray BROOK Flight Lieutenant DFC Salmon Arm, B.C.	5 - 0 - 5 plus three V-1's	Citation to DFC lists two victories with No. 239 Sqn. Other claims are with No. 418 Sqn.
Mark Henry BROWN Wing Commander DFC and Bar Portage la Prairie, Man.	7 1/2 - 5 1/2 - 3	CAN/RAF. KIA 12 Nov 1941. See Ch. 38, pp. 280.

Name-Rank-Awards-Hometown	*Score*	*Remarks*
Robert Andrew BUCKHAM Wing Commander DFC and Bar. Golden, B.C.	6 1/2 - 0 - 3	Nos. 416 and 421 Sqns. KFA 15 Jan 1947. Also held DFC (US).
John Todd CAINE Flight Lieutenant DFC and two Bars Edmonton, Alta.	20 - 0 - 7	Five victories in air; all others on ground. See Ch. 7.
Gregory Donald Angus Tunnicliffe CAMERON Flight Lieutenant DFC Toronto, Ont.	5 1/5 - 1 - 3	No. 401 Sqn.
Lorne Maxwell CAMERON Squadron Leader DFC Roland, Man.	6 - 0 - 2	Nos. 401 and 402 Sqns. Shot down 3 Jul 1944 but evaded capture.
Lloyd Vernon CHADBURN Wing Commander DSO and Bar, DFC Oshawa, Ont.	6 7/12 - 6 1/3 - 7	Also awarded French Legion of Honour and Croix de Guerre. KIA 13 Jun 1944. See Ch. 8.
Edward Francis John CHARLES Wing Commander DSO, DFC and Bar Lashburn, Sask.	15 1/2 - 6 1/2 - 5	CAN/RAF. See Ch. 9.
Philip Marcel CHARRON Flight Lieutenant Nil Ottawa, Ont.	5 - 0 - 1	No. 412 Sqn. KIA 19 Nov 1944.
William Lawrence CHISHOLM Squadron Leader DFC and Bar Berwick, N.S.	7 - 4 - 4	No. 92 Sqn. in North Africa.
Howard Douglas CLEVELAND Wing Commander DFC Vancouver, B.C.	10 - 0 - 2	See Ch. 10.

Name-Rank-Awards-Hometown	Score	Remarks
Arthur Charles COCHRANE Flight Lieutenant DFC Vernon, B.C.	5 - 1 - 2	CAN/RAF. Citation to DFC gives a total of seven. See Ch. 38, pg. 283.
Homer Powell COCHRANE Squadron Leader DFC Vernon, B.C.	5 - 2 - 1	CAN/RAF. No. 112 Sqn. One report gives him nine victories. Ch. 38, pp. 282.
Walter Allen Grenville CONRAD Wing Commander DFC and Bar Melrose, Ont.	5 1/2 - 2 - 4	Nos. 274, 145 and 403 Sqns. Shot down 17 Aug 1943 but evaded capture.
Stanley Herbert Ross COTTERILL Flight Lieutenant DFC Beamsville, Ont.	4 - 0 - 1 plus 4 V-1's	No. 418 Sqn. KIA 18 Oct 1944.
Harold Alexander CRAWFORD Flight Lieutenant DFC Revelstoke, B.C.	5 - 0 - 3	Served in Mediterranean and with No. 411 Sqn.
John Harvey CURRY Squadron Leader OBE, DFC Dallas, Texas	8 - 0 - 0	American in the RCAF. Served in Mediterranean
David Blake DACK Flying Officer Nil Calgary, Alta.	5 - 0 - 1/12	No. 401 Sqn. Three of his victories were Ju 52's destroyed on the ground.
Robert Tremayne Pillsbury DAVIDSON Wing Commander DFC Vancouver, B.C.	6 - 3 - 10	See Ch. 38, pg. 283.
Wilbert George DODD Squadron Leader DFC Rennie, Man.	5 7/12 - 1 - 2	No. 185 Sqn. (Malta) and No. 402 Sqn.
Harry James DOWDING Squadron Leader DFC and Bar Sarnia, Ont.	6 1/3 - 0 - 3	Nos. 403 and 442 Sqns.

Name-Rank-Awards-Hometown	Score	Remarks
William Watson DOWNER Pilot Officer DFC Wybridge, Ont.	6 - 0 - 1	No. 93 Sqn., Italy. KIA 16 Apr 1944.
John William Patterson DRAPER Flight Lieutenant DFC Toronto, Ont.	3 1/2 - 0 - 0 plus 6 V-1's	Nos. 111 and 91 Sqns.
Charles Emanuel EDINGER Flight Lieutenant DFC Hillsdale, Michigan	6 - 0 - 1	No. 410 Sqn. Born in Barrie, Ont. American citizen on enlistment in RCAF.
James Francis EDWARDS Wing Commander DFC and Bar, DFM Nokomis, Sask.	13 1/2 - 5 - 8	A press release gives him 15 destroyed, 8-10 prob- ables, 8-10 damaged, plus 8 destroyed on ground. See Ch. 11.
Phillipe Elwyn ETIENNE Flight Lieutenant DFC St. Lambert, P.Q.	5 - 0 - 1	No. 406 Sqn. A former 'Hurricat' pilot.
Colin John EVANS Flight Lieutenant Nil Hamilton, Ont.	1 1/2 - 1 - 0 plus 8 V-1's	No. 418 Sqn.
David Charles FAIRBANKS Squadron Leader DFC and two Bars Ithaca, N.Y.	14 - 1 - 4 plus two V-1's	See Ch. 12.
Harry Elmore FENWICK Flying Officer DFC Transcona, Man.	5 1/2 - 3 1/2 - 5	No. 81 Sqn., N. Africa. KIA with No. 401 Sqn. on 21 Jun 1944.
Leslie Sydney FORD Wing Commander DFC and Bar Liverpool, N.S.	6 - 0 - 2 1/3	Nos. 402 and 403 Sqns. KIA 4 Jun 1943.
David Esplin FORSYTH Flight Lieutenant DFC Winnipeg, Man.	4 - 0 - 0 plus four V-1's	No. 418 Sqn.

Name-Rank-Awards-Hometown	Score	Remarks
John Philip Wiseman FRANCIS Flying Officer DFC Winnipeg, Man.	6 - 0 - 3	Nos. 442 and 401 Sqns.
Robert Carl FUMERTON Wing Commander DFC and Bar, AFC Fort Coulonge, P.Q.	14 - 0 - 1	See Ch. 13.
Lionel Manley GAUNCE Squadron Leader DFC Lethbridge, Alta.	5 1/2 - 2 1/2 - 4	CAN/RAF. Nos. 615, 46 and 41 Sqns. KIA 19 Nov 1941.
Edward Lester GIMBEL Squadron Leader DFC Chicago, Illinois	5 - 1 1/2 - 1 1/2	Nos. 401, 403 and 421 Sqns. Missing 4 Mar 1943; reported safe (evader) 4 Aug 1943. Transferred to USAAF 13 Jun 1944.
Hugh Constant GODEFROY Wing Commander DSO, DFC and Bar Toronto, Ont.	7 - 0 - 2	Nos. 401 and 403 Sqns., and No. 127 Wing.
Donald Cameron GORDON Squadron Leader DFC and Bar Edmonton, Alta.	11 1/2 - 4 - 5	See Ch. 14.
Leslie Cyril GOSLING Flight Lieutenant DFC and Bar Battleford, Sask.	7 1/2 - 0 - 3	Citation to Bar to DFC credits him with nine destroyed. KIA 14 Jul 1943.
Malcolm Grant GRAHAM Flying Officer DFC Exeter, Ont.	5 - 0 - 0	No. 411 Sqn.
Ross Garstang GRAY Wing Commander DFC and Bar Edmonton, Alta.	10 - 0 - 12 plus two V-1's	No. 418 Sqn. Two air- craft destroyed and one damaged in air; all others on ground. See Ch. 15.

Name-Rank-Awards-Hometown	Score	Remarks
Fouglas Irving HALL Flight Lieutenant DFC and Bar Timmins, Ont.	7 - 0 - 2	Nos. 400 and 414 Sqns.
Archibald Allan HARRINGTON Lieutenant DSO, DFC Atlantic City, N.J.	7 - 0 - 0	No. 410 Sqn. Member of RCAF who transferred to USAAF, but flew a tour with RCAF unit. See Ch. 38, pg. 291.
Robert Kitchener HAYWARD Squadron Leader DSO, DFC St. John's, Nfld.	5 1/2 - 1/4 - 5 1/2	Nos. 401 and 411 Sqns.
George Urquhart HILL Squadron Leader DFC and two Bars Pictou, N.S.	11 4/5 - 3 - 11	Citation to second Bar to DFC credited him with 14 destroyed. See Ch. 17.
Thomas Harvey HOARE Squadron Leader DFC Lang, Sask.	2 - 0 - 0 plus three V-1's	Nos. 56 and 421 Sqns.
Garth Edward HORRICKS Flight Lieutenant DFM Pembroke, Ont.	5 - 2 - 4 1/7	Nos. 185 and 417 Sqns. KFA 1 Jul 1951.
Albert Ulric HOULE Squadron Leader DFC and Bar Massey, Ont.	11 - 1 - 7	See Ch. 18.
Douglas Franklin HUSBAND Flight Lieutenant DFC Toronto, Ont.	5 1/2 - 0 - 2	Nos. 81 and 401 Sqns.
Bruce Johnston INGALLS Flight Lieutenant DFC Danville, Ont.	7 1/2 - 0 - 2	Nos. 72 and 417 Sqns. KIA 16 Jun 1944.
David Robert Charles JAMIESON Flight Lieutenant DFC and Bar Toronto, Ont.	8 - 0 - 1	No. 412 Sqn.

Name-Rank-Awards-Hometown	Score	Remarks
Clarence Murl JASPER Flight Lieutenant DFC Spokane, Wash.	6 - 1 - 1	No. 418 Sqn.
George William JOHNSON Flight Lieutenant DFC and Bar Hamilton, Ont.	9 - 0 - 4	Nos. 411 and 401 Sqns.
Paul Gilbert JOHNSON Flight Lieutenant DFC Bethel, Conn.	5 - 0 - 4	No. 421 Sqn. KIA 18 Jul 1944.
Milton Eardley JOWSEY Squadron Leader DFC Ottawa, Ont.	5 - 2 - 3	Nos. 33 and 92 Sqns., North Africa; and No. 442 Sqn. POW 22 Feb 1945.
George Clinton KEEFER Wing Commander DSO and Bar, DFC and Bar Charlottetown, P.E.I.	18 - 2 - 7 1/7	Score includes five destroyed on ground. See Ch. 19.
George Noel KEITH Flying Officer DFC Cardston, Alta.	8 1/2 - 2 - 2	Nos. 402 and 72 Sqns. KIA 4 Aug 1943.
Irving Farmer KENNEDY Squadron Leader DFC and Bar Cumberland, Ont.	12 7/12 - 1 - 0	See Ch. 20.
John Alexander KENT Wing Commander DFC and Bar, AFC Winnipeg, Man.	13 - 2 - 3	See Ch. 21.
James Bernard KERR Squadron Leader Nil Campellford, Ont.	4 3/4 - 0 - 3 plus one V-1	No. 418 Sqn. Two destroyed on ground.
Donald Harold KIMBALL Flight Lieutenant DFC Oromocto, N.B.	6 - 0 - 1	No. 441 Sqn.

Name-Rank-Awards-Hometown	Score	Remarks
Robert Allan KIPP Squadron Leader DSO, DFC Kamloops, B.C.	12 1/2 - 1/2 - 3	Includes two aircraft destroyed on ground. See Ch. 22.
Walter Gordon KIRKWOOD Flying Officer DFC Vegreville, Alta.	5 - 0 - 0	Nos. 409 and 406 Sqns.
William Thomas KLERSY Squadron Leader DSO, DFC and Bar Brantford, Ont.	16 1/2 - 0 - 3 1/2	KFA 22 May 1945. See Ch. 23.
Esli Gordon LAPP Flight Lieutenant DFC Redcliffe, Alta.	5 - 0 - 1	No. 411 Sqn.
Joseph Emile Paul LARICHELIERE Pilot Officer Nil Montreal, P.Q.	6 - 0 - 0	CAN/RAF. KIA 16 Aug 1940. See Ch. 38, pg. 282.
John Blandford LATTA Flying Officer DFC Vancouver, B.C.	6 1/2 - 1 - 0	CAN/RAF. No. 242 Sqn. KIA 12 Jan 1941.
Donald Currie LAUBMAN Squadron Leader DFC and Bar Provost, Alta.	15 - 0 - 3	See Ch. 24.
Peter Strathearne LEGGAT Squadron Leader Nil Montreal, P.Q.	Five V-1's	No. 418 Sqn.
James Douglas LINDSAY Flight Lieutenant DFC Arnprior, Ont.	7 - 0 - 5	No. 403 Sqn. Also shot down two MiG-15's and damaged three, Korea, 1953.
James Forrest LUMA Lieutenant DFC Belt, Montana	7 - 0 - 4	Scored 2-0-4 on ground. American in RCAF, transferred to USAAF 29 Jun 1943 but flew tour with No. 418 Sqn.

Name-Rank-Awards-Hometown	*Score*	*Remarks*
Harry Deane MacDONALD Flight Lieutenant DFC and Bar Toronto, Ont.	7 1/2 - 1 - 5	Nos. 401 and 402 Sqns. KIA 30 Nov 1943.
John Frederick McELROY Squadron Leader DFC and Bar Kamloops, B.C.	13 1/2 - 2 1/2 - 9	See Ch. 25.
Donald Aikins MacFADYEN Squadron Leader DSO, DFC and Bar Toronto, Ont.	12 - 2 - 16 plus 5 V-1's	Score includes 5-1-16 on ground. See Ch. 26.
Gordon Roy McGREGOR Group Captain OBE, DFC Montreal, P.Q.	5 - 2 - 5	No. 1 (Can) Sqn., RCAF. Score includes one claim upgraded from 'probable' to 'destroyed' in 1977. See Ch. 38, pp. 281.
John MacKAY Flight Lieutenant DFC and Bar Cloverdale, B.C.	10 7/10 - 0 - 6 1/2	Also destroyed one MiG-15 in Korea, 1953. See Ch. 27.
Andrew Robert MacKENZIE Flight Lieutenant DFC Montreal, P.Q.	8 1/4 - 0 - 1	Nos. 421 and 403 Sqns.
William Lidstone McKNIGHT Flying Officer DFC and Bar Edmonton, Alta.	16 1/2 - 0 - 1	KIA 12 Jan 1941. See Ch. 28.
Ian Roy MacLENNAN Flight Lieutenant DFM Regina, Sask.	7 - 0 - 6	No. 1435 Sqn., Malta. POW 7 Jun 1944, with No. 443 Sqn.
Henry Wallace McLEOD Squadron Leader DSO, DFC and Bar Regina, Sask.	19 - 1 - 9 1/4	KIA 27 Sep 1944. See Ch. 29.
Ernest Archibald McNAB Group Captain OBE, DFC Regina, Sask.	5 - 1 - 3	No. 1 (Can) Sqn., RCAF. First RCAF ace. See Ch. 38, pg. 281.

Name-Rank-Awards-Hometown	Score	Remarks
Robert Wendell McNAIR Wing Commander DFC and two Bars Battleford, Sask.	14 - 2 - 14	Records conflict. DSO citation says 16 destroyed. Author C.S. Shores agrees. See Ch. 30.
Charles McLaughlin MAGWOOD Squadron Leader DFC Toronto, Ont.	5 - 0 - 3 1/2	Nos. 403 and 421 Sqns.
Newton Stuart MAY Flight Lieutenant Nil Guelph, Ont.	Five V-1's	No. 418 Sqn. POW 17 Oct 1944.
Harry Thorne MITCHELL Flight Lieutenant DFC Port Hope, Ont.	6 1/2 - 0 - 1	CAN/RAF. No. 87 Sqn.
John Davidson MITCHNER Squadron Leader DFC and Bar Saskatoon, Sask.	10 1/2 - 1 5/6 - 3	See Ch. 31.
Donald Robert MORRISON Flight Lieutenant DFC, DFM Toronto, Ont.	5 1/3 - 4 1/2 - 5	No. 401 Sqn. Citation to DFC says 15 destroyed, but this clearly lumps together all categories of claims. POW 8 Nov 1942.
Guy Elwood MOTT Flight Lieutenant DFC Oil Springs, Ont.	5 1/2 - 0 - 1/3	No. 441 Sqn. Missing 6 Aug 1944, but evaded capture.
Frederick Thomas MURRAY Flight Lieutenant DFC Windsor, Ont.	5 - 1 - 2 1/12	Nos. 412 and 401 Sqns. POW 22 Feb 1945.
John William NEIL Flight Lieutenant DFC Nanaimo, B.C.	5 - 3 - 6	Nos. 274 and 421 Sqns. POW 23 Aug 1944.

Name-Rank-Awards-Hometown	*Score*	*Remarks*
William Henry NELSON Flying Officer DFC Montreal, P.Q.	5 - 0 - 2	Won his DFC as bomber pilot. Switched to fighters and flew with No. 74 Sqn. KIA 1 Nov 1940.
David Edward NESS Flying Officer DFC Westmount, P.Q.	5 1/2 - 0 - 0 plus 2 1/2 V-1's	No. 56 Sqn.
Daniel Edward NOONAN Flight Lieutenant DFC Kingston, Ont.	5 1/4 - 0 - 0	No. 416 Sqn.
Geoffrey Wilson NORTHCOTT Wing Commander DSO, DFC and Bar Minnedosa, Man.	7 1/2 - 0 - 5	Nos. 401, 603, 229 and 416 Sqns. Citations credit him with nine destroyed.
Alfred Keith OGILVIE Flight Lieutenant DFC Ottawa, Ont.	6 - 3 - 3	CAN/RAF. No. 609 Sqn. POW 4 Jul 1941.
Thomas Lawrence PATTERSON Pilot Officer Nil Toronto, Ont.	7 - 1 - 1	CAN/RAF. No. 274 Sqn., N. Africa. KIA 25 Apr 1941.
Warren Brock PEGLAR Flight Lieutenant DFC Toronto, Ont.	4 - 0 - 0 (air) 4 - 0 - 0 (ground)	Score based on citation to DFC. Served in Nos. 501 and 274 Sqns., and with 335 Fighter Group (USAAF).
George PEPPER Flying Officer DFC and Bar Belleville, Ont.	6 - 0 - 1	No. 29 Sqn. KFA 17 Nov 1942. See Ch. 38, pp. 291.
Rodney Thirsk PHIPPS Flight Lieutenant DFC Strome, Alta.	5 1/2 - 0 - 2 (air) 10 - 0 - 1 (ground)	No. 272 Sqn., Mediterranean. Details scarce. See Ch. 38, pg. 292.

Name-Rank-Awards-Hometown	Score	Remarks
Donald Mathew PIERI Flight Lieutenant DFC Toronto, Ont.	6 - 0 - 2	Nos. 442 and 412 Sqns. Born in Texas.
Benjamin Erwin PLUMER Squadron Leader DFC Bassano, Alta.	5 - 0 - 0	Nos. 410 and 409 Sqns. Includes one destroyed on ground.
Gerald Geoffrey RACINE Flight Lieutenant DFC St. Boniface, Man.	7 - 0 - 0	No. 263 Sqn. Shot down 31 Mar 1944, and evaded capture. At least three victories were against aircraft on ground.
Gordon Learmouth RAPHAEL Group Captain DSO, DFC and Bar Brantford, Ont.	7 - 1 - 1 plus two V-1's	Won first DFC as a bomber pilot. Switched to night fighters, No. 85 Sqn. KFA 10 Apr 1945. See Ch. 38, pg. 289.
Donald George REID Pilot Officer DFM Lacombe, Alta.	5 - 0 - 1	No. 185 Sqn., Malta. KIA 22 Jul 1942.
Joseph Guillaume Laurent ROBILLARD Flight Lieutenant DFM Ottawa, Ont.	7 - 0 - 1	See Ch. 38, pp. 285.
Joseph Jean Paul SABOURIN Flight Lieutenant DFC St. Isidore, Ont.	6 1/2 - 0 - 3	KIA 16 Sep 1942. See Ch. 38, pp. 284.
Dallas Wilber SCHMIDT Flight Lieutenant DFC and Bar Wetaskiwan, Alta.	8 1/2 - 1 - 4 1/2	No. 236, 227 and 404 Sqns.
Rayne Dennis SCHULTZ Flight Lieutenant DFC and Bar Bashaw, Alta.	8 - 0 - 0	See Ch. 38, pp. 289.

Name-Rank-Awards-Hometown	Score	Remarks
Lloyd Gilbert SCHWAB Wing Commander DFC Niagara Falls, Ont.	11 - 1 - 0	Details of score are few. DFC citation is basis for total shown. See Ch. 32.
Sidney Platt SEID Flying Officer DFC San Francisco, Calif.	8 - 0 - 7 plus four V-1's	No. 418 Sqn. All victories on ground.
Jackson Eddis SHEPPARD Squadron Leader DFC Vancouver, B.C.	5 - 0 - 0	Nos. 401 and 412 Sqns. A former 'Hurricat' pilot.
Mervin Harold SIMS Flying Officer DFC Vancouver, B.C.	6 - 2 - 2 plus one V-1	No. 418 Sqn. Two destroyed and two damaged on ground.
Forgrave Marshall SMITH Wing Commander DFC Edmonton, Alta.	5 - 0 - 3	CAN/RAF. Total number destroyed based on citation to DFC.
James Duncan SMITH Flight Lieutenant Nil Winnipeg, Man.	7 1/3 - 1 - 2	CAN/RAF. Nos. 73 and 274 Sqns. France, Battle of Britain and N. Africa. KIA 14 Apr 1941.
Roderick Illingsworth Alpine SMITH Squadron Leader DFC and Bar Regina, Sask.	13 1/5 - 1/2 - 1	See Ch. 33.
Robert Rutherford SMITH Flight Lieutenant DFC London, Ont.	7 - 1 - 2	CAN/RAF. Nos. 229 and 112 Sqns. Citation to DFC gives 8 destroyed.
James Dean SOMERVILLE Wing Commander DSO, DFC Toronto, Ont.	7 - 0 - 1	Nos. 409 and 410 Sqns.
Noel Karl STANSFELD Squadron Leader DFC Vancouver, B.C.	5 1/2 - 2 - 0	CAN/RAF. No. 242 Sqn. DFC citation says seven destroyed; it appears to include all claims.

Name-Rank-Awards-Hometown	*Score*	*Remarks*
Hugh Norman TAMBLYN Flying Officer DFC Watrous, Sask.	5 - 1 - 2	CAN/RAF. Nos. 141 and 242 Sqns. KIA 3 Apr 1941.
Reade Franklin TILLEY Pilot Officer DFC Clearwater, Texas	7 - 0 - 0	American in RCAF. No. 126 Sqn. Transferred to USAAF 12 Oct 1942.
Hugh Charles TRAINOR Squadron Leader DSO, DFC Charlottetown, P.E.I.	8 1/2 - 1 - 0	Nos. 401 and 411 Sqns. POW 19 Sep 1944.
Gordon William TROKE Squadron Leader DFC Sydney, N.S.	6 1/4 - 1 - 5	Nos. 250 and 443 Sqns. May also have several destroyed on ground. KFA 24 Jun 1952.
John Howard TURNBULL Flight Lieutenant DFC and Bar St. Thomas, Ont.	12 1/2 - 0 - 0	See Ch. 34.
Percival Stanley TURNER Group Captain DSO, DFC and Bar Toronto, Ont.	14 - 2 - 6	The figures represent a minimum score. See Ch. 35.
James Arthur WALKER Squadron Leader DFC Gleichen, Alta.	6 - 1/2 - 1	CAN/RAF. No. 111 Sqn. Also shared one victory with 'several' pilots. KIA 8 Feb 1944.
James Elmslie WALKER Wing Commander DFC and two Bars Claresholm, Alta.	10 - 3 - 4	Score may have been as high as 11-6-12 1/2. See Ch. 36.
Claude WEAVER Pilot Officer DFC, DFM Oklahoma City, Ok.	13 1/2 - 1 - 0	American in the RCAF. No. 185 Sqn. Shot down 9 Sep 1942; evaded, and flew again with No. 403 Sqn. KIA 28 Jan 1944.
James Henry WHALEN Flight Lieutenant DFC Vancouver, B.C.	6 - 0 - 0	Nos. 411 and 129 Sqns. KIA 18 Apr 1944. See Ch. 38, pg. 286.

Name-Rank-Awards-Hometown	Score	Remarks
John William WILLIAMS Pilot Officer DFC Kamloops, B.C.	9 - 2 - 8	No. 249 Sqn., Malta. KFA 31 Oct 1942.
Frederick Albert William Johnson WILSON Flying Officer DFC Port Arthur, Ont.	5 1/2 - 0 - 7	Nos. 80 and 441 Sqns.
Gordon WONNACOTT Squadron Leader DFC and Bar Edmonton, Alta.	5 - 0 - 1	No. 414 Sqn.
Vernon Crompton WOODWARD Squadron Leader DFC and Bar Victoria, B.C.	20 - 5 - 11	See Ch. 37.
Jacob Hyson WYMAN Flight Lieutenant Nil Sexsmith, Alta.	5 - 0 - 4	No. 406 Sqn. All victories on ground.
Henry Paul Michael ZARY Squadron Leader DFC New York, N.Y.	5 - 0 - 5	Nos. 421 and 403 Sqns. American in the RCAF.

Appendix 2

Leading Canadian Observers and Radar Operators

The reader will have realized from various chapters that the radar operators in night fighters and the navigator/observers in intruder aircraft were full partners with their pilots when victories were achieved. The following would not be "aces" if the definition of that term were restricted to pilots, but their contributions were so significant that to overlook them would do a disservice to themselves and to the less famous of their trade.

Name-Rank-Awards-Hometown	Score	Remarks
Leslie Patrick Sandford BING Flight Lieutenant DFC and Bar Regina, Sask.	13 - 0 - 1	With R.C. Fumerton.
William Aaron BOAK Flight Lieutenant DFC Regina, Sask.	7 - 0 - 2	With Etienne (5-0-1) and Bannock (2-0-1).
Earl William BOAL Flight Lieutenant DFC Weyburn, Sask.	17 - 0 - 5	All with Caine.
George Philip Alcide BODARD Flying Officer DFC Lethbridge, Alta.	6 - 0 - 0	No. 410 Sqn. With S/L C.A.S. Anderson (2) and F/O D.M. MacKenzie (4 destroyed).
John Stewart CHRISTIE Flight Lieutenant DFC Montreal, P.Q.	6 - 0 - 1	No. 410 Sqn. With S/L S.B. Huppert (3-0-1) and F/L R.D. Schultz (3-0-0) CAN/RAF.

Name-Rank-Awards-Hometown	Score	Remarks
Frank Leroy COCHRANE Flight Lieutenant Nil Brantford, Ont.	Five V-1's	No. 418 Sqn. With F/L P.S. Leggatt.
Leo Elton FOWNES Flight Lieutenant DFC Baddeck, N.S.	5 - 0 - 1	No. 409 Sqn. With F/L R.I.E. Britten.
Colin Gowans FINLAYSON Flying Officer DFC and Bar Victoria, B.C.	16 1/2 - 0 - 5	No. 418 Sqn. With F/L C.C. Scherf (RAAF) (10 1/2-0-1) and Lt. J.F. Luma (USAAF) (6-0-1).
Noel James GIBBONS Flight Lieutenant DFC and Bar West Vancouver, B.C.	13 1/2 - 1/2 - 13 plus two V-1's	No. 418 Sqn. With F/L J.R.F. Johnson (3 1/2- 1/2-3) and S/L R.G. Gray (10-0-12 and two V-1's).
John James GREENE Flight Lieutenant DFC Toronto, Ont.	7 - 0 - 10	No. 418 Sqn. With S/L D.B. Freeman (2-0-6) and F/O J.H. Wyman (5-0-4).
Peter HULETSKY Flight Lieutenant DFC and Bar Montreal, P.Q.	12 1/2 - 1/2 - 4	No. 418 Sqn. With S/L R.A. Kipp.
Clarence Joseph KIRKPATRICK Flight Lieutenant DFC Hamilton, Ont.	6 1/2 - 0 - 2	No. 406 Sqn. With S/L D.J. Williams (4 1/2-0-0) and W/C R. Bannock (2-0-2).
Oscar Archibald Joseph MARTIN Flight Lieutenant DFC Ottawa, Ont.	6 - 0 - 1	No. 418 Sqn. With F/L C.M. Jasper.
Colin Neil MATHESON Pilot Officer DFC Winnipeg, Man.	5 - 0 - 0	No. 409 Sqn. With F/O W.G. Kirkwood.
David Norman McINTOSH Flying Officer DFC Stanstead, P.Q.	8 - 0 - 7 plus four V-1's	No. 418 Sqn. With F/O S.P. Seid.

Name-Rank-Awards-Hometown	Score	Remarks
Alister Donald McLAREN Flying Officer Nil Toronto, Ont.	3 - 0 - 5 plus three V-1's	No. 418 Sqn. With F/L P.R. Brook.
John Drever RITCH Flying Officer Nil Saskatoon, Sask.	Five V-1's	No. 418 Sqn. With F/O N.S. May.
George Douglas ROBINSON Flying Officer DFC Transcona, Man.	6 - 0 - 1	Nos. 409 and 410 Sqns. With W/C J.D. Somerville.
Vernal Garnet SHAIL Flight Lieutenant DFC New Westminster, B.C.	6 - 1 - 8	No. 406 Sqn. With S/L D.A. MacFadyen.
James David SHARPLES Flying Officer DFC Toronto, Ont.	7 1/2 - 3 - 2 plus one V-1	No. 418 Sqn. With F/O M.H. Sims (6-2-2 plus 1 V-1) and Stn. Manston with F/O K.V. Panter (RAF) (1 1/2-1-0).
Alexander Reid STEWART Flying Officer DFC Toronto, Ont.	12 - 0 - 2	No. 418 Sqn. With F/L C.C. Scherf (RAAF).
Charles Leo VAESSEN Flying Officer DFC Leipzig, Sask.	6 - 0 - 1	No. 410 Sqn. With F/L C.E. Edinder.
Vernon Albert WILLIAMS Flight Lieutenant DFC Hamilton, Ont.	5 - 0 - 0	No. 410 Sqn. With F/L R.D. Schultz.
James Davidson WRIGHT Flying Officer DFC Rosthern, Sask.	6 - 1 - 8	No. 418 Sqn. With S/L D.A. MacFadyen.

A

Abbeville, Fr, 36m, 144, 211
Abu Sueir, Egypt, 86m, 98, 100, 136
Acklington, Eng, UK, 36m, 96
Acton Down, Eng, UK, 36m, 245
Agrinion, Greece, 86m, 240
Aikman DFC; S/L A.F., 284
Akyab Island, Burma, 116m, 287
Alencon, Fr, 36m, 190
Alexandria, Egypt, 86m, 133, 143, 263, 273
Altenfjord, Norway, 118
Amiens, Fr, 36m, 144
Ancienne Lorette, PQ, 25, 108m
Andersen, L., 143
Anzio, It, 86m, 137
Anglesey, Wales, UK, 100
Angus DFC; F/O A.B., 280
Antigonish, NS, 121
Arbakka, Man, 204
Ardennes, Belg, 14, 206, 210
Argos, Greece, 275
Atkinson DSC; S/Lt W.H.I., 287-289
Augsburg, Ger, 94m, 166
Audet DFC; F/L R.J. 'Dick', 23-28, 63
Aurora, Ont, 64
Avord, Fr, 31, 36m, 196
Aylmer, Ont, 108m, 287

B

Bad Aibling, Ger, 94m, 112
Baden-Söllingen, W.Ger, 36m, 94m, 230
Bader; S/L D., 210, 213-216, 259, 260-265
Bagotville, PQ, 19, 100, 108m, 174, 220
Baldy Hughes, (BC?), 85
Banks; J., 246
Bannock DSO, DFC; W/C R. 'Russ', 16, 29, 30-36, 59, 101, 114, 121, 128, 199
Barker; W/C A., 167
Barrick DFM; Sgt J.F. 'Tex', 287
Barton OBE, DFC, DFM; W/C R.A. 'Butch', 37-43
Bashaw, Alta, 289
Beachy Head, Eng, UK, 36m, 160
Beaumont-le-Roger, Fr, 13, 36m, 228
Bell; J., 29
Belleville, Ont, 108m, 205, 291, 292
Bennell DFC; W/C R.J., 58
Beny-sur-Mer, Fr, 36m, 176, 205, 245
Benzie; P/O J., 259
Berlin, Ger, 41, 94m, 169, 200
Beurling; F., 54
Beurling DSO, DFC, DFM; F/L G.F. 'Buzz', 18, 45-54, 188, 210, 217
Biggin Hill, Eng, UK, 36m, 72, 97, 174, 181
Bing; Sgt L.P.S. 'Pat', 95, 98-100
Bir Hacheim, Libya, 86m, 143
Bir el Zidan, Libya, 82

Birmingham, Eng, UK, 36m, 251
Bishop VC, DSC, MC, DFC; A/M W.A. 'Billy', 97, 149, 289
Blatchford; F/O H.P. 'Cowboy', 8, 37
Blatchford; K., 29
Boak; F/L W.A., 33
Boal; Sgt E., 56-59
Bone, Algeria, 86m, 253, 269
Boomer; S/L K.A., 10
Boscombe Down, Eng, UK, 36m, 39
Borden, Ont, 30, 108m, 121, 194, 217, 284
Boulogne, Fr, 32, 36m, 224
Boulton; S/L F., 65, 144
Boundary Bay, BC, 181
Bourges, Fr, 36m, 58
Bournemouth, Eng, UK, 36m, 181, 251
Boyle; F/L J.J., 26
Bradwell Bay, Eng, UK, 36m, 114
Brae, Eng, UK, 96
Brandon, Man, 25, 108m, 132, 232, 250, 290
Brantford, Ont, 76, 108m, 173, 289
Breadner; A/M L., 155, 167
Breithaupt DFC; F/O W.R., 279, 280
Brintnell; L., 29
Bristol, Eng, UK, 36m, 101
Brook; F/L P., 112
Brown; S/L H.L.I., 240
Brown DFC; W/C M.H. 'Hilly', 210, 216, 242, 259, 280, 281
Brown; R., 37
Bruce; F/O R.R., 31, 33
Brussels, Belg, 26, 36m
Buchanan, Sask, 290
Buckham; F/L R.A., 53
Buckley; C., 277
Budejovice, Bohemia-Moravia, 94m, 113
Buffalo, NY, USA, 89
Burden; W/C H.J. 'Hank', 104
Burgsteinfurt, Ger, 94m
Burma, 116m, 284, 286, 287

C

Caen, Fr, 36m, 72, 177
Caine DFC; F/L J.T. 'Johnny', 4, 55-61, 112, 169
Cairo, Egypt, 82, 86m, 136, 143
Calais, Fr, 36m, 46
Caldwell; J., 29
Caldwell; P., 29
Calgary, Alta, 25, 108m, 110, 180, 268, 291, 292
Cambrai, Fr, 36m, 211
Cameron DFC; S/L L.M., 153, 245
Campbell; F/L D.F., 14
Campbell; A/V/M H.L., 63
Canne, It, 137

317

GLOSSARY OF ABBREVIATIONS IN THE INDEX

DECORATIONS:
- AFC - Air Force Cross
- DFC - Distinguished Flying Cross
- DFM - Distinguished Flying Medal
- DSC - Distinguished Service Cross
- DSO - Distinguished Service Order
- MC - Military Cross
- OBE - Order of the British Empire
- VC - Victoria Cross

RANKS:
- A/C - Air Commodore
- A/C/M - Air Chief Marshal
- A/M - Air Marshal
- A/V/M - Air Vice Marshal
- F/L - Flight Lieutenant
- F/O - Flying Officer
- G/C - Group Captain
- Hptm - Hauptmann
- Lt - Lieutenant
- Maj.Gen - Major General
- Obstlt - Oberstleutnant
- P/O - Pilot Officer
- Sgt - Sergeant
- S/L - Squadron Leader
- S/Lt - Sub-Lieutenant
- W/C - Wing Commander
- WO - Warrant Officer

LOCATIONS:
- Alta - Alberta
- BC - British Columbia
- Belg - Belgium
- Eng - England
- Fr - France
- Ger - Greater Germany
- It - Italy
- Man - Manitoba
- NB - New Brunswick
- Neth - Netherlands
- Nfld - Newfoundland
- NS - Nova Scotia
- NY - New York
- Ont - Ontario
- PQ - Quebec
- PEI - Prince Edward Island
- Sask - Saskatchewan
- Scot - Scotland
- UK - United Kingdom
- USA - United States of America
- USSR - Union of Soviet Socialist Republics
- W.Ger - West Germany (Federal Republic of Germany)